PRAISE FOR *Wine Folly*

———

"The best introductory book on wine
to come along in years."

—*The Washington Post*

"Wine is fun. It's complex, vibrant, and meaningful.
It should be part of your life . . . and so should this book."

—Geoff Kruth, Master Sommelier, Guildsomm.com

"With clever graphics, Madeline has created
a wine navigator that effortlessly guides
new wine lovers to a better understanding."

—Dr. Andrew Waterhouse, UC Davis

"I wish I had had a smart, fast, super-easy-to-understand
book like *Wine Folly* when I was starting out."

—Karen MacNeil, author of *The Wine Bible*

"A magically vivid wine guide for our information age—
cuts through the complexity of wine like a Champagne saber."

—Mark Oldman, author of *Oldman's Guide to Outsmarting Wine*
and *How to Drink Like a Billionaire*

Wine Folly

Magnum Edition

Wine Folly

Magnum Edition

THE MASTER GUIDE

Madeline Puckette and Justin Hammack

Avery
an imprint of Penguin Random House
New York

an imprint of
Penguin Random
House LLC • 375
Hudson Street • New York,
New York 10014 • Copyright
© 2018 Wine Folly, LLC • Penguin
supports copyright. Copyright fuels
creativity, encourages diverse voices,
promotes free speech, and creates a
vibrant culture. Thank you for buying an
authorized edition of this book and for
complying with copyright laws by not
reproducing, scanning, or distributing any
part of it in any form without permission.
You are supporting writers and allowing
Penguin to continue to publish books
for every reader. •
Most Avery books are
available at special quantity discounts
for bulk purchase for sales promotions,
premiums, fund-raising, and educational
purposes. Special books or book excerpts
also can be created to fit specific needs.
For details, write SpecialMarkets@
penguinrandomhouse.com • Library of
Congress Cataloging-in-Publication Data
• Puckette, Madeline, author • Wine folly:
magnum edition / Madeline Puckette and
Justin Hammack • ISBN 9780525533894
(hardback) • 1. Wine and wine making.
I. Puckette, Madeline, author. II. Title. •
p. cm • Printed in Canada. • Book design
by Madeline Puckette and Federica
Fragapane • Cover by Nick Misani
18 17 16 15 14 13

Contents

Introduction

What makes wine special? Why is it considered one of the best beverages on the planet?

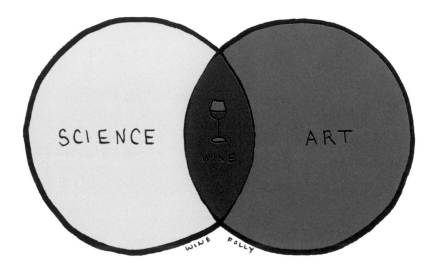

Why Love Wine?

The obvious reason to be interested in wine is because a small portion of it—say about 10–15%—is a mind-altering substance called ethanol. Yep, alcohol. However, the mere presence of ethanol (a simple chemical compound) doesn't explain the level of scientific rigor that goes into understanding wine. There is so much to know, including how wine is made and the science behind its tastes and flavors. Not to mention the health benefits, cultural traditions, and how wine fits into our history and evolution. In short, wine is interesting because it is complex.

The more you know, the more you know you don't know.

The topic of wine will go as deep as you're willing to dive. That is why there are hundreds of books on the subject. Some are erudite, some are heavyweight and technical, and some are drunken escapades!

This book is unlike any of the aforementioned styles. *Wine Folly: Magnum Edition* is the pragmatist's tool, designed to guide you on your path into wine, wherever it takes you. It will show you the basics and give you a solid foundation.

Who Made This Book?

This book was created by the co-founders of *Wine Folly*. Madeline Puckette is a wine sommelier, writer, and visual designer. Justin Hammack is a digital strategist, web developer, and entreprenuer.

Part of the effort in creating this book was verifying accuracy of information. Additional contributions were made by Kanchan Schindlauer, Mark Craig, Hilarie Larson, Vincent Rendoni, Haley Mercedes, and Stephen Reiss. Information sources can be viewed in the back of this book.

About Wine Folly

The first edition of this book, *Wine Folly: The Essential Guide to Wine* is on the *New York Times* Bestseller list, is an Amazon Cookbook of 2015, has a 4.8 star rating on Amazon (at the time of this writing), and has been printed in more than 20 languages (even Mongolian!)

Wine Folly is used by wine educators, sommeliers, and restaurant managers around the world to teach people about wine.

winefolly.com is the #1 ranking wine education site in the world. The best part? It's free.

Wine Folly isn't just the thoughts of one individual. The site's knowledge base has contributions from many wine professionals, writers, winemakers, scientists, and doctors.

Magnum Edition

You'll love *Wine Folly: Magnum Edition* if you've...

- Wanted to improve your knowledge of wine, but don't know how to start.
- Ever felt overwhelmed by the choices in the wine aisle.
- Bought disappointing wines or felt hesitant to try new wines.
- Ever felt intimidated by others' knowledge of wine.
- Ever been uncertain if you're drinking good wine or if it's all just marketing.

Wine Folly: Magnum Edition will help you...

- Learn how to assess wine quality.
- Handle, serve, store, and age wine.
- Find new wines that you're likely to enjoy.
- Gain professional sommelier-level knowledge of wine.
- Avoid buying poor-quality wines, even on a small budget.
- Drink wine more responsibly.
- Make great food and wine pairings.
- Gain confidence with wine

Wine Folly: Magnum Edition is the improved and expanded edition of *Wine Folly: The Essential Guide to Wine.*

Magnum Edition contains more than two times the content of the first volume, including new chapters, wine maps, infographics, and updated data sources.

Get the Most Out of This Book

Your homework assignment each time you try a new wine:

- Practice actively tasting the wine. (p. 24)
- Look up the wine or variety in the Grapes & Wines Section of this book. (pp. 66–191)
- Learn about the region where the wine is from. (pp. 192–299)
- Learn the best foods to pair with the wine. (p. 52)
- Gain confidence handling wine. (p. 36)
- Rinse and repeat!

SECTION
....
1

Wine
Basics

This section explores the
fundamental aspects of wine
including:
- How wine is made
- How to taste wine
- How to serve wine
- How to store wine

What Is Wine?

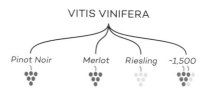

Wine is an alcoholic beverage made with fermented grapes. Technically, wine can be made with any fruit, but most wine is made with wine grapes.

Wine grapes are different than table grapes. They are smaller, sweeter, contain seeds, and have thicker skins. These traits have proven to be better for making wine.

There are thousands of different **wine varieties** and most are cultivars of just one species of grapevine: *Vitis vinifera.*

Grapevines are woody, perennial plants that produce a crop once a year. The different climates where grapes grow affect how sweet (or tart) the resulting wine tastes.

Vintage refers to the year that the grapes were harvested.

Non-vintage or "NV" wines are a blend of several vintages.

A single-varietal wine is a wine made with mostly or only one grape variety (e.g., Merlot, Assyrtiko, etc.).

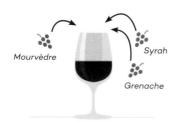

A **wine blend** is made by blending several different varietal wines together.

A **field blend** is made with different varieties that are harvested and vinified together.

There are several different styles of wine including **still, sparkling, fortified,** and **aromatized wines** (also known as vermouth).

In the US, **an organic wine** must be made with organically grown grapes and no added sulfites. In the EU, organic wines may contain sulfites but with lower maximums than non-organic wines.

3 Ways Wines Are Labeled

By Variety

Varietal wines (wines labeled by grape) are made with one or mostly one grape variety. Countries require a minimum of the listed variety to be included in the bottle.

75%
United States

85%
Australia, Austria, Argentina, Chile, France, Germany, Italy, New Zealand, Portugal, South Africa, Hungary, Greece, Canada

By Region

Wines that are labeled by region follow the strict legal rules of that region to dictate what's inside the bottle. For example, Sancerre is mostly Sauvignon Blanc.

Regional labeling is common in:

- France
- Italy
- Spain
- Portugal
- Greece
- Hungary

By Name

Wines that are labeled by name use a made-up name.

The fantasy name can be either made up by the winery to specify a special wine blend, or be the name of a vineyard or a place.

For example, *"Les Clos"* is the name of a vineyard in Chablis, France.

Drinking Facts

5 oz
(150 ml)

A standard serving of wine is 5 ounces (150 ml) and a standard bottle (750 ml) contains 5 servings of wine.

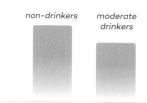

non-drinkers *moderate drinkers*

According to the American Heart Association, the incidence of **heart disease** is lower in people who practice moderation than in non-drinkers.

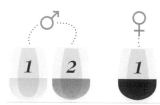

1   2   1

What is moderation? The American Cancer Institute recommends no more than 2 drinks per day for men (14 per week) and 1 drink per day for women (7 total per week).

1   2
1   2   3

What if I'm having a party? Men should not exceed more than 3 servings in a single day. Women should have no more than 2. Take **an alcohol-free day** to make up the difference.

The primary **cause of a wine headache** is not sulfites—it's dehydration! The other major cause is thought to be from fermentation-derived biogenic amines like tyramine.

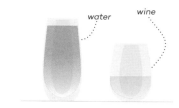

water   *wine*

Avoid headaches caused by dehydration by drinking one full 8-oz (250 ml) glass of water with every serving of wine.

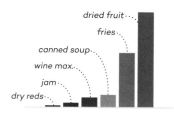

dried fruit
fries
canned soup
wine max
jam
dry reds

Wines are labeled **"contains sulfites"** if they contain more than 10 ppm (parts per million). Legal limits are as high as 350 ppm and most range between 50–150 ppm. For comparison's sake, a can of soda contains 350 ppm.

RED   WHITE   SWEET

Often, **red wines contain less sulfites** than white wines and dry wines contain less sulfites than sweet wines. Also in most cases, lower-quality wines contain more sulfites than higher-quality wines.

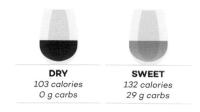

DRY	**SWEET**
103 calories	*132 calories*
0 g carbs	*29 g carbs*

Calories in wine? One standard serving of dry wine with 13% ABV has zero carbs and 103 calories. A standard serving of sweet wine with 5% sweetness and 13% ABV has 29 g carbs (from sugars) and 132 calories.

A Bottle of Wine

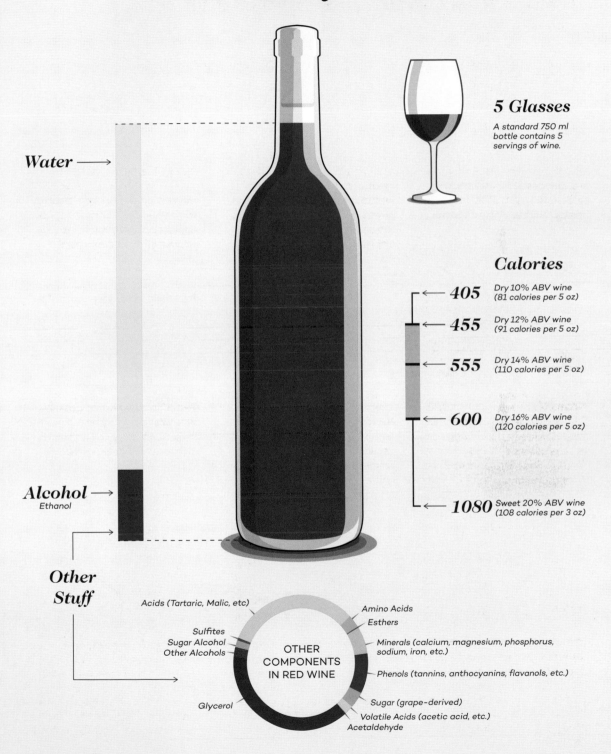

Water →

Alcohol →
Ethanol

Other Stuff

5 Glasses
A standard 750 ml bottle contains 5 servings of wine.

Calories

405 — Dry 10% ABV wine (81 calories per 5 oz)

455 — Dry 12% ABV wine (91 calories per 5 oz)

555 — Dry 14% ABV wine (110 calories per 5 oz)

600 — Dry 16% ABV wine (120 calories per 5 oz)

1080 — Sweet 20% ABV wine (108 calories per 3 oz)

OTHER COMPONENTS IN RED WINE

Acids (Tartaric, Malic, etc)
Sulfites
Sugar Alcohol
Other Alcohols
Glycerol
Amino Acids
Esthers
Minerals (calcium, magnesium, phosphorus, sodium, iron, etc.)
Phenols (tannins, anthocyanins, flavanols, etc.)
Sugar (grape-derived)
Volatile Acids (acetic acid, etc.)
Acetaldehyde

13

Wine Traits

Learn how each trait in wine will affect the quality and taste. This book characterizes wines by five traits: Body, Sweetness, Tannin, Acidity, and Alcohol.

BODY RANKED 1–5

This book ranks wines from 1 to 5 based on their presence of tannin, alcohol, and sweetness compared to other wines.

TASTING BODY

Imagine "light" vs "full" body in wine similar to the difference between skim and whole milk.

Body

Body is not a scientific term but rather a way to categorize wine by intensity level from lightest to richest.

Identifying "light-bodied" and "full-bodied" wines is akin to identifying the differences in skim and whole milk: The more fat in milk, the more full it will taste.

Though this concept applies to all beverages, with wine in particular, our taste receptors sense body in wine using the traits of tannin, sweetness, acidity, and alcohol.

Each trait affects the body of wine somewhat differently:

- Tannin increases the body in wine. Since red wines contain tannin and white wines do not, red wine tend to taste more full-bodied than white wines.
- Sweetness increases body in wine. This is why sweet wines tend to taste more full-bodied than dry wines. It's also why some dry wines often keep a small level of sweetness in order to increase body.
- Acidity decreases the body in wine.
- Alcohol increases the body in wine. This is why higher-alcohol wines (including fortified wines) taste more full-bodied than lighter-alcohol wines.
- Carbonation decreases the body in wine. This is why sparkling wines usually taste lighter than still wines.

There are some other tricks up the winemaker's sleeve to play around with body. For example, a winemaker can choose to age wines in oak barrels or use oxidative wine aging to increase the body in wine. We'll talk about winemaking methods more in How Wine Is Made (pp. 44–51).

Wines by Body

Sparkling

PROSECCO
CAVA
CRÉMANT
CHAMPAGNE
FRANCIACORTA
MELON
PIQUEPOUL
VINHO VERDE
PINOT BLANC
ASSYRTIKO
COLOMBARD
ALBARIÑO
FRIULANO
VERDICCHIO
CORTESE
MUSCAT BLANC
FURMINT
RIESLING
VERDEJO
FIANO
GRECHETTO
SILVANER
PINOT GRIS
TORRONTÉS
FERNAO PIRES
MOSCHOFILERO
CHENIN BLANC
ARINTO
GRÜNER VELTLINER
SAUVIGNON BLANC
GARGANEGA
VERMENTINO
FALANGHINA
SÉMILLON
VIURA
AIREN
TREBBIANO TOSCANO
SAVATIANO
GRENACHE BLANC
GEWÜRZTRAMINER
MARSANNE
ROUSSANNE
VIOGNIER
CHARDONNAY

White Wines

BRACHETTO
FRAPPATO
GAMAY
LAMBRUSCO
SCHIAVA
ZWEIGELT
CINSAULT
PINOT NOIR
NERELLO MASCALESE
CASTELÃO
CARMÉNÈRE
VALPOLICELLA
BOBAL
CARIGNAN
BLAUFRÄNKISCH
CABERNET FRANC
CONCORD
AGIORGITIKO
BAGA
BARBERA
BONARDA
DOLCETTO
GRENACHE
MENCÍA
MERLOT
MONTEPULCIANO
NEBBIOLO
NEGROAMARO
RHÔNE / GSM BLEND
SANGIOVESE
TEMPRANILLO
XINOMAVRO
AGLIANICO
ALICANTE BOUSCHET
BORDEAUX BLEND
CABERNET SAUVIGNON
MALBEC
MONASTRELL
NERO D'AVOLA
PETIT VERDOT
PETITE SIRAH
PINOTAGE
SAGRANTINO
SYRAH
TANNAT
TOURIGA NACIONAL
ZINFANDEL

Red Wines

SHERRY
SAUTERNAIS
ICE WINE
MADEIRA
MARSALA
MOSCATEL DE S.
VIN SANTO
MUSCAT ALEX.
PORT

Dessert Wines

*Some wines will prove to be
lighter or bolder than shown here!*

BODY

SWEETNESS

TANNIN

ACIDITY

ALCOHOL

SWEETNESS RANKED 1–5

This book ranks wines based on their common perceptible sweetness level. Since its possible to control sweetness in wine, you may see a range.

tastes sweeter

2.7 pH
HIGHER ACIDITY

17 g/L
RESIDUAL SUGAR

3 pH
LOWER ACIDITY

17 g/L
RESIDUAL SUGAR

OUR PERCEPTION OF SWEETNESS IS NOT PARTICULARLY ACCURATE

It's difficult to sense wine sweetness accurately because the other wine traits can distort our perception! For example, wines with higher tannin and/or higher acidity will taste less sweet than they actually are.

Sweetness

Sweetness in wine is called residual sugar (RS). Residual sugar is the unfermented grape sugars left over in the wine after fermentation has completed.

There is a very wide range of sweetness in wine, which starts at absolutely nothing—0 grams per liter—to up to 600 grams per liter. For perspective, milk contains about 50 g/L, Coca-Cola contains approximately 113 g/L and syrup is nearly all sugar at 70% or 700 g/L. Wine appears more viscous with higher residual sugar. For example, a 100-year-old bottle of Pedro Ximénez moves as slowly as maple syrup!

Still Wines

The following terms are the common language used by most professionals to describe wine sweetness levels:

- **Bone-Dry:** 0 calories per serving (<1 g/L)
- **Dry:** 0–6 calories per serving (1–17 g/L)
- **Off-Dry:** 6–21 calories per serving (17–35 g/L)
- **Medium Sweet:** 21–72 calories per serving (35–120 g/L)
- **Sweet:** 72+ calories per serving (>120 g/L)

Our palates are not particularly sensitive at tasting sugar. Dry-tasting wines often contain up to 17 g/L of residual sugar, which is 10 additional calories/carbs per serving. So, if you're trying to carb-count, scour the Internet for a "technical sheet" if available—wineries often list the residual sugar content in the wine.

Sparkling Wines

Unlike still wines, sparkling wines (including Champagne, Prosecco, and Cava), will add a small amount of sugar, usually in the form of concentrated grape must, during the last step of winemaking. For this reason, sparkling wines will absolutely have sweetness levels indicated on the bottle:

- **Brut Nature:** 0–3 g/L (no added sugar)
- **Extra Brut:** 0–6 g/L
- **Brut:** 0–12 g/L
- **Extra Dry:** 12–17 g/L
- **Dry:** 17–32 g/L
- **Demi-Sec:** 32–50 g/L
- **Doux:** Over 50 g/L

Sweetness Levels

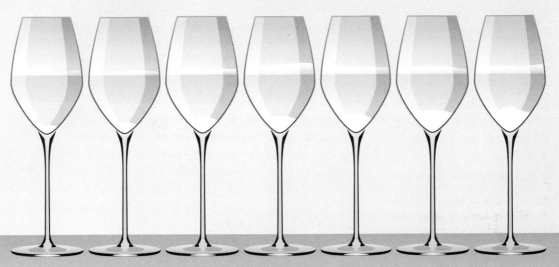

Brut Nature
0–2 cal.*
(0–3 g/L)

Extra Brut
0–5 cal.*
(0–6 g/L)

Brut
0–7 cal.*
(0–12 g/L)

Extra Dry
7–10 cal.*
(12–17 g/L)

Dry
10–20 cal.*
(17–32 g/L)

Demi-Sec
20–30 cal.*
(32–50 g/L)

Doux
30+ cal.*
(50+ g/L)

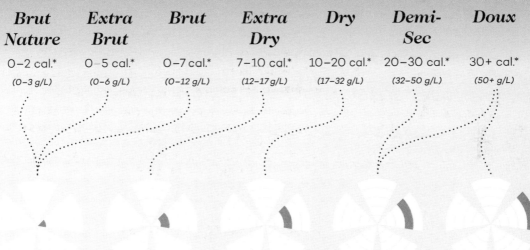

Bone Dry
0 calories*
(less than 1 g/L)

Dry
0–10 calories*
(1–17 g/L)

Off-Dry
10–21 calories
(17–35 g/L)

Sweet
21–72 calories*
(35–120 g/L)

Very Sweet
72+ calories*
(120+ g/L)

*Calories per 5oz / 150 ml serving.

Tannin

Tannin plays a very important role in wine quality and is the primary source of wine's health benefits. Yet, tannin is probably one of the least loved of all of wine's traits. Why? Simple: It's because tannin tastes bitter.

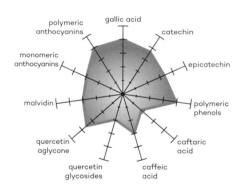

TANNIN RANKED FROM 1–5

Wines have the highest tannin when they are young. This book ranks wine tannin based on how bitter and astringent the wine tastes. Tannin can be controlled with winemaking and drops as wine ages.

PHENOLICS CHART

This radar chart displays a phenolic analysis of a Pinot Noir wine:

Catechin and epicatechin are condensed tannins. They are the "good for you" tannins.

Malvidin and monomeric anthocyanins produce color in red wine.

Caftaric and caffeic acid are thought to produce white wine's color.

Gallic acid comes from grape seeds but mostly comes from oak aging.

Quercetin reacts with anthocyanin, increasing color intensity.

What Is Tannin?

Tannins are naturally occurring polyphenols found in plants, seeds, bark, wood, leaves, and fruit skins. It's found in many plants and foods, notably green tea, super dark chocolate, walnut skins, and hachiya persimmons. In wine, tannins are found in the grape skins and seeds and they're also found in wooden barrels. Tannins are beneficial because they help stabilize wine and buffer it against oxidation.

Tasting Tannin

Want to experience unadulterated tannin for yourself? Place a wet tea bag on your tongue. The astringent, bitter sensation you get is the sensation of tannin!

In wine, tannin is a bit more subtle and feels like a gritty or drying sensation that makes your lips stick to your teeth. In this book, tannins are rated on a scale from 1 to 5 by how astringent they are, how bitter they taste, and how long they endure after swallowing.

Tannin and Your Health

Many scientific studies have explored the effects of tannin on health. The majority of this research suggests the following benefits:

- Procyanidins (aka condensed tannins) inhibit cholesterol, which in turn, helps fight heart disease.
- In a petri dish, ellagitannins (found in oak barrels) have stopped cancer cells from expanding.
- In test mice, ellagitannins reduced the effects of fatty liver disease and fought obesity.
- In human trials, catechin and epicatechin (two types of procyanidins) have lowered total cholesterol and improved the ratio of "good," or HDL, cholesterol to "bad," or LDL, cholesterol.
- As of yet, no studies have found tannin to cause headaches or migraines. Of course, there is always more to learn!

Tannin in Wine

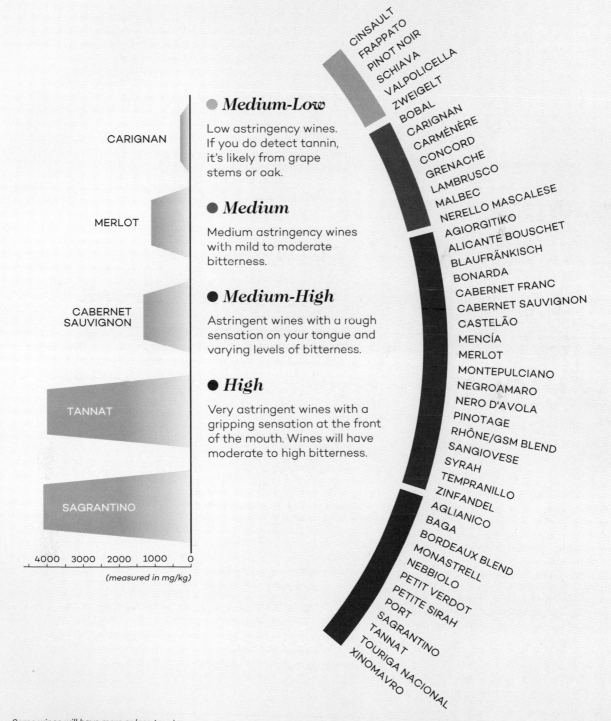

CARIGNAN

MERLOT

CABERNET SAUVIGNON

TANNAT

SAGRANTINO

4000   3000   2000   1000   0

(measured in mg/kg)

● *Medium-Low*
Low astringency wines. If you do detect tannin, it's likely from grape stems or oak.

● *Medium*
Medium astringency wines with mild to moderate bitterness.

● *Medium-High*
Astringent wines with a rough sensation on your tongue and varying levels of bitterness.

● *High*
Very astringent wines with a gripping sensation at the front of the mouth. Wines will have moderate to high bitterness.

CINSAULT
FRAPPATO
PINOT NOIR
SCHIAVA
VALPOLICELLA
ZWEIGELT
BOBAL
CARIGNAN
CARMÉNÈRE
CONCORD
GRENACHE
LAMBRUSCO
MALBEC
NERELLO MASCALESE
AGIORGITIKO
ALICANTE BOUSCHET
BLAUFRÄNKISCH
BONARDA
CABERNET FRANC
CABERNET SAUVIGNON
CASTELÃO
MENCÍA
MERLOT
MONTEPULCIANO
NEGROAMARO
NERO D'AVOLA
PINOTAGE
RHÔNE/GSM BLEND
SANGIOVESE
SYRAH
TEMPRANILLO
ZINFANDEL
AGLIANICO
BAGA
BORDEAUX BLEND
MONASTRELL
NEBBIOLO
PETIT VERDOT
PETITE SIRAH
PORT
SAGRANTINO
TANNAT
TOURIGA NACIONAL
XINOMAVRO

Some wines will have more or less tannin than what's indicated on this chart.

Acidity

Acidity is what gives wine its tart and sour taste. All wines lie on the acidic side of the pH scale ranging from about 3 to 4 pH (water is neutral at 7 pH). Acidity is important for wine quality because it slows the rate of chemical reactions, which cause wine to go bad.

ACIDITY RANKED FROM 1–5

In this book you'll find wines are ranked in terms of their perceptible acidity, or how acidic they typically taste.

Tasting Acidity

Imagine drinking lemonade. Notice all the mouth-watering, puckering, and tingly sensations flinging around your mouth? That's acidity at work. Terms like zesty, bright, tart, zippy, and fresh are often used in tasting notes to describe higher-acidity wines.

- Wines with higher acidity taste lighter bodied and also less sweet.
- Wines with lower acidity taste fuller bodied and more sweet.
- When acidity is too low, wines are often described as tasting flat, dull, soft, or flabby.
- When acidity is too high, wines are often described as tasting spicy, sharp, or too sour.
- Wines above 4 pH (low acidity) are not as stable as wines below 4 pH and more likely to develop faults.

So, the next time you taste wine, pay attention to how it makes your mouth water and tingle. With practice, you will create your own mental benchmark of acidity levels. Of course, each person has their own personal preference—some like acid more than others.

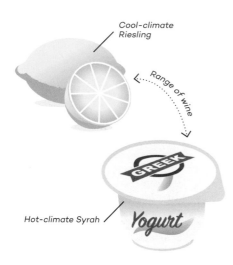

Cool-climate Riesling

Range of wine

Hot-climate Syrah

GREEK

Yogurt

WINE COMPARED TO OTHER FOODS

High-acid wines are as sour as lemons at around 2.6 pH. Lower-acid wines may be as flat as Greek yogurt at around 4.5 pH.

Acids in Wine

The most prevalent wine acids are tartaric acid (softer, found in bananas), malic acid (fruity, found in apples), and citric acid (tingly, found in citrus). Of course, there are many more acids, and each affect the taste differently. Generally:

- Acids change as wine ages and eventually are mostly acetic acid (the primary acid in vinegar).
- Some regions allow acidification (in hotter climates) which is the addition of acids (powdered tartaric and malic acid) to increase acidity. Most quality-minded producers do this as sparingly as possible.
- Wine contains anywhere from 4–12% total acids. (Sparkling wines are on the high side!)

Acidity in Wine

pH vs Acidity

Wines that are lower on the pH scale (i.e., farther from neutral) taste more sour.

Technically, pH does not measure the amount of acids in wine, it simply measures the concentration of free hydrogen ions. Our taste receptors perceive hydrogen ions as sourness.

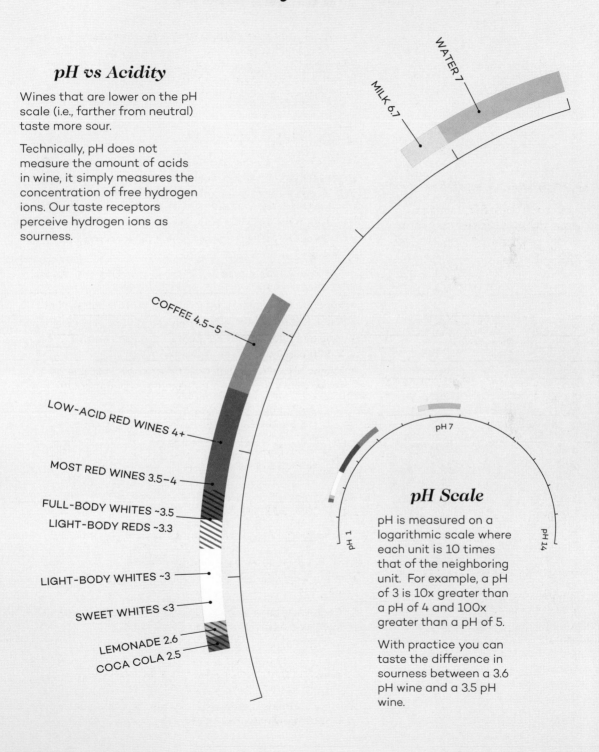

WATER 7

MILK 6.7

COFFEE 4.5–5

LOW-ACID RED WINES 4+

MOST RED WINES 3.5–4

FULL-BODY WHITES ~3.5

LIGHT-BODY REDS ~3.3

LIGHT-BODY WHITES ~3

SWEET WHITES <3

LEMONADE 2.6

COCA COLA 2.5

pH 7

pH 1

pH 14

pH Scale

pH is measured on a logarithmic scale where each unit is 10 times that of the neighboring unit. For example, a pH of 3 is 10x greater than a pH of 4 and 100x greater than a pH of 5.

With practice you can taste the difference in sourness between a 3.6 pH wine and a 3.5 pH wine.

ALCOHOL IS RANKED 1–5

This book ranks wines based on their typical alcohol content:

1 = Low, 5–10% ABV

2 = Medium-Low, 10–11.5% ABV

3 = Medium, 11.5–13.5% ABV

4 = Medium-High, 13.5–15% ABV

5 = High, Over 15% ABV

THE TASTE OF ALCOHOL

We interpret alcohol using many taste receptors, which is why alcohol tastes bitter, sweet, spicy and oily all at once. Based on genetics, some of us taste alcohol as bitter and others taste it as sweet.

Alcohol

The average glass of wine contains 12–15% ethanol. This simple compound has a profound effect on the taste and ageability of wine, as well as human health.

Alcohol and Your Health

Moderation may be the key to "healthy" drinking, but what is moderation exactly? Well, the concept is simple: Don't drink more than your body can metabolize.

Ethanol becomes toxic when it is metabolized in the liver and stomach. During the process, hydrogen atoms are removed from ethanol molecules and the compound turns into acetaldehyde. Acetaldehyde is toxic in large amounts (why binge drinking can kill you), but the body can metabolize small amounts of it using enzymes.

Of course, everyone's physiology is a bit different. You may need to consume less than others based on your own unique traits. For example:

- Women have fewer alcohol-digesting enzymes than men. Thus, it's recommended that women consume less.
- Some people (such as those with East Asian and American Indian lineage) produce enzymes that aren't as good at metabolizing acetaldehyde. If you get rashes, red flushing, headaches, and nausea easily when drinking, then plan to moderate more.
- Alcohol may cause a slight rise in blood sugar when ingested but ultimately it causes blood sugar to drop. So, if you're being treated for blood sugar abnormalities (diabetes) you'll want to be extra careful.
- Some people cannot control their consumption of alcohol (one drink *always* leads to more). If this is you, abstaining is likely the best solution. You are not alone: Alcohol use disorder affects about 1 in 16 US adults.

Alcohol in Wine

The alcohol level in wine is directly related to the sweetness levels in grapes. The sweeter the grapes, the higher the potential alcohol.

In some cool-climate countries grapes don't always ripen, so it's legal to add sugar to increase the alcohol level. The practice is called *chaptalization* and is allowed in places like France and Germany. Many consider chaptalization controversial because it directly manipulates the finished wine. Thus, most quality-minded producers avoid it.

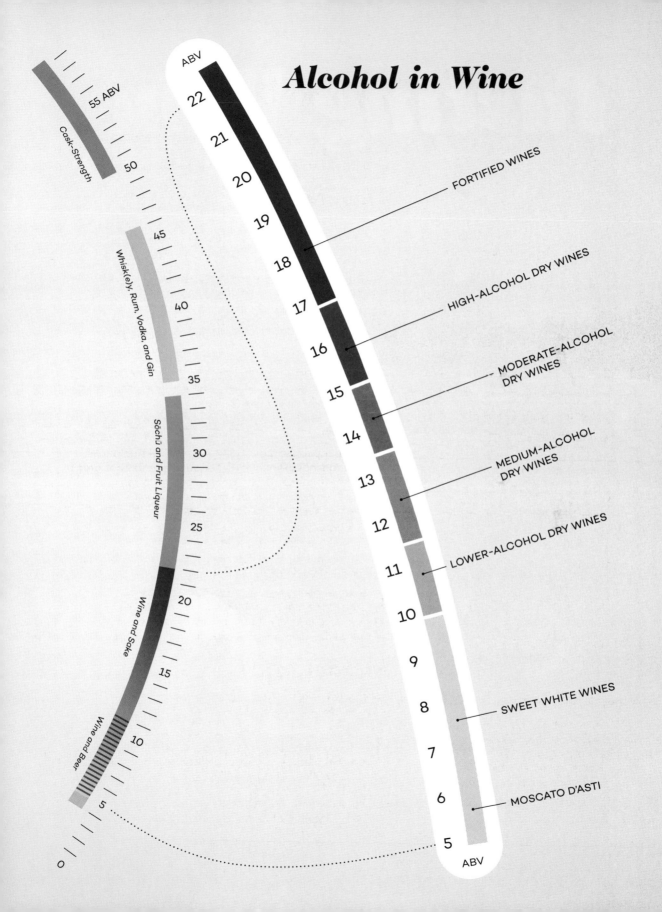

Alcohol in Wine

ABV

22
21
20
19
18
17
16
15
14
13
12
11
10
9
8
7
6
5

ABV

FORTIFIED WINES

HIGH-ALCOHOL DRY WINES

MODERATE-ALCOHOL
DRY WINES

MEDIUM-ALCOHOL
DRY WINES

LOWER-ALCOHOL DRY WINES

SWEET WHITE WINES

MOSCATO D'ASTI

Cask-Strength

55 ABV

50

Whisk(e)y, Rum, Vodka, and Gin

45

40

35

Sōchū and Fruit Liqueur

30

25

Wine and Sake

20

15

Wine and Beer

10

5

0

Tasting Wine

You don't need a big nose or a special number of taste buds to be a great wine taster. All you need is a consistent tasting technique to build upon. Each new wine you try is an opportunity to practice!

The **4-step tasting method** illustrated in this chapter is the same technique used by wine professionals. It's easy to learn but takes practice to master. Here are the basic steps:

Look

Hold your glass of wine over a white background under neutral lighting and take 3 observations:

- Hue
- Intensity of color
- Viscosity

Smell

Smell your wine and attempt to create a profile of its aromas before tasting it. Look for:

- 2–3 fruit flavors (be descriptive)
- 2–3 herbal or other flavors
- Any oak or earth flavors (if present)

Taste

Take a sizeable sip of wine and pass all over your palate before swallowing. Try to identify:

- The structure of wine (tannin, acidity, etc.)
- The flavors
- The wine's overall balance

Think

Finally, it's time to put all your observations together and assess the overall experience.

- Write down your tasting notes
- Rate the wine (optional)
- Compare with other wines (optional)

Look

Hue & Intensity

White Wines: A deeper color in white wine is usually an indication of aging or oxidation. For example, white wines aged in oak have a deeper color than white wines aged in stainless steel, which doesn't let oxygen in.

Rosé Wines: Since color intensity in rosé is controlled by the winemaker, a deeper color simply means the wine was macerated in grape skins for longer.

Red Wines: Look toward the edge of the wine to see the hue. Look toward the center to see how opaque the color is.

- Wines with a red-colored tint likely have a higher acidity (lower pH).
- Wines that are more purple or blue will have a lower acidity.
- A deeply colored, opaque red wine is likely to be youthful with higher tannin.
- Red wines become more pale and tawny as they age.

Viscosity

Wines with higher viscosity have higher alcohol, higher sugar, or both.

Wine Legs/Tears: Wine "legs" or "tears" is a phenomenon called the Gibbs-Marangoni effect. It is caused by fluid surface tension created from evaporating alcohol. In a controlled environment, many "tears" indicate a wine with higher alcohol. Temperature and humidity will affect results.

Sediment: Unfiltered wines often leave particles at the bottom of your glass. They are harmless but can be easily removed by pouring through a stainless-steel filter (such as a tea strainer).

STRAW   YELLOW   GOLD   AMBER

PINK   SALMON   COPPER   BROWN

PURPLE   RUBY   GARNET   TAWNY

RED TINT

BLUE TINT

AGED

GIBBS-MARANGONI EFFECT

Color of Wine

PALE STRAW
Vinho Verde, Muscadet, Verdejo

MEDIUM STRAW
Riesling, Torrontés, Moscato

DEEP STRAW
Albariño, Verdicchio

PALE YELLOW
Grüner Veltliner

MEDIUM YELLOW
Sauv. Blanc, Sémillon, Vermentino

DEEP YELLOW
Sauternes, Aged Riesling

PALE GOLD
Chenin Blanc, Pinot Gris

MEDIUM GOLD
Viognier, Trebbiano

DEEP GOLD
Chardonnay, Aged White Rioja

PALE COPPER
Provence Rosé, Pinot Gris

PALE AMBER
Orange Wine, White Port

MEDIUM AMBER
Tokaji Aszú, Vin Santo

DEEP AMBER
Tawny Port, Vinsanto

MEDIUM COPPER
Pinot Noir Rosé

PALE BROWN
Aged White, Sherry

MEDIUM BROWN
Sherry, White Port

DEEP BROWN
Pedro Ximénez

DEEP COPPER
Tibouren Rosé, Syrah Rosé

Use this chart to help identify and define hue and intensity in the wines you taste.

The examples included in this chart are here to help get you started and are not exhaustive.

Note: The color-corrected version of this chart is available as a poster online at winefolly.com

PALE PINK
Bandol Rosé

MEDIUM PINK
Garnacha Rosé

DEEP PINK
Tavel

PALE PURPLE
Gamay, Valpolicella Blend

MEDIUM PURPLE
Malbec, Syrah, Teroldego

DEEP PURPLE
Alicante Bouschet, Pinotage

PALE SALMON
Provence Rosé, White Zinfandel

PALE RUBY
Pinot Noir

MEDIUM RUBY
Tempranillo, GSM Blend

DEEP RUBY
Cabernet Sauvignon, Tannat

MEDIUM SALMON
Sangiovese Rosé

PALE GARNET
Nebbiolo

MEDIUM GARNET
Aged Reds, Brunello di Montalcino

DEEP GARNET
Aged Amarone, Barolo

DEEP SALMON
Syrah Rosé, Merlot Rosé

PALE TAWNY
Tawny Port, Aged Nebbiolo

MEDIUM TAWNY
Aged Sangiovese, Bual Madeira

DEEP TAWNY
Old Vintage Port

Smell

There are hundreds of aroma compounds found in wine. The best way to identify individual aromas is to smell before you taste.

Smelling Tips

Hold your glass under your nose and take a small sniff to "prime" your senses. Then, swirl your wine and take slow, delicate whiffs of the wine. Switch between thoughtfully smelling and pausing to give yourself time to pick out each aroma.

Position your nose above the glass and slowly move in until you pick out individual smells.

The top rim reveals more delicate floral aromas and the lower rim reveals richer fruit aromas.

Swirling the wine will concentrate the aromas.

What to Look For

Fruit: First, try to pick out a fruit aroma. Second, see if you can add in an adjective. If you're getting strawberry, what kind of strawberry is it? Fresh, ripe, stewed, dried? Two to three fruits is a good objective.

Herb / Other: Some wines are more savory than others and have many non-fruit smells including herbs, flowers, and minerals. Be descriptive. There are no wrong answers!

Oak: If a wine has aromas of vanilla, coconut, allspice, milk chocolate, cola, cedar, dill, or tobacco it might have spent time aging in oak barrels! Different species of oak (and different oak preparation methods) have different flavors. American oak (Quercus alba) tends to add more dill and coconut flavors, whereas European oak (Quercus petrea) offers more vanilla, allspice, and nutmeg aromas.

Earth: When you taste earthiness, try to figure out if it smells organic (loam, mushroom, forest floor), or inorganic (slate, chalk, gravel, clay). This group of aromas is thought to be microbe-derived and can provide clues to the wine's origin. Make note of the type of earthiness you taste, organic or inorganic.

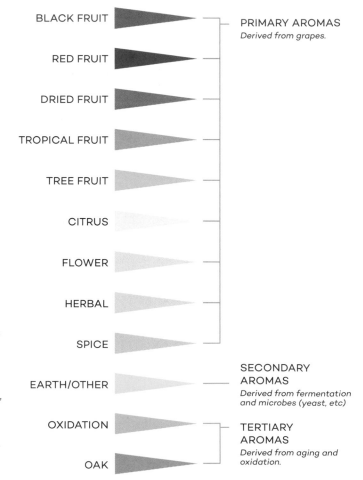

BLACK FRUIT
RED FRUIT
DRIED FRUIT
TROPICAL FRUIT
TREE FRUIT
CITRUS
FLOWER
HERBAL
SPICE
EARTH/OTHER
OXIDATION
OAK

PRIMARY AROMAS
Derived from grapes.

SECONDARY AROMAS
Derived from fermentation and microbes (yeast, etc)

TERTIARY AROMAS
Derived from aging and oxidation.

Wine Faults

When you taste test wine at a restaurant, you're testing for wine faults! Wine faults are typically due to poor storage and handling. Here are the most common faults and how to sniff them out.

Cork Taint

(TCA, 2,4,6-Trichloroanisole, TBA, etc.)

If the wine smells strongly of wet cardboard, wet dog, or a musty cellar, your wine is corked. This fault can be caused by chlorine coming in contact with corks and is thought to affect 1–3% of corked bottles. At a restaurant, most wine servers can help identify this fault. There is no easy fix. Return the wine.

Reduction

(Reduction, Mercaptans, Sulfur Compounds)

If the wine smells distinctly of garlic, cooked cabbage, rotten eggs, cooked corn, or burnt match, it has sulfur flavors (aka reduction). Reduction happens when wine doesn't get enough oxygen during winemaking. Decanting the wine will greatly improve the smell, and if not, you can try stirring your wine with a silver spoon. If this doesn't help, return the wine.

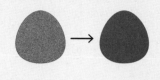

Oxidation

(Sotolon and various Aldehydes)

If the wine smells sharply of bruised apples, jackfruit, and linseed oil and looks partially brown (and isn't old Marsala or Madeira), then it's oxidized. Oxidation happens over time to all wines, but can occur before it should due to improper storage conditions. Try to find out if the wine is meant to be oxidized before returning it.

Volatile Acidity

(VA, Acetic Acid, Ethyl Acetate)

If the wine smells sharply of vinegar or nail polish remover, it likely suffers from of volatile acidity. Legally, wines may contain up to 1.2 g/L of volatile acidity. In small amounts, VA contributes to the complexity of wine. That said, some individuals are hyper sensitive to VA and don't like it. If this is you, find out if you can exchange the wine for something different.

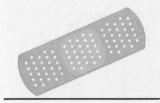

Brettanomyces

(aka "Brett")

If the wine smells like a bandage, sweaty saddle leather, a barnyard, or cardamom it has Brettanomyces. Brett is a wild yeast that ferments alongside wine yeast (Saccharomyces cerevisiae). Some wineries fully embrace it since Brett isn't technically bad. Many tasters enjoy the earthy, rustic aromas that Brett adds. Others detest it. If this is you, try to exchange the wine for something else.

UV Damage

(aka "Light Strike")

Light strike happens when wines are exposed to direct sunlight or left under artificial lighting for too long. Light increases chemical reactions in wine, which can cause premature aging. White and sparkling wines are the most affected. Return the wine.

Wine Aromas

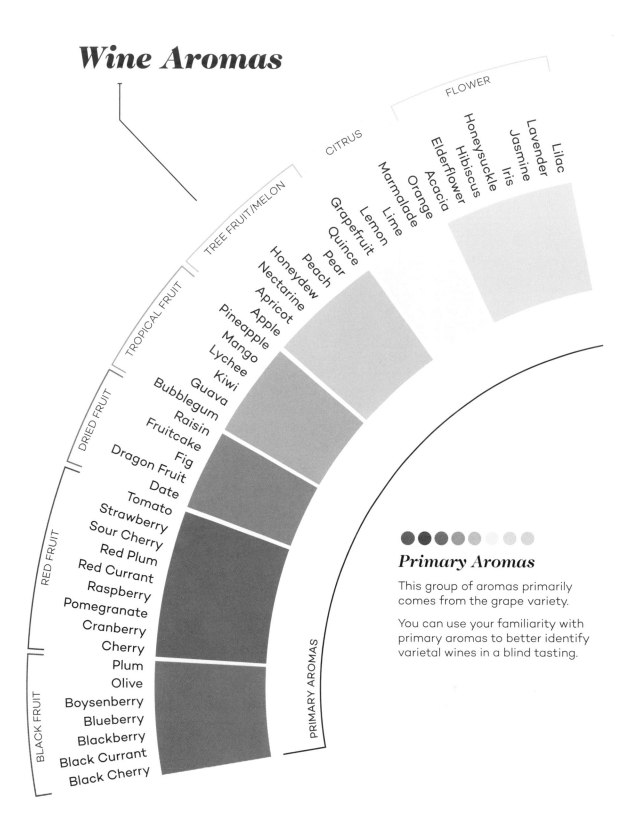

FLOWER

CITRUS

TREE FRUIT/MELON

TROPICAL FRUIT

DRIED FRUIT

RED FRUIT

BLACK FRUIT

Lilac
Lavender
Jasmine
Iris
Honeysuckle
Hibiscus
Elderflower
Acacia
Orange
Marmalade
Lemon
Lime
Grapefruit
Quince
Pear
Peach
Nectarine
Apricot
Apple
Pineapple
Mango
Lychee
Kiwi
Guava
Bubblegum
Raisin
Fruitcake
Fig
Dragon Fruit
Date
Tomato
Strawberry
Sour Cherry
Red Plum
Red Currant
Raspberry
Pomegranate
Cranberry
Cherry
Plum
Olive
Boysenberry
Blueberry
Blackberry
Black Currant
Black Cherry

PRIMARY AROMAS

Primary Aromas

This group of aromas primarily comes from the grape variety.

You can use your familiarity with primary aromas to better identify varietal wines in a blind tasting.

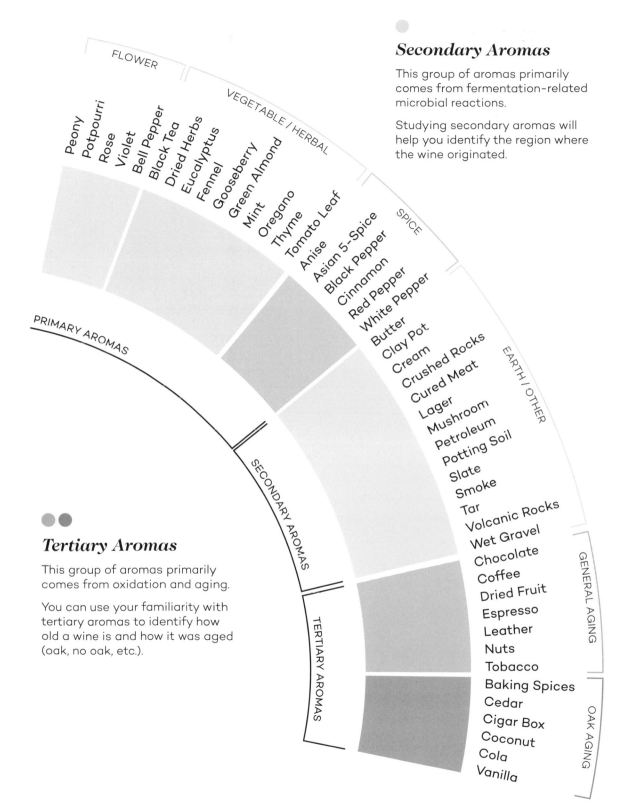

FLOWER

VEGETABLE / HERBAL

SPICE

EARTH / OTHER

PRIMARY AROMAS

SECONDARY AROMAS

TERTIARY AROMAS

GENERAL AGING

OAK AGING

Peony
Potpourri
Rose
Violet
Bell Pepper
Black Tea
Dried Herbs
Eucalyptus
Fennel
Gooseberry
Green Almond
Mint
Oregano
Thyme
Tomato Leaf
Anise
Asian 5-Spice
Black Pepper
Cinnamon
Red Pepper
White Pepper
Butter
Clay Pot
Cream
Crushed Rocks
Cured Meat
Lager
Mushroom
Petroleum
Potting Soil
Slate
Smoke
Tar
Volcanic Rocks
Wet Gravel
Chocolate
Coffee
Dried Fruit
Espresso
Leather
Nuts
Tobacco
Baking Spices
Cedar
Cigar Box
Coconut
Cola
Vanilla

Secondary Aromas

This group of aromas primarily comes from fermentation-related microbial reactions.

Studying secondary aromas will help you identify the region where the wine originated.

Tertiary Aromas

This group of aromas primarily comes from oxidation and aging.

You can use your familiarity with tertiary aromas to identify how old a wine is and how it was aged (oak, no oak, etc.).

Taste

Grab your glass of wine and take a medium-sized sip. "Chew" it. Allow it to touch every nook and cranny. Then, swallow the sample (or spit it out). Then, take a slow breath through your mouth and exhale through your nose.

Structure

Sweetness: Is the wine sweet or dry? Sweetness is the first trait you'll taste on the tip of your tongue.

Acidity: Does the wine make your mouth water? High acidity makes your mouth salivate and tingle.

Tannin: How astringent (mouth-drying) or bitter is the wine? Tannins are felt in the middle of your tongue and between your lips and teeth. Wines with high grape-based tannins tend to have more astringency toward the front of your mouth. Oak tannins are usually felt more toward the middle of the tongue.

Alcohol: Do you feel a warming or hot sensation in your throat? That's the alcohol!

Body: Does the wine fill your mouth with flavor (full-bodied) or is it barely there (light-bodied)?

Finish: What flavor does the wine end on? Is it bitter, sour, oily, or somewhat salty? Note other flavors as well (smoky, herbal, perfumed, etc.).

Length: How long does it take for the aftertaste to diminish?

Complexity: Is it easy or hard to pick out several different flavors and aromas? Lots of flavors = complex.

Layers: Do the wine's flavors change over the course of a single sip? Some critics poetically refer to this sensation as "layers" or "dimensions" in the wine.

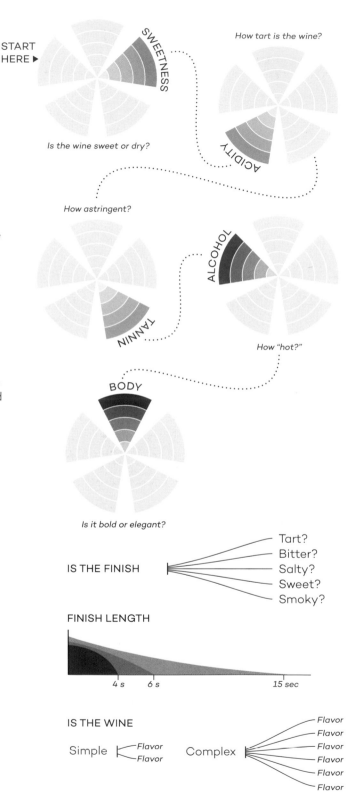

What Kind of Taster Are You?

Your sense of taste and preferences are influenced by both your environment and genetics. Some tasters are naturally more sensitive than others. Fortunately, everyone improves with practice.

HOW MANY TASTEBUDS DO YOU COUNT IN A HOLE-PUNCH SIZED SPACE ON YOUR TONGUE?

< 15 TASTEBUDS

15-30 TASTEBUDS

30+ TASTEBUDS

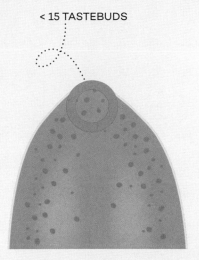 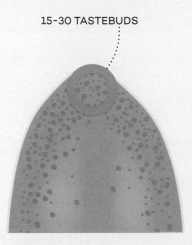 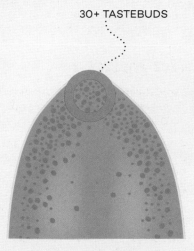

Nonsensitive

10–25% of people

If you count fewer than 15 tastebuds in the area of a hole punch on your tongue, you might be a nonsensitive.

You don't taste bitter the same way others do. In fact, some non-tasters don't taste bitter at all! You're more exploratory with your diet and enjoy rich and strongly flavored foods.

Wines to Try

- High-tannin red wines
- Full-bodied white wines
- Sweet white wines

Between 1–2% of the population suffers from anosmia—the inability to detect or perceive smells.

Average

50–75% of people

If you count between 15 and 30 tastebuds in the area of a hole punch on your tongue, it's likely you're an average taster.

An average taster can still taste the same bitter flavors that a hypersensitive tastes, but it doesn't cause extreme discomfort. Average tasters can be picky or exploratory.

Wines to Try

- Wines with savory flavors
- All wines. Keep exploring!

Women are over two times more likely to be hypersensitive tasters than men.

Hypersensitive

10–25% of people

If you have more than 30 tastebuds in the area of a hole punch on your tongue, you're a hypersensitive (aka "supertaster").

All flavors taste intense to you. It's also likely that you are sensitive to food textures, spiciness, and temperature. You are likely a picky eater.

Wines to Try

- Sweet white wines
- Low-tannin red wines

Asians, Africans, and South Americans have a higher proportion of hypersensitive tasters than Caucasians.

Think

Developing your palate will not happen overnight. It's a process of actively tasting and, more important, thinking about what you like and why.

Wine Ratings

Wine ratings were first popularized in the 1980s with the introduction of Robert Parker's 100-point wine rating system. Today, there are several rating scales, including a 5-star system, the 100-point scale, and a 20-point scale.

A high rating doesn't guarantee you'll love a wine. Instead, it gives you a general idea of a wine's quality level, as determined by the critic's opinion. The best ratings always include detailed tasting notes.

Rating wines consistently can take years of practice. One way to accelerate your skill is to practice comparative tasting.

Comparative Tasting

Comparative tastings pair related wines to be tasted side-by-side. This process makes it easier to identify similarities and differences in wines. Here are a few comparative tastings to try:

- Argentine vs French Malbec
- Oaked Chardonnay vs unoaked Chardonnay
- Sauvignon Blanc vs Grüner Veltliner
- Merlot vs Cabernet Franc vs Cabernet Sauvignon
- Pinot Noir from different countries
- Syrah from different countries
- Same wine, multiple vintages (aka a "vertical")

Wine Rating Scales

LEGENDARY

EPIC

GOOD

AVERAGE

POOR   MEH

50   60   70   80   85   90   95   100

10   12   14   16   17   18   19   20

—   ★   ★   ★   3.5   ★   4.5   ★

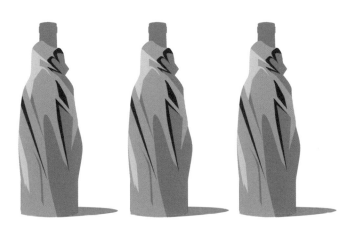

With comparative tasting practice you can learn to blind taste wines

Take Useful Tasting Notes

You're not going to remember every wine you taste. Fortunately, if you take useful tasting notes, you can quickly recall great wines and tasting experiences. Here's what a useful tasting note includes:

LARKMEAD 2014
CABERNET SAUVIGNON
NAPA VALLEY

TASTED FEB 25, 2017

DEEP PURPLE W/
STAINING OF THE TEARS.

HIGH INTENSITY AROMAS OF
BLACKBERRY, BLACK
CURRANT, VIOLETS, MILK
CHOCOLATE, CHERRY SAUCE
& CRUSHED GRAVEL.

ON THE PALATE: BOLD &
TOOTH-STAINING. MEDIUM
ACIDITY. POWDERY & SWEET
HIGH TANNINS. LAYERS OF
PURE CHERRY FRUIT, COCOA
POWDER & THEN VIOLETS
FINISHING WITH SWEET
POWDERY TANNINS.

93% CABERNET
7% PETIT VERDOT

MY FAVORITE FROM NAPA
VALLEY VINTNERS BARREL
AUCTION.

What you tasted

Producer, region, variety(ies), vintage, and any special designation (Riserva, Blanc de Blancs, etc.).

When you tasted it

Wines change as they age.

Your opinion

Stick to a rating system that works for you.

What you saw

Understand the wine before you even smell it!

What you smelled

Be as specific as possible, listing flavors from most to least dominant to create a hierarchy of importance.

What you tasted

Since we "taste" so much with our nose, try to focus this section on the structural qualities of sweetness, acidity, tannin, and alcohol. Also include anything not present in the smell.

What you did

Where were you? What did you eat? Who were you with?

Need help? Try these tasting mats:

🔗 **winefolly.com/tasting-mats/**

Handling, Serving, and Storing Wine

Opening Still Wine

Opening wine: It's tradition to cut the foil below the lip (although, to be honest, it doesn't really matter).

Insert the worm of the corkscrew and rotate it until it's almost all the way in. Pull the cork out slowly to reduce breakage.

Screw cap vs. cork: For wine drinkers, there is no practical difference between screw cap or cork. There are many amazing wines under screw cap.

Opening Sparkling Wine

Remove the foil and loosen the cage by turning it 6 times. Grip the bottle neck with your thumb over the top of the cage and cork. It's safer to remove the cage with the cork.

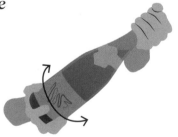

Firmly grip the cork and cage with one hand while rotating the bottom of the bottle with the other hand. Apply resistance as the cork begins to push out to slow it down.

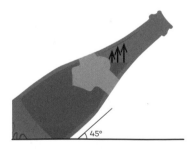

Slowly release the cork and cage with a subtle "pfffft." Continue holding the bottle at a 45° angle after opening the bottle to allow pressure to escape without bubbling over.

Decanting Wine

Decanting is simply pouring wine from a bottle into a vessel to "breathe." Decanting oxidizes wine, reducing the prevalance of certain acids and tannins—making wine taste smoother. It can also turn stinky sulfur compounds (see Wine Faults, p. 29) into less detectable smells. In short, it's magic!

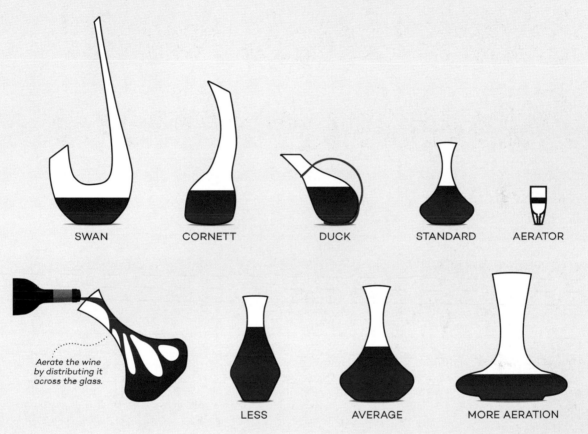

SWAN   CORNETT   DUCK   STANDARD   AERATOR

Aerate the wine by distributing it across the glass.

LESS   AVERAGE   MORE AERATION

What to Decant

Nearly all red wines benefit from decanting. The general rule is, if it has grippy tannins, or tastes sharp and spicy, decanting will help! Decanting is a great way to improve the taste of young wines and affordable wines.

By the way, decanting isn't just for red wines. It's possible to decant Champagne, full-bodied white wine, and orange wine.

How Long to Decant

Generally speaking, the bolder and more tannic the wine is, the longer it can be decanted. In this book there is a recommended decanting time for each wine ranging from no decanting (for light-bodied white wines) to over an hour (for full-bodied red wines with high tannin).

Be aware, it's possible to "over decant" a wine. Old wines are typically the most sensitive.

Choosing a Decanter

Nearly any inert vessel (glass, crystal, porcelain) can be used to decant, so get one you love! Simply consider how easy it will be to wash and store.

If space is an issue for you, wine aerators are a popular alternative. Aerators rapidly introduce excessive amounts of oxygen to wine, causing oxidation to occur instantaneously. While aerators might be too aggressive for old wines, they are fine for most daily drinkers.

Glassware

Size

Make sure your glasses are big enough to collect aromas. White wineglasses should range from about 13–20 oz. and red wineglasses from 17–30 oz. in total capacity.

Shape

A wide bowl exposes more surface area, increasing evaporation and aromatic intensity.

A narrow bowl behaves oppositely. Narrow bowls are useful for "spicy" or high ABV wines.

Opening

The opening size affects two things: how focused the aromas are when they enter your nose and whether or not you can fit your hand in the glass to clean it!

- Larger openings tend to express more floral aromas.
- Smaller openings tend to focus fruit and spice flavors.

Thickness

Thin-rimmed glasses increase exposure to liquid.

RIM

BOWL

STEM

FOOT

Crystal Glass

Crystal is a bit of a misnomer because this type of glass doesn't actually have a crystalline structure. Instead, crystal includes minerals such as lead, zinc, magnesium, and titanium.

The benefit of crystal is increased durability over standard glass. This means that crystal can be spun very thin. Additionally, the minerals in crystal glass refract light and sparkle.

Lead-based crystal glass is safe to drink from, just don't store liquids in them overnight.

Lead-based crystal is porous and should be hand-washed with fragrance-free soap.

If you can't hand wash, many lead-free crystal glasses are dishwasher safe.

Stems vs Stemless

Technically, stems do not affect the taste, although your hands will warm the glass. Feel free to choose whichever style works best for your situation.

Choosing Glassware

Choosing wineglasses is a personal choice. That said, here are some pointers:

- Consider how hard it will be to clean the glasses.
- Have rambunctious kids or pets in your house? Stemless glasses might be the best choice.
- Factor in the cost of losing a glass to breakage.
- Choose 1 or 2 glass styles that most match your wine preferences.
- Plan to buy enough glasses for your wine-drinking friends!

Types of Wineglasses

Sparkling Wines

The thinner and taller the glass, the better it will preserve the bubbles. Flutes are great for lean sparkling wines. Tulips are generally better for richer, or fruitier sparkling wines like Prosecco or aged sparklers. Coupes aren't ideal but they sure look pretty!

Coupe   Wide Tulip   Tulip   Flute

White/Rosé Wines

The smaller bowl keeps whites cooler and positions your nose closer to aromas. Larger bowls work better for oak-aged white wines like Chardonnay.

Light White   Aromatic White/Rosé   Full White

Red Wines

Wide, round bowls help collect aromas and are ideal for Pinot Noir. Medium-sized red glasses work well with spicy wines like Sangiovese or Zinfandel. Oversized glasses help mitigate high tannins with a wider lip (such as with Cabernet or Bordeaux blends).

Aromatic Red/Rosé   Light Red   Medium Red   Full Red

Other Glasses

There are many specialty glasses for wines such as Sherry and Port. Stemless also make a great choice for a water glass.

Port   Sherry   Sweet White / Sauternes   Stemless

Serving Wine

Serving Order

A simple tip when hosting a wine tasting: Order wines from lightest to richest, with the sweetest dessert wines served last.

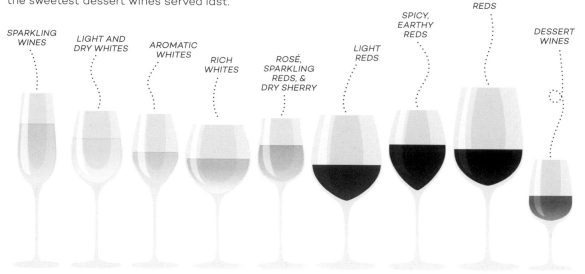

SPARKLING WINES

LIGHT AND DRY WHITES

AROMATIC WHITES

RICH WHITES

ROSÉ, SPARKLING REDS, & DRY SHERRY

LIGHT REDS

SPICY, EARTHY REDS

BOLD REDS

DESSERT WINES

START HERE →

Temperature

Like soda or beer, wine also has best practices for serving temperature.

ICE COLD
38–45° F

COLD
45–55° F

CELLAR
55–60° F

ROOM
60–68° F

Sparkling

Light-Bodied White

Full-Bodied White

Aromatic White

Rosé

Light-Bodied Red

Medium-Bodied Red

Full-Bodied Red

Dessert

Wine Etiquette Tips

Do tell!

Why? Etiquette is one of those things that, on the surface, seems silly, but can be quite useful in certain situations.

Hold your glass by the stem or base. Show off your cleanliness (no fingerprints!) and your ability to be careful around fragile things.

Smell your wine. Show onlookers how thoughtful you are! Also, researchers believe 80% of our sense of taste comes from smell.

Drink from the same position on the glass. Not only does this reduce lip marks on the glass, it also keeps you from smelling the inside of your mouth each you take a sip!

When opening a bottle, try do to it quietly...like a ninja. Of course, there are a few instances where making a "Pop!" will brighten everyone's mood.

When clinking, look your clinking partner in the eye as a sign of respect. Also, clink glasses bowl to bowl to reduce breakage.

When pouring, hold the bottle toward the base. Not only does this little trick show your dexterity, it's another point toward cleanliness.

Offer wine to others before pouring yourself seconds. This demonstrates your ability to be selfless. You're such the generous type!

Aeeeiiii!

Try your best not to be the drunkest one in the room. This is particularly useful in business situations when you might need to think on your feet!

Storing Open Wine

Sparkling Wine

1–3 days*

In the fridge with a sparkling wine stopper.

Light White & Rosé Wine

5–7 days*

In the fridge with a cork.

Full-Bodied White Wine

3–5 days*

In the fridge with a cork.

Red Wine

3–5 days*

In a cool dark place with a cork.

Fortified & Box Wine

28 days*

Corked or closed in a cool dark place.

Some wines stay fresher longer.

Cellaring Wine

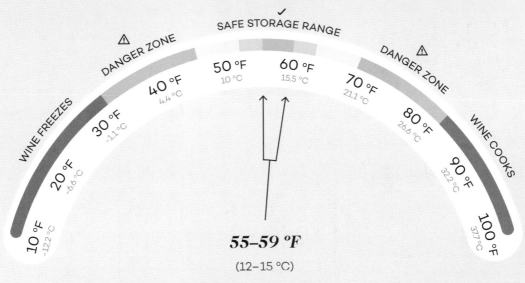

SAFE STORAGE RANGE

⚠ DANGER ZONE ⚠   ⚠ DANGER ZONE ⚠

WINE FREEZES

WINE COOKS

10 °F -12.2 °C
20 °F -6.6 °C
30 °F -1.1 °C
40 °F 4.4 °C
50 °F 10 °C
60 °F 15.5 °C
70 °F 21.1 °C
80 °F 26.6 °C
90 °F 32.2 °C
100 °F 37.7 °C

55–59 °F

(12–15 °C)

The ideal wine storage temperature is 55–59 °F and between 55–75% humidity.

time (oxidation) ⟶

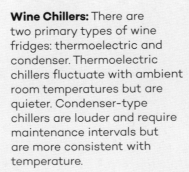
thermoelectric   condenser

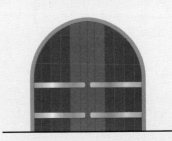

Wine deteriorates about four times faster when stored at ambient room temperatures compared to climate-controlled conditions. If you do not have a wine cellar or chiller, do your best to store your wine bottles in a cool, dark place.

Wine Chillers: There are two primary types of wine fridges: thermoelectric and condenser. Thermoelectric chillers fluctuate with ambient room temperatures but are quieter. Condenser-type chillers are louder and require maintenance intervals but are more consistent with temperature.

If you don't have a cellar or a wine fridge, plan to consume the wine you collect within a year or two of purchase. Bottles stored in variable temperature environments are more likely to develop wine faults.

How Wine Is Made

Great wines are made with high-quality grapes. Let's take a look at the life cycle of a grapevine and learn how each season affects that year's vintage.

...cane

Winter pruning: Last year's growth is cut back. The pruner chooses the best canes to grow new shoots for the coming year's harvest. This is a critical moment that determines the future of the vine.

Spring bud break: Sap rises up from the roots and the first signs of new growth occur in the vineyard. Buds are very delicate and spring hailstorms can destroy them and shorten the growing season (reducing ripeness in wines).

Spring flowering: If the buds survive, they creates shoots and flowers. Flowers of grapevines are called "perfect flowers" because they pollinate themselves without the need of bees.

Summer berry growth: Grape clusters remain green until late summer. Veraison ("vair-ray-shun") is when the berries change color from green to red. Before veraison, some growers remove green bunches to concentrate wine intensity in the remaining bunches.

Fall Harvest: Sugar levels rise and acidity lowers in grapes until they are perfectly ripe. Unlike other fruits, grapes do not ripen after they're picked, so harvesters always rush! Rain storms during this time are unlucky; they make for watery wines and rotten grapes.

Late harvest and winter dormancy: If all goes well, some producers leave a few bunches on the vine to raisinate (dry out) and press into a sweet, "late harvest" dessert wine. Foliage dies off and the vine goes into dormancy to survive the winter.

Red Winemaking

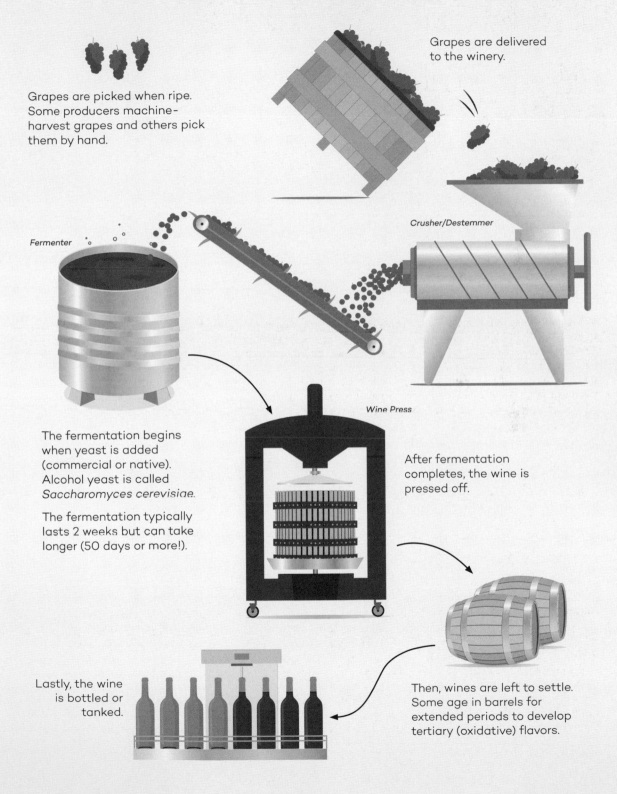

Grapes are picked when ripe. Some producers machine-harvest grapes and others pick them by hand.

Grapes are delivered to the winery.

Crusher/Destemmer

Fermenter

The fermentation begins when yeast is added (commercial or native). Alcohol yeast is called *Saccharomyces cerevisiae*.

The fermentation typically lasts 2 weeks but can take longer (50 days or more!).

Wine Press

After fermentation completes, the wine is pressed off.

Then, wines are left to settle. Some age in barrels for extended periods to develop tertiary (oxidative) flavors.

Lastly, the wine is bottled or tanked.

White Winemaking

White grapes are usually picked before red grapes, while they have plenty of acidity.

Crusher / Destemmer

Grapes are processed and pressed of their skins and seeds immediately.

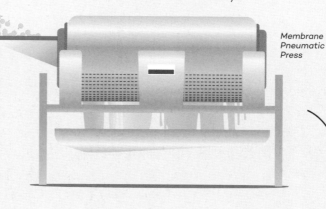

Membrane Pneumatic Press

The fermentation begins.

Typically, white wines ferment cooler than reds (in climate-controlled tanks) to preserve their delicate flavors.

Some wines continue to age in oak barrels or stainless-steel tanks for 6 or more months.

Diatomaceous Earth Filter

After the fermentation is done, the wines are filtered.

Lastly, the wines are bottled.

Stainless-Steel Fermentation Tank

Traditional Method Sparkling

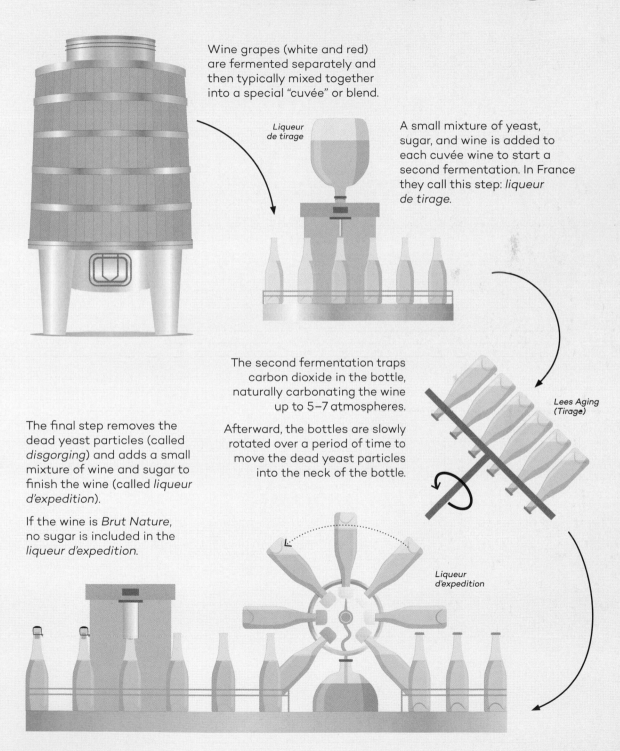

Wine grapes (white and red) are fermented separately and then typically mixed together into a special "cuvée" or blend.

Liqueur de tirage

A small mixture of yeast, sugar, and wine is added to each cuvée wine to start a second fermentation. In France they call this step: *liqueur de tirage*.

The second fermentation traps carbon dioxide in the bottle, naturally carbonating the wine up to 5–7 atmospheres.

Afterward, the bottles are slowly rotated over a period of time to move the dead yeast particles into the neck of the bottle.

Lees Aging (Tirage)

The final step removes the dead yeast particles (called *disgorging*) and adds a small mixture of wine and sugar to finish the wine (called *liqueur d'expedition*).

If the wine is *Brut Nature*, no sugar is included in the *liqueur d'expedition*.

Liqueur d'expedition

Other Wine Styles

Rosé Wines

There are several ways to make rosé wine but the most popular is maceration. For this, red grape skins are left to macerate in juice for a short time (on average from about 4–12 hours). Then, when the ideal color has been acheived, the juice is filtered off the skins and the fermentation is completed like a white wine.

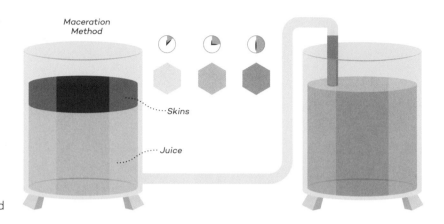

Maceration Method

Skins

Juice

Fortified Wines

Fortified wines or "Vin Doux Naturel" are made by adding neutral spirits (usually clear grape brandy) to wine. For Port, spirits are added midway through the fermentation. The alcohol stops the fermentation, stabilizes the wine, and leaves it partially sweet.

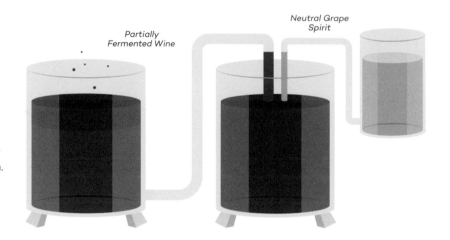

Partially Fermented Wine

Neutral Grape Spirit

Tank Method Sparkling

The tank method is a more affordable sparkling wine method commonly used for Prosecco and Lambrusco. Large, pressurized tanks complete the second fermentation (up to about 3 atmospheres) and then wines are filtered and bottled.

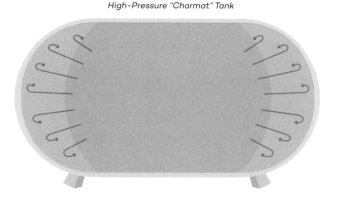

High-Pressure "Charmat" Tank

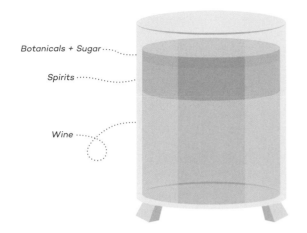

Botanicals + Sugar ·····
Spirits ·······
Wine ·····

Aromatized Wines

Aromatized wines like vermouth are a blend of wine, botanicals, some sugar (or grape juice) and spirits—to fortify the wine. Botanicals added include herbs, spices, and bitter roots and give aromatized wines their unique taste. The primary types of vermouth are dry (a dry white vermouth), sweet (a sweet red-colored vermouth), and blanc (a sweet white vermouth). Most vermouth in the market uses a white wine as its base.

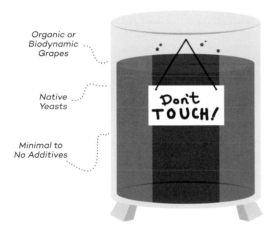

Organic or Biodynamic Grapes ···
Native Yeasts ···
Don't TOUCH!
Minimal to No Additives ···

"Natural" Wines

Today, there is still no official terminology to define natural wines. The generally accepted practices may include:

- Grapes grown either organically or biodynamically and harvested by hand.
- Fermentation with native or "wild" yeasts only.
- No enzymes or additives except for up to 50 ppm sulfites, if any.
- Wines are not filtered.

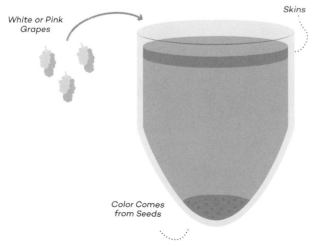

White or Pink Grapes
Skins ···
Color Comes from Seeds ···

"Orange" Wines

This colloquial term describes a subset of natural wines made with white grapes. Wines are fermented with their skins like red wines. The result is a wine that's dyed orange from the lignin in the seeds. Orange wines have tannin and body much like red wines.

Orange winemaking originated in Northeast Italy and Slovenia, where you can find great examples made with Pinot Grigio, Ribolla Gialla, and Malvasia grapes.

Winemaking Techniques

Many things in the winemaking process can drastically change the final product. Let's discuss some of the most used and talked-about winemaking techniques and how they affect the taste of wine.

Whole-Cluster Fermentation uses the entire grape bunch—including the stems. Stems add tannin and structure to typically delicate wines.

Cold Soaking is the process of resting the juice with the skins at a cold temperature prior to fermentation. This helps extract more color and flavors from the skin.

Saignée ("sahn-yay") or "Bleeding Off" is the process of draining some juice from a red wine fermentation to increase the concentration. Leftover juice is used for a deep-colored rosé wine.

Cool vs Hot Fermentations. Cool fermentations preserve delicate flower and fruit aromas (popular for white wines) and hot fermentations soften tannin and simplify flavors (popular with commercial wines).

Open-Top Fermentations allow more oxygen to enter during the fermentation and are most commonly used for red winemaking.

Closed Fermentations limit the amount of oxygen to facilitate during the fermentation and are popular with white wines in order to preserve delicate flavors.

Carbonic Maceration is a closed-top, whole-cluster fermentation, which reduces bitter grape tannins and preserves delicate floral aromas in red wines. This method is used with Gamay in Beaujolais.

Native Yeast. A fermentation that only uses yeast found in the winery or on the grapes. This method is rare and more common in small-production wines.

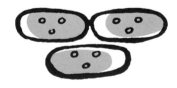

Commercial Yeast. Using commercially made yeasts to ferment wines. This method is very common, especially in large-production wines.

Pumpovers and Punchdowns are ways to mix the fermentation. Pumpovers extract red wine flavors aggressively. Punchdowns are more delicate and popular with light reds.

Microoxygenation. Red wines are bubbled with oxygen during the fermentation to help soften their tannins. This method is popular with red Bordeaux varieties.

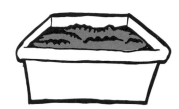

Extended Maceration. After the fermentation is completed, red wines are left on their skins for an extended period of time. This process can soften flavors and reduce harsh tannins.

Oak Aging. Two things are accomplished with oak aging: oxidation and oak flavors. New oak adds more oak flavors (vanilla, cola, clove) to wine.

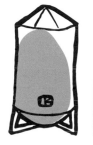

Stainless / Inert Aging. Stainless steel vessels slow oxidation and help preserve the primary flavors of a wine. This is a popular choice for white wines.

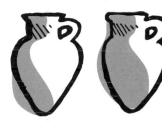

Concrete / Amphora. Raw concrete and clay amphora vessels often lower the acidity in wine, which can soften it's taste profile. This practice is still relatively uncommon.

Malolactic Fermentation. Almost all red wines go through MLF, in which a bacteria called *Oenococcus oeni* alters sharp malic acid (apples) into softer and smoother lactic acid (milk).

Fining and Racking. Fining adds enzymes to clarify wine. The enzymes glom to proteins that fall to the bottom of the barrel. Racking transfers wines to a fresh barrel.

Filtered vs. Unfiltered. Filtered wines are sent through microscopic filters to remove everything but the liquid. Unfiltered wines contain sediment, but it contributes to their complexity.

Food & Wine

This section explores the fundamentals of flavor pairing and how to pair food with wine. Included are several pairing charts for quick reference.

Wine Pairing

What makes a great food and wine pairing? Balance between the taste of a wine and the ingredients in the dish. Even though the science of flavor pairing is quite complex, anyone can learn the fundamentals. The very first thing to do is to start thinking about wine as an ingredient.

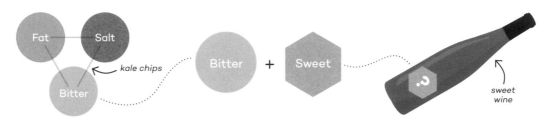

Identify the basic tastes (sweet, acid, salt, bitter, etc.) in the dish. For example, macaroni and cheese is fat and salt. Kale chips are bitter and salt.

Choose a pairing methodology for the wine to counterbalance the basic tastes in the food. For example, here are some classic pairings: sweet-salt, bitter-fat, salt-sour, fat-acid, and sweet-sour.

Select a style of wine that matches the pairing methodology. For example, if you are pairing fat + acid, you will want to choose a wine with higher acidity.

Next, identify the nuanced flavors in the food. These nuanced flavors could come from spices, herbs, or minor ingredients (olive, strawberry, bacon, etc.).

Then, select a wine that also contains similar nuanced flavors and fits the pairing method. For example, the wines above all have subtle herbal notes.

Test your pairing by consuming a little bit of food and wine together in your mouth. If the pairing is a winner, the tastes will be in balance.

Red wines taste more bitter due to tannin.

White, rosé and sparkling wines have more acidity.

Sweet wines are, well, sweeter!

Pairing Methodologies

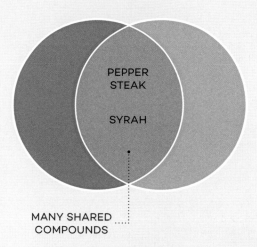

PEPPER
STEAK

SYRAH

MANY SHARED
COMPOUNDS

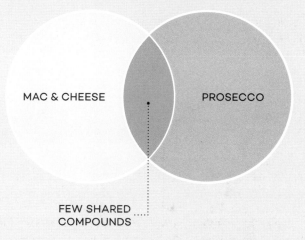

MAC & CHEESE

PROSECCO

FEW SHARED
COMPOUNDS

Congruent Pairing

A congruent pairing creates balance by amplifying shared flavor compounds. This style of flavor pairing is common in Western cultures.

For example, Syrah and seasoned steak share many compounds including rotundone, which is present in both pepper and Syrah.

Examples:

- Buttered Popcorn with Oaked Chardonnay
- Barbecue Pork with Zinfandel
- Cucumber Salad with Sauvignon Blanc
- Pineapple Upside-Down Cake with Tokaji Aszu
- Turkey and Cranberry Sauce with Pinot Noir
- Bresaola with Chianti Classico

Contrasting Pairing

A complementary pairing creates balance by contrasting tastes and flavors. This type of flavor pairing is the base of many Eastern culture cuisines (e.g., sweet and sour, etc.).

For example, rich, gooey mac and cheese is contrasted with a high acidity wine to cleanse the palate.

Examples:

- Blue Cheese with Ruby Port
- Pork Chop with Riesling
- Mushroom Risotto with Nebbiolo
- Grilled Trout with Manzanilla Sherry
- Maple Bacon with Champagne
- Coconut Curry and Grüner Veltliner

Pairing Tips

If you're just getting started, you'll find these tried-and-true practices to be extra helpful. As you get more familiar with different wines, you can experiment with breaking the rules! (Gamay with trout, anyone?)

The wine should be more acidic than the food.

The wine should be sweeter than the food.

The wine should have the same intensity as the food.

Bitter foods tend not to pair well with bitter wines (such as dry red wines).

Fats and oils counterbalance high-tannin wines.

Tannin in wine clashes with fish oils. That's why red wines don't typically pair well with seafood.

Wines with sweetness help counteract spicy foods.

More often than not, white, sparkling, and rosé wines create contrasting pairings.

More often than not, red wines create congruent pairings.

Taste Chart

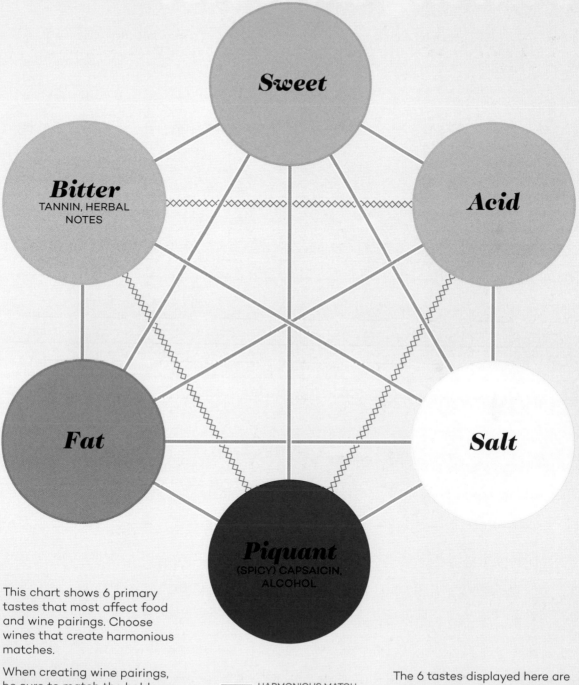

Sweet

Bitter
TANNIN, HERBAL NOTES

Acid

Fat

Salt

Piquant
(SPICY) CAPSAICIN, ALCOHOL

This chart shows 6 primary tastes that most affect food and wine pairings. Choose wines that create harmonious matches.

When creating wine pairings, be sure to match the boldness level of the food. For example, delicately flavored foods pair best with delicately flavored wines.

—— HARMONIOUS MATCH
XXXX DISCORDANT MATCH

The 6 tastes displayed here are just a portion of what humans can sense. Other tastes include fizziness, umami (meaty), numbness, electricity, soapiness, and coolness (menthol).

Pairing Exercise

In this exercise, you'll try 6 simple foods with 4 wine styles (full-bodied red, sweet white, light-bodied white, and sparkling). The purpose of this exercise is to learn how food and wine pairing works on a physical level.

Select Wines: Choose based on what's available. For example, you could choose Cava, Pinot Grigio, Malbec, and an off-dry Chenin Blanc.

Step 1: Take a bite of one of the ingredients (see facing page), chew it, and then, before you swallow, sip one of the wines.

Step 2: Evaluate the pairings as you go. Use a scale of 1 to 5. (1 = poor, 5 = great.)

Step 3: Try multiple taste combinations (sweet + fat, sour + salt, fat + bitter, etc.) and retry wines.

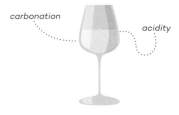

Sparkling Q: Does carbonation help with the pairing? Are their any flavor pairings that work really well with sparklers?

White Q: Does elevated acidity add to the pairing? How does the white compare to the red for pairing?

Red Q: How does the tannin in the wine interact with the 6 tastes? What pairings absolutely don't work?

Sweet Q: Any surprises here with sweetness? How many tastes does this style pair with?

Remember: There are no wrong answers and you will be surprised by what you discover!

Pairing Exercise

WINE AND INGREDIENT LIST

Salt
POTATO CHIP

Acid
PICKLE

Fat
BRIE

FULL-BODIED RED WINE

SWEET WHITE WINE

LIGHT-BODIED WHITE WINE

SPARKLING WINE

Malbec, Cabernet Sauvignon, Syrah, Petite Sirah, etc.

Late-harvest wines, Sweet Riesling Gewürztraminer, etc.

Sauvignon Blanc, Pinot Gris, Grechetto, Melon, etc.

Cava, Prosecco, Crémant, etc.

Bitter
KALE

Sweet
HONEY

Piquant
HOT SAUCE

Pairing with Cheese

Legend:
- ✓ = great
- ● = average
- ✗ = bad

Wine	Salty, Crumbly Cheese (Feta, Cotija, Queso Fresco, Halloumi, Mizithra)	Pungent Blue Cheese (Stilton, Blue, Roquefort, Gorgonzola)	Sour Cheese & Cream (Sour Cream, Cream Cheese, Ricotta, Havarti, Chèvre, Cottage Cheese)	Delicate, Buttery Cheese (Brie, Camembert, Époisses, Burrata, Delice de Bourgogne)	Nutty, Hard Cheese (Gruyere, Comte, Provolone, Edam, Emmental, Mozzarella, Scamorza)	Fruity, Umami Cheese (Cheddar, Gouda, Smoked Gouda, Colby, Ossau-Iraty, Muenster)	Dry, Salty, Umami Cheese (Parmesan, Grana Padano, Pecorino, Asiago, Aged Manchego)
SPARKLING WINE	✓	●	✓	✓	✓	●	✓
LIGHT-BODIED WHITE WINE	✓	✗	✓	✓	✓	✓	✓
FULL-BODIED WHITE WINE	●	✗	●	✓	✓	●	●
AROMATIC WHITE WINE	●	✓	●	✓	✓	●	●
ROSÉ WINE	✓	●	●	●	●	●	●
LIGHT-BODIED RED WINE	●	✗	●	●	✓	●	●
MED.-BODIED RED WINE	✗	✗	●	●	✓	✓	✓
FULL-BODIED RED WINE	✗	●	✗	●	●	✓	●
DESSERT WINE	✗	✓	●	✓	●	●	✗

Pairing with Protein

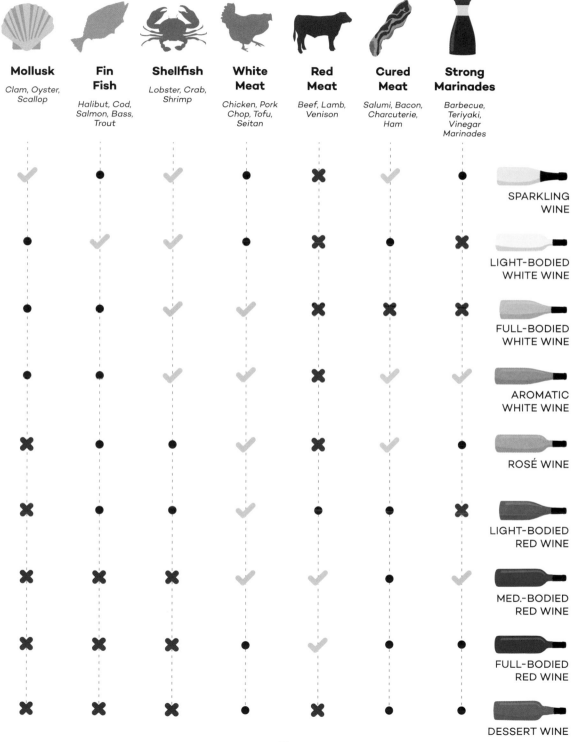

	Mollusk (Clam, Oyster, Scallop)	Fin Fish (Halibut, Cod, Salmon, Bass, Trout)	Shellfish (Lobster, Crab, Shrimp)	White Meat (Chicken, Pork Chop, Tofu, Seitan)	Red Meat (Beef, Lamb, Venison)	Cured Meat (Salumi, Bacon, Charcuterie, Ham)	Strong Marinades (Barbecue, Teriyaki, Vinegar Marinades)
SPARKLING WINE	✓	●	✓	●	✗	✓	●
LIGHT-BODIED WHITE WINE	●	✓	✓	●	✗	●	✗
FULL-BODIED WHITE WINE	●	●	✓	✓	✗	✗	✗
AROMATIC WHITE WINE	●	●	✓	✓	✗	✓	✓
ROSÉ WINE	✗	●	●	✓	✗	✓	●
LIGHT-BODIED RED WINE	✗	●	●	✓	●	●	✗
MED.-BODIED RED WINE	✗	✗	✗	✓	✓	●	✓
FULL-BODIED RED WINE	✗	✗	✗	●	✓	●	●
DESSERT WINE	✗	✗	✗	●	✗	●	●

Pairing with Vegetables

= great
= average
= bad

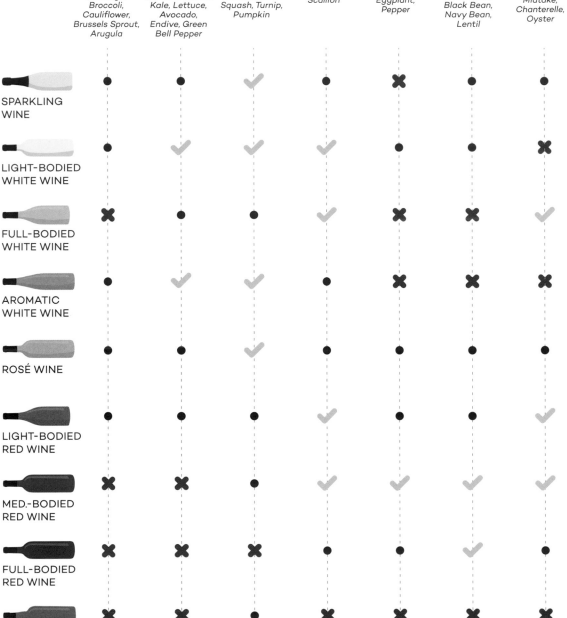

Wine	Cruciferous Vegetable (Cabbage, Broccoli, Cauliflower, Brussels Sprout, Arugula)	Green Vegetable (Green Bean, Pea, Kale, Lettuce, Avocado, Endive, Green Bell Pepper)	Harvest Vegetable (Yam, Carrot, Squash, Turnip, Pumpkin)	Allium (Onion, Garlic, Shallot, Scallion)	Nightshade (Capsicum, Tomato, Eggplant, Pepper)	Bean / Legume (Pinto Bean, Black Bean, Navy Bean, Lentil)	Funghi (Crimini, Porcini, Shitake, Miatake, Chanterelle, Oyster)
SPARKLING WINE	average	average	great	average	bad	average	average
LIGHT-BODIED WHITE WINE	average	great	great	great	average	average	bad
FULL-BODIED WHITE WINE	bad	average	average	great	bad	bad	great
AROMATIC WHITE WINE	average	great	great	average	bad	bad	bad
ROSÉ WINE	average	average	great	average	average	average	average
LIGHT-BODIED RED WINE	average	average	average	great	average	average	great
MED.-BODIED RED WINE	bad	bad	average	great	great	great	average
FULL-BODIED RED WINE	bad	bad	bad	average	average	great	average
DESSERT WINE	bad	bad	average	bad	bad	bad	bad

Pairing with Spices and Herbs

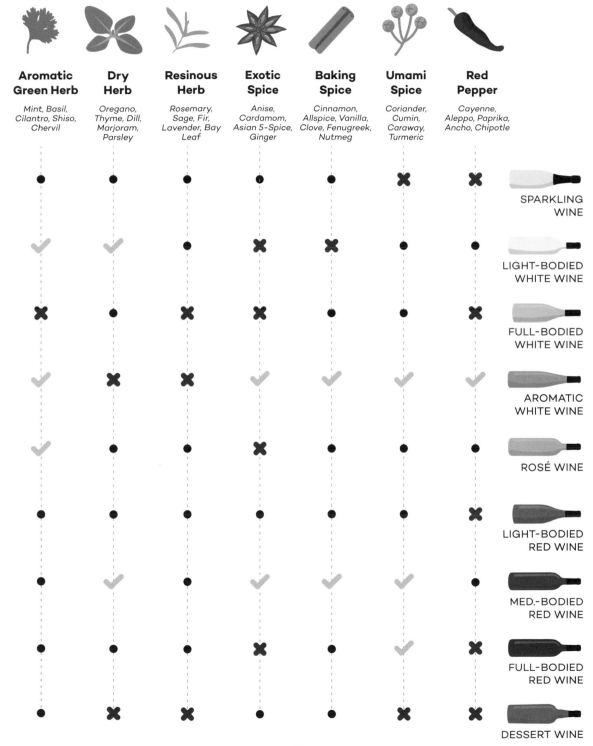

	Aromatic Green Herb (Mint, Basil, Cilantro, Shiso, Chervil)	Dry Herb (Oregano, Thyme, Dill, Marjoram, Parsley)	Resinous Herb (Rosemary, Sage, Fir, Lavender, Bay Leaf)	Exotic Spice (Anise, Cardamom, Asian 5-Spice, Ginger)	Baking Spice (Cinnamon, Allspice, Vanilla, Clove, Fenugreek, Nutmeg)	Umami Spice (Coriander, Cumin, Caraway, Turmeric)	Red Pepper (Cayenne, Aleppo, Paprika, Ancho, Chipotle)
SPARKLING WINE	●	●	●	●	●	✗	✗
LIGHT-BODIED WHITE WINE	✓	✓	●	✗	✗	●	●
FULL-BODIED WHITE WINE	✗	●	✗	✗	●	●	✗
AROMATIC WHITE WINE	✓	✗	✗	✓	✓	✓	✓
ROSÉ WINE	✓	●	●	✗	●	●	●
LIGHT-BODIED RED WINE	●	●	●	●	●	●	✗
MED.-BODIED RED WINE	●	✓	●	✓	✓	✓	●
FULL-BODIED RED WINE	●	●	●	✗	●	✓	✗
DESSERT WINE	●	✗	✗	●	●	✗	✗

Cooking with Wine

Not only is wine fun to cook with, it does a great job of enhancing flavors in food. There are three ways to use wine in cooking: reduction sauces, marinades, and deglazes/cooking liquids.

Reduction Sauces

1 cup of wine = ¼ cup of reduction sauce

Wine reduction sauces are an excellent way to use wine's unique flavors, acidity, and fruitiness to complement both savory and sweet dishes. For the truest flavor, simmer the wine slowly over low heat. While the wine simmers the alcohol will burn off, but low heat will help preserve the delicacy of the wine's aromatics in the sauce.

Marinades

2 parts wine, 1 part fat, and seasoning

A marinade is a concoction of acid, oil, herb, and spice (and sometimes sugar) designed to tenderize and flavor proteins. Wine has both tannin and acid, making it a great tenderizer to fill the role of acid in a marinade. When flavoring your marinade, think carefully about how all the ingredients will pair together. Marination times will depend on the protein—too much time can make the protein mushy. Fish need only 15 minutes to 45 minutes whereas brisket may require an overnight soak.

2 PARTS WINE   1 PART FAT   SEASONING

Deglazes/Cooking Liquids

A splash or 1–2 tablespoons per cup

The benefit of adding wine to a dish as a cooking liquid is that you get the benefits of wine's natural acidity as well as its flavors. Deglazing is when you toss cool liquid in a hot pan. The process captures all the brown bits (caused by Maillard reaction) stuck to the bottom of your sauté pan. You can use this deglazing liquid to create a gravy or a soup base.

Additionally, you can add wine directly to slow-cooked stews. Just be sure to add the wine early enough to cook out the alcohol (takes at least an hour).

Wines for Cooking

Dry White and Red Wines

Perfect for using with beef stews, cream soups, white wine butter sauces, mussels, clams, and deglazes.

These are your everyday-drinking white and red wines. The best wine to use in your dish will often be one that best pairs with your meal. Generally speaking, you should opt for fruity, light-bodied white wines and fruity, light- to medium-bodied red wines (and rosé) with higher acidity.

Examples: Pinot Gris, Sauvignon Blanc, Albariño, Verdejo, Colombard, Chenin Blanc, Riesling

Nutty, Oxidized Wines

Perfect for use in gravies, on chicken and pork, rich fish like halibut and shrimp, and soups.

Oxidation in wine adds many complex and robust flavors of nuts, baked fruit, as well as subtle browned sugar-like notes. Many oxidized wines are also fortified, which creates very concentrated reduction sauces. While traditionally oxidized wines are used in classic European dishes, they also do well with rich Asian and Indian flavors.

Examples: Sherry, Madeira, Marsala, Orange Wine, Vin Jaune

Rich, Sweet Dessert Wines

Perfect for syrups on desserts with nuts, caramel, and vanilla ice cream.

Sweet red and white wines make delicious wine reduction sauces. When choosing a wine, remember to match the intensity of the dish. For example, a rich, chocolaty dessert is better matched with a sauce made from a rich and bold wine like Ruby Port.

Examples: Sauternes, Port, Ice Wine, Sweet Riesling, Muscat Beaumes de Venise, Vin Santo, Gewürztraminer, P.X. (Pedro Ximénez)

Grapes & Wines

This section contains 100 common wines, grapes, and blends along with tasting notes, food pairing and serving recommendations, and regional distribution.

Wine Grapes of the World

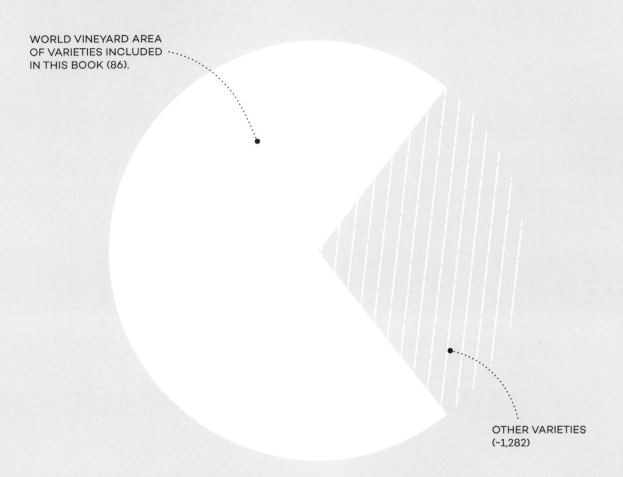

WORLD VINEYARD AREA
OF VARIETIES INCLUDED
IN THIS BOOK (86).

OTHER VARIETIES
(~1,282)

The most in-depth book on wine grapes available today includes 1,368 varieties used in commercial wine production (*Wine Grapes*, Robinson, Harding, Vouillamoz, 2012). Of these varieties, just a small fraction account for the vast majority of vineyards planted throughout the world.

So, to accelerate your understanding of wine, we've included just 100 grapes and wines (86 grapes and 14 wines, to be exact). These varieties represent the most popular grapes used for drinking wines as well as the most planted varieties, representing 71% of the world's vineyard area.

When you come across a rare variety not included in this volume, you can visit the free resource on winefolly.com. We hope to continue to add more of the wines and varieties of the world.

Wines by Style

White Wines

ZWEIGELT
SCHIAVA
LAMBRUSCO
GAMAY
FRAPPATO
BRACHETTO
CHARDONNAY
VIOGNIER
ROUSSANNE
MARSANNE
GEWÜRZTRAMINER
GRENACHE BLANC
SAVATIANO
TREBBIANO TOSCANO
AIRÉN
VIURA
SÉMILLON
FALANGHINA
VERMENTINO
SAUVIGNON BLANC
GRÜNER VELTLINER
ARINTO
CHENIN BLANC
MOSCHOFILERO
FERNÃO PIRES
TORRONTÉS
PINOT GRIS
SILVANER
GRECHETTO
FIANO
VERDEJO
RIESLING
FURMINT
MUSCAT BLANC
CORTESE
VERDICCHIO
FRIULANO
ALBARIÑO
COLOMBARD
ASSYRTIKO
PINOT BLANC
VINHO VERDE
PIQUEPOUL
MELON
FRANCIACORTA
CHAMPAGNE
CRÉMANT
CAVA
PROSECCO

Sparkling Wines

Individual wines may be lighter or bolder than depicted in this chart.

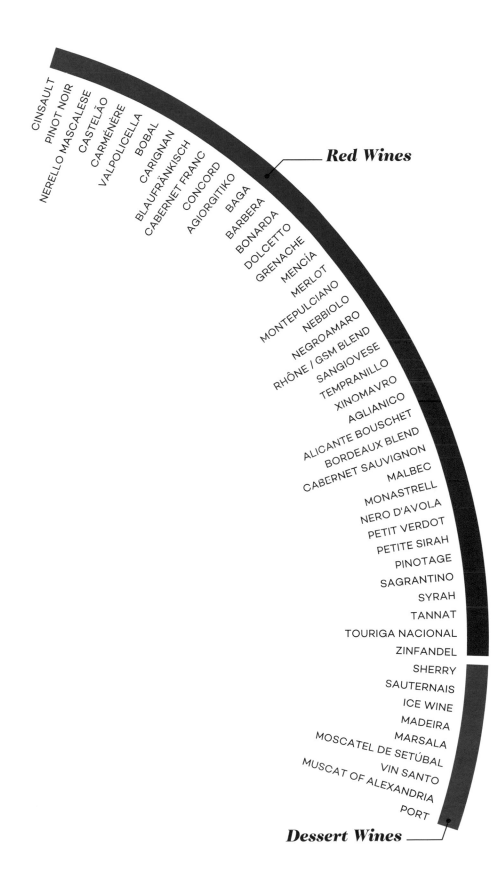

Red Wines

CINSAULT
PINOT NOIR
NERELLO MASCALESE
CASTELÃO
CARMÉNÈRE
VALPOLICELLA
BOBAL
CARIGNAN
BLAUFRÄNKISCH
CABERNET FRANC
CONCORD
AGIORGITIKO
BAGA
BARBERA
BONARDA
DOLCETTO
GRENACHE
MENCÍA
MERLOT
MONTEPULCIANO
NEBBIOLO
NEGROAMARO
RHÔNE / GSM BLEND
SANGIOVESE
TEMPRANILLO
XINOMAVRO
AGLIANICO
ALICANTE BOUSCHET
BORDEAUX BLEND
CABERNET SAUVIGNON
MALBEC
MONASTRELL
NERO D'AVOLA
PETIT VERDOT
PETITE SIRAH
PINOTAGE
SAGRANTINO
SYRAH
TANNAT
TOURIGA NACIONAL
ZINFANDEL
SHERRY
SAUTERNAIS
ICE WINE
MADEIRA
MARSALA
MOSCATEL DE SETÚBAL
VIN SANTO
MUSCAT OF ALEXANDRIA
PORT

Dessert Wines

Section Guide

Grape or wine name

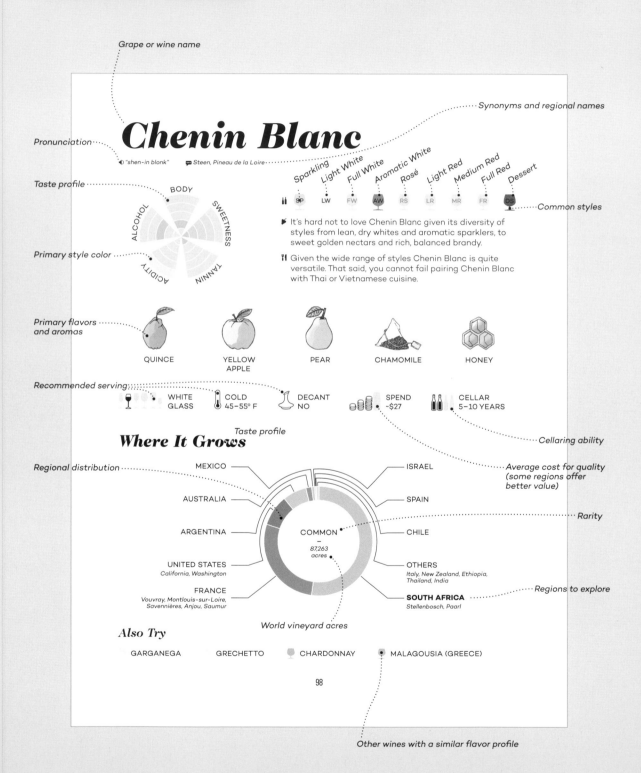

Chenin Blanc

Synonyms and regional names

Pronunciation ···· 🔊 "shen-in blonk"   💬 Steen, Pineau de la Loire ····

Taste profile ····

BODY
SWEETNESS
ALCOHOL
TANNIN
ACIDITY

Primary style color ····

Sparkling · Light White · Full White · Aromatic White · Rosé · Light Red · Medium Red · Full Red · Dessert

SP · LW · FW · AW · RS · LR · MR · FR · DS ···· Common styles

🍴 It's hard not to love Chenin Blanc given its diversity of styles from lean, dry whites and aromatic sparklers, to sweet golden nectars and rich, balanced brandy.

🍴 Given the wide range of styles Chenin Blanc is quite versatile. That said, you cannot fail pairing Chenin Blanc with Thai or Vietnamese cuisine.

Primary flavors and aromas ····

QUINCE   YELLOW APPLE   PEAR   CHAMOMILE   HONEY

Recommended serving ····

WHITE GLASS   COLD 45–55° F   DECANT NO   SPEND ~$27   CELLAR 5–10 YEARS

Cellaring ability

Average cost for quality (some regions offer better value)

Where It Grows

Taste profile

Regional distribution ····

MEXICO
AUSTRALIA
ARGENTINA
UNITED STATES
California, Washington
FRANCE
Vouvray, Montlouis-sur-Loire, Savennières, Anjou, Saumur

COMMON
–
87,263
acres

ISRAEL
SPAIN
CHILE
OTHERS
Italy, New Zealand, Ethiopia, Thailand, India
SOUTH AFRICA
Stellenbosch, Paarl

Rarity

Regions to explore

World vineyard acres

Also Try

GARGANEGA   GRECHETTO   🍷 CHARDONNAY   🍷 MALAGOUSIA (GREECE)

Other wines with a similar flavor profile

Agiorgitiko

🔊 ""ah-your-yeek-tee-ko" 💬 *St. George, Nemea*

BODY
SWEETNESS
TANNIN
ACIDITY
ALCOHOL

| | SP | LW | FW | AW | RS | LR | MR | FR | DS |

🥂 The top red of Greece offers a wide range of styles from rosé to deep red. The most exceptional Agiorgitiko are the full-bodied red wines from Nemea in Peloponnese.

🍴 With subtle flavors of nutmeg and cinnamon, Agiorgitiko pairs wonderfully with roasted meats, tomato sauces, and spiced cuisines from the Middle East to India.

| RASPBERRY | BLACKBERRY | PLUM SAUCE | BLACK PEPPER | NUTMEG |

🍷 OVERSIZED GLASS 🌡️ ROOM 60–68° F 🍶 DECANT 60+ MIN 🪙 SPEND ~$15 🍾 CELLAR 5–25 YEARS

Where It Grows

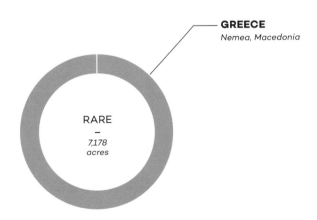

GREECE
Nemea, Macedonia

RARE
–
7,178
acres

Also Try

🍷 XINOMAVRO   🍷 MERLOT   🍷 BARBERA   🍷 NERO D'AVOLA

71

Aglianico

 "olli-yawn-nee-ko" *Taurasi*

SP   LW   FW   AW   RS   LR   MR   FR   DS

Nebbiolo may be king in Northern Italy, but down south, Aglianico reigns supreme. It's a wine with incredible quality and a unique savory flavor that's best aged.

A savory wine like Aglianico goes well with gamey dishes or even Texas-style barbecue. A well-aged Aglianico is best enjoyed slow, like fine Islay Scotch.

 WHITE PEPPER

 BLACK CHERRY

 SMOKE

 GAME

 SPICED PLUM

 OVERSIZED GLASS

 ROOM 60–68° F

 DECANT 60+ MIN

 SPEND ~$26

 CELLAR 5–25 YEARS

Where It Grows

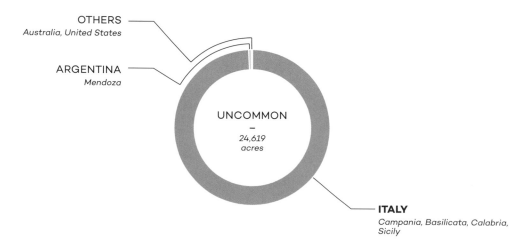

OTHERS
Australia, United States

ARGENTINA
Mendoza

UNCOMMON
–
24,619
acres

ITALY
Campania, Basilicata, Calabria, Sicily

Also Try

 NEBBIOLO    MONASTRELL   NEGROAMARO   TEMPRANILLO

Airén

◀) *"air-ren"*

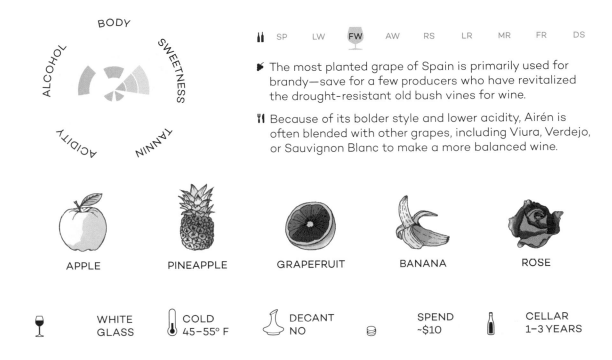

SP　LW　**FW**　AW　RS　LR　MR　FR　DS

🌱 The most planted grape of Spain is primarily used for brandy—save for a few producers who have revitalized the drought-resistant old bush vines for wine.

🍴 Because of its bolder style and lower acidity, Airén is often blended with other grapes, including Viura, Verdejo, or Sauvignon Blanc to make a more balanced wine.

APPLE　　PINEAPPLE　　GRAPEFRUIT　　BANANA　　ROSE

WHITE GLASS　　COLD 45–55° F　　DECANT NO　　SPEND ~$10　　CELLAR 1–3 YEARS

Where It Grows

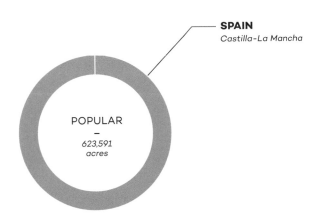

SPAIN
Castilla-La Mancha

POPULAR
–
623,591 acres

Also Try

🍷 SAVATIANO　　　TREBBIANO TOSCANO　　　ROUSSANNE

Albariño

 "alba-reen-yo"   *Alvarinho*

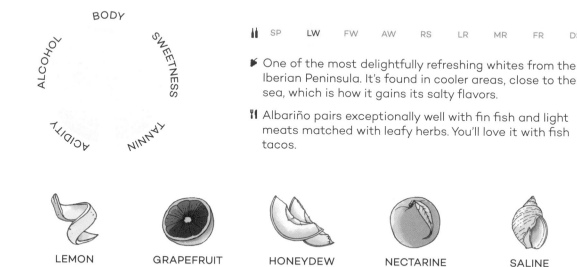

BODY
SWEETNESS
TANNIN
ACIDITY
ALCOHOL

	SP	LW	FW	AW	RS	LR	MR	FR	DS

🐟 One of the most delightfully refreshing whites from the Iberian Peninsula. It's found in cooler areas, close to the sea, which is how it gains its salty flavors.

🍴 Albariño pairs exceptionally well with fin fish and light meats matched with leafy herbs. You'll love it with fish tacos.

LEMON ZEST	GRAPEFRUIT	HONEYDEW	NECTARINE	SALINE

WHITE GLASS	ICE COLD 38–45° F	DECANT NO		SPEND ~$12	CELLAR 1–5 YEARS

Where It Grows

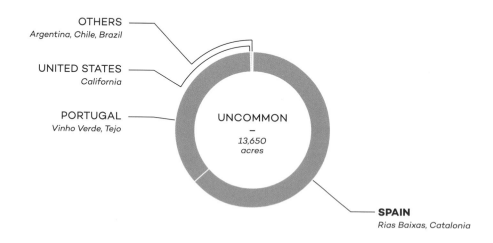

OTHERS
Argentina, Chile, Brazil

UNITED STATES
California

PORTUGAL
Vinho Verde, Tejo

UNCOMMON
–
13,650 acres

SPAIN
Rias Baixas, Catalonia

Also Try

   LOUREIRO (PORTUGAL)   RIESLING   FURMINT   VERDEJO   VINHO VERDE

Alicante Bouschet

 "olly-kan-tay boo-shey"   *Garnacha Tintorera*

BODY
SWEETNESS
TANNIN
ACIDITY
ALCOHOL

							FR	
SP	LW	FW	AW	RS	LR	MR	**FR**	DS

🥩 A rare type of grape called a teinturier with red skins and red flesh. It was created when botanist Henri Bouschet crossed Garnacha with Petit Bouschet in Southern France.

🍴 The intense smoky-sweet flavors of Alicante Bouschet beg for equally intense foods including barbecue, teriyaki, carne asada, and grilled vegetables.

BLACK CHERRY	BLACKBERRY BRAMBLE	BLACK PLUM	BLACK PEPPER	SWEET TOBACCO

OVERSIZED GLASS	ROOM 60–68° F	DECANT 30 MIN	SPEND ~$10	CELLAR 3–7 YEARS

Where It Grows

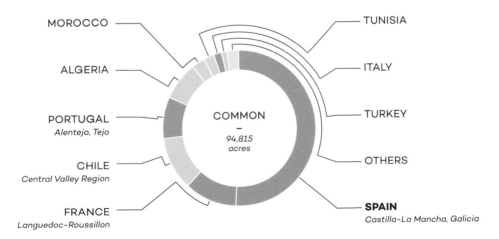

MOROCCO

ALGERIA

PORTUGAL
Alentejo, Tejo

CHILE
Central Valley Region

FRANCE
Languedoc-Roussillon

COMMON
–
94,815
acres

TUNISIA

ITALY

TURKEY

OTHERS

SPAIN
Castilla-La Mancha, Galicia

Also Try

🍷 MONASTRELL   🍷 SYRAH   🍷 PETITE SIRAH   🍷 ZINFANDEL   🍷 TOURIGA NACIONAL

Arinto

🔊 *"ah-reen-too"*   💬 *Paderna*

BODY
SWEETNESS
TANNIN
ACIDITY
ALCOHOL

| SP | LW | **FW** | AW | RS | LR | MR | FR | DS |

🏹 An indigenous grape to Portugal that produces exceptional, age-worthy whites that can evolve over time (7+ years) to reveal flavors of beeswax and nuts.

🍴 Arinto makes an excellent pairing with richer seafood including Portugal's famous Bacalhao (salt cod) due to its high acidity and lemon zest–like flavors.

 LEMON ZEST

 GRAPEFRUIT

 HAZELNUT

 BEESWAX

 CHAMOMILE

🍷 **WHITE GLASS**

🌡️ **COLD 45–55° F**

⚗️ **DECANT NO**

 SPEND ~$10

🍾 **CELLAR 5–10 YEARS**

Where It Grows

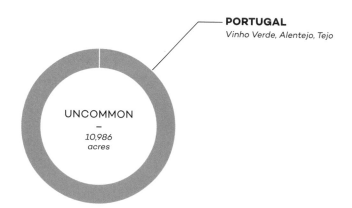

PORTUGAL
Vinho Verde, Alentejo, Tejo

UNCOMMON
–
10,986 acres

Also Try

GARGANEGA   FALANGHINA   TREBBIANO TOSCANO   GRENACHE BLANC   SÉMILLON

Assyrtiko

◀) *"ah-seer-teeko"*

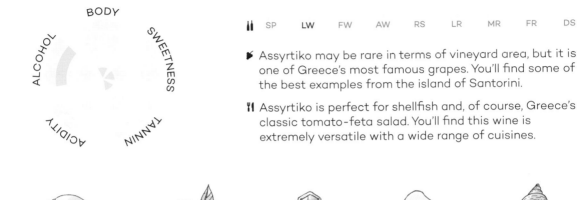

BODY
SWEETNESS
TANNIN
ACIDITY
ALCOHOL

| SP | LW | FW | AW | RS | LR | MR | FR | DS |

🌾 Assyrtiko may be rare in terms of vineyard area, but it is one of Greece's most famous grapes. You'll find some of the best examples from the island of Santorini.

🍴 Assyrtiko is perfect for shellfish and, of course, Greece's classic tomato-feta salad. You'll find this wine is extremely versatile with a wide range of cuisines.

| LIME | PASSION-FRUIT | BEESWAX | FLINT | SALINE |

| WHITE GLASS | ICE COLD 38–45° F | DECANT NO | SPEND ~$20 | CELLAR 5–10 YEARS |

Where It Grows

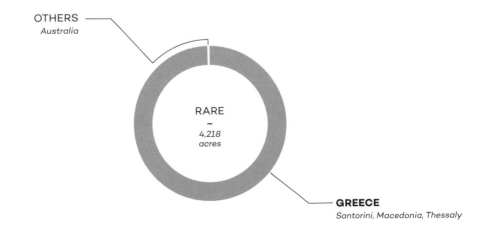

OTHERS
Australia

RARE
–
4,218 acres

GREECE
Santorini, Macedonia, Thessaly

Also Try

DRY RIESLING   ALBARIÑO   FURMINT   PICPOUL   ARINTO

Baga

🔊 *"bah-gah"*   💬 *Tinta Bairrada*

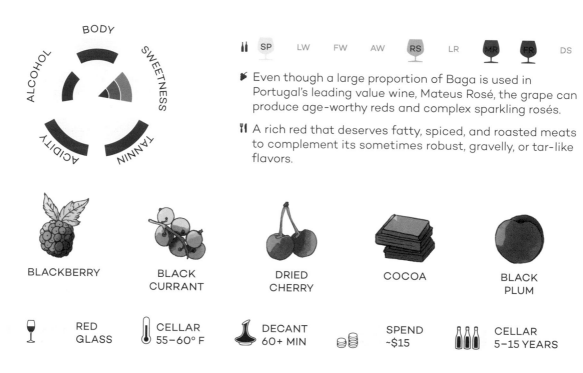

| | SP | LW | FW | AW | RS | LR | MR | FR | DS |

🏹 Even though a large proportion of Baga is used in Portugal's leading value wine, Mateus Rosé, the grape can produce age-worthy reds and complex sparkling rosés.

🍴 A rich red that deserves fatty, spiced, and roasted meats to complement its sometimes robust, gravelly, or tar-like flavors.

BLACKBERRY   BLACK CURRANT   DRIED CHERRY   COCOA   BLACK PLUM

🍷 RED GLASS   🌡 CELLAR 55–60° F   DECANT 60+ MIN   💰 SPEND ~$15   🍾 CELLAR 5–15 YEARS

Where It Grows

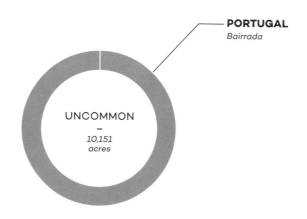

PORTUGAL
Bairrada

UNCOMMON
–
10,151 acres

Also Try

 DOLCETTO    BONARDA    MONASTRELL   NEGROAMARO   PINOTAGE

Barbera

🔊 *"bar-bear-ruh"*

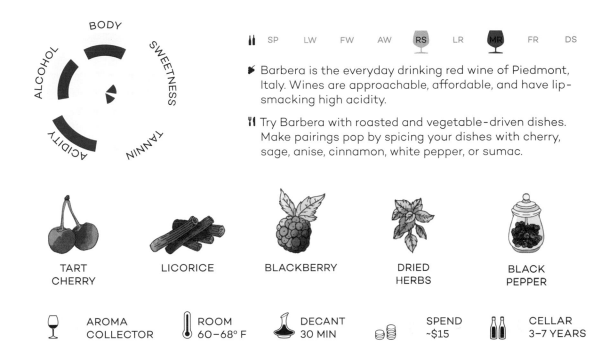

SP   LW   FW   AW   **RS**   LR   **MR**   FR   DS

🌿 Barbera is the everyday drinking red wine of Piedmont, Italy. Wines are approachable, affordable, and have lip-smacking high acidity.

🍴 Try Barbera with roasted and vegetable-driven dishes. Make pairings pop by spicing your dishes with cherry, sage, anise, cinnamon, white pepper, or sumac.

TART CHERRY | LICORICE | BLACKBERRY | DRIED HERBS | BLACK PEPPER

AROMA COLLECTOR | ROOM 60–68° F | DECANT 30 MIN | SPEND ~$15 | CELLAR 3–7 YEARS

Where It Grows

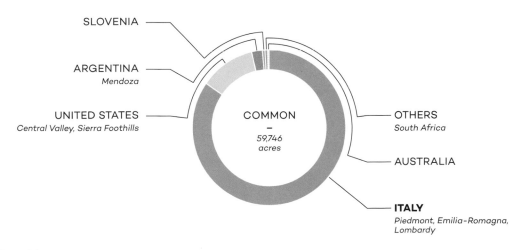

SLOVENIA

ARGENTINA
Mendoza

UNITED STATES
Central Valley, Sierra Foothills

COMMON
–
59,746
acres

OTHERS
South Africa

AUSTRALIA

ITALY
Piedmont, Emilia-Romagna, Lombardy

Also Try

🍷 AGIORGITIKO   🍷 MENCÍA   🍷 DOLCETTO   🍷 BLAUFRÄNKISCH   🍷 MONTEPULCIANO

Blaufränkisch

🔊 *"blauw-fronk-keesh"*   💬 *Lemberger, Kékfrankos*

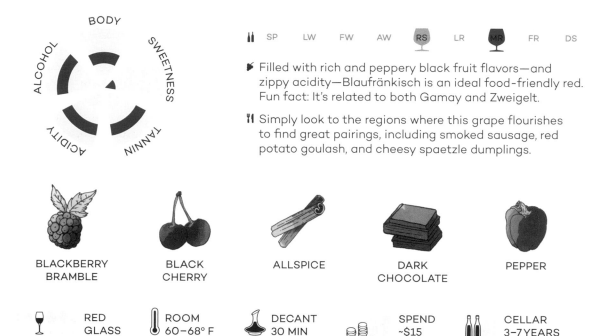

BODY · SWEETNESS · TANNIN · ACIDITY · ALCOHOL

| SP | LW | FW | AW | **RS** | LR | **MR** | FR | DS |

🍷 Filled with rich and peppery black fruit flavors—and zippy acidity—Blaufränkisch is an ideal food-friendly red. Fun fact: It's related to both Gamay and Zweigelt.

🍴 Simply look to the regions where this grape flourishes to find great pairings, including smoked sausage, red potato goulash, and cheesy spaetzle dumplings.

BLACKBERRY BRAMBLE · BLACK CHERRY · ALLSPICE · DARK CHOCOLATE · PEPPER

RED GLASS · ROOM 60–68° F · DECANT 30 MIN · SPEND ~$15 · CELLAR 3–7 YEARS

Where It Grows

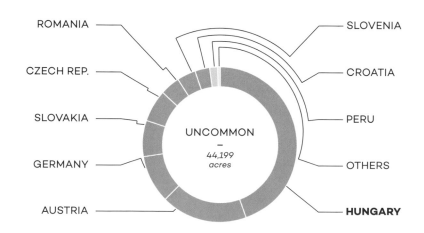

ROMANIA · CZECH REP. · SLOVAKIA · GERMANY · AUSTRIA · SLOVENIA · CROATIA · PERU · OTHERS · **HUNGARY**

UNCOMMON
–
44,199
acres

Also Try

🍷 SYRAH   🍷 BONARDA   🍷 MALBEC   🍷 MONASTRELL   🍷 PINOTAGE

Bobal

◀) *"bo-bal"*

SP LW FW AW RS LR **MR** FR DS

🥄 This under-the-radar grape happens to be the second most planted red wine in Spain. Wines are loved for their fruity flavors, soft tannins, and velvety finish.

🍴 Bring out Bobal's fruity flavors by using actual fruit in your dish, such as orange chicken or roast chicken with pomegranate-molasses sauce.

BLACKBERRY	POMEGRANATE	LICORICE	BLACK TEA	COCOA POWDER

RED GLASS	ROOM 60–68° F	DECANT 30 MIN		SPEND ~$10	CELLAR 3–7 YEARS

Where It Grows

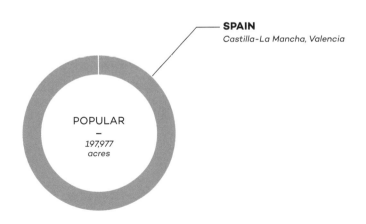

SPAIN
Castilla-La Mancha, Valencia

POPULAR
–
197,977 acres

Also Try

 GAMAY   DORNFELDER   DOLCETTO   ZWEIGELT   BLAUFRÄNKISCH

Bonarda

🔊 *"bo-nard-duh"*   💬 *Douce Noir, Charbono*

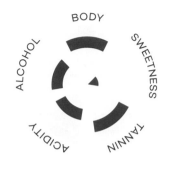

BODY
SWEETNESS
TANNIN
ACIDITY
ALCOHOL

| SP | LW | FW | AW | RS | LR | MR | FR | DS |

🍷 Not the same Bonarda that grows in Northern Italy. This Bonarda (aka Douce Noir) grows alongside Malbec in Argentina, where it produces smooth and fruity wines.

🍴 Bonarda is a great choice for dishes with mole sauces, and curried potatoes. You'll also love it alongside empanadas and tacos al pastor.

PLUM SAUCE	CHERRY	CARDAMOM	FIG PASTE	GRAPHITE

 RED GLASS   🌡 ROOM 60–68° F   ⚱ DECANT 30 MIN   SPEND ~$10   🍾 CELLAR 3–7 YEARS

Where It Grows

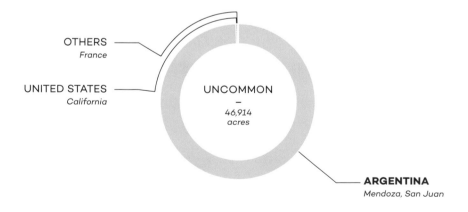

OTHERS
France

UNITED STATES
California

UNCOMMON
–
46,914
acres

ARGENTINA
Mendoza, San Juan

Also Try

🍷 MERLOT   🍷 SYRAH   🍷 DOLCETTO   🍷 PETITE SIRAH

Bordeaux Blend (Red)

◀) *"bore-doe"*   💬 *Meritage, Cabernet-Merlot*

SP   LW   FW   AW   **RS**   LR   **MR**   **FR**   DS

🍷 A red blend that's primarily Cabernet Sauvignon and Merlot along with several other grape varieties that originated in Bordeaux, France.

🍴 The tannins in this blend make it an excellent choice to match with steak and other red meat dishes. Keep seasoning simple—think salt and pepper.

 BLACK CURRANT

 BLACK CHERRY

 GRAPHITE

 CHOCOLATE

 DRIED HERBS

 OVERSIZED GLASS

 ROOM 60–68° F

 DECANT 60+ MIN

 SPEND ~$25

 CELLAR 5–25 YEARS

The Blend

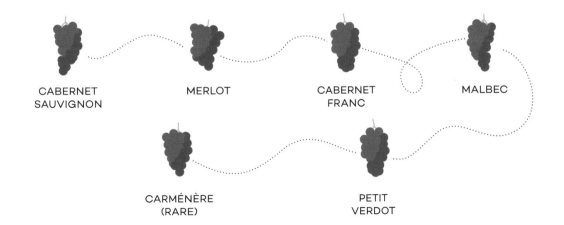

CABERNET SAUVIGNON

MERLOT

CABERNET FRANC

MALBEC

CARMÉNÈRE (RARE)

PETIT VERDOT

Also Try

 CABERNET SAUVIGNON    MERLOT   CABERNET FRANC   MALBEC   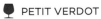 PETIT VERDOT

Bordeaux Blend (Red)

ADDITIONAL TASTING NOTES

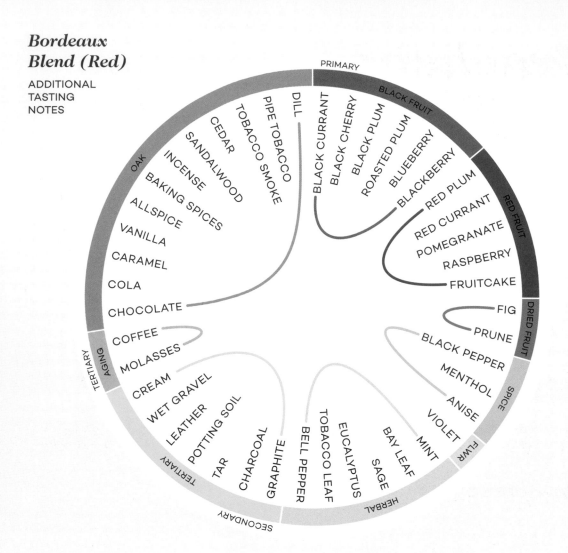

Bordeaux, France

Summers are hot in Bordeaux, but are often cut short. Fall temperatures restrain fruit flavors, maintain acidity, and add herbaceous notes to the resulting wines. The gravel-clay soils in Médoc and Graves give wines more tannin and the clay soils in Libournais allow for bolder fruit.

‣ BLACK CURRANT
‣ ANISE
‣ TOBACCO LEAF
‣ PLUM SAUCE
‣ BAKING SPICES

Western Australia

Australia's top region for Bordeaux blends receives cooling breezes from the Indian Ocean, giving wines more red fruit flavors and elegance. The decomposing granite gravel and clay-based soils of the region are cited for influencing the region's trademark sage and bay leaf notes.

‣ RED CURRANT
‣ BLACK CHERRY
‣ SAGE
‣ COFFEE
‣ BAY LEAF

Bolgheri, Tuscany

Better known as "Super Tuscans," these Merlot and Cabernet-dominant blends of Tuscany sometimes feature Sangiovese blended in as well. In Bolgheri, the most famous Bordeaux blend area, the best soils are a rich, brown, gravelly clay, which gives wines bold fruit and dusty leather notes.

‣ BLACK CHERRY
‣ BLACKBERRY
‣ SANDALWOOD
‣ LEATHER
‣ ANISE

Brachetto

◀) *"brak-kett-toe"*   💬 *Brachetto d'Acqui*

BODY
ALCOHOL
SWEETNESS
ACIDITY
TANNIN

| | SP | LW | FW | AW | RS | LR | MR | FR | DS |

🌾 A rare, sweet red wine from Piedmont that's famous for it's perfumed aromatics and frothy, creamy bubbles.

🍴 A perfect match with rich, creamy chocolate truffles, ganache, and mousse. Additionally, try it with gelato if you're looking for an unbelievably classy ice cream float.

CANDIED STRAWBERRY

ORANGE ZEST

BLACK CURRANT

APRICOT

CREAM

 RED GLASS   🌡 CELLAR 55–60° F   DECANT NO   SPEND ~$12   CELLAR 1–3 YEARS

Where It Grows

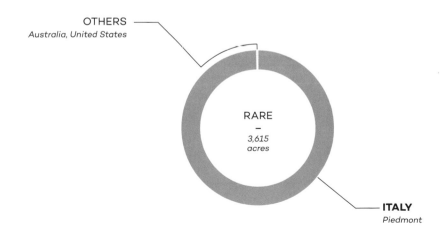

OTHERS
Australia, United States

RARE
—
3,615 acres

ITALY
Piedmont

Also Try

🍷 LAMBRUSCO   🍷 BLACK MUSCAT   🍷 FREISA (ITALY)   🍷 CONCORD

Cabernet Franc

🔊 *"kab-err-nay fronk"* 💬 *Breton, Chinon, Bourgueil*

BODY
SWEETNESS
TANNIN
ACIDITY
ALCOHOL

| SP | LW | FW | AW | RS | LR | MR | FR | DS |

🗡 Cabernet Franc is the parent grape of both Merlot and Cabernet Sauvignon. It may have originated in the Basque Country of Spain but this fact is up for debate.

🍴 Higher acidity makes it possible to pair Cabernet Franc with tomato-based dishes, vinegar-based sauces (smoky BBQ, anyone?), or rich black beluga lentils.

| STRAWBERRY | RASPBERRY | BELL PEPPER | CRUSHED GRAVEL | CHILI PEPPER |

 RED GLASS   🌡 ROOM 60–68° F   DECANT 30 MIN   SPEND ~$20   🍾 CELLAR 5–10 YEARS

Where It Grows

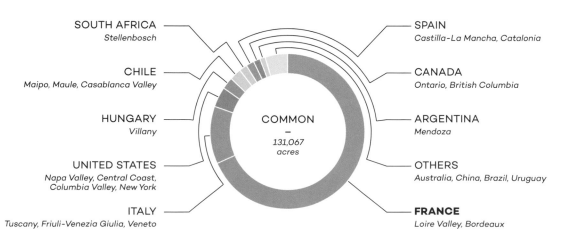

SOUTH AFRICA
Stellenbosch

CHILE
Maipo, Maule, Casablanca Valley

HUNGARY
Villany

UNITED STATES
Napa Valley, Central Coast, Columbia Valley, New York

ITALY
Tuscany, Friuli-Venezia Giulia, Veneto

COMMON
–
131,067
acres

SPAIN
Castilla-La Mancha, Catalonia

CANADA
Ontario, British Columbia

ARGENTINA
Mendoza

OTHERS
Australia, China, Brazil, Uruguay

FRANCE
Loire Valley, Bordeaux

Also Try

 CARMÉNÈRE    SANGIOVESE    TEMPRANILLO   ZINFANDEL   CASTELÃO

Cabernet Franc

ADDITIONAL
TASTING
NOTES

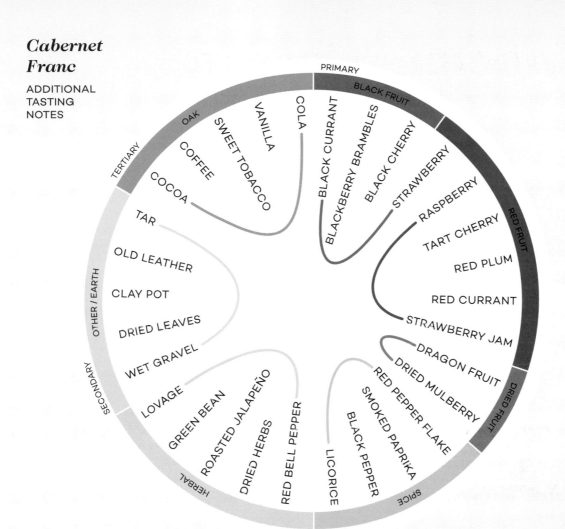

Chinon, France

The Loire Valley is known for producing exceptional single-varietal Cabernet Franc wines in and around the Middle Loire Valley (Chinon, Bourgueil, Anjou, etc.). The cooler climate lends itself to wines with lighter color, lighter body, higher acidity, and distinct herbal flavors.

▸ RED BELL PEPPER
▸ RED CHILI FLAKE
▸ RASPBERRY SAUCE
▸ WET GRAVEL
▸ DRIED HERBS

Tuscany, Italy

Tuscany's warmer climate gives Cabernet Franc richer fruit flavors. The region's red clay soils generally increase tannin. Since Cabernet Franc is not an indigenous variety of Italy, wines are declassified to IGP (see p. 253) and labeled by variety or made-up name.

▸ CHERRY
▸ LEATHER
▸ STRAWBERRY
▸ LICORICE
▸ COFFEE

Sierra Foothills, CA

The regions of Shenandoah Valley, El Dorado, Fair Play, and Fiddletown have warm, stable climates that make for ripe, sweet grapes with lower acidity. Wines are typically fruit-forward and jammy with higher alcohol and subtle whiffs of dried leaves.

▸ DRIED STRAWBERRY
▸ RASPBERRY
▸ TOBACCO LEAF
▸ CEDAR
▸ VANILLA

Cabernet Sauvignon

◄) "kab-er-nay saw-vin-yawn"

 SP   LW   FW   AW   RS   LR   MR   FR   DS

🗡 The world's most popular wine is a natural cross between Cabernet Franc and Sauvignon Blanc that originated in Bordeaux. Wines are concentrated and age-worthy.

🍴 The rich flavor and high tannin content in Cabernet Sauvignon make it a perfect partner to rich grilled meats, peppery sauces, and dishes with high flavor.

BLACK CHERRY

BLACK CURRANT

CEDAR

BAKING SPICES

GRAPHITE

 OVERSIZED GLASS   TEMP 60–68° F   DECANT 60+ MIN   SPEND ~$20   CELLAR 5–25 YEARS

Where It Grows

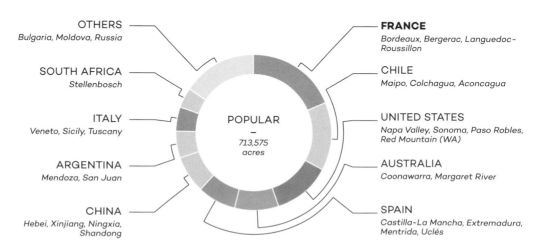

OTHERS
Bulgaria, Moldova, Russia

SOUTH AFRICA
Stellenbosch

ITALY
Veneto, Sicily, Tuscany

ARGENTINA
Mendoza, San Juan

CHINA
Hebei, Xinjiang, Ningxia, Shandong

POPULAR
–
713,575 acres

FRANCE
Bordeaux, Bergerac, Languedoc-Roussillon

CHILE
Maipo, Colchagua, Aconcagua

UNITED STATES
Napa Valley, Sonoma, Paso Robles, Red Mountain (WA)

AUSTRALIA
Coonawarra, Margaret River

SPAIN
Castilla-La Mancha, Extremadura, Mentrida, Uclés

Also Try

 BORDEAUX BLEND   MERLOT    CABERNET FRANC   CARMÉNÈRE   NERO D'AVOLA

Cabernet Sauvignon

ADDITIONAL
TASTING
NOTES

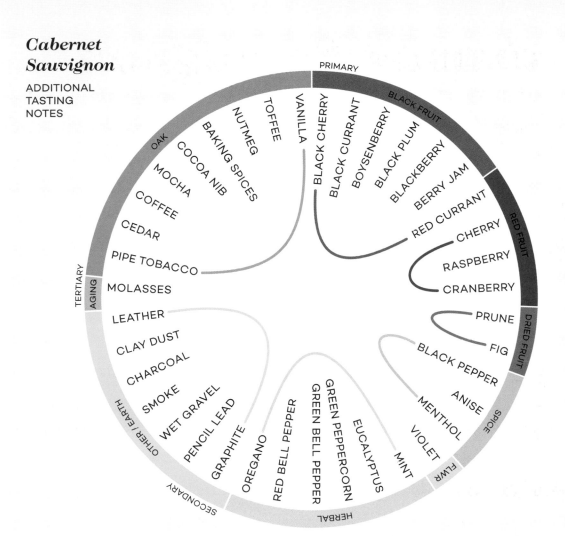

Chile

Cabernet Sauvignon excels in the Aconcagua, Maipo, Cachapoal, and Colchagua Valleys. In Maipo, the cooling winds from the Pacific create an ideal Mediterranean climate, which makes the most full-bodied Cabernet Sauvignons in Chile. The Alto Maipo is a famous subregion for this grape.

▸ BLACKBERRY
▸ BLACK CHERRY
▸ FIG PASTE
▸ BAKING SPICES
▸ GREEN PEPPERCORN

Napa Valley, CA

One of Napa Valley's most notable features is volcanic soils, which give its wines a distinct dusty and minerally character. Wines from the valley floor tend to offer more black cherry with lush tannins. Hillside wines have more acidity, blackberry notes, and rustic tannins.

▸ BLACK CURRANT
▸ PENCIL LEAD
▸ TOBACCO
▸ BLACKBERRY
▸ MINT

South Australia

Coonawarra in South Australia is marked by a warmer climate and red clay soils with high iron-oxide content (called "terra rossa"). Cabernet wines are bold and fruity but evenly balanced, with higher tannin and rustic notes of white pepper and bay leaf.

▸ BLACK PLUM
▸ WHITE PEPPER
▸ CURRANT CANDY
▸ CHOCOLATE
▸ BAY LEAF

Carignan

 "kare-rin-yen"   Mazuelo, Samsó, Carignano

| SP | LW | FW | AW | RS | LR | MR | FR | DS |

 A productive, drought-resistant vine that had a poor reputation until recently when several winemakers started making great wines sourced from old vineyards.

Carignan works well with cinnamon-spiced dishes, berry-based sauces and smoky meats. In other words, it's an amazing choice for Thanksgiving and holiday fare.

DRIED CRANBERRY

RASPBERRY

TOBACCO LEAF

BAKING SPICES

CURED MEAT

 RED GLASS

ROOM 60–68° F

DECANT 30 MIN

 SPEND ~$15

 CELLAR 5–10 YEARS

Where It Grows

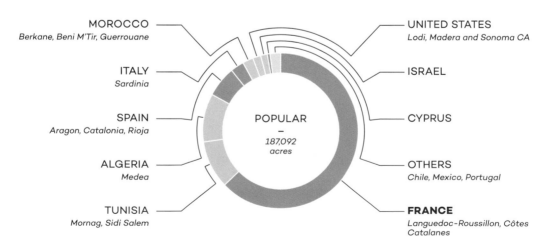

MOROCCO
Berkane, Beni M'Tir, Guerrouane

ITALY
Sardinia

SPAIN
Aragon, Catalonia, Rioja

ALGERIA
Medea

TUNISIA
Mornag, Sidi Salem

POPULAR
–
187,092
acres

UNITED STATES
Lodi, Madera and Sonoma CA

ISRAEL

CYPRUS

OTHERS
Chile, Mexico, Portugal

FRANCE
Languedoc-Roussillon, Côtes Catalanes

Also Try

 GRENACHE   SANGIOVESE   GSM / RHÔNE BLEND   CASTELÃO   ZINFANDEL

90

Carménère

◀ "kar-men-nair"   💬 Grand Vidure, Cabernet Gernischt

SP   LW   FW   AW   **RS**   LR   **MR**   FR   DS

🌶 Once thought to be a nearly extinct Bordeaux variety, we now know that nearly 50% of the Merlot planted in Chile is actually Carménère!

🍴 The herbal, peppercorn flavors in Carménère are a great embellishment to roast meats (from chicken to beef) and pretty much anything spiced with cumin.

RASPBERRY

BELL PEPPER

BLACK PLUM

PAPRIKA

VANILLA

 RED GLASS

🌡 ROOM 60–68° F

DECANT 30 MIN

 SPEND ~$15

CELLAR 5–15 YEARS

Where It Grows

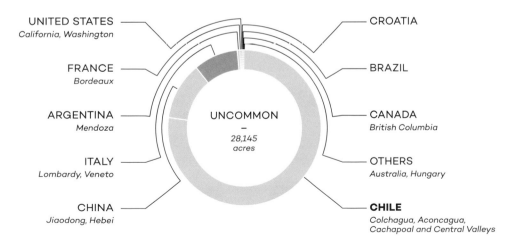

UNITED STATES
California, Washington

FRANCE
Bordeaux

ARGENTINA
Mendoza

ITALY
Lombardy, Veneto

CHINA
Jiaodong, Hebei

CROATIA

BRAZIL

CANADA
British Columbia

OTHERS
Australia, Hungary

CHILE
Colchagua, Aconcagua, Cachapoal and Central Valleys

UNCOMMON
–
28,145
acres

Also Try

 CABERNET FRANC

 CABERNET SAUVIGNON

 HONDARRIBI BELTZA (SPAIN)

 BORDEAUX BLEND

 MERLOT

Castelão

🔊 *"kast-tall-ow"*　💬 *Perequita*

BODY · SWEETNESS · TANNIN · ACIDITY · ALCOHOL

🍶 SP　LW　FW　AW　RS　LR　**MR**　FR　DS

🌿 Widely planted in Portugal—but rarely seen elsewhere—Castelão creates rich, fruity wines with subtle smoky flavors. The grape is typically in "vinho regional" blends.

🍴 If you can't get your hands on Portuguese octopus "à lagareiro" (roasted with potatoes), make some shredded chicken tacos with black beans and you'll find happiness.

RED CURRANT　PLUM　STRAWBERRY　DRIED MEAT　MOCHA

 RED GLASS　 ROOM 60–68° F　 DECANT 30 MIN　 SPEND ~$10　 CELLAR 5–10 YEARS

Where It Grows

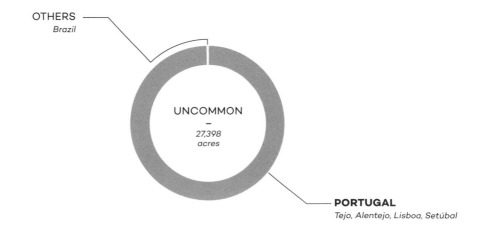

OTHERS
Brazil

UNCOMMON
–
*27,398
acres*

PORTUGAL
Tejo, Alentejo, Lisboa, Setúbal

Also Try

🍷 CARIGNAN　🍷 ZINFANDEL　🍷 GRENACHE　🍷 CINSAULT

Cava

🔊 *"kah-vah"*

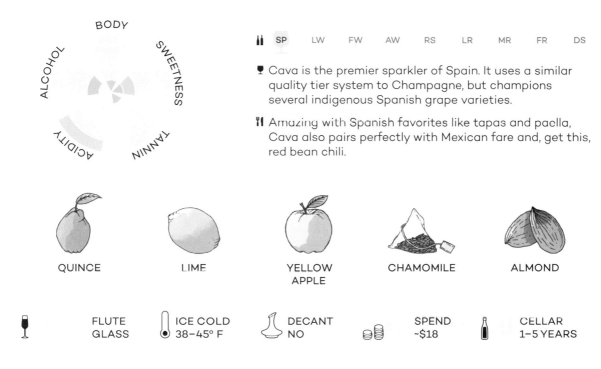

BODY
ALCOHOL
SWEETNESS
ACIDITY
TANNIN

| 🍾 | SP | LW | FW | AW | RS | LR | MR | FR | DS |

🍷 Cava is the premier sparkler of Spain. It uses a similar quality tier system to Champagne, but champions several indigenous Spanish grape varieties.

🍴 Amazing with Spanish favorites like tapas and paella, Cava also pairs perfectly with Mexican fare and, get this, red bean chili.

QUINCE   LIME   YELLOW APPLE   CHAMOMILE   ALMOND

| 🥂 FLUTE GLASS | 🌡 ICE COLD 38–45° F | DECANT NO | SPEND ~$18 | CELLAR 1–5 YEARS |

Grapes & Styles

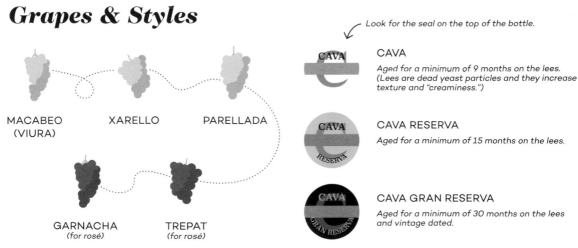

MACABEO (VIURA)   XARELLO   PARELLADA

GARNACHA *(for rosé)*   TREPAT *(for rosé)*

Look for the seal on the top of the bottle.

CAVA
Aged for a minimum of 9 months on the lees. (Lees are dead yeast particles and they increase texture and "creaminess.")

CAVA RESERVA
Aged for a minimum of 15 months on the lees.

CAVA GRAN RESERVA
Aged for a minimum of 30 months on the lees and vintage dated.

Also Try

 CRÉMANT   CHAMPAGNE   SEKT (AUSTRIA & GERMANY)    METODO CLASSICO   CAP CLASSIQUE (SOUTH AFRICA)

Champagne

◄)) *"sham-pain"*

	SP	LW	FW	AW	RS	LR	MR	FR	DS

🍷 The most iconic sparkling wine is made with Chardonnay, Pinot Noir, and Pinot Meunier. The most treasured wines age for 3 or more years.

🍴 Anything that's salty or fried pairs magically with Champagne. Champagne isn't just an aperitif—try pairing it with the main course as well!

CITRUS　　YELLOW APPLE　　CREAM　　ALMOND　　TOAST

🥂 FLUTE GLASS　　🌡 ICE COLD 38–45° F　　⚗ DECANT NO　　🪙 SPEND ~$52　　🍾 CELLAR 5–20 YEARS

Where It Grows

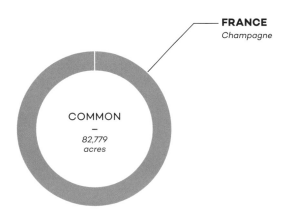

FRANCE
Champagne

COMMON
–
82,779
acres

Also Try

🥂 CRÉMANT　　🥂 CAVA　　🥂 METODO CLASSICO　　🥂 SEKT (AUSTRIA & GERMANY)　　🥂 CAP CLASSIQUE (SOUTH AFRICA)

Champagne

ADDITIONAL
TASTING
NOTES

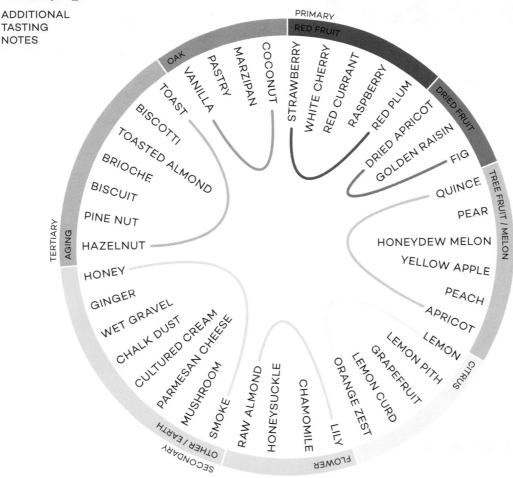

Montagne de Reims

The hills are sunny enough to ripen Pinot Noir and Pinot Meunier. With the increase of red grapes in the blend, sparklers often have a richer and fruitier style. Many top Champagne houses source their best grapes from the 10 Grand Cru vineyards found here.

▸ WHITE CHERRY
▸ GOLDEN RAISIN
▸ LEMON ZEST
▸ PARMESAN CHEESE
▸ BRIOCHE

Côte des Blancs

This east-facing chalk-covered slope is famous for single-varietal *Blanc de Blancs* Champagne. The region is planted to 98% Chardonnay and boasts 6 Grand Cru vineyards. To many, this slope offers the purest expression of Champagne.

▸ YELLOW APPLE
▸ LEMON CURD
▸ HONEYSUCKLE
▸ CULTURED CREAM
▸ MARZIPAN

Vallée de la Marne

The valley along the Marne river has just one Grand Cru vineyard, Aÿ, located right outside of the city of Épernay. The focus here is on Pinot Meunier, which ripens more easily than Pinot Noir. Expect richer, more unctuous sparkling wines with smoke and mushroom aromas.

▸ YELLOW PLUM
▸ QUINCE
▸ CULTURED CREAM
▸ MUSHROOM
▸ SMOKE

Chardonnay

🔊 "shar-dun-nay" 💬 *Chablis, Morillion, Bourgogne Blanc*

| | SP | LW | FW | AW | RS | LR | MR | FR | DS |

🍾 One of the world's most popular grapes, Chardonnay is made in a wide range of styles from sparkling *Blanc de Blancs* to rich, creamy white wines aged in oak.

🍴 Chardonnay pairs best with subtle spices and flavors. For example, try matching it with creamy, buttery flavors and soft textures. Lobster is a winning match.

YELLOW APPLE

STARFRUIT

PINEAPPLE

VANILLA

BUTTER

🍷 AROMA COLLECTOR   🌡 COLD 45–55° F   DECANT NO   SPEND ~$40   CELLAR 5–10 YEARS

Where It Grows

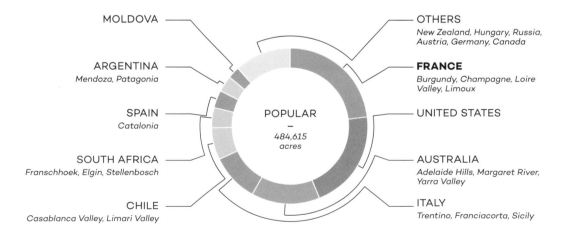

MOLDOVA

ARGENTINA
Mendoza, Patagonia

SPAIN
Catalonia

SOUTH AFRICA
Franschhoek, Elgin, Stellenbosch

CHILE
Casablanca Valley, Limari Valley

POPULAR
—
484,615 acres

OTHERS
New Zealand, Hungary, Russia, Austria, Germany, Canada

FRANCE
Burgundy, Champagne, Loire Valley, Limoux

UNITED STATES

AUSTRALIA
Adelaide Hills, Margaret River, Yarra Valley

ITALY
Trentino, Franciacorta, Sicily

Also Try

 MARSANNE   ROUSSANNE   VIOGNIER   SAVATIANO    TREBBIANO TOSCANO

Chardonnay

ADDITIONAL
TASTING
NOTES

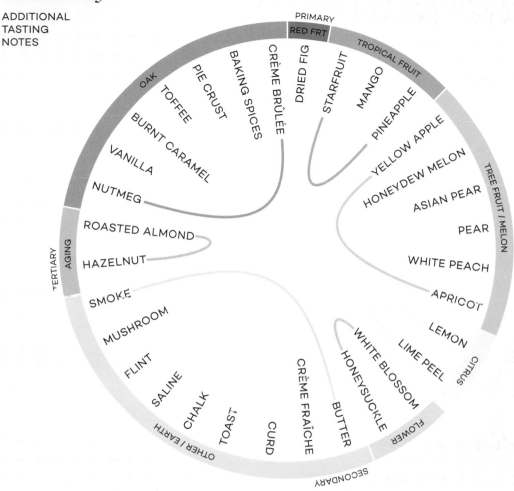

Chablis, France

While much of Burgundy produces a richer, oaked style of Chardonnay, Chablis is leaner and typically unoaked with higher acidity. The region's chalk-white soils are often attributed as the source of the wine's crisp, mineral-driven texture.

- QUINCE
- STARFRUIT
- LIME PEEL
- WHITE BLOSSOM
- CHALK

Santa Barbara, CA

The regions of Sta. Rita Hills and Santa Maria are cool enough for excellent Chardonnay. The style here is much riper, often with ripe apple and tropical fruit flavors. Oak aging and malolactic fermentation give these wines a buttery, creamy texture with flavors of nutmeg and baking spices.

- YELLOW APPLE
- PINEAPPLE
- LEMON ZEST
- PIE CRUST
- NUTMEG

Western Australia

The granite-based soils in Margaret River produce a more elegant, aromatic style of Chardonnay. However, it's still warm enough to produce ripe fruit. Several producers create blends with a small portion of oaked wine with unoaked wine to create a fantastic balance between fruit and creaminess.

- WHITE PEACH
- TANGERINE
- HONEYSUCKLE
- VANILLA
- LEMON CURD

Chenin Blanc

🔊 *"shen-in blonk"*   💬 *Steen, Pineau de la Loire*

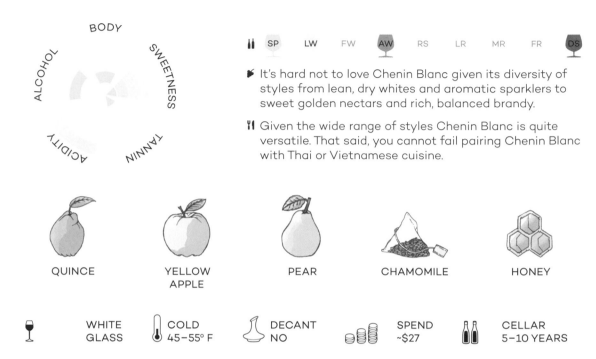

SP   LW   FW   AW   RS   LR   MR   FR   DS

🍷 It's hard not to love Chenin Blanc given its diversity of styles from lean, dry whites and aromatic sparklers to sweet golden nectars and rich, balanced brandy.

🍴 Given the wide range of styles Chenin Blanc is quite versatile. That said, you cannot fail pairing Chenin Blanc with Thai or Vietnamese cuisine.

QUINCE   YELLOW APPLE   PEAR   CHAMOMILE   HONEY

WHITE GLASS   COLD 45–55° F   DECANT NO   SPEND ~$27   CELLAR 5–10 YEARS

Where It Grows

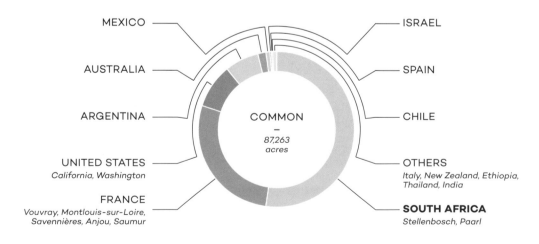

MEXICO

AUSTRALIA

ARGENTINA

UNITED STATES
California, Washington

FRANCE
*Vouvray, Montlouis-sur-Loire,
Savennières, Anjou, Saumur*

COMMON
–
*87,263
acres*

ISRAEL

SPAIN

CHILE

OTHERS
*Italy, New Zealand, Ethiopia,
Thailand, India*

SOUTH AFRICA
Stellenbosch, Paarl

Also Try

 GARGANEGA   GRECHETTO   CHARDONNAY   MALAGOUSIA (GREECE)

Chenin Blanc

ADDITIONAL
TASTING
NOTES

PRIMARY
DRIED FRUIT
TROPICAL FRUIT
TREE FRUIT / MELON

OAK
VANILLA
NUTMEG
BRIOCHE
YELLOW RAISIN
MARMALADE
PINEAPPLE
PASSIONFRUIT
PEAR
QUINCE
YELLOW APPLE
HONEYDEW MELON
WHILE PEACH

TERTIARY
AGING
BRUISED APPLE
HAZELNUT
SALTED BUTTER
BREAD YEAST
CREAM
LEMON CURD
CHALK
OILY
TARRAGON
ACACIA
JASMINE

CITRUS
LIME
LEMON
CITRUS PEEL
POMELO
GINGER

SECONDARY
OTHER / EARTH
HERBAL

CITRUS BLOSSOM
CHAMOMILE
HONEYSUCKLE
ALLSPICE
MARZIPAN
HONEY
SAFFRON

SPICE

FLOWER

Rich and Off-Dry

Each region specializing
in Chenin Blanc produces
multiple styles. The richest
style comes from the ripest
grapes. These wines have bold,
sweet fruit aromas and an
oily palate. In some places,
such as in Paarl, South Africa,
producers oak-age wines to
impart subtle allspice flavors.

‣ ASIAN PEAR
‣ YELLOW APPLE
‣ HONEYSUCKLE
‣ ORANGE BLOSSOM
‣ ALLSPICE

Lean and Dry

Lean and dry styles use less
ripe grapes and are common in
cooler climate growing regions
such as Vouvray in the Loire
Valley. This style is also the
norm with value-driven Chenin
from South Africa. Wines have
more tart fruit characteristics
with higher acidity and subtle
green notes.

‣ QUINCE
‣ PEAR
‣ POMELO
‣ GINGER
‣ TARRAGON

Sparkling

Brut (dry) or Demi-Sec (fruity
and off-dry) are the primary
styles of sparkling Chenin
Blanc. Examples to try include
South Africa's Cap Classique,
and there are also single-
varietal Chenin Blanc sparklers
from Vouvray in the Loire
Valley.

‣ HONEYDEW MELON
‣ LEMON
‣ JASMINE
‣ LEMON CURD
‣ CREAM

Cinsault

 "sin-so"   *Cinsaut*

BODY
SWEETNESS
TANNIN
ACIDITY
ALCOHOL

| | SP | LW | FW | AW | RS | LR | MR | FR | DS |

- Cinsault is one of the minor blending grapes in Rhône / GSM blends and Provence rosé. Expect fresh, punchy reds that are just as floral as they are fruity.

- Try Cinsault with lighter but nevertheless well-spiced vegetarian Indian fare. This is a versatile food-pairing red wine because of its low tannin.

| RASPBERRY | RED CURRANT | TART CHERRY | VIOLET | BLACK TEA |

| AROMA COLLECTOR | ROOM 60–68° F | DECANT 30 MIN | SPEND ~$15 | CELLAR 3–7 YEARS |

Where It Grows

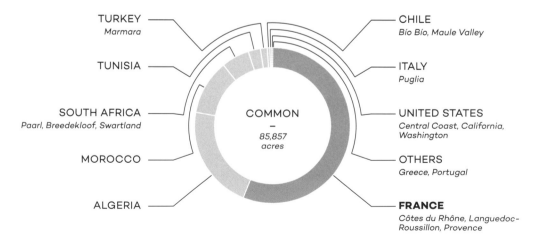

COMMON
–
85,857
acres

TURKEY
Marmara

TUNISIA

SOUTH AFRICA
Paarl, Breedekloof, Swartland

MOROCCO

ALGERIA

CHILE
Bío Bío, Maule Valley

ITALY
Puglia

UNITED STATES
Central Coast, California, Washington

OTHERS
Greece, Portugal

FRANCE
Côtes du Rhône, Languedoc-Roussillon, Provence

Also Try

 PINOT NOIR   ZWEIGELT   GAMAY   CASTELÃO

Colombard

🔊 *"kall-lum-bar"*   💬 *Colombar*

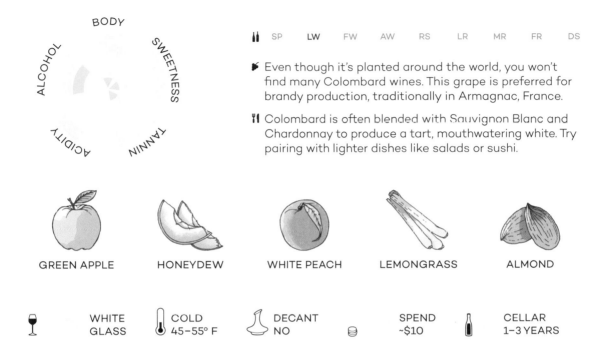

BODY
ALCOHOL
SWEETNESS
ACIDITY
TANNIN

🍾	SP	LW	FW	AW	RS	LR	MR	FR	DS

🌱 Even though it's planted around the world, you won't find many Colombard wines. This grape is preferred for brandy production, traditionally in Armagnac, France.

🍴 Colombard is often blended with Sauvignon Blanc and Chardonnay to produce a tart, mouthwatering white. Try pairing with lighter dishes like salads or sushi.

GREEN APPLE	HONEYDEW	WHITE PEACH	LEMONGRASS	ALMOND

🍷 WHITE GLASS   🌡️ COLD 45–55° F   🍶 DECANT NO   🪙 SPEND ~$10   🍾 CELLAR 1–3 YEARS

Where It Grows

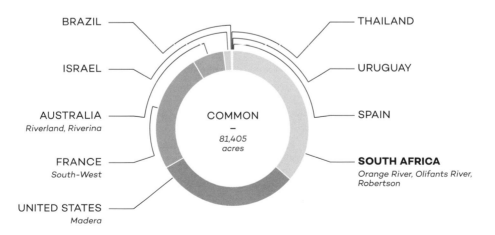

BRAZIL
THAILAND
ISRAEL
URUGUAY
AUSTRALIA
Riverland, Riverina
SPAIN
FRANCE
South-West
SOUTH AFRICA
Orange River, Olifants River, Robertson
UNITED STATES
Madera

COMMON
—
81,405
acres

Also Try

⬤ SAUVIGNON BLANC   ⬤ FRIULANO   ⬤ PICPOUL

Concord

◀) *"kahn-kord"*

SP　LW　FW　AW　RS　LR　**MR**　FR　DS

🍷 An American grape of the native Vitis labrusca species, from Concord, Massachusetts, it is the most planted grape in New York and used for juices and flavoring.

🍴 There might be nothing better than a peanut butter sandwich and a glass of Concord grape wine. Together they make a PB&J.

GRAPE	PLUM SAUCE	MUSK	POTTING SOIL	CUMIN

RED GLASS　　CELLAR 55–60° F　　DECANT 30 MIN　　SPEND ~$8　　CELLAR 1–3 YEARS

Where It Grows

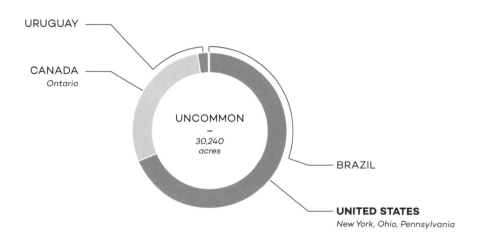

URUGUAY

CANADA
Ontario

UNCOMMON
–
30,240 acres

BRAZIL

UNITED STATES
New York, Ohio, Pennsylvania

Also Try

🍷 CATAWBA (USA)　　🍷 NIAGARA (USA)　　🍷 MUSCADINE (USA)　　🍷 LAMBRUSCO

Cortese

 "kort-tay-zay"   💬 *Gavi*

BODY
SWEETNESS
TANNIN
ACIDITY
ALCOHOL

🍾 SP **LW** FW AW RS LR MR FR DS

🦅 Known as Cortese de Gavi or just Gavi, which is where this grape grows in Piedmont, Italy. Wines are zesty and lean with green almond notes on the finish.

🍴 An awesome choice with foods inspired by Northern Italy's coastal cuisine including fragrant pesto pastas and seafood dishes with basil and lemon.

| MEYER LEMON | GALA APPLE | HONEYDEW | SEASHELL | ALMOND |

 WHITE GLASS   🌡 COLD 45–55° F   DECANT NO   SPEND ~$15   🍾 CELLAR 1–5 YEARS

Where It Grows

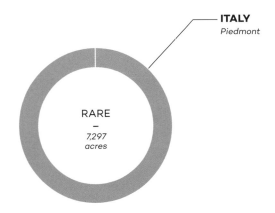

ITALY
Piedmont

RARE
–
7,297
acres

Also Try

GRECHETTO   GARGANEGA   ARNEIS   GRILLO (SICILY)   🍷 FALANGHINA

Crémant

🔊 *"krem-mont"*

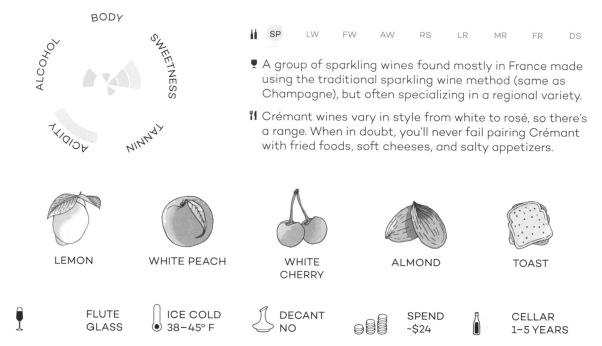

	SP	LW	FW	AW	RS	LR	MR	FR	DS

🍷 A group of sparkling wines found mostly in France made using the traditional sparkling wine method (same as Champagne), but often specializing in a regional variety.

🍴 Crémant wines vary in style from white to rosé, so there's a range. When in doubt, you'll never fail pairing Crémant with fried foods, soft cheeses, and salty appetizers.

LEMON	WHITE PEACH	WHITE CHERRY	ALMOND	TOAST

FLUTE GLASS	ICE COLD 38–45° F	DECANT NO	SPEND ~$24	CELLAR 1–5 YEARS

Popular Styles

CRÉMANT D'ALSACE
Pinot Noir, Pinot Blanc, Pinot Gris, Chardonnay, etc.

CRÉMANT DE LIMOUX
Chardonnay, Chenin Blanc, Mauzac, etc.

CRÉMANT DE BOURGOGNE
Chardonnay, Pinot Noir, etc.

CRÉMANT DE LOIRE
Chenin Blanc, Cabernet Franc, Pinot Noir

CRÉMANT DE BORDEAUX
Merlot, etc.

CRÉMANT DE DIE
Clairette

CRÉMANT DE SAVOIE
Jacquère, Altesse, Chasselas, etc.

CRÉMANT DU JURA
Chardonnay, Pinot Noir, Poulsard, etc.

Also Try

🥂 CHAMPAGNE　　🥂 CAVA　　🥂 SEKT (AUSTRIA & GERMANY)　　🥂 FRANCIACORTA　　🥂 METODO CLASSICO

Dolcetto

🔊 *"dol-chet-to"*

| | SP | LW | FW | AW | RS | LR | **MR** | FR | DS |

🗡 Dolcetto means "little sweet one" in Nothern Italy. Surprisingly, wines are typically tart with loads of black fruit flavors and occasionally aggressive tannins.

🍴 One of Italy's classic food wines that's best with richer, darker meats and vegetable dishes with roasted tomatoes, eggplant, and garlic.

PLUM   BLACKBERRY   COCOA   BLACK PEPPER   VIOLET

🍷 RED GLASS   🌡 ROOM 60–68° F   🍾 DECANT 30 MIN   🪙 SPEND ~$16   🍾 CELLAR 1–5 YEARS

Where It Grows

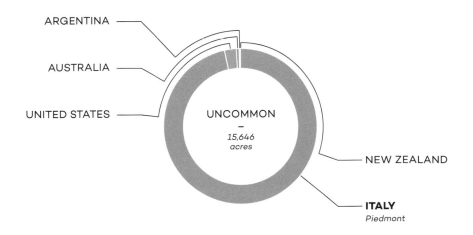

ARGENTINA

AUSTRALIA

UNITED STATES

UNCOMMON
–
15,646 acres

NEW ZEALAND

ITALY
Piedmont

Also Try

🍷 BLAUFRÄNKISCH   🍷 BONARDA   🍷 MERLOT   🍷 MONTEPULCIANO   🍷 MALBEC

Falanghina

◀)) *"fah-lahng-gee-nah"*

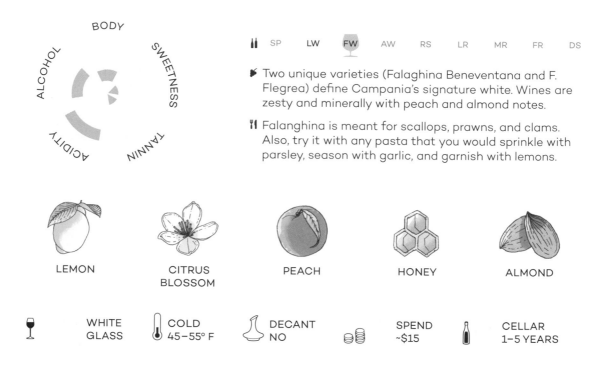

| ▯▯ | SP | LW | FW | AW | RS | LR | MR | FR | DS |

🍷 Two unique varieties (Falaghina Beneventana and F. Flegrea) define Campania's signature white. Wines are zesty and minerally with peach and almond notes.

🍴 Falanghina is meant for scallops, prawns, and clams. Also, try it with any pasta that you would sprinkle with parsley, season with garlic, and garnish with lemons.

LEMON   CITRUS BLOSSOM   PEACH   HONEY   ALMOND

🍷 WHITE GLASS   🌡 COLD 45–55° F   ⚗ DECANT NO   💰 SPEND ~$15   🍾 CELLAR 1–5 YEARS

Where It Grows

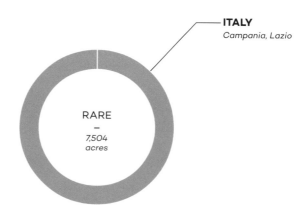

ITALY
Campania, Lazio

RARE
—
7,504 acres

Also Try

 MARSANNE   🍷 ROUSSANNE   GARGANEGA   🍷 CHARDONNAY   TREBBIANO TOSCANO

Fernão Pires

 "fer-now peer-esh" *Maria Gomes*

BODY
ALCOHOL
SWEETNESS
ACIDITY
TANNIN

 SP LW FW AW RS LR MR FR DS

🔖 A top white grape in Portugal that delivers wines with high-intensity floral aromas and medium body. More recently, it's been blended successfully with Viognier.

🍴 This wine begs for fresh green foods with an herbal note such as cucumber dill salad, classic California sushi rolls, or Vietnamese fresh spring rolls.

LIME

PEACH

ORANGE BLOSSOM

HONEYSUCKLE

CLOVE

🍷 WHITE GLASS

🌡️ COLD 45–55° F

DECANT NO

SPEND ~$10

🍾 CELLAR 1–3 YEARS

Where It Grows

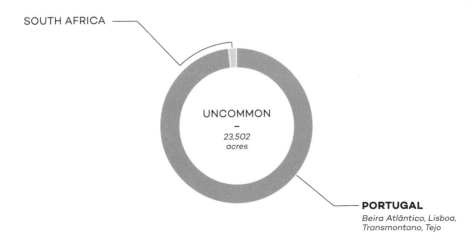

SOUTH AFRICA

UNCOMMON
–
23,502 acres

PORTUGAL
Beira Atlântico, Lisboa, Transmontano, Tejo

Also Try

 TORRONTES    MOSCHOFILERO   GRAŠEVINA (CROATIA)   MÜLLER-THURGAU    PINOT BLANC

Fiano

🔊 *"fee-ahn-no"*　　💬 *Fiano di Avellino*

BODY
SWEETNESS
ALCOHOL
ACIDITY
TANNIN

🍷	SP	**LW**	FW	AW	RS	LR	MR	FR	DS

🗡 A fascinating, age-worthy Southern Italian white with a rich, almost waxy texture. Easy to find (and surprisingly affordable) labeled as Fiano di Avellino from Campania.

🍴 A richer, and more flavorful white wine like Fiano matches well with savory glazed light meats like orange-rosemary roasted chicken and soy-glazed salmon.

HONEYDEW

ASIAN PEAR

HAZELNUT

ORANGE PEEL

PINE

🍷 **WHITE GLASS**　　🌡 **COLD 45–55° F**　　⚱ **DECANT NO**　　🪙 **SPEND ~$18**　　🍾 **CELLAR 5–10 YEARS**

Where It Grows

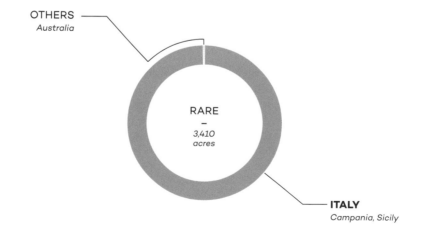

OTHERS — *Australia*

RARE
–
3,410
acres

ITALY
Campania, Sicily

Also Try

 VERMENTINO　　 RKATSITELI　　 SAVATIANO　　 GRENACHE BLANC　　 ROUSSANNE

Franciacorta

◄) *"fran-cha-kor-tah"*

BODY · SWEETNESS · TANNIN · ACIDITY · ALCOHOL

SP LW FW AW RS LR MR FR DS

🍷 A region in Lombardy, Italy, dedicated to the production of traditional method sparkling wine using the same grapes as Champagne with the addition of Pinot Blanc.

🍴 A fruity sparkling wine like Franciacorta pairs perfectly with soft ripened cheeses (like brie), dried fruits (like apricot and cherry), and roasted, salted nuts.

 LEMON

 PEACH

 WHITE CHERRY

 ALMOND

 TOAST

 FLUTE GLASS

 ICE COLD 38–45° F

 DECANT NO

 SPEND ~$40

 CELLAR 5–20 YEARS

Styles

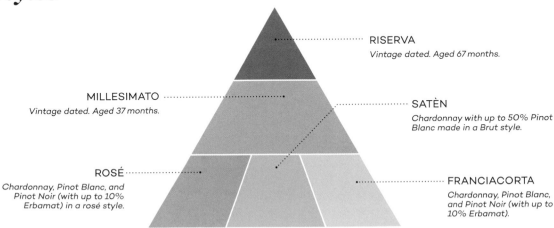

RISERVA
Vintage dated. Aged 67 months.

MILLESIMATO
Vintage dated. Aged 37 months.

SATÈN
Chardonnay with up to 50% Pinot Blanc made in a Brut style.

ROSÉ
Chardonnay, Pinot Blanc, and Pinot Noir (with up to 10% Erbamat) in a rosé style.

FRANCIACORTA
Chardonnay, Pinot Blanc, and Pinot Noir (with up to 10% Erbamat).

Also Try

CHAMPAGNE   CRÉMANT   CAVA   METODO CLASSICO   CAP CLASSIQUE

Frappato

 "fra-pat-toe"

BODY
ALCOHOL
SWEETNESS
ACIDITY
TANNIN

A rare find from Sicily that bursts with aromas of sweet red berries and incense spice. It's sometimes blended with Nero d'Avola to add complexity.

Frappato is a great wine to pair with dishes that feature roasted red pepper and sun-dried tomato. Also, try it with roast turkey and cranberry sauce.

| DRIED STRAWBERRY | POMEGRANATE | WHITE PEPPER | TOBACCO | CLOVE |

 AROMA COLLECTOR   CELLAR 55–60° F   DECANT NO   SPEND ~$16   CELLAR 1–3 YEARS

Where It Grows

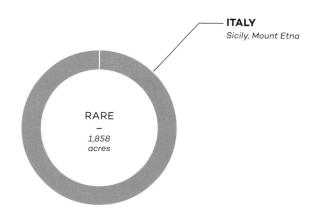

ITALY
Sicily, Mount Etna

RARE
–
1,858 acres

Also Try

 SCHIAVA   ZINFANDEL   PINOT NOIR   NERELLO MASCALESE   BRACHETTO

Friulano

🔊 *"free-yu-lawn-oh"* 💬 *Sauvignon Vert, Sauvignonasse*

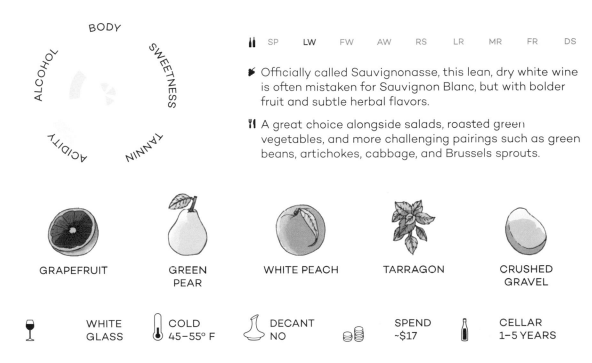

BODY
SWEETNESS
ALCOHOL
TANNIN
ACIDITY

🍾 SP **LW** FW AW RS LR MR FR DS

🥄 Officially called Sauvignonasse, this lean, dry white wine is often mistaken for Sauvignon Blanc, but with bolder fruit and subtle herbal flavors.

🍴 A great choice alongside salads, roasted green vegetables, and more challenging pairings such as green beans, artichokes, cabbage, and Brussels sprouts.

GRAPEFRUIT	GREEN PEAR	WHITE PEACH	TARRAGON	CRUSHED GRAVEL

🍷 WHITE GLASS	🌡️ COLD 45–55° F	DECANT NO	🪙	SPEND ~$17	🍾 CELLAR 1–5 YEARS

Where It Grows

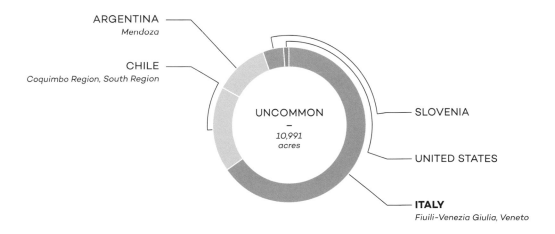

ARGENTINA
Mendoza

CHILE
Coquimbo Region, South Region

UNCOMMON
–
10,991 acres

SLOVENIA

UNITED STATES

ITALY
Fiuili-Venezia Giulia, Veneto

Also Try

SAUVIGNON BLANC   MELON   VERDEJO   ALBARIÑO   FURMINT

Furmint

◀) *"furh-meent"*   💬 *Tokay*

BODY

	SP	LW	FW	AW	RS	LR	MR	FR	DS

🌿 Furmint is Hungary's most famous grape. It's famously used in Tokaji Aszú dessert wines, but is also available as a dry white wine that tastes similar to Riesling.

🍴 With green, spicy flavors and brace-yourself acidity, Furmint is a superb match with herb-crusted poultry or fish. Also, try it with sushi and Chinese dumplings.

 MEYER LEMON   GREEN APPLE   GINGER   SMOKE   PEPPEROCINI

 WHITE GLASS   COLD 45–55° F   DECANT NO   SPEND ~$20   CELLAR 5–20 YEARS

Where It Grows

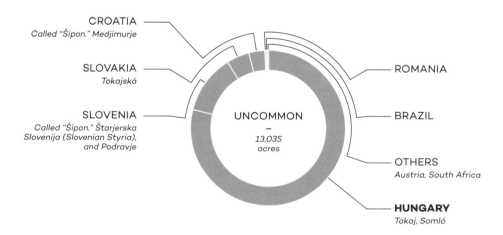

CROATIA
Called "Šipon." Medjimurje

SLOVAKIA
Tokajská

SLOVENIA
Called "Šipon." Štarjerska Slovenija (Slovenian Styria), and Podravje

UNCOMMON
–
13,035
acres

ROMANIA

BRAZIL

OTHERS
Austria, South Africa

HUNGARY
Tokaj, Somló

Also Try

 RIESLING   ASSYRTIKO   RKATSITELI   LOUREIRO (PORTUGAL)   ALBARIÑO

Gamay

🔊 *"gam-may"*   💬 *Gamay Noir*

BODY · ALCOHOL · SWEETNESS · ACIDITY · TANNIN

SP LW FW AW **RS** **LR** MR FR DS

🍷 A fruity, floral, and sometimes earthy light-bodied red that is the main variety planted in Beaujolais. Outside of France, Gamay has a tiny but devoted following.

🍴 One of the red wines that pairs with all manner of dishes from sweet-and-sour salmon to beef stroganoff or even sesame tempeh.

POMEGRANATE | BLACKBERRY BRAMBLE | VIOLET | POTTING SOIL | BANANA

🍷 AROMA COLLECTOR | 🌡️ CELLAR 55–60° F | DECANT 30 MIN | 🪙 SPEND ~$15 | 🍾 CELLAR 1–5 YEARS

Where It Grows

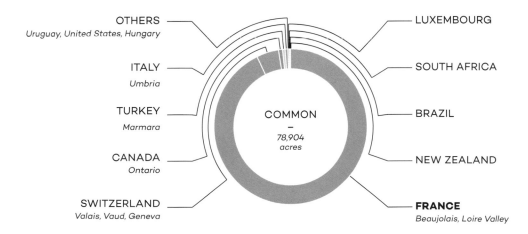

OTHERS
Uruguay, United States, Hungary

ITALY
Umbria

TURKEY
Marmara

CANADA
Ontario

SWITZERLAND
Valais, Vaud, Geneva

COMMON
–
78,904 acres

LUXEMBOURG

SOUTH AFRICA

BRAZIL

NEW ZEALAND

FRANCE
Beaujolais, Loire Valley

Also Try

 ZWEIGELT   SCHIAVA   PINOT NOIR   VALPOLICELLA   FRAPPATO

Garganega

🔊 *"gar-gah-neh-gah"* 💬 *Grecanico, Soave, Gambellara*

BODY

SWEETNESS

ALCOHOL

TANNIN

ACIDITY

| 🍷 | SP | **LW** | FW | AW | RS | LR | MR | FR | **DS** |

🔖 An important Italian white that's loved for its lean, dry style and the rich tangerine and toasted almond notes it gains as it ages. Garganega is the main grape of Soave.

🍴 Try pairing Soave with lighter meats, tofu, or fish and season with citrus-tarragon dressing and other aromatic green herbs.

| PEACH | HONEYDEW | TANGERINE | MARJORAM | SALINE |

| 🍷 WHITE GLASS | 🌡️ COLD 45–55° F | DECANT NO | 🪙 | SPEND ~$12 | 🍾 CELLAR 3–7 YEARS |

Where It Grows

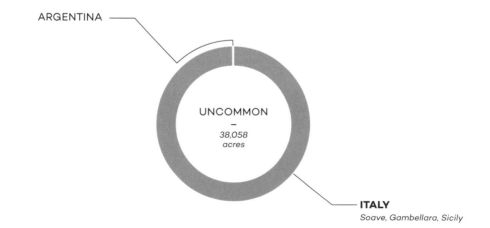

ARGENTINA

UNCOMMON
–
*38,058
acres*

ITALY
Soave, Gambellara, Sicily

Also Try

CHENIN BLANC   GRECHETTO   ALBARIÑO   FRIULANO   ARNEIS

Gewürztraminer

🔊 *"ga-vurtz-tra-me-ner"* 💬 *Traminer*

| 🍾 | SP | LW | FW | AW | RS | LR | MR | FR | DS |

🌿 Treasured for its intense floral aromas, Gewürztraminer has thrived for centuries in Europe. Wines are best enjoyed in their youth when acidity is highest.

🍴 The sweet floral aromatics and ginger-like spice paired with a fuller body make Gewürztraminer a great partner to Indian and Moroccan Cuisine.

| LYCHEE | ROSE | GRAPEFRUIT | TANGERINE | GINGER |

 WHITE GLASS   ICE COLD 38–45° F   DECANT NO   SPEND ~$15   CELLAR 1–5 YEARS

Where It Grows

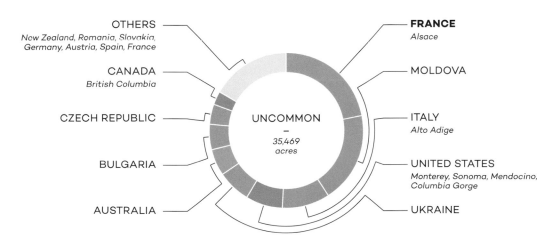

OTHERS
New Zealand, Romania, Slovakia, Germany, Austria, Spain, France

CANADA
British Columbia

CZECH REPUBLIC

BULGARIA

AUSTRALIA

UNCOMMON
—
35,469 acres

FRANCE
Alsace

MOLDOVA

ITALY
Alto Adige

UNITED STATES
Monterey, Sonoma, Mendocino, Columbia Gorge

UKRAINE

Also Try

 MOSCHOFILERO   MUSCAT BLANC TORRONTÉS CSERSZEGI FŰSZERES (HUNGARY) MÜLLER-THURGAU

Grechetto

🔊 *"greh-ketto"*   💬 *Orvieto*

🍾	SP	LW	FW	AW	RS	LR	MR	FR	DS

🥩 The primary grape in Italy's well-known Orvieto wines from Umbria and Lazio. Even though the wines are white, if you close your eyes, they almost taste like dry rosé.

🍴 Grechetto may grow in the land-locked province of Umbria but that doesn't preclude it from pairing excellently with tuna and other steak-like sea fare.

WHITE PEACH	HONEYDEW	STRAWBERRY	WILD FLOWERS	SEASHELL

WHITE GLASS	COLD 45–55° F	DECANT NO	SPEND ~$18	CELLAR 1–5 YEARS

Where It Grows

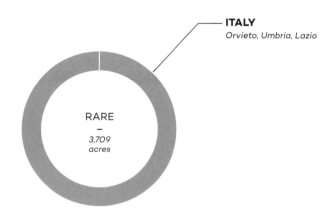

ITALY
Orvieto, Umbria, Lazio

RARE
–
3,709 acres

Also Try

FRIULANO   ALBARIÑO   CHENIN BLANC   GARGANEGA   MELON

Grenache

🔊 *"grenn-nosh"*　　💬 *Garnacha, Cannonau*

ALCOHOL · BODY · SWEETNESS · TANNIN · ACIDITY

| SP | LW | FW | AW | RS | LR | MR | FR | DS |

🌿 Grenache produces rich, flavorful red wines as well as deep ruby-tinted rosé. Grenache is the most important variety in Châteauneuf-du-Pape and the Rhône / GSM Blend.

🍴 The high-intensity flavors of Grenache match roasted meats and vegetables that include exotic spices like cumin, allspice, and Asian five-spice.

STEWED STRAWBERRY

GRILLED PLUM

LEATHER

DRIED HERBS

BLOOD ORANGE

 RED GLASS　　🌡 **ROOM 60–68° F**　　 **DECANT 30 MIN**　　 **SPEND ~$23**　　 **CELLAR 5–10 YEARS**

Where It Grows

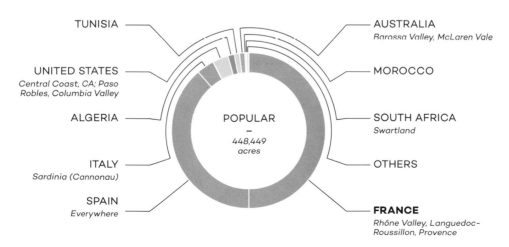

TUNISIA

UNITED STATES
Central Coast, CA; Paso Robles, Columbia Valley

ALGERIA

ITALY
Sardinia (Cannonau)

SPAIN
Everywhere

POPULAR
–
448,449
acres

AUSTRALIA
Barossa Valley, McLaren Vale

MOROCCO

SOUTH AFRICA
Swartland

OTHERS

FRANCE
Rhône Valley, Languedoc-Roussillon, Provence

Also Try

🍷 CARIGNAN　　🍷 ZINFANDEL　　🍷 MERLOT　　🍷 VALPOLICELLA

Grenache

ADDITIONAL
TASTING
NOTES

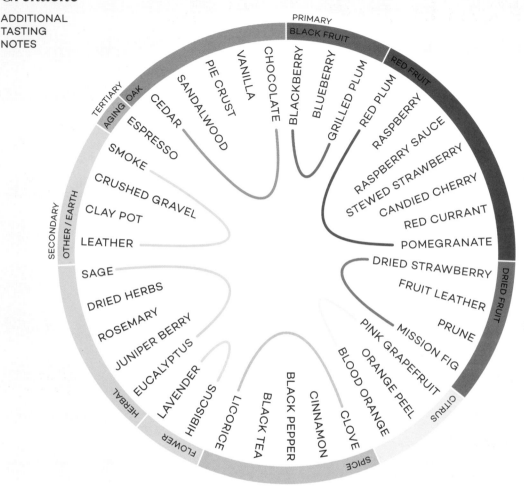

Aragon, Spain

The Northern Spanish regions (Somontano, Campo de Borja, Cariñena, Calatayud) produce fantastic, fruit-forward, high alcohol styles of Garnacha with punchy red fruit flavors and subtle notes of sweet pink grapefruit and hibiscus flowers.

▸ RASPBERRY
▸ HIBISCUS
▸ PINK GRAPEFRUIT
▸ DRIED HERBS
▸ CLOVE

Rhône Valley, France

The Southern Rhône and Châteauneuf-du-Pape is famous for its Grenache-Syrah-Mourvèdre blends. Surprisingly, many of the top wines made here feature a heavy proportion of Grenache. Expect wines with more savory, herbal, and floral flavors.

▸ GRILLED PLUM
▸ RASPBERRY SAUCE
▸ BLACK TEA
▸ LAVENDER
▸ CRUSHED GRAVEL

Sardegna

The island of Sardegna specializes in Grenache, or as it's called there: Cannonau. The style here is lighter-bodied and very rustic with flavors of leather, dried red fruits, and wild game. There are fruitier examples as well, but the rustic version is well worth a taste.

▸ LEATHER
▸ RED PLUM
▸ GAME
▸ BLOOD ORANGE
▸ CLAY POT

Grenache Blanc

🔊 *"gren-nash blonk"* 💬 *Garnacha Blanca*

BODY
ALCOHOL
SWEETNESS
ACIDITY
TANNIN

| | SP | LW | FW | AW | RS | LR | MR | FR | DS |

🌾 Grenache Blanc is a color mutation of Grenache that produces full-bodied white wines that are sometimes aged in oak to delivery toasty, creamy, dill-like flavors.

🍴 A great choice with more steak-like fish including tuna steaks, swordfish, grilled snapper, and mahi mahi.

YELLOW PLUM	PEAR	LEMON ZEST	HONEYSUCKLE	TOAST

🍷 WHITE GLASS 🌡️ COLD 45–55° F DECANT NO 💰 SPEND ~$22 🍾 CELLAR 1–5 YEARS

Where It Grows

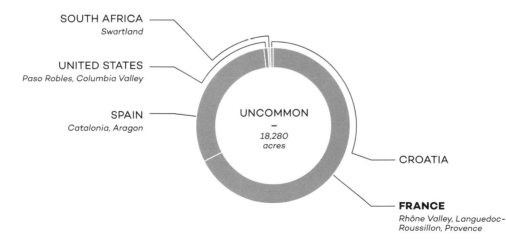

SOUTH AFRICA
Swartland

UNITED STATES
Paso Robles, Columbia Valley

SPAIN
Catalonia, Aragon

UNCOMMON
—
18,280 acres

CROATIA

FRANCE
Rhône Valley, Languedoc-Roussillon, Provence

Also Try

ROUSSANNE SAVATIANO RKATSITELI VIURA GARGANEGA

Grüner Veltliner

◀ "grew-ner felt-lee-ner"

| | SP | LW | FW | AW | RS | LR | MR | FR | DS |

🌱 Austria's most important wine is produced in a myriad of styles, the most popular of which are lean, herbaceous, and peppery wines with mouth-watering acidity.

🍴 A very versatile food wine that makes an ideal palate cleanser. Try Grüner Veltliner with light meats and seafood such as tarragon chicken and sashimi.

YELLOW APPLE

PEAR

ASPARAGUS

WHITE PEPPER

FLINT

WHITE GLASS

COLD 45–55° F

DECANT NO

SPEND ~$20

CELLAR 5–15 YEARS

Where It Grows

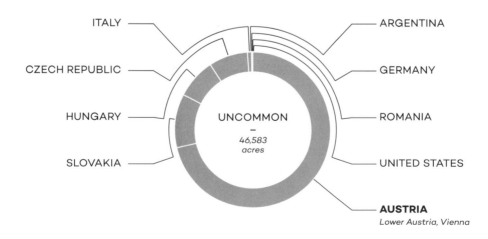

ITALY

CZECH REPUBLIC

HUNGARY

SLOVAKIA

ARGENTINA

GERMANY

ROMANIA

UNITED STATES

AUSTRIA
Lower Austria, Vienna

UNCOMMON
–
46,583
acres

Also Try

SAUVIGNON BLANC   VINHO VERDE   VERMENTINO   FRIULANO   VERDEJO

Ice Wine

 Eiswein

BODY
ALCOHOL
SWEETNESS
TANNIN
ACIDITY

 SP · LW · FW · AW · RS · LR · MR · FR · **DS**

A late harvest sweet wine that can only be made when grapes naturally freeze in the vineyard. Popular varieties include Riesling, Vidal Blanc, and Cabernet Franc.

Ice wines are perfect with fruit tarts, cheesecake, ice cream, and soft and pungent cheeses such as Brie and Camembert.

| PINEAPPLE | LEMON CURD | HONEYSUCKLE | APRICOT | LYCHEE |

DESSERT GLASS   COLD 45–55° F   DECANT NO   SPEND ~$40   CELLAR 5–10 YEARS

Grapes and Styles

RIESLING   GRÜNER VELTLINER   VIDAL BLANC

CABERNET FRANC   CHENIN BLANC   GEWÜRZTRAMINER

To be labeled ice wine, grapes must be picked and pressed while frozen naturally. This only happens in cool climates where temperatures get below 20° F (-7° C) in the late harvest period.

Canada is the largest producer of Ice Wine followed by Germany, Austria, and the United States.

Because the juice is so sweet, fermentations are quite long, taking about 2–6 months.

Ice wines have low alcohol and high sweetness (10% ABV and 160–220 g/L residual sugar).

Also Try

 SAUTERNES   FURMINT (TOKAJI ASZÚ)   LATE HARVEST RIESLING

Lambrusco

🔊 *"lam-broos-co"*

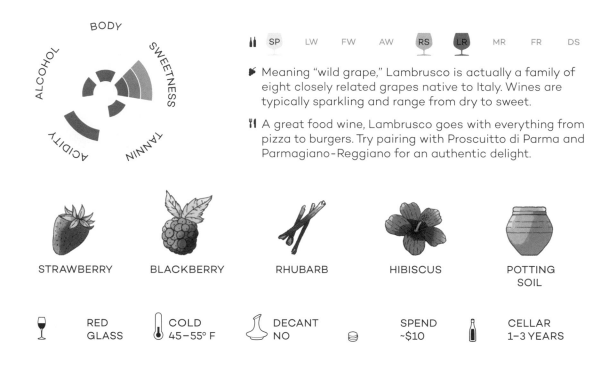

| | SP | LW | FW | AW | RS | LR | MR | FR | DS |

🌾 Meaning "wild grape," Lambrusco is actually a family of eight closely related grapes native to Italy. Wines are typically sparkling and range from dry to sweet.

🍴 A great food wine, Lambrusco goes with everything from pizza to burgers. Try pairing with Proscuitto di Parma and Parmagiano-Reggiano for an authentic delight.

STRAWBERRY · BLACKBERRY · RHUBARB · HIBISCUS · POTTING SOIL

RED GLASS · COLD 45–55° F · DECANT NO · SPEND ~$10 · CELLAR 1–3 YEARS

Where It Grows

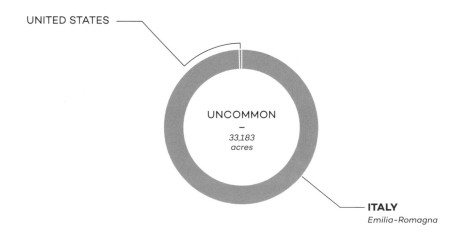

UNITED STATES

UNCOMMON
–
33,183 acres

ITALY
Emilia-Romagna

Also Try

🍷 SCHIAVA 🍷 BRACHETTO D'ACQUI 🍷 ZWEIGELT 🍷 CONCORD

Lambrusco

ADDITIONAL
TASTING
NOTES

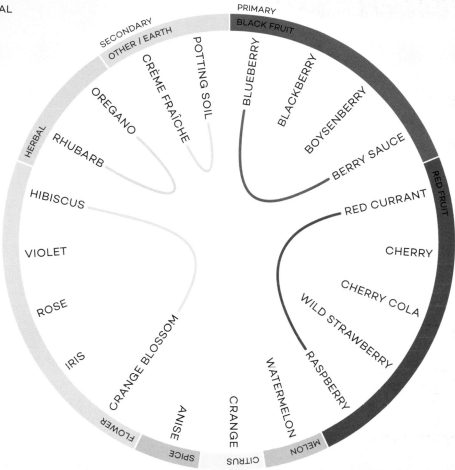

Lambrusco di Sorbara

This grape produces the most delicate and floral of the Lambrusco varieties, often in a pale pink hue. The best versions are in a dry and refreshing style with delightfully sweet aromas of orange blossom, mandarins, cherries, violets, and watermelon.

▸ ORANGE BLOSSOM
▸ MANDARIN ORANGE
▸ CHERRY
▸ VIOLET
▸ WATERMELON

Lambrusco Grasparossa

The boldest Lambrusco grape features blueberry and blackcurrant flavors with moderately high, mouth-drying tannin. The tank sparkling method imparts a wonderous, palate-balancing creaminess as well! You'll find this wine labeled as Lambrusco Grasparossa di Castelvetro (includes 85% of this grape).

▸ BLACK CURRANT
▸ BLUEBERRY
▸ OREGANO
▸ COCOA POWDER
▸ CULTURED CREAM

Sweetness Levels

Lambrusco can range in style from dry to sweet using the following terms:

- **Secco:** Dry wines with floral or herbal notes.
- **Semisecco:** Just off-dry styles with more fruitiness.
- **Amabile and Dolce:** Noticeably sweet styles, great for pairing dessert, particularly milk chocolate.

Madeira

🔊 *"ma-deer-uh"*

 SP LW FW AW RS LR MR FR

🍷 These oxidized and fortified dessert wines are made exclusively on the Portuguese Island of Madeira. Wines are incredibly stable and some will age over 100 years.

🍴 Madeira is a popular choice for reduction sauces because of its walnut flavors. Still, you'll be surprised at how well it pairs with artichokes, pea soup, and asparagus.

BURNT CARAMEL	WALNUT OIL	PEACH	HAZELNUT	ORANGE PEEL

 DESSERT GLASS   CELLAR 55–60° F   DECANT NO   SPEND ~$43  CELLAR 5–100 YEARS

Styles

RAINWATER	SERCIAL	VERDELHO	BUAL / BOAL	MALMSEY
A common style blended with Tinta Negramole.	The lightest style made with Sercial grapes.	A light and aromatic style made with Verdelho grapes.	The second sweetest style made with Malvasia grapes.	The sweetest style made with Malvasia grapes.

Sweetness Levels

- EXTRA DRY: 0–50 g/L RS
- DRY: 50–65 g/L RS
- MEDIUM DRY: 65–80 g/L RS
- MED. RICH / SWEET: 80–96 g/L RS
- RICH / SWEET: 96+ g/L RS

Production Methods

CANTEIRO METHOD
Wine ages naturally in barrels or large glass bottles in a warm room or under the sun.

ESTUFA METHOD
Wine is heated in tanks for a short period.

Vintage Styles

COLHEITA / HARVEST
A single vintage Madeira aged 5+ years. Typically a single variety.

SOLERA
A multi-vintage blend by Canteiro. Rare.

FRASQUEIRA / GARRAFEIRA
Single vintage aged 20+ years by Canteiro method. Very rare.

Also Try

🍷 DRY MARSALA

Non-Vintage Styles

FINEST / CHOICE / SELECT
Aged 3 years by Estufa. Affordable choice for cooking wines. Tinta Negramole.

RAINWATER
Medium Dry style aged 3 years. Great affordable cooking wine. Tinta Negramole.

5-YEAR / RESERVE / MATURE
Aged 5–10 years. Sipping quality.

10-YEAR / SPECIAL RESERVE
Aged 10–15 years by Canteiro. Typically a single variety. High quality.

15-YEAR / EXTRA RESERVE
Aged 15–20 years by Canteiro. Typically a single variety. High quality.

Malbec

 "mal-bek"   Côt

SP LW FW AW **RS** LR MR **FR** DS

Argentina's most important variety came by way of France, where it's commonly called Côt. Wines are loved for their bold fruit flavors and smooth chocolaty finish.

Unlike Cabernet, Malbec doesn't have a long finish, making it a great choice with leaner red meats (ostrich, anyone?) and does wonders with melted blue cheese.

| RED PLUM | BLACKBERRY | VANILLA | SWEET TOBACCO | COCOA |

 RED GLASS   ROOM 60–68° F   DECANT 30 MIN   SPEND ~$15   CELLAR 5–10 YEARS

Where It Grows

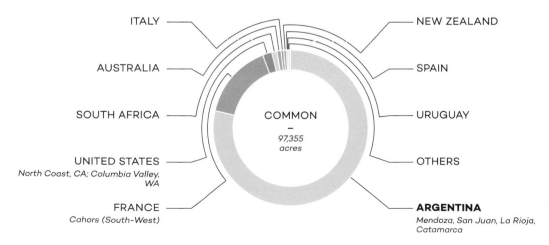

ITALY

AUSTRALIA

SOUTH AFRICA

UNITED STATES
North Coast, CA; Columbia Valley, WA

FRANCE
Cahors (South-West)

NEW ZEALAND

SPAIN

URUGUAY

OTHERS

ARGENTINA
Mendoza, San Juan, La Rioja, Catamarca

COMMON
—
97,355 acres

Also Try

 MONASTRELL   SYRAH   BONARDA   PETIT VERDOT   MERLOT

Malbec

ADDITIONAL
TASTING
NOTES

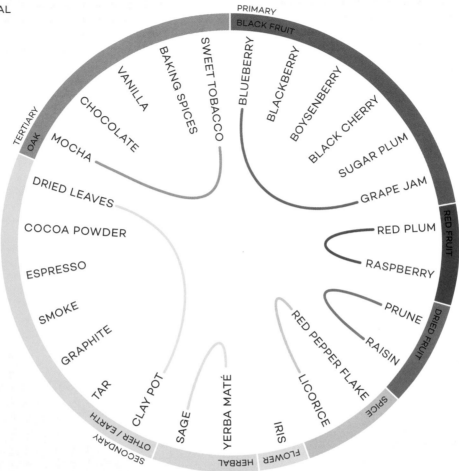

Mendoza, Argentina

These entry-level Malbec wines receive minimal oak aging, delivering a much fresher and juicier style. Most have more red fruit notes (tart cherry, raspberry, red plum) with soft tannins and herbal notes of raspberry leaf or yerba mate.

▸ RED PLUM
▸ BOYSENBERRY
▸ RED PEPPER FLAKE
▸ PRUNE
▸ RASPBERRY LEAF

Mendoza "Reserva"

Higher-end examples of Mendoza Malbec use the highest-quality grapes, often from old vines or the higher elevation vineyards in Luján de Cuyo and Uco Valley. Wines are bolder, with black fruit flavors with chocolate, mocha, and blueberry notes from oak aging.

▸ BLACKBERRY
▸ SUGAR PLUM
▸ MOCHA
▸ RED PEPPER FLAKE
▸ SWEET TOBACCO

Cahors, France

France produces Malbec in both the Loire Valley (where it's called Côt) and in southwest France in Cahors. The Cahors region produces wines with more earthy-berry flavors and wines typically have a lighter and more elegant body with higher acidity compared to Argentinean examples.

▸ RED PLUM
▸ DRIED LEAVES
▸ BOYSENBERRY
▸ IRIS
▸ COCOA POWDER

Marsala

◀) *"mar-sal-uh"*

 SP   LW   FW   AW   RS   LR   MR   FR   DS

🍷 Marsala is a fortified wine from Sicily commonly used in cooking to create rich, caramelized sauces, but the higher-quality tiers also make exceptional sipping wines.

🍴 You can use dry Marsala for most cooking applications. Sweet styles are preferred for desserts such as zabaglione or as a reduction sauce over ice cream.

STEWED APRICOT

VANILLA

TAMARIND

BROWN SUGAR

TOBACCO

🍷 DESSERT GLASS   🌡 CELLAR 55–60° F   ⚗ DECANT NO   🪙 SPEND ~$17   🍾 CELLAR 5–25 YEARS

GRILLO   CATTARATTO   INZOLIA   GRECANICO   NERO D'AVOLA   NERELLO MASCALESE   FRAPPATO

● VIRGIN STRAVECCHIO / VIRGIN RESERVE
Aged 10+ years. Only in dry.

● VIRGIN / VIRGEN SOLERA
Aged 5+ years. Only in dry.

● ● ● SUPERIOR RESERVE
Aged 4+ years. Not available in sweet.

● ● ● SUPERIOR
Aged 2 years.

● ● ● FINE / FINE I.P.
Aged 1 year.

● GOLD (ORO): *A blend of white grapes. The finest of Marsala styles.*

● AMBER (AMBRA): *A blend of white grapes and cooked grape must (mosto cotto).*

● RED (RUBINO): *Rare. A blend made with up to 30% red grapes.*

● DRY (SECCO): *0–40 g/L RS*

● SEMISWEET (SEMISECCO): *40–100 g/L RS*

● SWEET (DOLCE): *100+ g/L RS*

Also Try

 MADEIRA   PALO CORTADO SHERRY   AMONTILLADO SHERRY

Marsanne

🔊 *"mar-sohn"*   💬 *Châteauneuf-du-Pape Blanc, Côtes du Rhône Blanc*

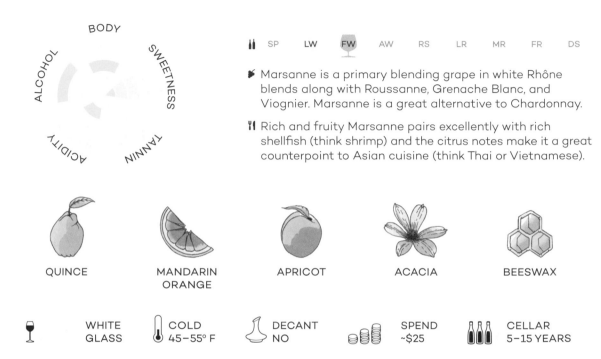

	SP	LW	**FW**	AW	RS	LR	MR	FR	DS

🍷 Marsanne is a primary blending grape in white Rhône blends along with Roussanne, Grenache Blanc, and Viognier. Marsanne is a great alternative to Chardonnay.

🍴 Rich and fruity Marsanne pairs excellently with rich shellfish (think shrimp) and the citrus notes make it a great counterpoint to Asian cuisine (think Thai or Vietnamese).

QUINCE   MANDARIN ORANGE   APRICOT   ACACIA   BEESWAX

WHITE GLASS   COLD 45–55° F   DECANT NO   SPEND ~$25   CELLAR 5–15 YEARS

Where It Grows

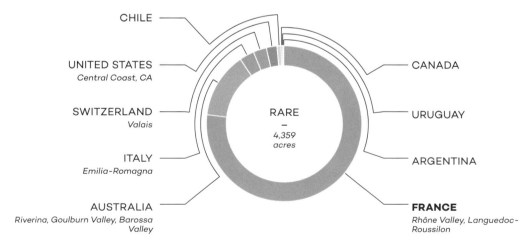

CHILE

UNITED STATES
Central Coast, CA

SWITZERLAND
Valais

ITALY
Emilia-Romagna

AUSTRALIA
Riverina, Goulburn Valley, Barossa Valley

RARE
–
4,359 acres

CANADA

URUGUAY

ARGENTINA

FRANCE
Rhône Valley, Languedoc-Roussilon

Also Try

🍷 ROUSSANNE   🍷 CHARDONNAY   🍷 VIOGNIER

Melon

◀) *"mel-oh"* 💬 *Muscadet, Melon de Bourgogne*

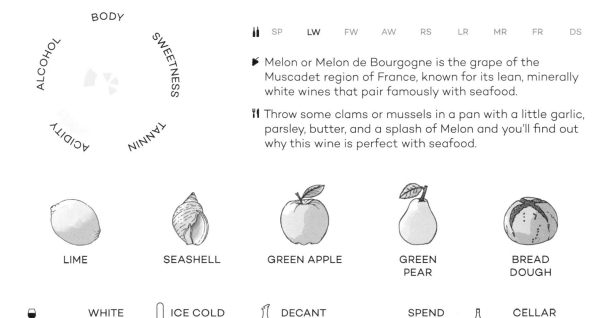

🍶	SP	LW	FW	AW	RS	LR	MR	FR	DS

🌿 Melon or Melon de Bourgogne is the grape of the Muscadet region of France, known for its lean, minerally white wines that pair famously with seafood.

🍴 Throw some clams or mussels in a pan with a little garlic, parsley, butter, and a splash of Melon and you'll find out why this wine is perfect with seafood.

LIME	SEASHELL	GREEN APPLE	GREEN PEAR	BREAD DOUGH

🍷 WHITE GLASS — 🌡️ ICE COLD 38–45° F — ⚗️ DECANT NO — 🪙 — SPEND ~$14 — 🍾 CELLAR 1–5 YEARS

Where It Grows

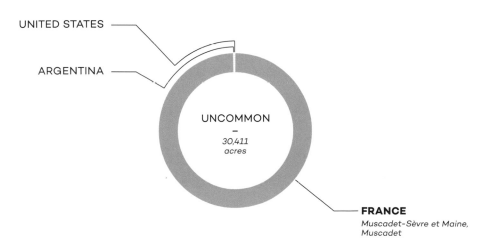

UNITED STATES

ARGENTINA

UNCOMMON
–
30,411
acres

FRANCE
Muscadet-Sèvre et Maine, Muscadet

Also Try

FRIULANO   GRECHETTO   VERDEJO   CHASSELAS (SWITZERLAND)

Mencía

🔊 *"men-thee-uh"*   💬 *Jaen, Bierzo, Riberia Sacra*

SP　LW　FW　AW　RS　LR　**MR**　FR　DS

🍖 A red variety from the Iberian peninsula (Spain and Portugal) that's quickly developing a following for its heady aromatics and potential to age.

🍴 Due to its acidity and structure, you'll want to lean toward richer white meats like turkey and pork or cured, peppery meats (pastrami!) to balance intensity.

TART CHERRY	POMEGRANATE	BLACKBERRY	LICORICE	CRUSHED GRAVEL

🍷 RED GLASS	🌡 CELLAR 55–60° F	⚗ DECANT 60+ MIN	🪙 SPEND ~$15	🍾 CELLAR 5–20 YEARS

Where It Grows

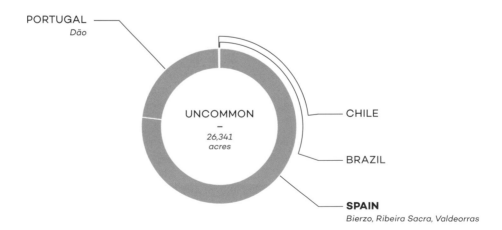

PORTUGAL
Dão

UNCOMMON
–
26,341 acres

CHILE

BRAZIL

SPAIN
Bierzo, Ribeira Sacra, Valdeorras

Also Try

🍷 XINOMAVRO　🍷 NERO D'AVOLA　🍷 BARBERA　🍷 SYRAH

Merlot

🔊 *"murr-low"*

BODY · SWEETNESS · TANNIN · ACIDITY · ALCOHOL

🍷 SP LW FW AW **RS** LR **MR** **FR** DS

🌿 Merlot is loved for it's boisterous black cherry flavors, supple tannins, and smoky or chocolaty finish. It's often found in a Bordeaux blend with Cabernet Franc.

🍴 Merlot tastes great alongside roasted foods like pork shoulder, roasted mushrooms, or braised short ribs. Try complementing the fruit notes with chimichurri sauce!

CHERRY   PLUM   CHOCOLATE   DRIED HERBS   VANILLA

 OVERSIZED GLASS   🌡 ROOM 60–68° F   🍷 DECANT 30 MIN   SPEND ~$15   CELLAR 5–20 YEARS

Where It Grows

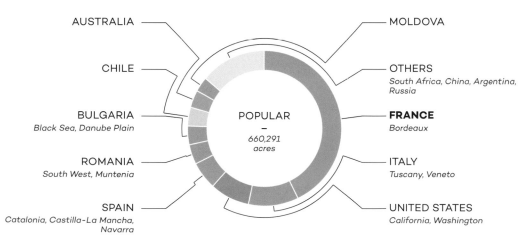

AUSTRALIA

CHILE

BULGARIA
Black Sea, Danube Plain

ROMANIA
South West, Muntenia

SPAIN
Catalonia, Castilla-La Mancha, Navarra

POPULAR
–
660,291 acres

MOLDOVA

OTHERS
South Africa, China, Argentina, Russia

FRANCE
Bordeaux

ITALY
Tuscany, Veneto

UNITED STATES
California, Washington

Also Try

 CABERNET SAUVIGNON   MALBEC   PETIT VERDOT    MONTEPULCIANO   VALPOLICELLA

Merlot

ADDITIONAL
TASTING
NOTES

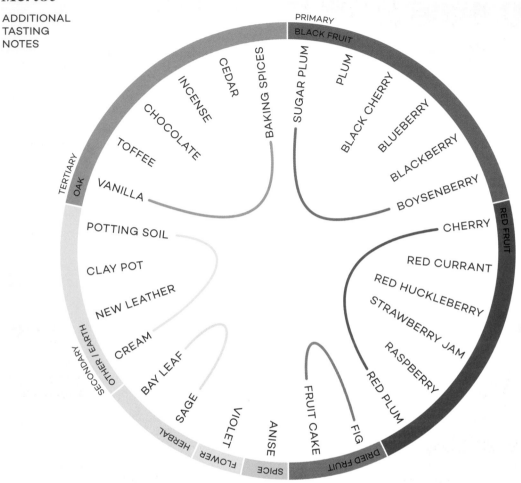

"Right Bank" Bordeaux

The Bordeaux regions of Pomerol and Saint-Émilion on the northeast bank of the Dordogne River have pockets of rich, clay-based soils that are ideal for ripening Merlot and Cabernet Franc. Great examples have rich, cherry fruit flavors balanced with cedar, leather, and incense notes.

▸ CHERRY
▸ NEW LEATHER
▸ CEDAR
▸ INCENSE
▸ BAY LEAF

Columbia Valley, WA

The region's hot daytime temperatures can drop by 40° F or more at night, which results in wines with sweet fruit, but elevated acidity. Merlot is a champion in Washington's soils, producing crisp, lighter-bodied cherry fruit along with floral and minty flavors.

▸ BLACK CHERRY
▸ BOYSENBERRY
▸ CHOCOLATE CREAM
▸ VIOLET
▸ MINT

North Coast, CA

The North Coast encompasses both Napa Valley and Sonoma. Believe it or not, Merlot is still an underappreciated value here when compared to Cabernet Sauvignon. Wines offer boisterous sweet black cherry fruit with moderate, fine-grained tannins, and subtle notes of baking chocolate.

▸ SWEET CHERRY
▸ SUGAR PLUM
▸ BAKING CHOCOLATE
▸ VANILLA
▸ DESERT DUST

Monastrell

🔊 *"Moan-uh-strel"*   💬 *Mourvèdre, Mataro*

🍷 A deeply bold, smoky red wine found in abundance in Central Spain. It's known as Mourvèdre in Southern France, where it's an essential grape in the Rhône / GSM blend.

🍴 A perfect wine with smoked meats and barbecue where the wine's peppery and gamey flavors seem to vanish, revealing layers of black fruits and chocolate.

BLACKBERRY

BLACK PEPPER

COCOA

TOBACCO

ROASTED MEAT

🍷 RED GLASS   🌡 ROOM 60–68° F   ⚗ DECANT 60+ MIN   💲 SPEND ~$14   🍾 CELLAR 5–15 YEARS

Where It Grows

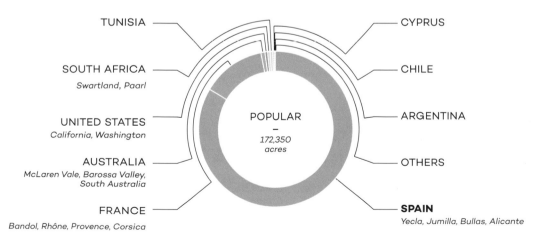

TUNISIA

SOUTH AFRICA
Swartland, Paarl

UNITED STATES
California, Washington

AUSTRALIA
McLaren Vale, Barossa Valley, South Australia

FRANCE
Bandol, Rhône, Provence, Corsica

POPULAR
–
172,350 acres

CYPRUS

CHILE

ARGENTINA

OTHERS

SPAIN
Yecla, Jumilla, Bullas, Alicante

Also Try

🍷 PETITE SIRAH   🍷 TANNAT   🍷 SYRAH   🍷 PETIT VERDOT   🍷 ALICANTE BOUSCHET

Monastrell

ADDITIONAL
TASTING
NOTES

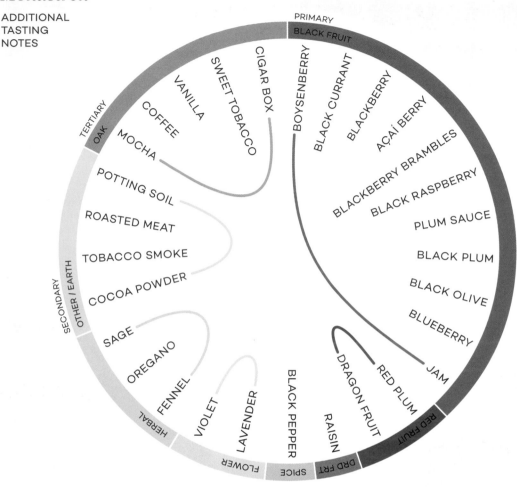

PRIMARY
BLACK FRUIT

BOYSENBERRY
BLACK CURRANT
BLACKBERRY
AÇAÍ BERRY
BLACKBERRY BRAMBLES
BLACK RASPBERRY
PLUM SAUCE
BLACK PLUM
BLACK OLIVE
BLUEBERRY
JAM
RED PLUM
DRAGON FRUIT
RAISIN
BLACK PEPPER
LAVENDER
VIOLET
FENNEL
OREGANO
SAGE
COCOA POWDER
TOBACCO SMOKE
ROASTED MEAT
POTTING SOIL
MOCHA
COFFEE
VANILLA
SWEET TOBACCO
CIGAR BOX

TERTIARY
OAK
SECONDARY
OTHER / EARTH
HERBAL
FLOWER
SPICE
DRD FRT
RED FRUIT

Bandol, France

It's said that Mourvèdre
("more-ved" – as the French
say) thrives with it's head in
the sun and feet in the sea, so
it's no wonder the grape shines
on the south-facing slopes of
Bandol in Provence. By law, the
wine must spend at least 18
months in oak barrels, lending
to this wine's rustic elegance.

‣ BLACK PLUM
‣ ROASTED MEAT
‣ BLACK PEPPER
‣ COCOA POWDER
‣ HERBS DE PROVENCE

Southeastern Spain

A major variety in the regions
of Jumilla, Yecla, Alicante,
and Bullas, where the grape is
called Monastrell. The warm,
dry climate produces wines
with bold fruit flavors and even
some tar and black olive! That
said, there is exceptional value
to be found here.

‣ BLACKBERRY
‣ BLACK RAISIN
‣ MOCHA
‣ TOBACCO SMOKE
‣ BLACK PEPPER

Bandol Rosé

Despite the depths of the
red wines produced with
Monastrell, the rosé wines are
surprisingly light with delicate
flavors of fresh strawberry and
a pink-rose colored hue. Along
with the delicate fruit, you're
likely to notice subtle notes
of violet and white or black
pepper.

‣ STRAWBERRY
‣ WHITE PEACH
‣ WHITE PEPPER
‣ WHITE BLOSSOM
‣ VIOLET

Montepulciano

🔊 *"mon-ta-pull-chee-anno"*

BODY

ALCOHOL

SWEETNESS

ACIDITY

TANNIN

🍷 SP LW FW AW RS LR **MR** **FR** DS

🥩 A high-quality Italian red found mostly in Abruzzo, where it produces wines with black fruit flavors and a smoky-sweet finish when it's made with care.

🍴 Montepulciano is an amazing wine to pair alongside sausages of all kinds. Smoked Andouille and sweet fennel salsiccia are the first that come to mind.

RED PLUM

BLACKBERRY

DRIED THYME

BAKING SPICES

MESQUITE

🍷 OVERSIZED GLASS

🌡️ ROOM 60–68° F

🫗 DECANT 60+ MIN

 SPEND ~$15

🍾 CELLAR 5–15 YEARS

Where It Grows

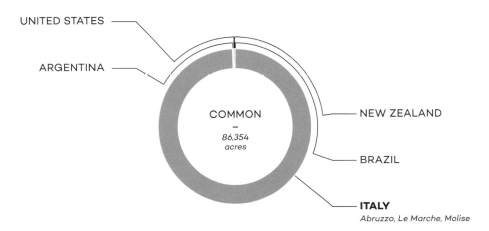

UNITED STATES

ARGENTINA

COMMON
–
86,354
acres

NEW ZEALAND

BRAZIL

ITALY
Abruzzo, Le Marche, Molise

Also Try

🍷 NEGROAMARO 🍷 MERLOT 🍷 BORDEAUX BLEND 🍷 AGIORGITIKO 🍷 NERO D'AVOLA

Moscatel de Setúbal

◀) *"Mos-ka-tell de Seh-too-bal"* 💬 *Moscatel Roxo*

	SP	LW	FW	AW	RS	LR	MR	FR	**DS**

🍖 A rich and honeyed fortified dessert wine made primarily with Muscat of Alexandria grapes grown on the Setúbal peninsula in Southern Portugal.

🍴 Moscatel de Setúbal is amazing alongside Portuguese cheeses with a gooey middle such as Queijo de Ovelha. Or, pair it with any dessert drizzled with a caramel topping.

MANDARIN ORANGE	GRAPE	DRIED APRICOT	HONEY	CARAMEL

 DESSERT GLASS | CELLAR 55–60° F | DECANT NO | SPEND ~$13 | CELLAR 1–5 YEARS

Grapes & Styles

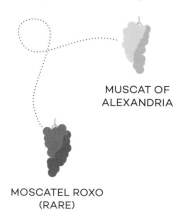

MUSCAT OF ALEXANDRIA

MOSCATEL ROXO (RARE)

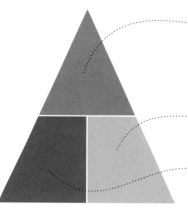

MOSCATEL DE SETÚBAL SUPERIOR

Aged more than 5 years. Wines are typically richer and sweeter with more dried fruit and nut flavors. Sometimes wines will be labeled by 20, 30, and 40 años (years), indicating the minimum age of the blend.

MOSCATEL DE SETÚBAL

Aged up to 5 years. Wines are typically more floral and with more citrus and fresh grape notes.

MOSCATEL ROXO

A rare style made mostly or only of Moscatel Roxo grapes.

Also Try

🍷 TAWNY PORT | 🍷 VIN SANTO | 🍷 MUSCAT OF ALEXANDRIA | 🍷 MUSCAT DE RIVESALTES | 🍷 MUSCAT OF SAMOS (GREECE)

Moschofilero

 "moosh-ko-fee-lair-oh"

BODY
SWEETNESS
TANNIN
ACIDITY
ALCOHOL

A richly aromatic white wine that hails from the small region of Mantineia close to Tripoli in Peloponnese, Greece. The grape has pink skins and can be made into rosé.

Anything you might serve at high tea, including cucumber sandwiches, lox with cream cheese, or fruit tarts, pairs well with this wonderfully aromatic wine.

POTPOURRI	HONEYDEW	PINK GRAPEFRUIT	LEMON	ALMOND

WHITE GLASS	COLD 45–55° F	DECANT NO		SPEND ~$14	CELLAR 1–3 YEARS

Where It Grows

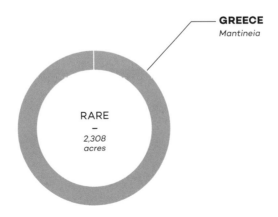

GREECE
Mantineia

RARE
—
2,308 acres

Also Try

 FERNAO PIRES   TORRONTÉS   CSERSZEGI FŰSZERES (HUNGARY)    GEWÜRZTRAMINER   MÜLLER-THURGAU

Muscat Blanc

🔊 *"muss-kot blonk"* 💬 *Moscato Bianco, Moscatel, Muscat Blanc à Petit Grains, Muskateller*

🥂 An ancient aromatic white variety originally from Greece that's available in all styles from dry to sweet, still to sparkling, and even fortified.

🍴 Drier styles pair well with salads, sushi, and fresh fruit. Sparkling Moscato d'Asti is excellent with almond cake. Fortified Muscat tastes great with cheeses and nuts.

ORANGE BLOSSOM

MEYER LEMON

MANDARIN ORANGE

RIPE PEAR

HONEYSUCKLE

| 🍷 WHITE GLASS | 🌡️ COLD 45–55° F | DECANT NO | 🪙 SPEND ~$17 | 🍾 CELLAR 1–5 YEARS |

Where It Grows

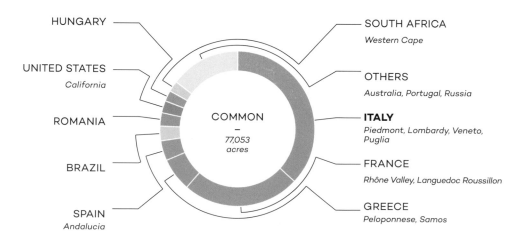

HUNGARY

UNITED STATES
California

ROMANIA

BRAZIL

SPAIN
Andalucia

COMMON
–
77,053
acres

SOUTH AFRICA
Western Cape

OTHERS
Australia, Portugal, Russia

ITALY
Piedmont, Lombardy, Veneto, Puglia

FRANCE
Rhône Valley, Languedoc Roussillon

GREECE
Peloponnese, Samos

Also Try

 MUSCAT OF ALEXANDRIA

 MÜLLER-THURGAU

 GEWÜRZTRAMINER

 TORRONTÉS

 CSERSZEGI FŰSZERES (HUNGARY)

Muscat Blanc

ADDITIONAL
TASTING
NOTES

PRIMARY

TERTIARY · AGING

RD FRT · DRIED FRUIT · TROPICAL FRUIT

PECAN · HAZELNUT · CARAMEL · TOFFEE · ROSE PETAL · ORANGE BLOSSOM · HONEYSUCKLE · PERFUME

FRESH GRAPE · RAISIN · WHITE MULBERRY · PASSIONFRUIT · PINEAPPLE · LYCHEE · MANGO

FLOWER

NUTMEG · GINGER · HONEY · VANILLA BEAN · CORIANDER · TANGERINE · MANDARIN ORANGE · MEYER LEMON · APRICOT · PEACH · PEAR

QUINCE · HONEYDEW MELON · PINK LADY APPLE · ASIAN PEAR

TREE FRUIT / MELON

SPICE · CITRUS

Moscato d'Asti

A very delicate and lightly sparkling Muscat Blanc from the Asti region in Piedmont, Italy. Moscato d'Asti has one of the lowest alcohol levels of all wines (at around 5.5% ABV), reserving the grape sugars for sweetness in this highly aromatic white wine.

‣ MANDARIN ORANGE
‣ HONEYSUCKLE
‣ MEYER LEMON
‣ ROSE PETAL
‣ VANILLA BEAN

Alsace Muscat

France produces several styles of Muscat from lighter Alsatian Muscat to richer, fortified dessert wines like Muscat de Rivesaltes and Muscat de Beaumes de Venise. In Alsace, the wines are light-bodied, just off-dry, with aromas of perfume, lemongrass, and a kick of brown spices.

‣ FRESH GRAPE
‣ PERFUME
‣ LEMONGRASS
‣ CORIANDER
‣ NUTMEG

Rutherglen Muscat

One of the sweetest dessert wines in the world (or "Stickies" as they say in Australia) hails from Victoria. This unctous wonder is made a the rare "Rouge" variant of Muscat Blanc. Wines are a deep amber to golden brown color with aromas of caramelized cherry, coffee, sassafras, and vanilla.

‣ CARAMEL
‣ CANDIED CHERRY
‣ COFFEE
‣ SASSAFRAS
‣ VANILLA BEAN

Muscat of Alexandria

Hanepoot, Moscatel

BODY
SWEETNESS
ALCOHOL
TANNIN
ACIDITY

▮▮	SP	LW	FW	AW	RS	LR	MR	FR	🍷 DS

Another important Muscat variety used primarily for dessert wines and off-dry white wines (like Spanish Moscatel). Muscat of Alexandria offers slightly more orange zest and sweet rose notes than Muscat Blanc.

A great match with almond biscotti, charcuterie plates, or soft or pungent cheeses like Roquefort.

MANDARIN ORANGE	HONEY	LYCHEE	PEACH SKIN	WHITE FLOWERS

| 🍷 DESSERT GLASS | 🌡 CELLAR 55–60° F | ⚗ DECANT NO | 🪙 | SPEND ~$13 | 🍾 CELLAR 1–5 YEARS |

Where It Grows

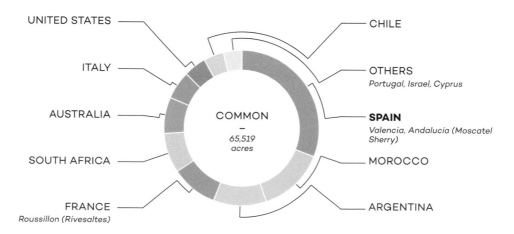

UNITED STATES

ITALY

AUSTRALIA

SOUTH AFRICA

FRANCE
Roussillon (Rivesaltes)

COMMON
–
65,519
acres

CHILE

OTHERS
Portugal, Israel, Cyprus

SPAIN
Valencia, Andalucía (Moscatel Sherry)

MOROCCO

ARGENTINA

Also Try

 MUSCAT BLANC MOSCATEL DE SETÚBAL  RUTHERGLEN MUSCAT  BLACK MUSCAT

Nebbiolo

 "nebby-oh-low"  *Barolo, Barbaresco, Spanna, Chiavennasca*

BODY
ALCOHOL
SWEETNESS
ACIDITY
TANNIN

| SP | LW | FW | AW | RS | LR | MR | FR | DS |

🏴 One of Italy's top reds made famous by the Barolo region of Piedmont. It's here where wines deliver both delicate aromas and rigorous tannins the grape is famous for.

🍴 Seek out creamy, cheesy dishes with a high fat content to counteract the wine's natural intense tannin. Dishes like truffle risotto or butternut ravioli are a revelation.

CHERRY

ROSE

LEATHER

ANISE

CLAY POT

 AROMA COLLECTOR

🌡 CELLAR 55–60° F

🍷 DECANT 60+ MIN

🪙 SPEND ~$30

🍾 CELLAR 5–25 YEARS

Where It Grows

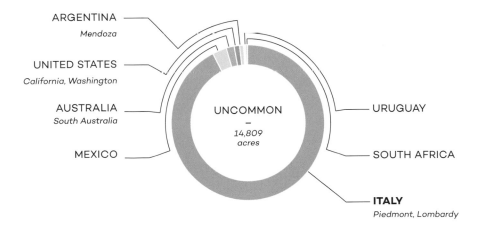

ARGENTINA
Mendoza

UNITED STATES
California, Washington

AUSTRALIA
South Australia

MEXICO

UNCOMMON
—
14,809
acres

URUGUAY

SOUTH AFRICA

ITALY
Piedmont, Lombardy

Also Try

🍷 XINOMAVRO   🍷 AGLIANICO   🍷 TEMPRANILLO   🍷 SANGIOVESE

Nebbiolo

ADDITIONAL
TASTING
NOTES

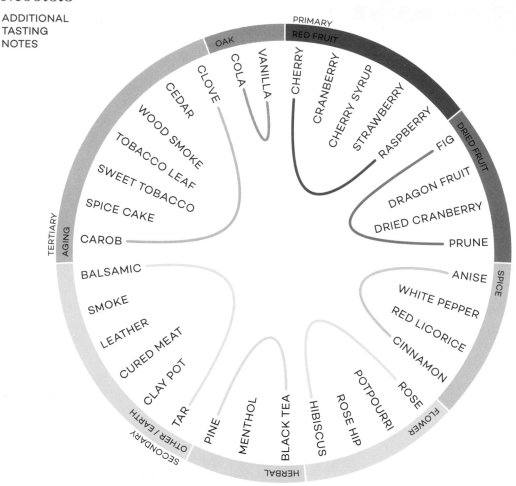

Southern Piedmont

The boldest and highest tannin expressions of Nebbiolo come from the regions of Barolo, Barbaresco, and Roero. Each region also makes a more intense "Riserva" version, which has more rigorous production standards, including extended aging. Barolo produces the highest tannins of all.

- ‣ BLACK CHERRY
- ‣ SPICE CAKE / TAR
- ‣ ROSE
- ‣ LICORICE
- ‣ CAROB

Northern Piedmont

Includes the regions of Ghemme and Gattinara and north-facing vineyards around Barolo. (Declassified to Langhe.) The wines from this part of Piedmont produce a lighter, more elegant style of Nebbiolo with softer tannin. It can vary between fruity and herbaceous depending on the vintage.

- ‣ SOUR CHERRY
- ‣ ROSE HIP
- ‣ TOBACCO LEAF
- ‣ LEATHER
- ‣ BLACK TEA

Valtellina, Italy

In neighboring Lombardy, Nebbiolo grows in a Northern alpine valley that opens to Lake Como. The temperatures are much cooler here, which results in very elegant Nebbiolo wines with herbal and floral notes and medium tannin, similar to a cool-climate Pinot Noir.

- ‣ CRANBERRY
- ‣ HIBISCUS
- ‣ PEONY
- ‣ DRIED HERBS
- ‣ CLOVE

Negroamaro

🔊 *"neg-row-amaro"*

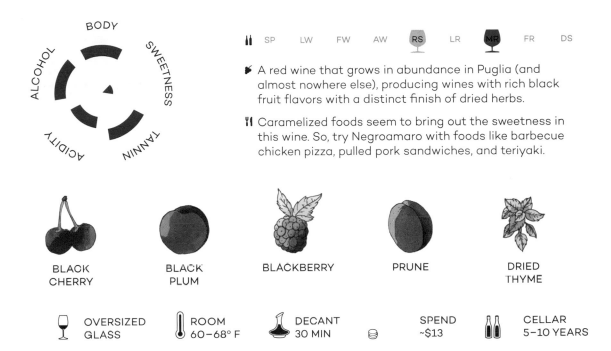

| | SP | LW | FW | AW | RS | LR | MR | FR | DS |

🌿 A red wine that grows in abundance in Puglia (and almost nowhere else), producing wines with rich black fruit flavors with a distinct finish of dried herbs.

🍴 Caramelized foods seem to bring out the sweetness in this wine. So, try Negroamaro with foods like barbecue chicken pizza, pulled pork sandwiches, and teriyaki.

BLACK CHERRY **BLACK PLUM** **BLACKBERRY** **PRUNE** **DRIED THYME**

OVERSIZED GLASS ROOM 60–68° F DECANT 30 MIN SPEND ~$13 CELLAR 5–10 YEARS

Where It Grows

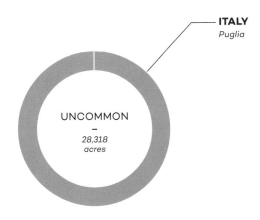

ITALY
Puglia

UNCOMMON
–
28,318 acres

Also Try

🍷 MONTEPULCIANO 🍷 MERLOT 🍷 NERO D'AVOLA 🍷 BAGA

Nerello Mascalese

🔊 *"nair-rello mask-uh-lay-say"*

BODY
SWEETNESS
TANNIN
ACIDITY
ALCOHOL

| | SP | LW | FW | AW | RS | LR | MR | FR | DS |

🍷 A rare red grape found on the slopes of Mount Etna in Sicily that produces high quality light-bodied reds that are surprisingly reminiscent of Pinot Noir.

🍴 Try Nerello Mascalese with roasted tomato and pepper flavors and lighter meats such as poultry and pork. It also pairs well with oregano, thyme, coriander, and sage.

| DRIED CHERRY | ORANGE ZEST | DRIED THYME | ALLSPICE | CRUSHED GRAVEL |

| AROMA COLLECTOR | 🌡 CELLAR 55–60° F | 🍷 DECANT 30 MIN | 🪙 SPEND ~$17 | 🍾 CELLAR 5–15 YEARS |

Where It Grows

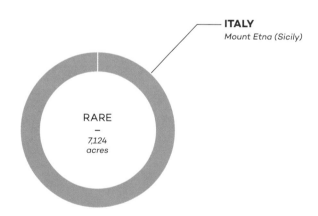

ITALY
Mount Etna (Sicily)

RARE
–
7,124
acres

Also Try

🍷 PINOT NOIR   🍷 GRENACHE   🍷 FRAPPATO   🍷 CARIGNAN

Nero d'Avola

🔊 *"nair-oh davo-la"* 💬 *Calabrese*

SP LW FW AW RS LR MR **FR** DS

🌾 Sicily's most important red wine variety is often likened to Cabernet Sauvignon due to its full-bodied style and flavors of black cherry and tobacco.

🍴 With its bold fruit flavors and robust tannin, Nero d'Avola is a great wine to match with rich meaty meats. Some classic pairings include oxtail soup and beef stew.

BLACK CHERRY | BLACK PLUM | LICORICE | TOBACCO | CHILI PEPPER

 OVERSIZED GLASS   ROOM 60–68° F   DECANT 60+ MIN   SPEND ~$15   CELLAR 5–15 YEARS

Where It Grows

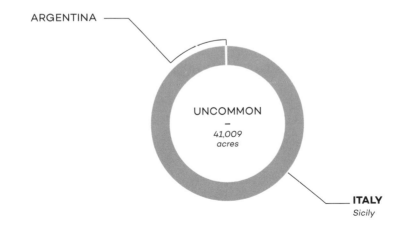

ARGENTINA

UNCOMMON
—
41,009
acres

ITALY
Sicily

Also Try

 BORDEAUX BLEND   CABERNET SAUVIGNON   MONTEPULCIANO   AGIORGITIKO   MENCÍA

145

Petit Verdot

◀) *"peh-tee vur-doe"*

🍷 Considered a minor blending grape in Bordeaux, Petit Verdot has shown promise as a single-varietal wine in warmer climates, where it makes smooth full-bodied reds.

🍴 A bold, tannic wine with a shorter finish like Petit Verdot will do well with roasted meats that have a pungent note, such as Cuban-style pork or even burgers with blue cheese.

BLACK CHERRY	PLUM	VIOLET	LILAC	SAGE

OVERSIZED GLASS	ROOM 60–68° F	DECANT 60+ MIN	SPEND ~$19	CELLAR 5–15 YEARS

Where It Grows

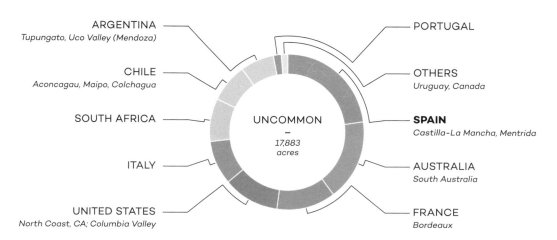

UNCOMMON — *17,883 acres*

ARGENTINA
Tupungato, Uco Valley (Mendoza)

CHILE
Aconcagau, Maipo, Colchagua

SOUTH AFRICA

ITALY

UNITED STATES
North Coast, CA; Columbia Valley

PORTUGAL

OTHERS
Uruguay, Canada

SPAIN
Castilla-La Mancha, Mentrida

AUSTRALIA
South Australia

FRANCE
Bordeaux

Also Try

🍷 TOURIGA NACIONAL   🍷 PETITE SIRAH   🍷 SAGRANTINO   🍷 TANNAT   🍷 BONARDA

Petite Sirah

◀) *"peh-teet sear-ah"* 💬 *Durif, Petite Syrah*

🔖 Petite Sirah is loved for its deeply colored wines with rich black fruit flavors and bold tannins. The grape is related to Syrah and the rare French-Alps grape, Peloursin.

🍴 Given Petite Sirah's sometimes aggressive tannin profile, it pairs best with fat- and umami-driven dishes—be it steaks from the grill or a plate of beef stroganoff.

SUGAR PLUM　　BLUEBERRY　　DARK CHOCOLATE　　BLACK PEPPER　　BLACK TEA

 RED GLASS　　 ROOM 60–68° F　　 DECANT 60+ MIN　　 SPEND ~$18　　 CELLAR 5–15 YEARS

Where It Grows

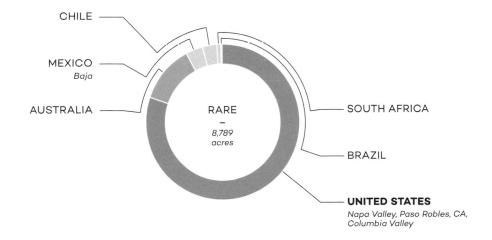

CHILE

MEXICO
Baja

AUSTRALIA

RARE
–
8,789
acres

SOUTH AFRICA

BRAZIL

UNITED STATES
Napa Valley, Paso Robles, CA, Columbia Valley

Also Try

 SYRAH　　 DOLCETTO　　TOURIGA NACIONAL　　SAGRANTINO　　 TANNAT

147

Pinot Blanc

🔊 *"pee-no blonk"*   💬 *Weissburgunder, Klevner*

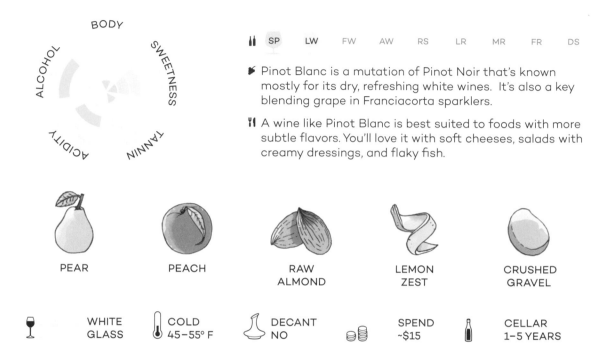

BODY   SWEETNESS   TANNIN   ACIDITY   ALCOHOL

| 🍾 | SP | LW | FW | AW | RS | LR | MR | FR | DS |

🏷 Pinot Blanc is a mutation of Pinot Noir that's known mostly for its dry, refreshing white wines. It's also a key blending grape in Franciacorta sparklers.

🍴 A wine like Pinot Blanc is best suited to foods with more subtle flavors. You'll love it with soft cheeses, salads with creamy dressings, and flaky fish.

PEAR   PEACH   RAW ALMOND   LEMON ZEST   CRUSHED GRAVEL

🍷 WHITE GLASS   🌡 COLD 45–55° F   DECANT NO   SPEND ~$15   🍾 CELLAR 1–5 YEARS

Where It Grows

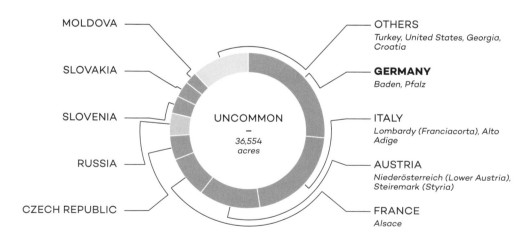

MOLDOVA

SLOVAKIA

SLOVENIA

RUSSIA

CZECH REPUBLIC

UNCOMMON
–
36,554
acres

OTHERS
Turkey, United States, Georgia, Croatia

GERMANY
Baden, Pfalz

ITALY
Lombardy (Franciacorta), Alto Adige

AUSTRIA
Niederösterreich (Lower Austria), Steiermark (Styria)

FRANCE
Alsace

Also Try

PINOT GRIS   AUXERROIS   SILVANER   VERDICCHIO   🍷 FERNAO PIRES

Pinot Gris

◀) *"pee-no gree"*   💬 *Pinot Grigio, Grauburgunder*

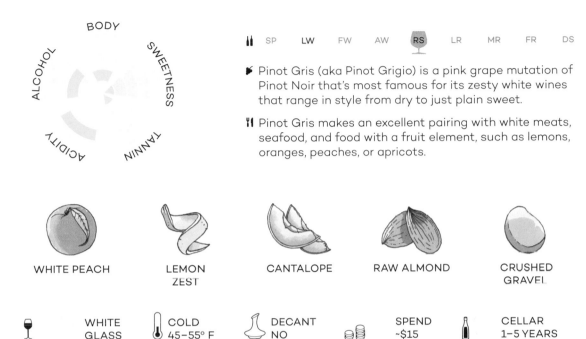

BODY · SWEETNESS · TANNIN · ACIDITY · ALCOHOL

| | SP | LW | FW | AW | RS | LR | MR | FR | DS |

🏷 Pinot Gris (aka Pinot Grigio) is a pink grape mutation of Pinot Noir that's most famous for its zesty white wines that range in style from dry to just plain sweet.

🍴 Pinot Gris makes an excellent pairing with white meats, seafood, and food with a fruit element, such as lemons, oranges, peaches, or apricots.

WHITE PEACH · LEMON ZEST · CANTALOPE · RAW ALMOND · CRUSHED GRAVEL

WHITE GLASS · COLD 45–55° F · DECANT NO · SPEND ~$15 · CELLAR 1–5 YEARS

Where It Grows

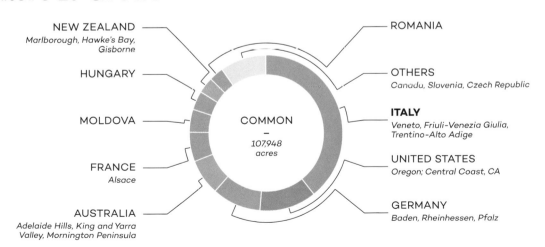

NEW ZEALAND
Marlborough, Hawke's Bay, Gisborne

HUNGARY

MOLDOVA

FRANCE
Alsace

AUSTRALIA
Adelaide Hills, King and Yarra Valley, Mornington Peninsula

COMMON
—
107,948
acres

ROMANIA

OTHERS
Canada, Slovenia, Czech Republic

ITALY
Veneto, Friuli-Venezia Giulia, Trentino-Alto Adige

UNITED STATES
Oregon; Central Coast, CA

GERMANY
Baden, Rheinhessen, Pfalz

Also Try

PINOT BLANC · ALBARIÑO · GRECHETTO · ARNEIS · FRIULANO

Pinot Noir

🔊 *"pee-no nwar"*　💬 *Spätburgunder*

BODY
ALCOHOL
SWEETNESS
ACIDITY
TANNIN

🌿 The world's most popular light-bodied red is loved for its red fruit and spice flavors that are accentuated by a long, smooth, soft-tannin finish.

🍴 A versatile red wine for food pairing given the higher acidity and lower tannin. Pinot Noir tastes like it was meant for duck, chicken, pork, and mushrooms.

CHERRY　　RASPBERRY　　CLOVE　　MUSHROOM　　VANILLA

 AROMA COLLECTOR　 CELLAR 55–60° F　 DECANT 30 MIN　 SPEND ~$30　 CELLAR 5–15 YEARS

Where It Grows

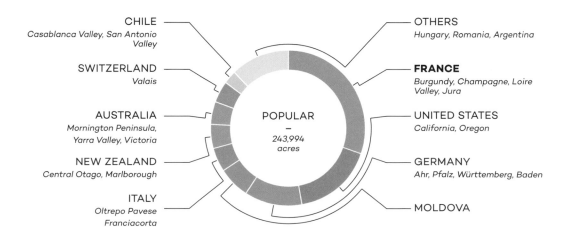

CHILE
Casablanca Valley, San Antonio Valley

SWITZERLAND
Valais

AUSTRALIA
Mornington Peninsula, Yarra Valley, Victoria

NEW ZEALAND
Central Otago, Marlborough

ITALY
Oltrepo Pavese Franciacorta

POPULAR
–
243,994
acres

OTHERS
Hungary, Romania, Argentina

FRANCE
Burgundy, Champagne, Loire Valley, Jura

UNITED STATES
California, Oregon

GERMANY
Ahr, Pfalz, Württemberg, Baden

MOLDOVA

Also Try

 ST. LAURENT　 GAMAY　 NERELLO MASCALESE　 SCHIAVA　 ZWEIGELT

Pinot Noir

ADDITIONAL
TASTING
NOTES

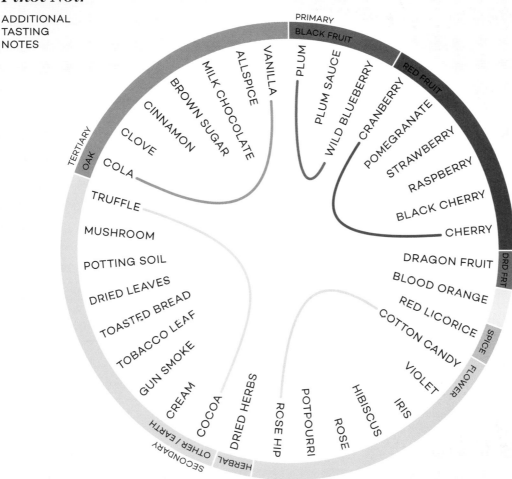

Burgundy, France

A small strip of land along the Côte d'Or includes 27 appellations (Nuits-St-Georges, Gevrey-Chambertin, etc.). These 27 regions are home to the most prestigious Pinot Noir vineyards in the world. The region is cooler and wines have earthy fruit and flower flavors with elevated acidity.

- MUSHROOM
- CRANBERRY
- PLUM SAUCE
- PASTILLE CANDY
- HIBISCUS

Central Coast, CA

In an otherwise hot climate, the Pacific Ocean creates a fog layer in the mornings almost every day, which helps keep the area cool enough to grow Pinot Noir vines. Still, wines are at the riper end of the spectrum with sweet fruit and softer acidity.

- RASPBERRY SAUCE
- PLUM
- GUN SMOKE
- VANILLA
- ALLSPICE

Other Regions

Try these other regions on for size.

Cooler climates offer more tart fruit flavors such as in Oregon; British Columbia, CA; Tasmania, AU; Marlborough, NZ; Oltrepo Pavese, IT; and of course, Germany.

Warmer climates offer ripe, boisterous fruit flavors such as in Mornington Peninsula and Yarra Yarra Valley, AU; Sonoma, CA; Central Otago, NZ; Casablanca Valley, Chile; and Patagonia, Argentina.

Pinotage

◀) *"pee-no-taj"*

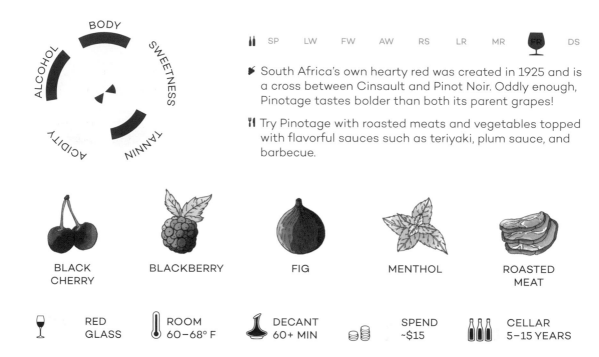

	SP	LW	FW	AW	RS	LR	MR	FR	DS

⚑ South Africa's own hearty red was created in 1925 and is a cross between Cinsault and Pinot Noir. Oddly enough, Pinotage tastes bolder than both its parent grapes!

🍴 Try Pinotage with roasted meats and vegetables topped with flavorful sauces such as teriyaki, plum sauce, and barbecue.

BLACK CHERRY	BLACKBERRY	FIG	MENTHOL	ROASTED MEAT

RED GLASS	ROOM 60–68° F	DECANT 60+ MIN	SPEND ~$15	CELLAR 5–15 YEARS

Where It Grows

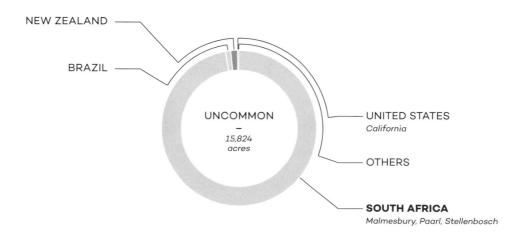

NEW ZEALAND

BRAZIL

UNCOMMON
–
15,824
acres

UNITED STATES
California

OTHERS

SOUTH AFRICA
Malmesbury, Paarl, Stellenbosch

Also Try

🍷 ALICANTE BOUSCHET   🍷 SYRAH   🍷 PETITE SIRAH   🍷 MONASTRELL   🍷 TANNAT

Picpoul

🔊 *"pik-pool"*   💬 *Picpoul Blanc, Piquepoul Blanc, Picpoul de Pinet*

BODY

ALCOHOL — SWEETNESS

ACIDITY — TANNIN

🍾	SP	LW	FW	AW	RS	LR	MR	FR	DS

🌱 An old French grape that's rising in popularity. Picpoul means "stings the lip" and makes lip-zapping white wines that have a distinct saline note.

🍴 It's almost like Picpoul was made to be paired with seafood, shellfish, and sushi as well as fried appetizers. Fried calamari might just be the perfect Picpoul pairing.

GREEN APPLE	CITRUS BLOSSOM	LEMON	THYME	SALINE

🍷 WHITE GLASS	🌡 ICE COLD 38–45° F	DECANT NO		SPEND ~$10	🍾 CELLAR 1–3 YEARS

Where It Grows

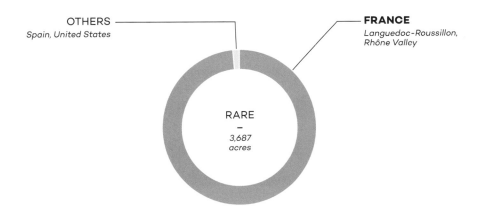

OTHERS
Spain, United States

FRANCE
Languedoc-Roussillon, Rhône Valley

RARE
–
3,687 acres

Also Try

ASSYRTIKO   MUSCADET (MELON)   VINHO VERDE   ALBARIÑO   GRILLO (SICILY)

Port

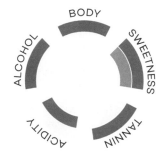

BODY
SWEETNESS
TANNIN
ACIDITY
ALCOHOL

SP LW FW AW RS LR MR FR **DS**

🍷 The most famous fortified wine of Portugal is a blend made in a range of styles including white, rosé, red, and tawny. Each style has a unique taste, so try them all!

🍴 If you want to experience what a perfect pairing tastes like, grab a bottle of LBV or Vintage Port and a hunk of Stilton cheese.

BLACK PLUM

DRIED CHERRY

CHOCOLATE

RAISIN

CINNAMON

🍷 DESSERT GLASS   🌡 CELLAR 55–60° F   DECANT 30 MIN   SPEND ~$35   CELLAR 50+ YEARS

TOURIGA FRANCA

TOURIGA NACIONAL

TINTA BARROCA

TINTA RORIZ
(Tempranillo)

TINTO CÃO

RABIGATO

+50 more

VIOSINHO

WHITE PORT ············
A white grape Port. Off-dry with flavors of dried peach, white pepper, tangerine zest, and incense.

ROSÉ PORT
Rosé style. Strawberry, cinnamon, honey, and raspberry candy.

RUBY PORT
Basic red Port. Sweet black fruits, chocolate and spice. Drink young.

LBV PORT
(Late Bottled Vintage Port) a ready to drink single-vintage Port.

TAWNY PORT
A barrel-aged Port that gets better (and more pricy) with age. Try a 20-year.

COLHEITA PORT
A single-vintage oxidative, barrel-aged Port.

CRUSTED PORT
A multi-vintage Port designed to age. Uncommon.

VINTAGE PORT
Single vintage Port wines from exceptional years. Drinks well in the first 5 years, then will continue to cellar from 30–50 or more years.

Also Try

🍷 RECIOTO DELLA VALPOLICELLA   🍷 BANYULS (FRANCE)   🍷 RIVESALTES (FRANCE)   🍷 VIN SANTO ROSSO   🍷 LATE HARVEST REDS

Prosecco

🔊 "pro-seh-co"

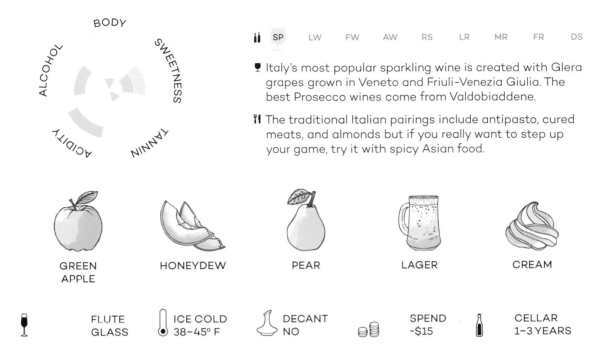

	SP	LW	FW	AW	RS	LR	MR	FR	DS

🍷 Italy's most popular sparkling wine is created with Glera grapes grown in Veneto and Friuli-Venezia Giulia. The best Prosecco wines come from Valdobiaddene.

🍴 The traditional Italian pairings include antipasto, cured meats, and almonds but if you really want to step up your game, try it with spicy Asian food.

GREEN APPLE	HONEYDEW	PEAR	LAGER	CREAM

🥂 FLUTE GLASS	🌡️ ICE COLD 38–45° F	DECANT NO	🪙 SPEND ~$15	🍾 CELLAR 1–3 YEARS

Quality Levels

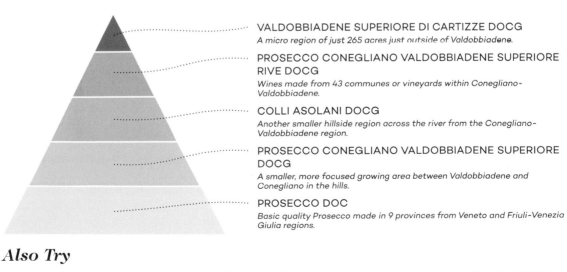

VALDOBBIADENE SUPERIORE DI CARTIZZE DOCG
A micro region of just 265 acres just outside of Valdobbiadene.

PROSECCO CONEGLIANO VALDOBBIADENE SUPERIORE RIVE DOCG
Wines made from 43 communes or vineyards within Conegliano-Valdobbiadene.

COLLI ASOLANI DOCG
Another smaller hillside region across the river from the Conegliano-Valdobbiadene region.

PROSECCO CONEGLIANO VALDOBBIADENE SUPERIORE DOCG
A smaller, more focused growing area between Valdobbiadene and Conegliano in the hills.

PROSECCO DOC
Basic quality Prosecco made in 9 provinces from Veneto and Friuli-Venezia Giulia regions.

Also Try

🥂 CAVA   🥂 CRÉMANT   🥂 SEKT (AUSTRIA, GERMANY)   🥂 CHAMPAGNE   🥂 CAP CLASSIQUE (SOUTH AFRICA)

Rhône / GSM Blend

🔊 "roan"　💬 Grenache-Syrah-Mourvèdre, Côtes du Rhône

🍷	SP	LW	FW	AW	RS	LR	MR	FB	DS

🗡 GSM stands for Grenache, Syrah, and Mourvèdre. These three grapes create the base of Southern France and Northern Spain's most important red wine blends.

🍴 The GSM Blend is a versatile food pairing wine that works particularly well with dishes featuring Mediterranean spices including red pepper, sage, rosemary, and olives.

RASPBERRY　BLACKBERRY　ROSEMARY　BAKING SPICES　LAVENDER

OVERSIZED GLASS　ROOM 60–68° F　DECANT 30 MIN　SPEND ~$15　CELLAR 5–15 YEARS

The Blend
The Rhône / GSM Blend may include some or all of these grapes!

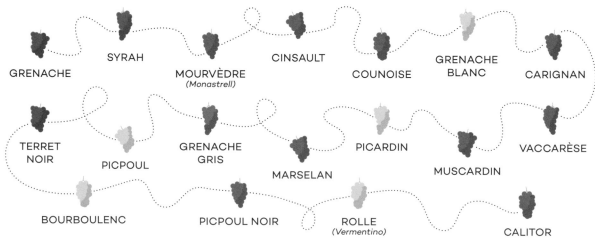

GRENACHE　SYRAH　MOURVÈDRE *(Monastrell)*　CINSAULT　COUNOISE　GRENACHE BLANC　CARIGNAN

TERRET NOIR　PICPOUL　GRENACHE GRIS　MARSELAN　PICARDIN　MUSCARDIN　VACCARÈSE

BOURBOULENC　PICPOUL NOIR　ROLLE *(Vermentino)*　CALITOR

Also Try

🍷 GRENACHE　 🍷 ZINFANDEL　 🍷 SANGIOVESE　 🍷 MENCÍA　 🍷 CARIGNAN

Rhône / GSM Blend

ADDITIONAL
TASTING
NOTES

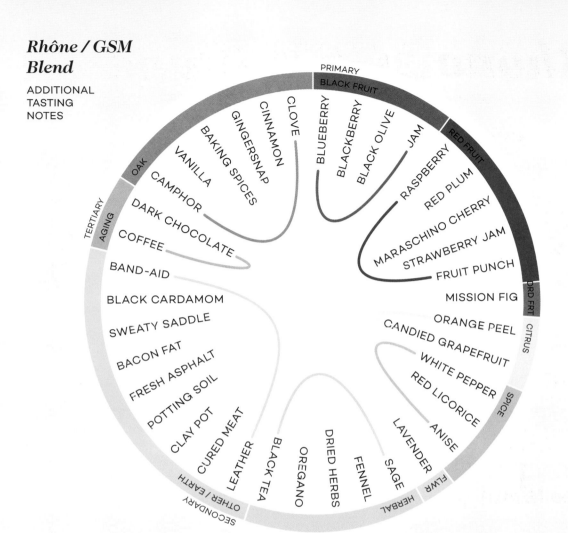

Côtes du Rhône

The Rhône and other parts of Southern France, including Coteaux de Languedoc and Provence, is where the Rhône / GSM Blend originated. It's here you'll find wines that balance brambly black and red fruit flavors with savory notes of black pepper, olives, Provencal herbs, and brown baking spices.

▸ BLACK OLIVE
▸ DRIED CRANBERRY
▸ DRIED HERBS
▸ CINNAMON
▸ LEATHER

Paso Robles, CA

The region of Paso Robles was really the first to whole-heartedly champion Rhône varieties in the United States. The hot, dry climate produces incredibly bold, smoky wines—particularly those that emphasize Syrah and Mourvèdre (Monastrell).

▸ BLACK RASPBERRY
▸ MISSION FIG
▸ GINGERSNAP
▸ BACON FAT
▸ CAMPHOR

Provence Rosé

The other side of the Rhône / GSM Blend is when it's made as rosé. This is the specialty of Provence and Southern France. The blend often includes some Rolle (aka Vermentino) to add bright acidity and crunchy bitterness to help liven up the blend.

▸ STRAWBERRY
▸ HONEYDEW MELON
▸ PINK PEPPERCORN
▸ CELERY
▸ ORANGE PEEL

Riesling

 "reese-ling"

BODY

ALCOHOL

SWEETNESS

ACIDITY

TANNIN

  SP LW FW AW RS LR MR FR DS

An aromatic white variety that can produce white wines ranging in style from bone-dry to very sweet. Germany is the world's most important producer of Riesling.

Off-dry Riesling wines make a great pairing to spicy Indian and Asian cuisines and do excellently alongside duck, pork, bacon, shrimp, and crab.

LIME GREEN APPLE BEESWAX JASMINE PETROLEUM

 WHITE GLASS   COLD 45–55° F   DECANT NO   SPEND ~$26   CELLAR 5–10 YEARS

Where It Grows

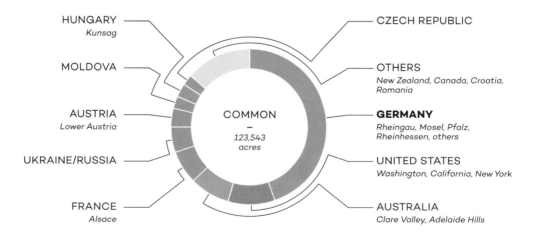

HUNGARY
Kunsag

MOLDOVA

AUSTRIA
Lower Austria

UKRAINE/RUSSIA

FRANCE
Alsace

COMMON
–
123,543
acres

CZECH REPUBLIC

OTHERS
New Zealand, Canada, Croatia, Romania

GERMANY
Rheingau, Mosel, Pfalz, Rheinhessen, others

UNITED STATES
Washington, California, New York

AUSTRALIA
Clare Valley, Adelaide Hills

Also Try

FURMINT   ASSYRTIKO   LOUREIRO (PORTUGAL)   MÜLLER-THURGAU

Riesling

ADDITIONAL
TASTING
NOTES

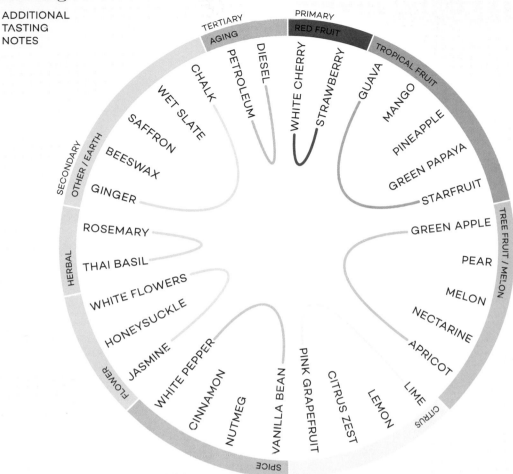

TERTIARY
AGING
PRIMARY
RED FRUIT
TROPICAL FRUIT
DIESEL
PETROLEUM
CHALK
WET SLATE
SAFFRON
BEESWAX
GINGER
ROSEMARY
THAI BASIL
WHITE FLOWERS
HONEYSUCKLE
JASMINE
WHITE PEPPER
CINNAMON
NUTMEG
VANILLA BEAN
PINK GRAPEFRUIT
CITRUS ZEST
LEMON
LIME
APRICOT
NECTARINE
MELON
PEAR
GREEN APPLE
STARFRUIT
GREEN PAPAYA
PINEAPPLE
MANGO
GUAVA
STRAWBERRY
WHITE CHERRY
SECONDARY
OTHER / EARTH
HERBAL
FLOWER
SPICE
CITRUS
TREE FRUIT / MELON

Germany

Riesling is Germany's specialty. The regions of Rheingau, Pfalz, and Mosel produce some of the most exceptional examples of Riesling in the world. Wines here are noted for their sky-high acidity, high aromatic intensity, minerality, and balanced off-dry style.

▸ APRICOT
▸ MEYER LEMON
▸ BEESWAX
▸ PETROLEUM
▸ WET SLATE

Alsace, France

Alsace is next to Germany and also specializes in Riesling. Like Germany, Alsace labels by variety. Alsace Riesling is lean, minerally, and quite dry! The best examples come from the southern parts, where there are 51 official Grand Cru vineyards found on the low slopes of the Vosges Mountains.

▸ GREEN APPLE
▸ LIME
▸ LEMON
▸ SMOKE
▸ THAI BASIL

South Australia

In the cooler spots of South Australia (Eden Valley, Clare Valley, and Adelaide Hills) you'll find a very distinct style of Riesling with unmistakable pertrol-like aromas. On the palate, wines are dry with minerally citrus flavors and tropical fruit notes.

▸ LIME PEEL
▸ GREEN APPLE
▸ GREEN PAPAYA
▸ JASMINE
▸ DIESEL

Roussanne

 "rooh-sahn"    *Bergeron, Fromental*

BODY
ALCOHOL
SWEETNESS
ACIDITY
TANNIN

| | SP | LW | **FW** | AW | RS | LR | MR | FR | DS |

🥄 A rare, intriguing full-bodied white wine found mostly in Southern France, where it's typically blended with Grenache Blanc, Marsanne, and sometimes Viognier.

🍴 Producers in the United States have taken to oaking this wine, which makes it a great match with buttery meats like lobster, crab, foie gras, and paté.

 MEYER LEMON    APRICOT   BEESWAX    CHAMOMILE   BRIOCHE

🍷 AROMA COLLECTOR   🌡 COLD 45–55° F   DECANT NO   🪙 SPEND ~$30   🍾 CELLAR 5–7 YEARS

Where It Grows

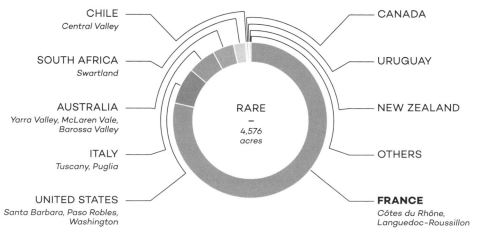

CHILE
Central Valley

SOUTH AFRICA
Swartland

AUSTRALIA
Yarra Valley, McLaren Vale, Barossa Valley

ITALY
Tuscany, Puglia

UNITED STATES
Santa Barbara, Paso Robles, Washington

RARE
–
4,576
acres

CANADA

URUGUAY

NEW ZEALAND

OTHERS

FRANCE
Côtes du Rhône, Languedoc-Roussillon

Also Try

🍷 MARSANNE   🍷 CHARDONNAY   🍷 GRENACHE BLANC   🍷 SAVATIANO   🍷 VIURA

Sagrantino

 "sah-grahn-tee-no"

SP LW FW AW RS LR MR **FR** **DS**

- A rare, deeply bold, central-Italian red that's recently been noted for having some of the highest levels of polyphenols (antioxidants) of any red wine.

- Given it's super-high tannin and astringency, look for dishes that feature more fat and umami including cream-based sauces, sausages, wild mushrooms, and cheese.

PLUM SAUCE	LICORICE	BLACK TEA	BLACK OLIVE	BLACK PEPPER

 OVERSIZED GLASS   ROOM 60–68° F   DECANT 60+ MIN   SPEND ~$32   CELLAR 5–25 YEARS

Where It Grows

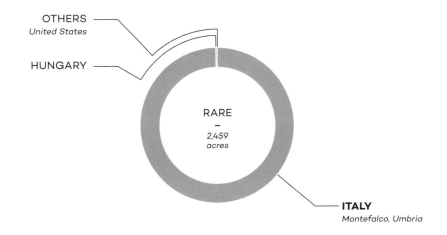

OTHERS
United States

HUNGARY

RARE
–
2,459 acres

ITALY
Montefalco, Umbria

Also Try

 TANNAT  PETITE SIRAH   TOURIGA NACIONAL   MONASTRELL   BORDEAUX BLEND

Sangiovese

 "san-jo-vay-zay"   *Prugnolo Gentile, Nielluccio, Morellino, Brunello*

BODY
SWEETNESS
TANNIN
ACIDITY
ALCOHOL

| | SP | LW | FW | AW | RS | LR | MR | FR | DS |

🦪 Sangiovese is Italy's most planted grape and the key variety in Tuscany's renowned Chianti. It's sensitive, tasting quite different depending on where it grows.

🍴 The high acidity allows Sangiovese to match well with all manner of well-spiced foods. It's one of the few wines that will not get lost when paired with tomato sauce.

| CHERRY | ROASTED TOMATO | SWEET BALSAMIC | OREGANO | ESPRESSO |

🍷 **RED GLASS**   🌡 **CELLAR 55–60° F**   **DECANT 30 MIN**   **SPEND ~$18**   **CELLAR 5–25 YEARS**

Where It Grows

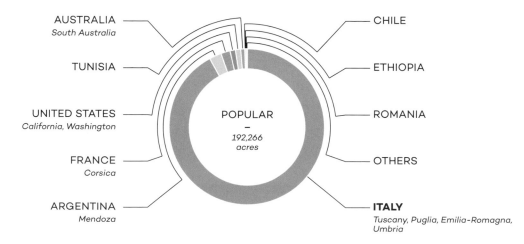

AUSTRALIA
South Australia

TUNISIA

UNITED STATES
California, Washington

FRANCE
Corsica

ARGENTINA
Mendoza

POPULAR
–
192,266
acres

CHILE

ETHIOPIA

ROMANIA

OTHERS

ITALY
Tuscany, Puglia, Emilia-Romagna, Umbria

Also Try

🍷 NEBBIOLO   🍷 TEMPRANILLO   🍷 AGIORGITIKO   🍷 AGLIANICO   🍷 MENCÍA

Sangiovese

ADDITIONAL
TASTING
NOTES

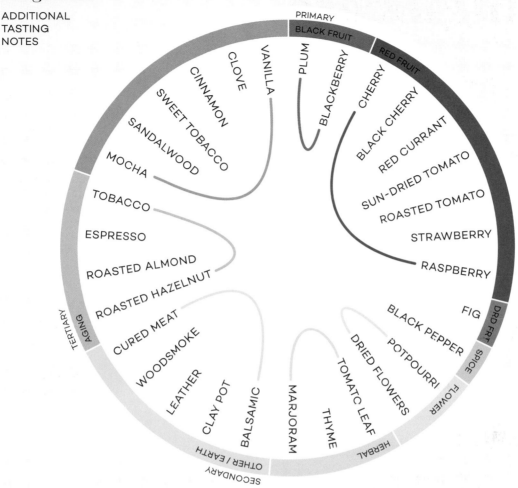

PRIMARY
BLACK FRUIT
RED FRUIT
PLUM
BLACKBERRY
CHERRY
BLACK CHERRY
RED CURRANT
SUN-DRIED TOMATO
ROASTED TOMATO
STRAWBERRY
RASPBERRY
FIG
VANILLA
CLOVE
CINNAMON
SWEET TOBACCO
SANDALWOOD
MOCHA
TOBACCO
ESPRESSO
ROASTED ALMOND
ROASTED HAZELNUT
CURED MEAT
WOODSMOKE
LEATHER
CLAY POT
BALSAMIC
MARJORAM
THYME
TOMATO LEAF
DRIED FLOWERS
POTPOURRI
BLACK PEPPER
DRD FRT
SPICE
FLOWER
HERBAL
OTHER / EARTH
SECONDARY
TERTIARY
AGING

Chianti

Chianti ("key-aunty") is a region in Tuscany that specializes in Sangiovese. Within Chianti, there are eight subzones, including the original Chianti Classico. Chianti classifies its wines based on region, quality, and aging specifications.

▸ "GRAN SELEZIONE" - 2.5 YEARS
▸ "RISERVA" - 2 YEARS
▸ "SUPERIORE" - 1 YEAR
▸ CH. CLASSICO, CH. COLLI FIORENTINI, CH. RUFINA - 1 YEAR
▸ CH. MONTESPERTOLI - 9 MOS.
▸ CHIANTI AND OTHERS - 6 MOS.

Montalcino

The Tuscan region of Montalcino grows a special clone called Sangiovese Grosso or Brunello. The region has three 100% Sangiovese wines:

▸ BRUNELLO DI MONTALCINO "RISERVA": Aged 2 years in oak, and 4 more years after that.

▸ BRUNELLO DI MONTALCINO: Aged 2 years in oak, and 3 additional years after that.

▸ ROSSO DI MONTALCINO: Aged 1 year.

Regional Names

Sangiovese has many regional names. Because many of these regions are lesser-known, you can find them for great values.

● CARMIGNANO
● CHIANTI
● MONTEFALCO ROSSO
● MORELLINO DI SCANSANO
● ROSSO CONERO
● ROSSO DI MONTALCINO
● TORGIANO ROSSO
● VINO NOBILE DI MONTEPULCIANO

Sauternais

🔊 "sow-turn-aye" 💬 Sauternes, Barsac, Cérons

| 🍾 | SP | LW | FW | AW | RS | LR | MR | FR | DS |

🍷 A group of dessert wine regions in Bordeaux that make wine with Sémillon, Sauvignon Blanc, and Muscadelle grapes infected with a fungus called Botrytis cinerea.

🍴 Sauternes (and others) are best with wash-rind soft cheeses where the sweetness of the wine can counteract the "funk." The most classic pairing is Roquefort.

LEMON CURD

APRICOT

QUINCE

HONEY

GINGER

 DESSERT GLASS   COLD 45–55° F   DECANT NO   SPEND ~$37    CELLAR 10–30 YEARS

Sauternais Appellations

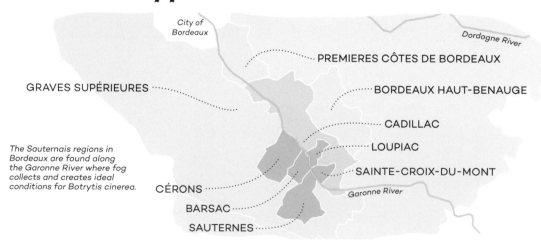

City of Bordeaux

Dordogne River

PREMIERES CÔTES DE BORDEAUX

GRAVES SUPÉRIEURES

BORDEAUX HAUT-BENAUGE

CADILLAC

LOUPIAC

SAINTE-CROIX-DU-MONT

The Sauternais regions in Bordeaux are found along the Garonne River where fog collects and creates ideal conditions for Botrytis cinerea.

CÉRONS

BARSAC

SAUTERNES

Garonne River

Also Try

 ICE WINE    LATE HARVEST WHITE WINES   🍷 TOKAJI ASZÚ

Sauvignon Blanc

🔊 *"saw-vin-yawn blonk"*   💬 *Fumé Blanc*

BODY

ALCOHOL

SWEETNESS

ACIDITY

TANNIN

 SP   LW   FW   AW   RS   LR   MR   FR   DS

🏹 A unique-tasting white wine with strong herbaceous flavors that are derived from compounds called methoxypyrazines (also found in bell peppers!).

🍴 Sauvignon Blanc is a wonderful pairing partner with herb-driven sauces, salty cheeses, light meats, and last but not least, Asian food.

GOOSEBERRY

HONEYDEW

GRAPEFRUIT

WHITE PEACH

PASSION-FRUIT

 WHITE GLASS   🌡 COLD 45–55° F   DECANT NO   SPEND ~$15   CELLAR 1–5 YEARS

Where It Grows

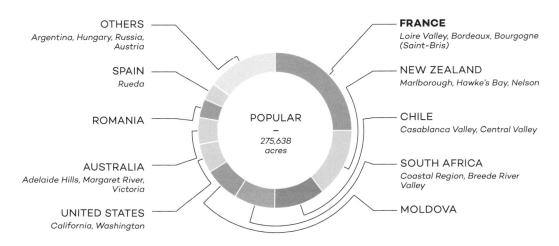

OTHERS
Argentina, Hungary, Russia, Austria

SPAIN
Rueda

ROMANIA

AUSTRALIA
Adelaide Hills, Margaret River, Victoria

UNITED STATES
California, Washington

POPULAR
–
275,638 acres

FRANCE
Loire Valley, Bordeaux, Bourgogne (Saint-Bris)

NEW ZEALAND
Marlborough, Hawke's Bay, Nelson

CHILE
Casablanca Valley, Central Valley

SOUTH AFRICA
Coastal Region, Breede River Valley

MOLDOVA

Also Try

GRÜNER VELTLINER   VERMENTINO   CHENIN BLANC   COLOMBARD   VERDEJO

Sauvignon Blanc

ADDITIONAL
TASTING
NOTES

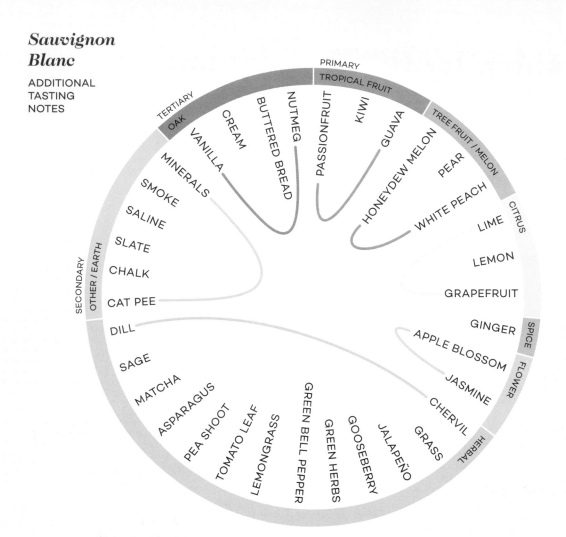

TERTIARY

PRIMARY

OAK

TROPICAL FRUIT

VANILLA
CREAM
BUTTERED BREAD
NUTMEG
PASSIONFRUIT
KIWI
GUAVA
HONEYDEW MELON

TREE FRUIT / MELON

PEAR
WHITE PEACH

MINERALS
SMOKE
SALINE
SLATE
CHALK
CAT PEE

SECONDARY
OTHER / EARTH

LIME
LEMON
GRAPEFRUIT

CITRUS

GINGER

SPICE

DILL
SAGE
MATCHA
ASPARAGUS
PEA SHOOT
TOMATO LEAF
LEMONGRASS
GREEN BELL PEPPER
GREEN HERBS
GOOSEBERRY
JALAPEÑO
GRASS
CHERVIL
JASMINE
APPLE BLOSSOM

FLOWER

HERBAL

Loire Valley, France

A specialty of the Loire Valley, Sauvignon Blanc grows primrarily in Centre and the overarching Touraine region. Wines tend to be lean and crisp with more herbal flavors, minerality, smoke, with an absence of oak. The most popular regional wine from the Loire is Sancerre.

‣ LIME
‣ GOOSEBERRY
‣ GRAPEFRUIT
‣ SLATE
‣ SMOKE

New Zealand

Sauvignon Blanc is New Zealand's most important grape and Marlborough is the top region for this variety. Wines offer more green tropical fruit notes that are often supported with a touch of residual sugar to help counterbalance the high acidity.

‣ PASSIONFRUIT
‣ KIWI
‣ PEA SHOOT
‣ JASMINE
‣ RIPE PEAR

North Coast, CA

Cooler spots in Sonoma and Napa produce much riper styles of Sauvignon Blanc, which are often blended with Sémillion to make a white blend inspired by white Bordeaux. Some wines are aged in oak, much like Chardonnay.

‣ WHITE PEACH
‣ MATCHA POWDER
‣ LEMONGRASS
‣ BUTTERED BREAD
‣ SALINE

Savatiano

◀) *"sav-vah-tee-ahno"*

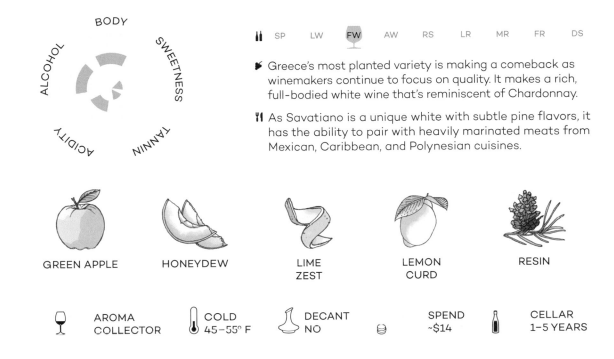

| | SP | LW | **FW** | AW | RS | LR | MR | FR | DS |

🏷 Greece's most planted variety is making a comeback as winemakers continue to focus on quality. It makes a rich, full-bodied white wine that's reminiscent of Chardonnay.

🍴 As Savatiano is a unique white with subtle pine flavors, it has the ability to pair with heavily marinated meats from Mexican, Caribbean, and Polynesian cuisines.

GREEN APPLE   HONEYDEW   LIME ZEST   LEMON CURD   RESIN

AROMA COLLECTOR   COLD 45–55° F   DECANT NO   SPEND ~$14   CELLAR 1–5 YEARS

Where It Grows

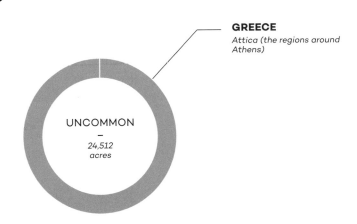

GREECE
Attica (the regions around Athens)

UNCOMMON
–
24,512 acres

Also Try

TREBBIANO TOSCANO   CHARDONNAY   FALANGHINA   FIANO   SÉMILLON

Schiava

🔊 *"skee-ah-vah"*   💬 *Vernatsch, Trollinger, Black Hamburg*

BODY
SWEETNESS
TANNIN
ACIDITY
ALCOHOL

| 🍾 | SP | LW | FW | AW | RS | LR | MR | FR | DS |

🍷 A group of several varieties, the finest of which is Schiava Gentile. It produces a sweetly aromatic light-bodied wine with aroma reminiscent of cherry candy.

🍴 A wonderful pairing with shrimp, chicken, and tofu, particularly with southeast Asian cuisines that feature basil, ginger, galangal, and other aromatic herbs.

| STRAWBERRY | RASPBERRY | ROSE CANDY | LEMON | SMOKE |

 AROMA COLLECTOR   🌡 CELLAR 55–60° F   DECANT NO   SPEND ~$15   CELLAR 1–3 YEARS

Where It Grows

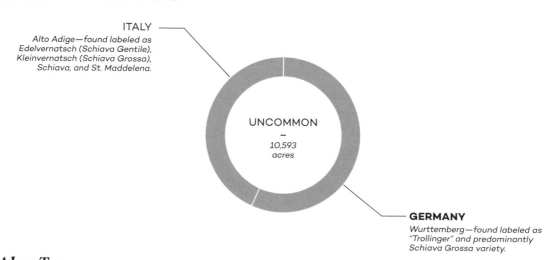

ITALY
Alto Adige—found labeled as Edelvernatsch (Schiava Gentile), Kleinvernatsch (Schiava Grossa), Schiava, and St. Maddelena.

UNCOMMON
–
10,593 acres

GERMANY
Wurttemberg—found labeled as "Trollinger" and predominantly Schiava Grossa variety.

Also Try

🍷 PINOT NOIR   🍷 ST. LAURENT   🍷 FRAPPATO   🍷 GAMAY   🍷 ZWEIGELT

Sémillon

◄) *"sem-ee-yawn"*   💬 *Hunter Valley Riesling*

BODY

ALCOHOL

SWEETNESS

ACIDITY

TANNIN

| | SP | LW | FW | AW | RS | LR | MR | FR | DS |

🍶 A major grape of Sauternes, which is Bordeaux's prized dessert wine. Dry Sémillon wines can be surprisingly rich when oaked, with a taste similar to Chardonnay.

🍴 Sémillon pairs best with richer fish entrées (black cod) and white meats (chicken and pork chops). Try spicing with fresh fennel and dill.

LEMON

BEESWAX

YELLOW PEACH

CHAMOMILE

SALINE

🍷 WHITE GLASS   🌡️ COLD 45–55° F   DECANT NO   SPEND ~$14   CELLAR 5–10 YEARS

Where It Grows

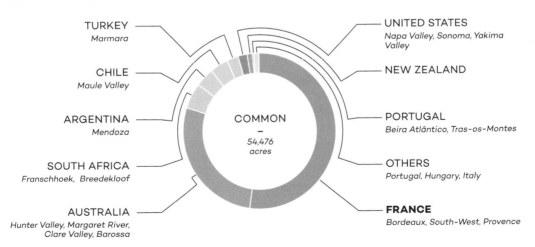

TURKEY
Marmara

CHILE
Maule Valley

ARGENTINA
Mendoza

SOUTH AFRICA
Franschhoek, Breedekloof

AUSTRALIA
Hunter Valley, Margaret River, Clare Valley, Barossa

COMMON
–
54,476
acres

UNITED STATES
Napa Valley, Sonoma, Yakima Valley

NEW ZEALAND

PORTUGAL
Beira Atlântico, Tras-os-Montes

OTHERS
Portugal, Hungary, Italy

FRANCE
Bordeaux, South-West, Provence

Also Try

GARGANEGA   VIURA   FRIULANO   SAVATIANO   RKATSITELI

Sherry

🔊 *"share-ee"*   💬 *Jerez, Xérès*

BODY

ALCOHOL
SWEETNESS

ACIDITY
TANNIN

🍷 Sherry is Spain's top fortified wine, made primarily with Palomino Fino grapes and extended oxidative aging. It's available in a range of styles of bone-dry to very sweet.

🍴 Serve a Fino or Manzanilla Sherry with smoked, fried, or grilled fish, or vegetables. Try Amontillado Sherry with barbecue. Try a PX or Cream Sherry with gooey cheeses.

JACKFRUIT	SALINE	PRESERVED LEMON	BRAZIL NUT	ALMOND

🍷 DESSERT GLASS	🌡 CELLAR 55–60° F	⚱ DECANT NO	🪙 SPEND ~$25	🍾 CELLAR 1–5 YEARS

How Sherry is Made

Sherry uses an aging method called a solera. Soleras are tiers of barrels with 3–9 steps called criaderas, or "scales."

3-criadera solera

Young wines go into the top scale and finished wine is taken from the bottom scale. Wines age for at least 2 years. (Some age more than 50!) There is also a rare single-vintage Sherry called Añada.

Also Try

 SERCIAL MADEIRA   DRY MARSALA

Dry Styles

FINO & MANZANILLA

The lightest styles from Jerez and Sanlúcar de Barrameda, with salty fruit flavors. Best served chilled.

AMONTILLADO

A slightly bolder, nutty style in between Fino and Oloroso.

PALO CORTADO

A richer style with roasted flavors of coffee and molasses.

OLOROSO

The boldest style made from oxidative oak aging. Seasoned Oloroso barrels are in high demand for making whisky.

Sweet Styles

P.X. (PEDRO XIMÉNEZ)

The sweetest style, having upward of 600 g/L RS. Wines are deep brown-colored, with fig and date flavors.

MOSCATEL

An aromatic style made with Muscat of Alexandria featuring caramel flavors.

SWEETENED SHERRY

The most affordable style is typically made by blending P.X. with Oloroso. Wines are labeled by sweetness level:

- *Dry: 5–45 g/L RS*
- *Medium: 5–115 g/L RS*
- *Pale Cream: 45–115 g/L RS*
- *Cream: 115–140 g/L RS*
- *Dulce: 160+ g/L RS*

Silvaner

◀) *"sihl-fahn-er"* 💬 *Gruner Silvaner, Sylvaner*

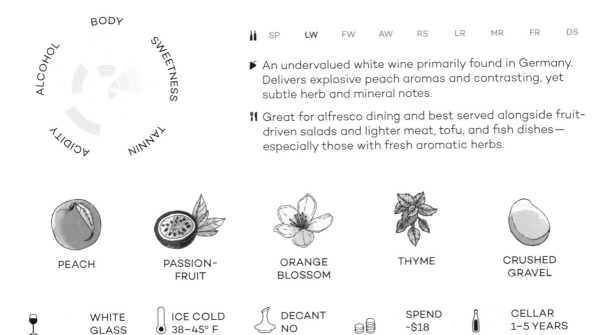

BODY · SWEETNESS · TANNIN · ACIDITY · ALCOHOL

▌▌ SP **LW** FW AW RS LR MR FR DS

🗡 An undervalued white wine primarily found in Germany. Delivers explosive peach aromas and contrasting, yet subtle herb and mineral notes.

🍴 Great for alfresco dining and best served alongside fruit-driven salads and lighter meat, tofu, and fish dishes—especially those with fresh aromatic herbs.

PEACH	PASSION-FRUIT	ORANGE BLOSSOM	THYME	CRUSHED GRAVEL

🍷 WHITE GLASS	🌡 ICE COLD 38–45° F	DECANT NO	💰 SPEND ~$18	🍾 CELLAR 1–5 YEARS

Where It Grows

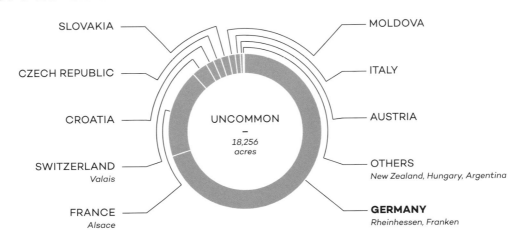

SLOVAKIA

CZECH REPUBLIC

CROATIA

SWITZERLAND
Valais

FRANCE
Alsace

UNCOMMON
–
18,256 acres

MOLDOVA

ITALY

AUSTRIA

OTHERS
New Zealand, Hungary, Argentina

GERMANY
Rheinhessen, Franken

Also Try

 PINOT BLANC    MALAGOUSIA (GREECE)   PINOT GRIS   VERDICCHIO    FERNÃO PIRES

Syrah

🔊 "sear-ah" 💬 Shiraz, Hermitage

BODY · SWEETNESS · TANNIN · ACIDITY · ALCOHOL

SP LW FW AW RS LR MR FR DS

🔖 A rich, powerful, and sometimes meaty red wine that originated in the Rhône Valley of France. It's the most planted grape of Australia, where it's called Shiraz.

🍴 Darker meats and exotic spices bring out the fruit notes of Syrah. Try it with lamb shawarma, gyros, Asian five-spice pork, and Indian tandoori.

BLUEBERRY	PLUM	MILK CHOCOLATE	TOBACCO	GREEN PEPPERCORN

🍷 RED GLASS	🌡 ROOM 60–68° F	⚗ DECANT 60+ MIN	🪙 SPEND ~$25	🍾 CELLAR 5–15 YEARS

Where It Grows

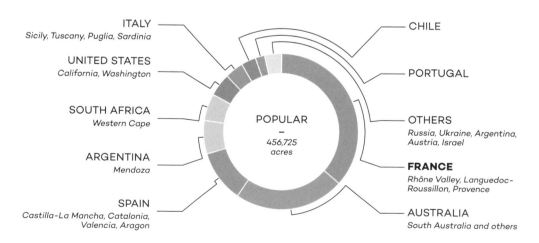

ITALY
Sicily, Tuscany, Puglia, Sardinia

UNITED STATES
California, Washington

SOUTH AFRICA
Western Cape

ARGENTINA
Mendoza

SPAIN
Castilla-La Mancha, Catalonia, Valencia, Aragon

POPULAR
–
456,725 acres

CHILE

PORTUGAL

OTHERS
Russia, Ukraine, Argentina, Austria, Israel

FRANCE
Rhône Valley, Languedoc-Roussillon, Provence

AUSTRALIA
South Australia and others

Also Try

🍷 TOURIGA NACIONAL   🍷 MONASTRELL   🍷 PETITE SIRAH   🍷 MENCÍA   🍷 ALICANTE BOUSCHET

Syrah

ADDITIONAL
TASTING
NOTES

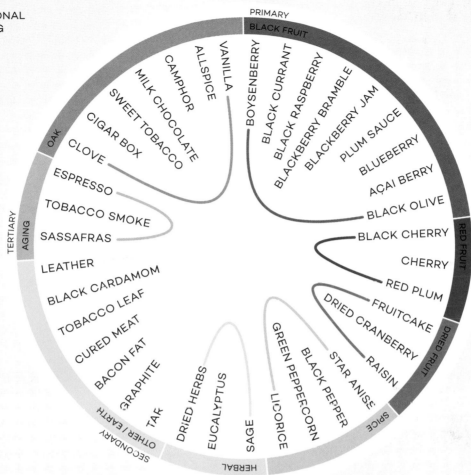

South Australia

Few wines can meet the intensity of a South Australian Shiraz. Historically, Barossa Valley grapes were used in fortified Port-style wines. Today, the 100-year-old vines make some of the most coveted Syrah in the world. Investigate McLaren Vale, Barossa Valley, and the value-driven Riverland region.

‣ BLACKBERRY SAUCE
‣ FRUIT CAKE
‣ SASSAFRAS
‣ CAMPHOR
‣ SWEET TOBACCO

Rhône Valley, France

The Northern Rhône has several appellations producing single-varietal Syrah wines, including Côte Rôtie, Cornas, St.-Joseph, Crozes-Hermitage, and Hermitage. Wines are medium-bodied with earthy fruit flavors, high tannin, and noticeable black pepper notes.

‣ PLUM
‣ BLACK PEPPER
‣ TOBACCO LEAF
‣ BACON FAT
‣ GRAPHITE

Chile

We're likely to see more Syrah exported from South America given its strikingly pure fruit flavors, elevated acidity, and easy-drinking character. Overall, the wines express tart-to-ripe black fruit flavors and not-too-intense tannin.

‣ BOYSENBERRY
‣ BLACK CHERRY
‣ STAR ANISE
‣ GRAPHITE
‣ GREEN PEPPERCORN

Tannat

🔊 *"tahn-naht"*   💬 *Madiran*

SP LW FW AW RS LR MR FR DS

🏹 Tannat has some of the highest polyphenols (antioxidants) of all red wines. The grape originated in South-West France and is the #1 wine of Uruguay.

🍴 Because Tannat can be so darn tannic and astringent, you'll want to pair it with rich, barbecue grilled meats, or other fatty dishes. Cassoulet is an awesome choice.

BLACK CURRANT	PLUM	LICORICE	SMOKE	CARDAMOM

🍷 OVERSIZED GLASS	🌡 ROOM 60–68° F	DECANT 60+ MIN	🪙 SPEND ~$15	CELLAR 5–25 YEARS

Where It Grows

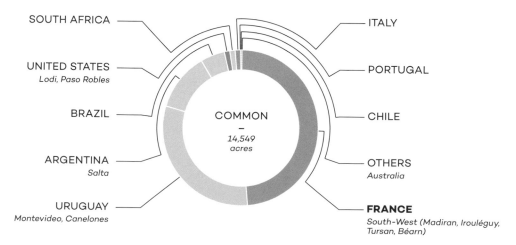

SOUTH AFRICA

UNITED STATES
Lodi, Paso Robles

BRAZIL

ARGENTINA
Salta

URUGUAY
Montevideo, Canelones

ITALY

PORTUGAL

CHILE

OTHERS
Australia

FRANCE
South-West (Madiran, Irouléguy, Tursan, Béarn)

COMMON
–
14,549
acres

Also Try

🍷 SAGRANTINO   🍷 ALICANTE BOUSCHET   🍷 TOURIGA NACIONAL   🍷 MONASTRELL   🍷 PETITE SIRAH

Tempranillo

◀) *"temp-rah-nee-oh"* 💬 *Cencibel, Tinta Roriz, Aragonêz, Tinta de Toro, Ull de Llebre, Tinta del Pais*

| SP | LW | FW | AW | RS | LR | MR | FR | DS |

🏹 Spain's top variety, made famous by the wines of Rioja, where wines are classified by how long they age in oak. Fine Tempranillo ages 20+ years but costs a little more.

🍴 Bolder, aged Tempranillo wines pair nicely with steak, gourmet burgers, and rack of lamb. Fresher styles match well with baked pasta and other tomato-based dishes.

BODY · SWEETNESS · TANNIN · ACIDITY · ALCOHOL

| CHERRY | DRIED FIG | CEDAR | TOBACCO | DILL |

RED GLASS · CELLAR 55–60° F · DECANT 60+ MIN · SPEND ~$14 · CELLAR 10–30 YEARS

Where It Grows

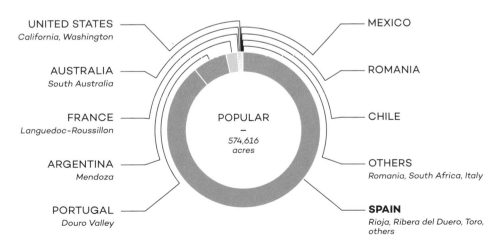

POPULAR
–
574,616
acres

UNITED STATES
California, Washington

AUSTRALIA
South Australia

FRANCE
Languedoc-Roussillon

ARGENTINA
Mendoza

PORTUGAL
Douro Valley

MEXICO

ROMANIA

CHILE

OTHERS
Romania, South Africa, Italy

SPAIN
Rioja, Ribera del Duero, Toro, others

Also Try

🍷 SANGIOVESE   🍷 NEBBIOLO   🍷 AGIORGITIKO   🍷 MONTEPULCIANO   🍷 AGLIANICO

Tempranillo

ADDITIONAL
TASTING
NOTES

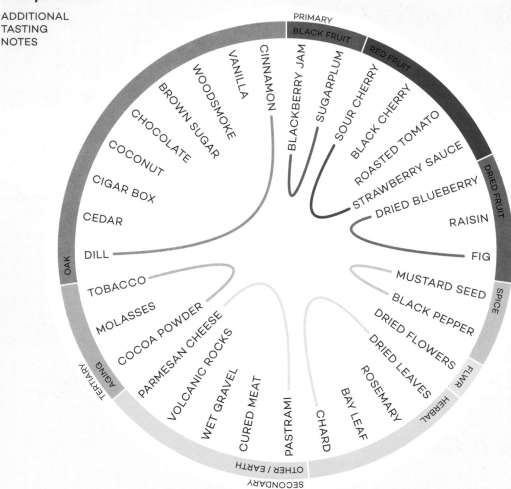

Northern Spain

Introductory Tempranillo from Spain typically hails from the regions of Rioja and Ribera del Duero. The most affordable examples are typically not oaked or aged for very long, producing a fresher and juicier wine with distinct meaty notes typical of the variety.

- ▸ DRIED CHERRY
- ▸ SOUR CHERRY
- ▸ PASTRAMI
- ▸ ROASTED TOMATO
- ▸ CHARD

Spanish "Reserva"

Tempranillo from the Spanish regions of Rioja, Toro, and Ribera del Duero categorize wines by aging regime. The shortest aged wines include "Roble" or "Tinto" (little or no aging), followed by "Crianza" (aged up to 1 year). Finally, Reserva and Gran Reserva are aged up to 3 and 6 years respectively.

- ▸ BLACK CHERRY
- ▸ DILL
- ▸ CIGAR BOX
- ▸ BROWN SUGAR
- ▸ FIG

Rosé Tempranillo

Tempranillo produces a much more savory, muscular style of rosé wine with meaty flavors. Wines typically have a salmon-colored hue with a richer, more oily palate expressing bold red fruit flavors.

- ▸ STRAWBERRY
- ▸ WHITE PEPPER
- ▸ CLOVE
- ▸ TOMATO
- ▸ BAY LEAF

Torrontés

🔊 *"torr-ron-TEZ"*   💬 *Torrontés Sanjuanino, T. Mendocino, T. Riojano*

BODY · SWEETNESS · TANNIN · ACIDITY · ALCOHOL

| SP | LW | FW | **AW** | RS | LR | MR | FR | DS |

🍷 Argentina's very own white is actually a group of 3 varieties that are natural crossings with Muscat of Alexandria. Torrontés Riojano is considered the best.

🍴 Even though Torrontés can smell sweet, it's usually dry to taste, making it a great match with savory dishes that feature exotic spices, fruit, and aromatic herbs.

| MEYER LEMON | PEACH | ROSE PETAL | GERANIUM | CITRUS ZEST |

| 🍷 WHITE GLASS | 🌡 COLD 45–55° F | DECANT NO | SPEND ~$12 | 🍾 CELLAR 1–5 YEARS |

Where It Grows

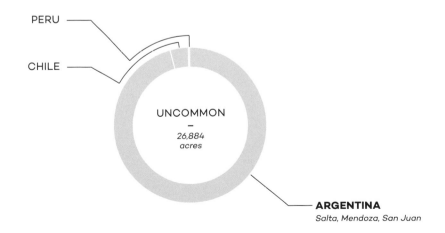

PERU

CHILE

UNCOMMON
–
26,884 acres

ARGENTINA
Salta, Mendoza, San Juan

Also Try

🍷 FERNAO PIRES   🍷 CSERSZEGI FŰSZERES (HUNGARY)   SILVANER   GRAŠEVINA (CROATIA)   PINOT BLANC

Touriga Nacional

🔊 *"tor-ree-guh nah-see-un-nall"* 💬 *Touriga de Dão, Carabruñera, Mortugua*

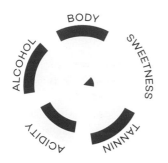

 ALCOHOL BODY SWEETNESS   TANNIN ACIDITY

SP LW FW AW RS LR MR FR DS

🍷 Originally used in Port wines, this increasingly important Portuguese grape is now featured in single-varietal red wines and blends from the Douro Valley and beyond.

🍴 Touriga Nacional's elegant floral fruit aromas and massive tannins will make you yearn for thick-cut steaks topped with compound butter or blue cheese.

VIOLET	BLUEBERRY	PLUM	MINT	WET SLATE

 OVERSIZED GLASS

ROOM 60–68° F

DECANT 60+ MIN

SPEND ~$25

CELLAR 5–25 YEARS

Where It Grows

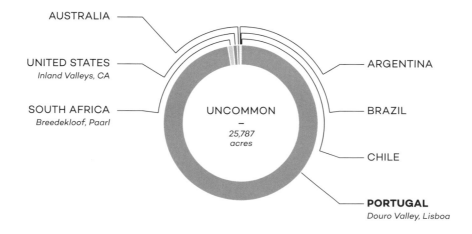

AUSTRALIA

UNITED STATES
Inland Valleys, CA

SOUTH AFRICA
Breedekloof, Paarl

UNCOMMON
–
25,787 acres

ARGENTINA

BRAZIL

CHILE

PORTUGAL
Douro Valley, Lisboa

Also Try

 SYRAH SAGRANTINO MONASTRELL PETIT VERDOT PETITE SIRAH

Trebbiano Toscano

💬 *Ugni Blanc ("oo-nee blonk")*

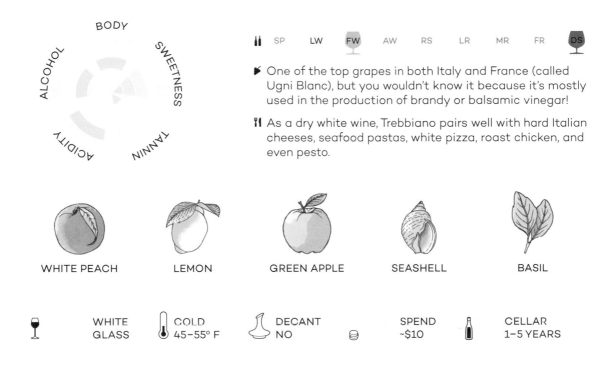

BODY
SWEETNESS
TANNIN
ACIDITY
ALCOHOL

SP LW **FW** AW RS LR MR FR **DS**

🏹 One of the top grapes in both Italy and France (called Ugni Blanc), but you wouldn't know it because it's mostly used in the production of brandy or balsamic vinegar!

🍴 As a dry white wine, Trebbiano pairs well with hard Italian cheeses, seafood pastas, white pizza, roast chicken, and even pesto.

WHITE PEACH	LEMON	GREEN APPLE	SEASHELL	BASIL

WHITE GLASS	COLD 45–55° F	DECANT NO		SPEND ~$10	CELLAR 1–5 YEARS

Where It Grows

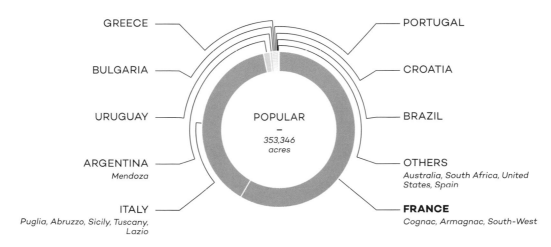

GREECE

BULGARIA

URUGUAY

ARGENTINA
Mendoza

ITALY
Puglia, Abruzzo, Sicily, Tuscany, Lazio

POPULAR
–
353,346
acres

PORTUGAL

CROATIA

BRAZIL

OTHERS
Australia, South Africa, United States, Spain

FRANCE
Cognac, Armagnac, South-West

Also Try

🍷 CHARDONNAY   🍷 SAVATIANO   🍷 SÉMILLON   🍷 ROUSSANNE   🍷 GRENACHE BLANC

Valpolicella Blend

🔊 *"val-polla-chellah"* 💬 *Amarone della Valpolicella, Recioto della Valpolicella, Valpolicella Superiore Ripasso*

BODY

ALCOHOL · SWEETNESS

ACIDITY · TANNIN

| 🍾 | SP | LW | FW | AW | RS | LR | MR | FR | DS |

🍷 The region's most famous wine, Amarone della Valpolicella, uses partially dried grapes (a process called *appasimento*) that are then fermented into a rich red wine.

🍴 The more simple Valpolicella wines pair with burgers and roast chicken. Finer Ripasso and Amarone styles deserve braised meats, steaks, mushrooms, and aged cheeses.

| TART CHERRY | CINNAMON | CHOCOLATE | GREEN PEPPERCORN | ALMOND |

| 🍷 RED GLASS | 🌡 CELLAR 55–60° F | DECANT 30 MIN | SPEND ~$30 | CELLAR 5–25 YEARS |

CORVINA · CORVINONE · MOLINARA · RONDINELLA

RECIOTO DELLA VALPOLICELLA
A dessert wine style made with the apassimento method where grapes are dried on straw mats to concentrate sugars. Features flavors of black raisin, black cherry, chocolate, clove, and roasted hazelnut.

AMARONE DELLA VALPOLICELLA
A dry wine made with the apassimento method. Wines take up to 50 days to ferment. Expect flavors of black cherry, fig, sassafras, and dark chocolate.

VALPOLICELLA SUPERIORE RIPASSO
Superiore Valpolicella wines blended with the leftover grape must of Amarone wine. Features cherry sauce, green peppercorn, and carob.

VALPOLICELLA SUPERIORE
Higher-quality Valpolicella grapes make more concentrated wines. Anticipate dark berries and spicy, high acidity.

VALPOLICELLA CLASSICO
Basic-quality grapes producing entry-level wines. Tart cherry and ash.

Also Try

🍷 BLAUFRÄNKISCH · 🍷 MENCÍA · 🍷 ZWEIGELT · RHÔNE / GSM BLEND · GRENACHE

Verdejo

 "ver-day-ho"   *Rueda, Verdeja*

BODY

ALCOHOL

SWEETNESS

ACIDITY

TANNIN

| | SP | **LW** | FW | AW | RS | LR | MR | FR | DS |

🏹 An herbaceous white wine that grows almost exclusively in the Rueda region of Spain. Not to be confused with Verdelho, a Portuguese grape used in Madeira.

🍴 With high acidity and a subtle bitterness, Verdejo makes a great food wine and palate cleanser. Try it with fish tacos, lime chicken, carnitas, and seitan steaks.

LIME

HONEYDEW

GRAPEFRUIT PITH

FENNEL

WHITE PEACH

🍷 WHITE GLASS

🌡 ICE COLD 38–45° F

DECANT NO

SPEND ~$15

CELLAR 1–5 YEARS

Where It Grows

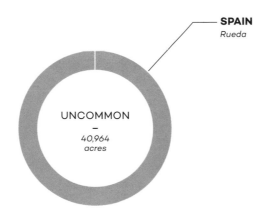

SPAIN
Rueda

UNCOMMON
—
40,964
acres

Also Try

SAUVIGNON BLANC   FRIULANO   MELON   VERMENTINO   COLOMBARD

Verdicchio

 "vair-dee-kee-yo"   💬 Trebbiano di Lugana

BODY
ALCOHOL
SWEETNESS
ACIDITY
TANNIN

🍾	SP	LW	FW	AW	RS	LR	MR	FR	DS

🍷 A fascinating white found primarily in Le Marche, Italy. Verdicchio wines are loved for their sweet, peachy aromas and somewhat oily texture.

🍴 A stellar apertif wine, Verdicchio is great alongside marcona almonds, proscuitto, quiche, and savory tarts and soufflés.

PEACH	LEMON CURD	ALMOND SKIN	OILY	SALINE

🍷 WHITE GLASS   🌡 ICE COLD 38–45° F   ⚗ DECANT NO   🪙 SPEND ~$18   🍾 CELLAR 1–3 YEARS

Where It Grows

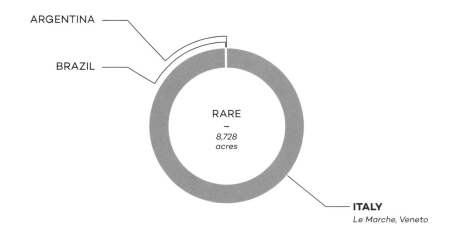

ARGENTINA

BRAZIL

RARE
—
8,728
acres

ITALY
Le Marche, Veneto

Also Try

PINOT BLANC   SILVANER   GRECHETTO   FERNAO PIRES   PINOT GRIS

Vermentino

🔊 "vur-men-tino"   💬 Rolle, Favorita, Pigato

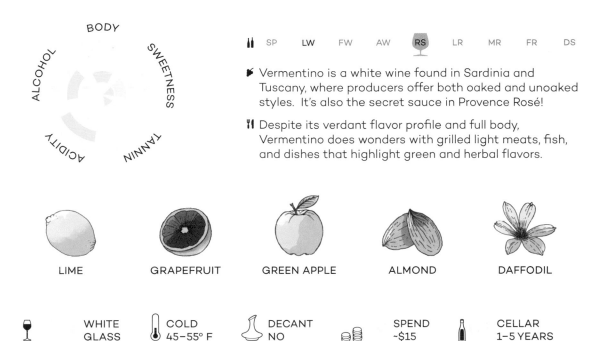

BODY · SWEETNESS · TANNIN · ACIDITY · ALCOHOL

🍷 SP · **LW** · FW · AW · **RS** · LR · MR · FR · DS

🌱 Vermentino is a white wine found in Sardinia and Tuscany, where producers offer both oaked and unoaked styles. It's also the secret sauce in Provence Rosé!

🍴 Despite its verdant flavor profile and full body, Vermentino does wonders with grilled light meats, fish, and dishes that highlight green and herbal flavors.

| LIME | GRAPEFRUIT | GREEN APPLE | ALMOND | DAFFODIL |

| 🍷 WHITE GLASS | 🌡 COLD 45–55° F | DECANT NO | 🪙 SPEND ~$15 | 🍾 CELLAR 1–5 YEARS |

Where It Grows

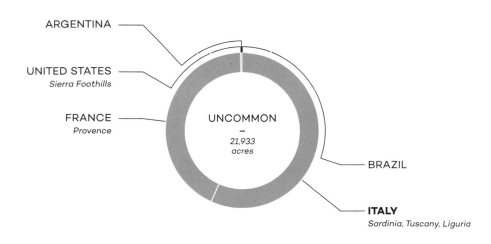

ARGENTINA

UNITED STATES
Sierra Foothills

FRANCE
Provence

UNCOMMON
–
21,933
acres

BRAZIL

ITALY
Sardinia, Tuscany, Liguria

Also Try

CHENIN BLANC · SAUVIGNON BLANC · GRÜNER VELTLINER · COLOMBARD · SÉMILLON

183

Vinho Verde

🔊 *"vino verr-day"* 💬 *Loureiro, Alvarinho, Trajadura, Azal*

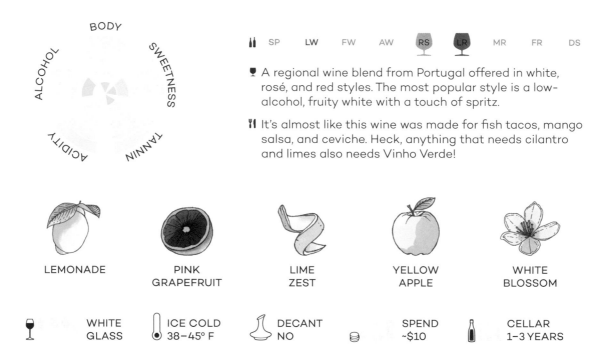

	SP	LW	FW	AW	RS	LR	MR	FR	DS

🍷 A regional wine blend from Portugal offered in white, rosé, and red styles. The most popular style is a low-alcohol, fruity white with a touch of spritz.

🍴 It's almost like this wine was made for fish tacos, mango salsa, and ceviche. Heck, anything that needs cilantro and limes also needs Vinho Verde!

LEMONADE	PINK GRAPEFRUIT	LIME ZEST	YELLOW APPLE	WHITE BLOSSOM

WHITE GLASS	ICE COLD 38–45° F	DECANT NO		SPEND ~$10	CELLAR 1–3 YEARS

Grapes

Vinho Verde is a blend of any or all of these Northern Portuguese grapes.

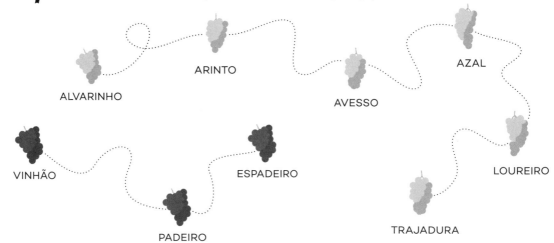

ARINTO

AZAL

ALVARINHO

AVESSO

LOUREIRO

VINHÃO

ESPADEIRO

TRAJADURA

PADEIRO

Also Try

🍷 ALBARIÑO   🍷 ARINTO   ASSYRTIKO   🍷 DRY RIESLING   COLOMBARD

Vin Santo

◀) *"vin son-tow"*

 SP   LW   FW   AW   RS   LR   MR   FR

🍷 Vin Santo ("holy wine") is a rare Italian dessert wine made of Trebbiano, Malvasia, and/or Sangiovese. Because Vin Santo is so sweet, fermentations can last for up to 4 years!

🍴 Vin Santo is a favorite with Italian pastries and almond biscotti. It also makes an excellent pairing partner with soft and funky cheeses like Taleggio.

PERFUME   FIG   RAISIN   ALMOND   TOFFEE

 DESSERT GLASS   CELLAR 55–60° F   DECANT NO   SPEND ~$40   CELLAR 5–10 YEARS

How Vin Santo Is Made

Grapes are laid out on mats or hung in rafters for months to raisinate—a method referred to as "passito." Then, the raisins are barreled, where they'll naturally ferment in spring. The fermentation rises and falls with the seasons and can take up to 4 years to complete!

A lower-quality Vin Santo is also available made with fortification called Vin Santo Liquoroso.

Lighter styles

Richer styles

VIN SANTO DI GAMBELLARA
Veneto wines made with Garganega grapes.

VINO SANTO TRENTINO
Trentino wines made with a rare aromatic white grape called Nosiola with candied grapefruit and honey notes.

VIN SANTO DEL CHIANTI CLASSICO
The most popular style. These Tuscan wines are made with white grapes such as Malvasia and Trebbiano Toscano.

VIN SANTO DI OFFIDA
A rare wine of the Marche region made with Passerina grapes in a dry style with meyer lemon and fennel notes.

VIN SANTO OCCHIO DI PERNICE
A rare red style from Tuscany made with mostly Sangiovese and a red variant of Malvasia called Malvasia Nera.

VINSANTO OF GREECE
A different wine altogether, made with Assyrtiko grapes in Santorini, Greece, with noticeable tannin and flavors of raspberry, dried apricot, and preserved cherries.

Also Try

 TAWNY PORT   MOSCATEL DE SETÚBAL   BOAL MADEIRA    MALMSEY MADEIRA    CREAM SHERRY

Viognier

 "vee-own-yay" 💬 Condrieu

BODY
ALCOHOL · SWEETNESS
ACIDITY · TANNIN

🐟 A rich, oily white wine that originated in the Northern Rhône and is rapidly growing in popularity in California, Australia, and beyond, where it's often aged in oak.

🍴 Want to bring out the best in Viognier? Try it with dishes flavored with almonds, citrus, stewed fruits, and aromatic herbs like Thai basil or tarragon.

| TANGERINE | PEACH | MANGO | HONEYSUCKLE | ROSE |

 WHITE GLASS   🌡 COLD 45–55° F   DECANT NO   🪙 SPEND ~$30   🍾 CELLAR 1–5 YEARS

Where It Grows

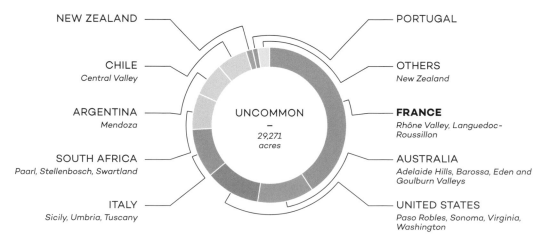

NEW ZEALAND

CHILE
Central Valley

ARGENTINA
Mendoza

SOUTH AFRICA
Paarl, Stellenbosch, Swartland

ITALY
Sicily, Umbria, Tuscany

UNCOMMON
–
29,271
acres

PORTUGAL

OTHERS
New Zealand

FRANCE
Rhône Valley, Languedoc-Roussillon

AUSTRALIA
Adelaide Hills, Barossa, Eden and Goulburn Valleys

UNITED STATES
Paso Robles, Sonoma, Virginia, Washington

Also Try

🍷 MALAGOUSIA (GREECE)   🍷 MARSANNE   🍷 FIANO   🍷 CHARDONNAY   🍷 FERNÃO PIRES

Viura

◀) *"vee-yur-ah"* 💬 *Macabeo, Macabeu*

BODY
SWEETNESS
TANNIN
ACIDITY
ALCOHOL

🍴 **SP** | LW | **FW** | AW | RS | LR | MR | FR | DS

🍾 Viura is the primary grape in Spanish Rioja Blanco and Cava sparkling wines (where it's called "Macabeo"). Viura wines become increasingly rich and nutty with age.

🍴 Younger Viura wines pair well with Southeast Asian cuisine (coconut curries, vermicelli noodle bowls). Aged Viura pairs nicely with roasted meats and resinous herbs.

 | | | |
HONEYDEW | LIME PEEL | LEMON VERBANA | TARRAGON | HAZELNUT

 WHITE GLASS   🌡️ **COLD** 45–55° F   **DECANT NO**   **SPEND** ~$15   **CELLAR** 5–15 YEARS

Where It Grows

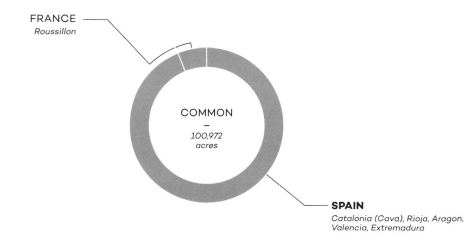

FRANCE
Roussillon

COMMON
–
100,972 acres

SPAIN
Catalonia (Cava), Rioja, Aragon, Valencia, Extremadura

Also Try

🍷 GRENACHE BLANC   🍷 ARINTO   🍷 TREBBIANO TOSCANO   🍷 CHARDONNAY   🍷 SÉMILLON

Xinomavro

🔊 *"ksino-mav-roh"*　💬 *Xynomavro*

ALCOHOL · BODY · SWEETNESS · TANNIN · ACIDITY

🍾 SP　LW　FW　AW　RS　LR　**MR**　**FR**　DS

🏷️ Xinomavro is the most important grape of Naoussa in Greece. Naoussa wines have been compared to Italian Nebbiolo and the coveted wines of Barolo.

🍴 Sop up the rigorous tannin and acidity in Xinomavro by pairing it with cheesy pastas, mushroom risotto, and rich, roasted meats.

| RASPBERRY | PLUM SAUCE | ANISE | ALLSPICE | TOBACCO |

🍷 OVERSIZED GLASS　🌡️ ROOM 60–68° F　🍶 DECANT 60+ MIN　🪙 SPEND ~$15　🍾 CELLAR 5–15 YEARS

Where It Grows

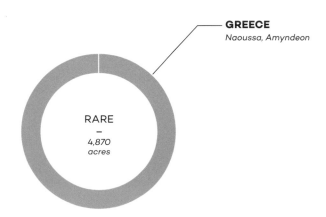

GREECE
Naoussa, Amyndeon

RARE
–
4,870 acres

Also Try

 NEBBIOLO　 TEMPRANILLO　 MENCÍA　 SANGIOVESE　 AGLIANICO

Zinfandel

🔊 *"zin-fan-dell"*   💬 *Primitivo, Tribidrag, Crljenak Kaštelanski*

🍷 SP   LW   FW   AW   RS   LR   **MR**   **FR**   DS

🥄 A fruit-forward yet bold red that's loved for its jammy fruit and smoky, exotic spice notes. Originally from Croatia, Zinfandel is related to Croatia's #1 red, Plavic Mali.

🍴 Zinfandel is ideal with Turkish, Moroccan, and Arabic cuisine, which bring out the grape's cinnamon-like spices. Try it with Asian barbecue.

BLACKBERRY	STRAWBERRY	PEACH PRESERVES	CINNAMON	SWEET TOBACCO

RED GLASS	ROOM 60–68° F	DECANT 30 MIN	SPEND ~$15	CELLAR 5–7 YEARS

Where It Grows

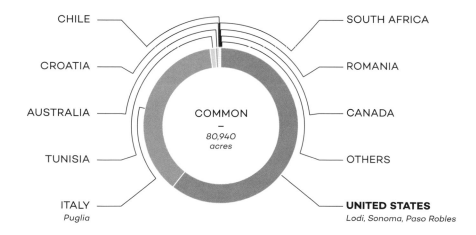

CHILE

CROATIA

AUSTRALIA

TUNISIA

ITALY
Puglia

COMMON
–
80,940
acres

SOUTH AFRICA

ROMANIA

CANADA

OTHERS

UNITED STATES
Lodi, Sonoma, Paso Robles

Also Try

🍷 PLAVIC MALI (CROATIA)   🍷 GRENACHE   🍷 CARIGNAN   🍷 CASTELÃO   🍷 FRAPPATO

Zinfandel

ADDITIONAL
TASTING
NOTES

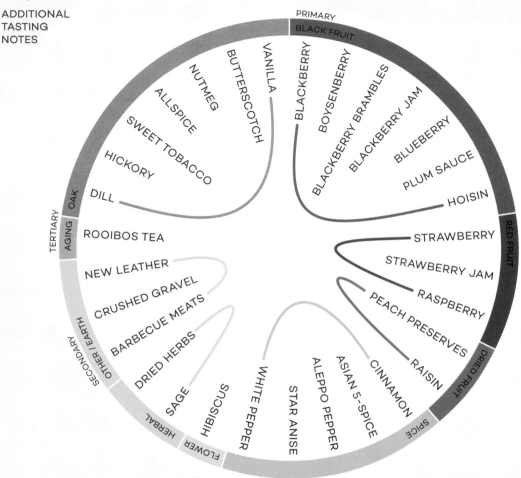

Puglia, Italy

In Puglia, Zinfandel goes by the name of Primitivo and the grape expresses similar bright, candied fruit, with much more leather and dried herbal notes found in Southern Italian reds. Primitivo di Manduria is one of the finest regions, producing the boldest examples.

▸ STRAWBERRY
▸ LEATHER
▸ CANDIED CURRANT
▸ DRIED HERBS
▸ SPICED ORANGE

Lodi, CA

The Lodi region hums along silently in California's Central Valley with over 100,000 acres of vineyards, many of which are dedicated to Zinfandel. Wines appear pale in color, but are highly aromatic with smoky-sweet fruit flavors and smooth tannins.

▸ RASPBERRY JAM
▸ PEACH PRESERVES
▸ BLACKBERRY BRAMBLE
▸ HICKORY
▸ STAR ANISE

North Coast, CA

Several regions within Sonoma and Napa are famous for Zinfandel including Rockpile, Dry Creek Valley, Chiles Valley, and Howell Mountain. Wines here offer bold tannins, colors, and rustic flavors thanks to the region's volcanic soils.

▸ BLACKBERRY
▸ BLACK PLUM
▸ CRUSHED GRAVEL
▸ ALLSPICE
▸ WHITE PEPPER

Zweigelt

🔊 *"zz-why-galt"* 💬 *Blauer Zweigelt, Rotburger*

BODY • SWEETNESS • TANNIN • ACIDITY • ALCOHOL

| 🍾 | SP | LW | FW | AW | RS | LR | MR | FR | DS |

🌾 Austria's most planted red wine grape is a cross between Blaufränkisch and St. Laurent (which tastes like Pinot Noir). Zweigelt wines are typically bright, tart, and fruity.

🍴 The ultimate picnic red, Zweigelt will moisten up even the driest barbecue-grilled chicken and will make that store-bought macaroni salad taste amazing!

| RED CHERRY | RASPBERRY | BLACK PEPPER | LICORICE | CHOCOLATE |

 AROMA COLLECTOR
 CELLAR 55–60° F
 DECANT 30 MIN
 SPEND ~$14
 CELLAR 1–5 YEARS

Where It Grows

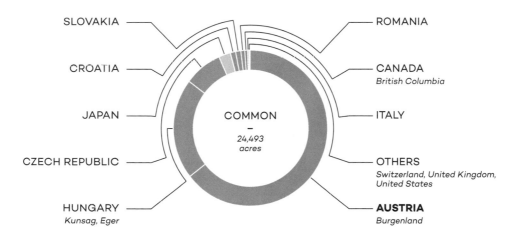

SLOVAKIA
CROATIA
JAPAN
CZECH REPUBLIC
HUNGARY
Kunsag, Eger

COMMON — 24,493 acres

ROMANIA
CANADA
British Columbia
ITALY
OTHERS
Switzerland, United Kingdom, United States
AUSTRIA
Burgenland

Also Try

 BLAUFRÄNKISCH   ST. LAURENT (GERMANY)   GAMAY FRAPPATO   SCHIAVA

Wine Regions

Wine Regions of the World

▬▬▬	ITALY
▬▬▬	FRANCE
▬▬	SPAIN
▬▬	UNITED STATES
▬	ARGENTINA
▪	AUSTRALIA
▪	CHILE
▪	SOUTH AFRICA
▪	CHINA
▪	GERMANY
▪	PORTUGAL
▪	RUSSIA
▪	ROMANIA
▪	HUNGARY
▪	BRAZIL
▪	GREECE
▪	NEW ZEALAND
▪	AUSTRIA
▪	SERBIA
▪	UKRAINE

Wine production of top 20 countries (% of world total). Trade Data & Analysis (2015)

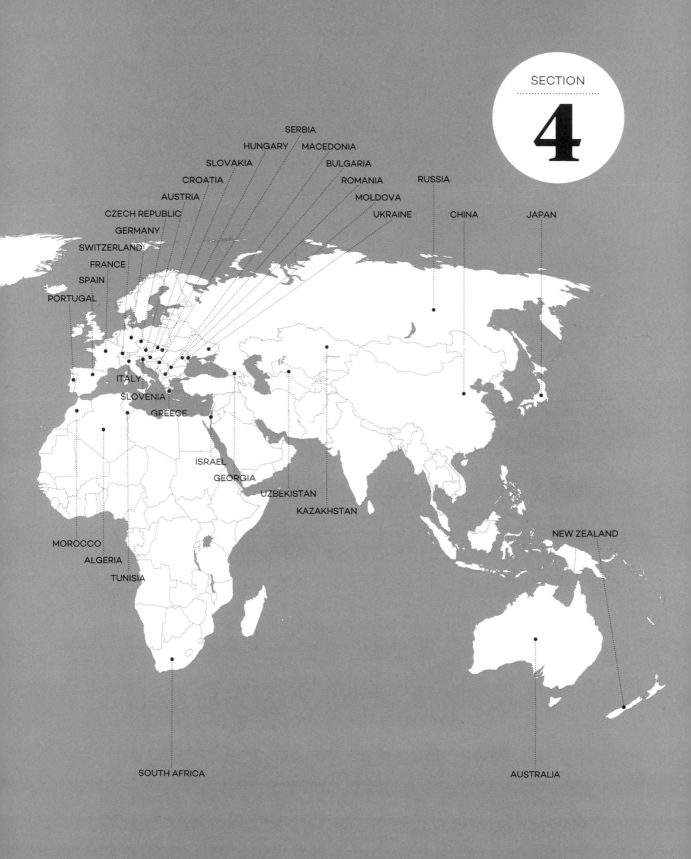

SECTION

4

SERBIA
HUNGARY   MACEDONIA
SLOVAKIA   BULGARIA
CROATIA   ROMANIA   RUSSIA
AUSTRIA   MOLDOVA
CZECH REPUBLIC   UKRAINE   CHINA   JAPAN
GERMANY
SWITZERLAND
FRANCE
SPAIN
PORTUGAL

ITALY
SLOVENIA
GREECE

ISRAEL
GEORGIA
UZBEKISTAN
KAZAKHSTAN

NEW ZEALAND

MOROCCO
ALGERIA
TUNISIA

SOUTH AFRICA   AUSTRALIA

World Wine Production by Country

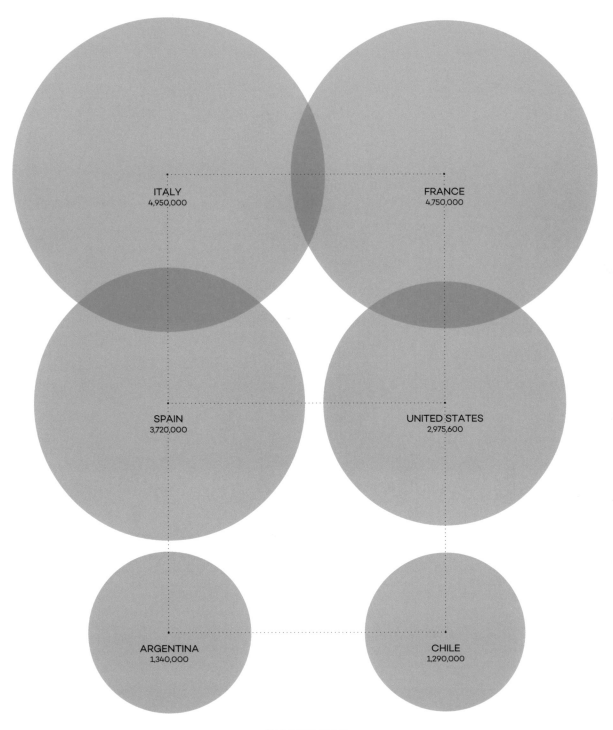

ITALY
4,950,000

FRANCE
4,750,000

SPAIN
3,720,000

UNITED STATES
2,975,600

ARGENTINA
1,340,000

CHILE
1,290,000

(IN LITERS '000)
Trade Data & Analysis (2015)

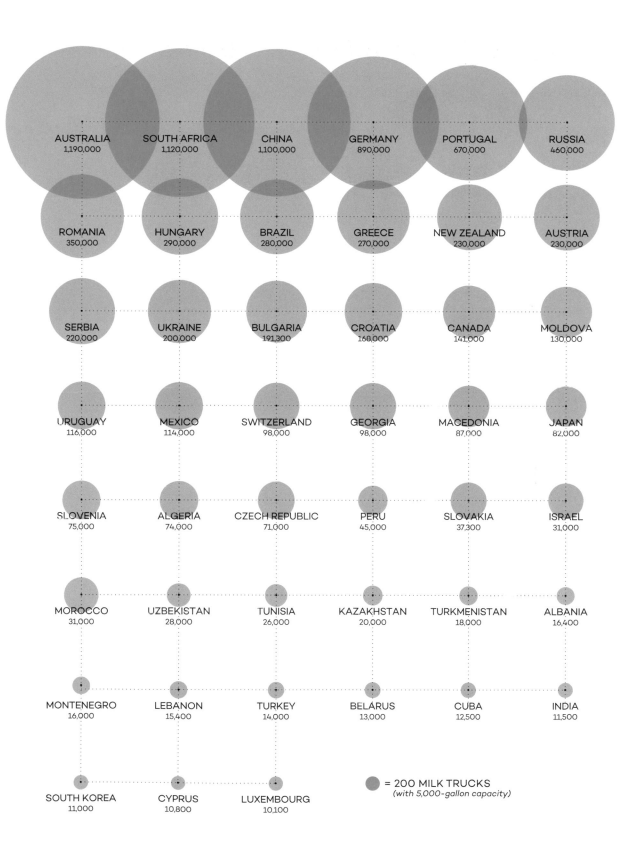

AUSTRALIA
1,190,000

SOUTH AFRICA
1,120,000

CHINA
1,100,000

GERMANY
890,000

PORTUGAL
670,000

RUSSIA
460,000

ROMANIA
350,000

HUNGARY
290,000

BRAZIL
280,000

GREECE
270,000

NEW ZEALAND
230,000

AUSTRIA
230,000

SERBIA
220,000

UKRAINE
200,000

BULGARIA
191,300

CROATIA
168,000

CANADA
141,000

MOLDOVA
130,000

URUGUAY
116,000

MEXICO
114,000

SWITZERLAND
98,000

GEORGIA
98,000

MACEDONIA
87,000

JAPAN
82,000

SLOVENIA
75,000

ALGERIA
74,000

CZECH REPUBLIC
71,000

PERU
45,000

SLOVAKIA
37,300

ISRAEL
31,000

MOROCCO
31,000

UZBEKISTAN
28,000

TUNISIA
26,000

KAZAKHSTAN
20,000

TURKMENISTAN
18,000

ALBANIA
16,400

MONTENEGRO
16,000

LEBANON
15,400

TURKEY
14,000

BELARUS
13,000

CUBA
12,500

INDIA
11,500

SOUTH KOREA
11,000

CYPRUS
10,800

LUXEMBOURG
10,100

● = 200 MILK TRUCKS
(with 5,000-gallon capacity)

Where Did Wine Come From?

Current evidence suggests that wine originated in the ancient Caucasus region, which includes the Caucasus and Zagros Mountains. This area includes modern-day Armenia, Azerbaijan, Georgia, northern Iran, southeastern Anatolia, and eastern Turkey. Evidence supporting wine's origin dates from between 8000 BC and 4200 BC, and includes an ancient winery in Armenia, wine grape residue unearthed in jars in Georgia, and signs of grape domestication in eastern Turkey.

An ancient people called the Shulaveri-Shomu culture inhabited Caucasus during the stone age (aka Neolithic period—about 8,000 years ago). They were farmers who used obsidian for tools, raised cattle and pigs, and, most important, made wine!

From Caucasus, wine grapes followed human civilization as it expanded southward and westward into the Mediterranean.

Evidence suggests that the ancient seafaring civilizations of the Phoenicias and Greeks spread wine throughout Europe.

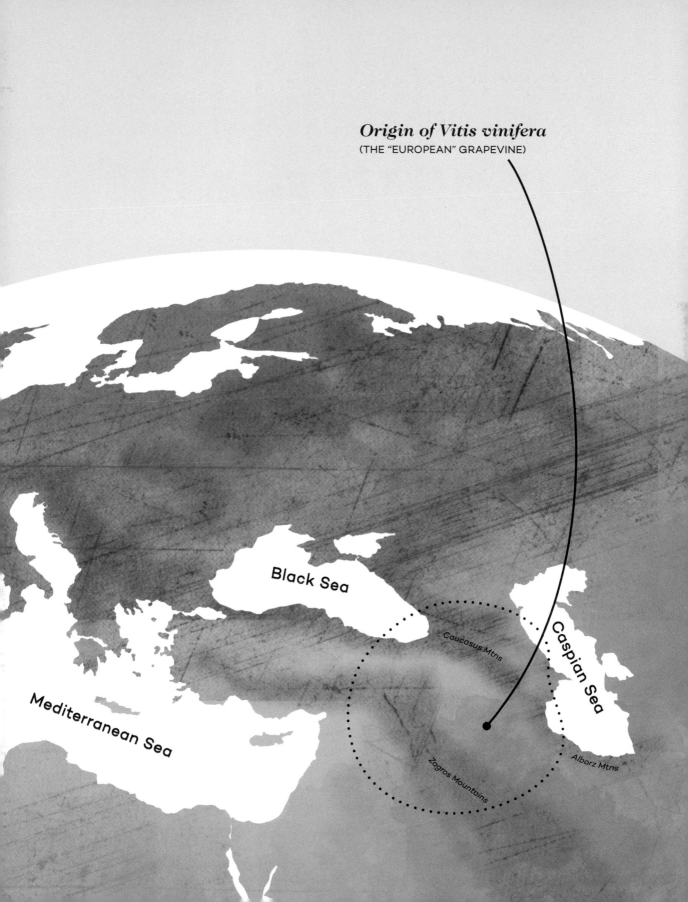

Origin of Vitis vinifera
(THE "EUROPEAN" GRAPEVINE)

Black Sea

Caspian Sea

Mediterranean Sea

Caucasus Mtns

Zagros Mountains

Alborz Mtns

Argentina

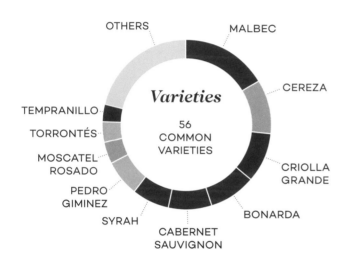

OTHERS · MALBEC · CEREZA · CRIOLLA GRANDE · BONARDA · CABERNET SAUVIGNON · SYRAH · PEDRO GIMINEZ · MOSCATEL ROSADO · TORRONTÉS · TEMPRANILLO

Varieties

56 COMMON VARIETIES

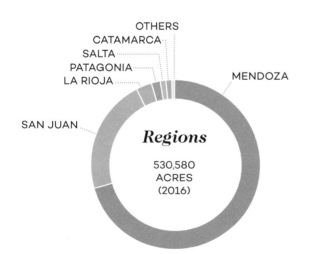

OTHERS · CATAMARCA · SALTA · PATAGONIA · LA RIOJA · SAN JUAN · MENDOZA

Regions

530,580 ACRES (2016)

The land of Malbec

The majority of Argentina's vineyards are located at the base of the Andes Mountains, in an area with both ample sunshine and snowmelt for irrigation. These conditions result in plump, deep-colored wines of which Malbec is the most important variety. High elevation vineyards (upward of 7,500 feet!) have cool nighttime temperatures that help to maintain acidity in the wines. Beyond Malbec, Cabernet Sauvignon, Bonarda, Syrah, Cabernet Franc, Pinot Noir, and an aromatic white called Torrontés are all well worth exploring.

Wine Regions

Mendoza is the largest, most important wine region, accounting for 75% of Argentina's vineyards. Red wines are the focus here and certain areas stand out above the rest in terms of quality. For example, the subregions of Maipú, Luján de Cuyo, and Uco Valley have the highest elevations, which result in wines with higher acidity. The acid adds freshness and age-ability. Other Mendoza regions offer terrific value, including San Rafael and Santa Rosa, where there are many old vines plots producing more concentrated wines.

Beyond Mendoza, the high elevation vineyards in Catamarca, La Rioja, and Salta produce wines with more elegance and minerality with a focus on Torrontés in a dry and lean style. In the South, Patagonia is up-and-coming for Pinot Noir.

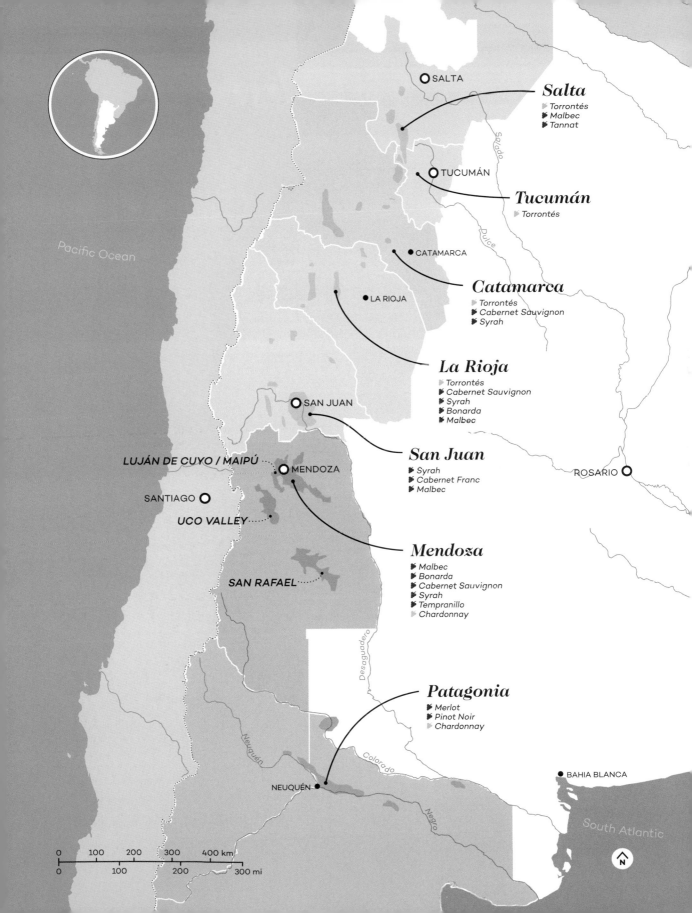

Pacific Ocean

SALTA

Salta
- Torrontés
- Malbec
- Tannat

TUCUMÁN

Tucumán
- Torrontés

CATAMARCA

LA RIOJA

Catamarca
- Torrontés
- Cabernet Sauvignon
- Syrah

La Rioja
- Torrontés
- Cabernet Sauvignon
- Syrah
- Bonarda
- Malbec

SAN JUAN

LUJÁN DE CUYO / MAIPÚ

MENDOZA

SANTIAGO

UCO VALLEY

ROSARIO

San Juan
- Syrah
- Cabernet Franc
- Malbec

SAN RAFAEL

Mendoza
- Malbec
- Bonarda
- Cabernet Sauvignon
- Syrah
- Tempranillo
- Chardonnay

Patagonia
- Merlot
- Pinot Noir
- Chardonnay

BAHIA BLANCA

NEUQUÉN

South Atlantic

Salado

Dulce

Desaguadero

Neuquén

Colorado

Negro

| 0 | 100 | 200 | 300 | 400 km |
| 0 | 100 | 200 | 300 mi | |

N

Wines to Explore

Bold red wines including Malbec, Cabernet Sauvignon, and Syrah are Argentina's specialty. You'll find great value in lesser-known varieties like Bonarda and Torrontés. Tempranillo, Cabernet Franc, and Pinot Noir are the best at championing Argentina's dusty-but-fruity terroir.

Uco Valley Malbec

Some of the highest elevation vineyards in Mendoza are found in the Uco Valley. The elevation results in wines with more savory flavors, dusty tannins, and layered black fruit. You'll often see wines labeled by a subzone such as Tupungato or Vista Flores.

 BLACK PLUM, RASPBERRY, OLIVE, RED PEPPER FLAKE, COCOA

Luján de Cuyo Malbec

Luján de Cuyo produces Malbec wines with more black fruit flavors in a more lush style. The subregions of Agrelo (elegance + power), Vistalba (minerality), Las Compuertas (elegance), and Perdriel (tannin) offer the most distinguishable differences.

 BLACKBERRY, PLUM SAUCE, BLACK CHERRY, ASIAN 5-SPICE, GRAPHITE

Maipú Malbec

Mendoza's classic wine-growing area produces more elegant Malbec wines with lighter red fruit flavors and often a touch of earthy cedar or tobacco. The subzone of Barrancas is slightly warmer, which results in wines with more black-fruit notes.

 RED PLUM, BOYSENBERRY, CHERRY, CEDAR, TOBACCO

Cabernet-Malbec Blend

An increasingly popular blend from Argentina features Cabernet Sauvignon with Malbec. Malbec adds a plush and opulent style with explosive berry fruit. Cabernet Sauvignon delivers more complexity with increased tannin and savory flavors.

 BLACKBERRY, PLUM, CHOCOLATE, BLACK PEPPER, TOBACCO

Cabernet Sauvignon

Grapes under Mendoza's sun develop bold, ripe fruit flavors that can handle judicious new oak aging programs (top wines are often aged for 18 months). The region's terroir offers exotic spice notes on top of the variety's flavor profile.

 BLACK CURRANT SAUCE, BLACK CHERRY, ASIAN 5-SPICE, TOBACCO SMOKE

Bonarda

(aka Deuce Noir or Charbono) A rare grape to the rest of the world, Bonarda grows in abundance in Argentina. It offers exceptional value as a single-varietal wine. Overall, Bonarda is similar to Malbec with an explosion of juicy red and black fruit with a slightly lighter taste profile.

 PLUM, CHERRY, LICORICE, COCOA, GRAPHITE

Good to Know

🍷 Single-varietal wines must contain at least 85% of the listed variety.

🍷 Wines labeled "Reserva" must be aged for at least 12 months for red wines or 6 months for white and rosé wines.

Patagonia Pinot Noir

Argentina offers a unique take on Pinot Noir with its wines from Neuquén and Río Negro in Patagonia. Wines balance sweet red fruit flavors with leafy herbal tea-like flavors. Patagonia is an up-and-coming frontier in Argentinian wine.

 RED CURRANT, CHERRY, SANDALWOOD, GRAPHITE, EARL-GRAY TEA

Tempranillo

A grape that's well-suited for arid climates, high elevation, and clay-dominant soils. These regional traits result in wines with higher intensity and structure (tannin). Argentinian Tempranillo is relatively hard to find and typically offered at great values.

 SMOKE, BLACK CHERRY, CINNAMON, CEDAR, VANILLA

Cabernet Franc

Often blended into Malbec wines to add subtle herbal notes, Cabernet Franc is increasingly made into single-varietal wines in and around Mendoza. Cabernet Franc takes on a much bolder style here than compared to its French cousins, with more body and tannin.

 BLACKBERRY, CHOCOLATE, GREEN PEPPERCORN, CHARCOAL, PLUM

Chardonnay

For those who love oaky and creamy styles of Chardonnay, Mendoza offers fruit-forward wines laced with baked pastry and nutmeg notes. Unfortunately, it's difficult to grow Chardonnay in such a hot climate, so seek out quality producers.

 BAKED APPLE, PINEAPPLE, CREAM, NUTMEG, TARRAGON

Torrontés

An underrated and affordable aromatic white wine that smells sweet but usually tastes dry. The best wines are made from the Torrontés Riojana variety (there are 3 distinct Torrontés varieties in all). Keep your eyes out for Salta and the subregion Cafayate.

 LYCHEE, LEMON-LIME, PERFUME, PEACH, CITRUS PITH

Sparkling Malbec

Bodegas have begun picking Malbec slightly earlier to make zesty, dry sparkling rosé wines. Malbec as a rosé wine has a delicate, pale pink color with aromas ranging from peach to raspberry and flavors from sweet melon to citrus pith.

 WHITE PEACH, RASPBERRY, CHALK, RHUBARB, TANGERINE

Australia

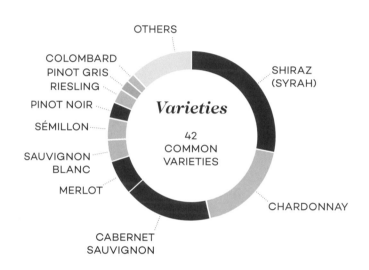

OTHERS

COLOMBARD
PINOT GRIS
RIESLING

PINOT NOIR

SÉMILLON

SAUVIGNON
BLANC

MERLOT

Varieties

42
COMMON
VARIETIES

SHIRAZ
(SYRAH)

CHARDONNAY

CABERNET
SAUVIGNON

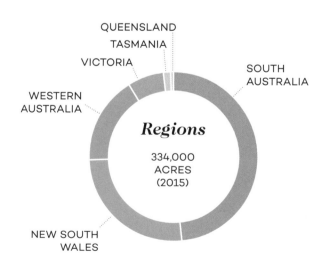

QUEENSLAND
TASMANIA
VICTORIA

WESTERN
AUSTRALIA

Regions

334,000
ACRES
(2015)

SOUTH
AUSTRALIA

NEW SOUTH
WALES

All hail Aussie Shiraz

Australia's warm, dry climate matched with the ingenuity of its people make for wines that stand on their own. For example, Australians coined the name "Shiraz" in order to highlight the unmistakable and unique taste of their Syrah wines. The Australian wine industry constantly innovates and drives technology. One intriguing result is that nearly all Aussie wines are stoppered with screw caps (aka "Stelvins")—even the super-premium bottles!

Wine Regions

Australia is a large country and each geographical area specializes in different wines. Here are some popular choices from Australia's most important growing regions:

- In South Australia's flagship region, Barossa Valley, there is a focus on Shiraz and Riesling.

- In Western Australia's Margaret River, you'll find a predominance of unoaked Chardonnay and elegant Bordeaux blends.

- In Victoria, there are many cooler regions making fruity Chardonnay and Pinot Noir.

- In Victoria's Rutherglen, there is a delightful aged sweet wine made with a red-skinned variant of Muscat Blanc.

- Ouside of Sydney in New South Wales, you'll find age-worthy, lean, and minerally Syrah and Sémillon from Hunter Valley.

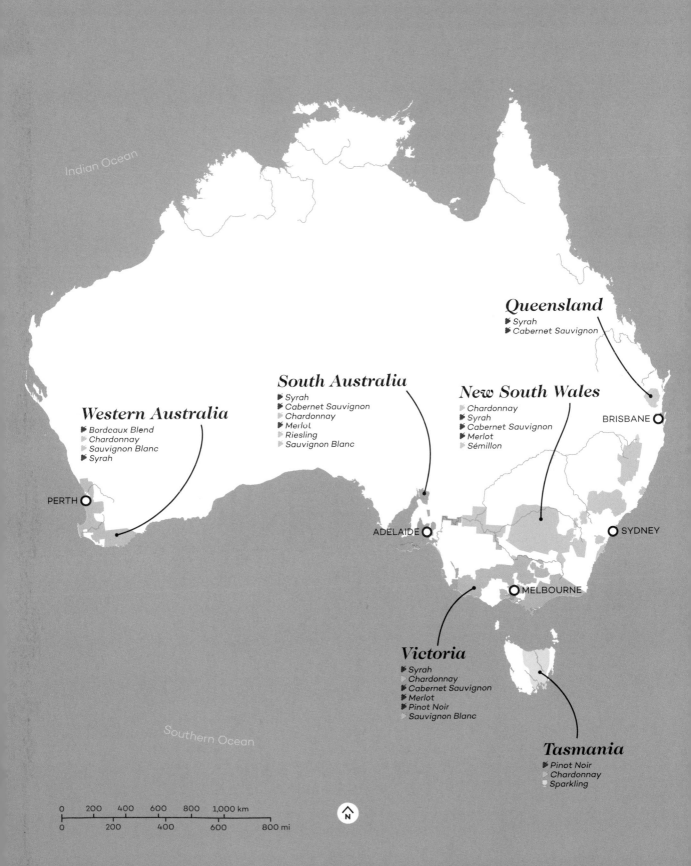

Indian Ocean

Queensland
- Syrah
- Cabernet Sauvignon

BRISBANE

South Australia
- Syrah
- Cabernet Sauvignon
- Chardonnay
- Merlot
- Riesling
- Sauvignon Blanc

New South Wales
- Chardonnay
- Syrah
- Cabernet Sauvignon
- Merlot
- Sémillon

Western Australia
- Bordeaux Blend
- Chardonnay
- Sauvignon Blanc
- Syrah

PERTH

ADELAIDE

SYDNEY

MELBOURNE

Victoria
- Syrah
- Chardonnay
- Cabernet Sauvignon
- Merlot
- Pinot Noir
- Sauvignon Blanc

Southern Ocean

Tasmania
- Pinot Noir
- Chardonnay
- Sparkling

0   200   400   600   800   1,000 km

0   200   400   600   800 mi

N

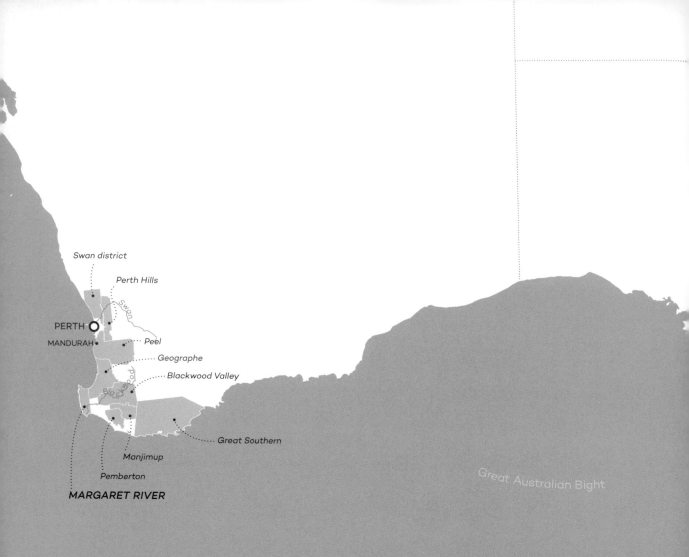

Swan district

Perth Hills

PERTH

MANDURAH • Peel

Geographe

Blackwood Valley

Great Southern

Manjimup

Pemberton

MARGARET RIVER

Swan

Blackwood

Great Australian Bight

0	150	300	450	600	750	900 km
0	150	300	450	600 mi		

N

BUNDABERG

South Burnett ⋯⋯⋯

SUNSHINE COAST

BRISBANE ◯

Granite Belt ⋯⋯⋯

GOLD COAST ◯

New England Australia ⋯⋯⋯

TAMWORTH •

Hastings River ⋯⋯⋯

PORT MACQUARIE

Southern Flinders Ranges ⋯⋯⋯

Darling

Macquarie

HUNTER VALLEY

Mudgee

• ORANGE

Lachlan

CLARE VALLEY ⋯⋯⋯

RIVERLAND

Orange

Cowra

NEWCASTLE ◯

BAROSSA VALLEY

MURRAY DARLING

Hilltops

RIVERINA

Adelaide Plains

Eden Valley

ADELAIDE HILLS

◯ ADELAIDE

Southern Highlands

MCLAREN VALE

◯ SYDNEY

LANGHORNE CREEK

Murray

Swan Hill

WAGGA WAGGA

Currency Creek

Goulburn Valley

Pericoota

RUTHERGLEN

• CANBERRA

Shoalhaven Coast

Kangaroo Is.

Southern Fleurieu

Heathcote

Canberra District

Padthaway

Bendigo

Gundagai

Mount Benson

Pyrenees

Tumbarumba

Robe

Grampians

Wrattonbully

COONAWARRA

Henty

Gippsland

Mount Gambier

MELBOURNE •

Beechworth

Macedon Ranges

Alpine Valleys

Sunbury

King Valley

Geelong

Glenrowan

Strathbogie Ranges

Upper Goulburn

MORNINGTON PENINSULA

YARRA VALLEY

• LAUNCESTON

TASMANIA

• HOBART

Wines to Explore

To get a great overivew of Australian wine, mix and match a case of wines from the major growing regions. You'll quickly discover that each region brings its own style, from Western Australia's elegant Bordeaux-style reds to South Australia's plush, smoky Shiraz.

South Australian Shiraz

The epitome of Shiraz is found in South Australia, a historic region where many vines are over 100 years old. In fact, Barossa Valley in South Australia is the only region that guarantees wines labeled "old vine" are from vines more than 35 years of age.

 BLACKBERRY, DRIED CURRANT, MOCHA, TOBACCO, CLAY POT

South Australia GSM Blends

Where there is great Syrah, there is also great Grenache and Monastrell (called Mataro here). You'll find them all over South Australia, but definitely investigate McLaren Vale and Barossa Valley for great quality.

 RASPBERRY, LICORICE, GRAPHITE, EXOTIC SPICES, ROAST MEAT

Coonawarra Cabernet

Coonawarra's best Cabernet vineyards spring out of dusty red clay soils that give these wines ample depth, powerful tannins, and a subtle dried herb quality. Besides Coonawarra (which is cooler than Bordeaux!), Langhorne Creek is another area worth investigating.

 BLACKBERRY, BLACK CURRANT, CEDAR, SPEARMINT, BAY LEAF

Margaret River Bordeaux Blend

Western Australia differentiates itself from the rest of Australia with its earthier and more elegant Bordeaux-style blends. Well-made wines are even better when aged 10 years. This region is a great choice for someone looking to collect longer term.

 BLACK CHERRY, BLACK CURRANT, BLACK TEA, ROSEHIP, LOAM

Victoria Pinot Noir

The regions in Victoria, including Mornington Peninsula, are hailed as some of the best places for Pinot Noir in the country. The best wines have rich fruit flavors and intriguing notes of orange peel and spice that come out in the finish.

 PLUM, RASPBERRY, LAVENDER, BLACK TEA, ALLSPICE

Yarra Valley Oaked Chardonnay

Victoria is also a great place to look for Australian Chardonnay. In the Yarra Valley, there are several great unoaked Chardonnay wines that offer a bouquet of juicy fruit aromas supported with a tangy, crisp finish.

 STARFRUIT, LEMON, PEAR, PINEAPPLE, WHITE FLOWERS

206

Good to Know

▮▮ Most Australian wines are bottled by screw cap, including the age-worthy bottlings. Wines can be stored upright.

▮▮ If a wine blend lists the included varieties they will be listed in order of proportion.

Margaret River Chardonnay

One of Australia's top-ranking regions for excellent quality Chardonnay in both oaked and unoaked styles. Wines tend to have more minerality and floral notes due, in part, to the region's sandy, granite-based soils.

 FW PEAR, PINEAPPLE, MINERALS, WHITE FLOWERS, HAZELNUT

Hunter Valley Sémillon

The oldest continually operating wine-growing region of Australia is known for both Shiraz and Sémillon. The real surprise are the Sémillon wines, which are complex whilst being lean and minerally at the same time.

LW LIME, LILAC, ASIAN PEAR, GREEN PINEAPPLE, CANDLE WAX

Clare Valley Riesling

There are some cooler micro-climates within South Australia, including Adelaide Hills and Clare Valley. While Adelaide Hills produces a range of white wines, Clare Valley focuses on delightfully refreshing dry Riesling.

 AW LEMON, BEESWAX, WHITE PEACH, LIME, PETROLEUM

Tasmanian Wines

Tasmania is still very much a new frontier in Australian wine, representing less than 0.5% of the country's wine grape harvest. The focus here is on cool-climate Pinot Noir, Chardonnay, and sparkling wines, which are lean and smoky, often with subtle mushroom notes.

 SP LEMON, ALMOND, CREAM, SMOKE, SALINE

Rutherglen Muscat

One of the rare sweet wines of the world made with a red variant of Muscat Blanc that's sometimes labeled as "Brown Muscat." Grapes hang on the vine long after the harvest to produce one of the sweetest "stickies" of Australia.

 DS DRIED LYCHEE, ORANGE PEEL, WALNUT, EXOTIC SPICES, COFFEE

Australian Tawny

Before Shiraz was popularized as a dry red wine in Australia, wineries were known for their dessert wines. The fortified Port-style wines are delightful to taste, especially the tawnies, which develop more candied pecan notes as they age.

 DS TOFFEE, INCENSE, DRIED CHERRY, PECAN, NUTMEG

Austria

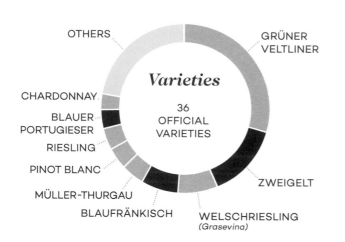

OTHERS
GRÜNER VELTLINER

Varieties

36 OFFICIAL VARIETIES

CHARDONNAY
BLAUER PORTUGIESER
RIESLING
PINOT BLANC
MÜLLER-THURGAU
BLAUFRÄNKISCH
ZWEIGELT
WELSCHRIESLING (Grasevina)

Say hello to Grüner Veltliner

Most never realize that Austria is obsessed with wine, but if you go to the capital of Vienna, you'll find several thousand acres of vineyards flanking the city (that have been there thousands of years!). Austria is most famous for its native grape, Grüner Veltliner or "green veltliner," which produces lip-smacking white wines with acidity that will hit your tongue like a lightning bolt. The region's other wines have a similar delightfully disarming and spicy quality, making Austrian wine an experience like no other.

Wine Regions

Niederösterreich (Lower Austria) is Austria's largest wine region. This is where you'll find the country's most popular and important wine varieties, including Grüner Veltliner and Riesling. Within Lower Austria, the regions of Wachau, Kremstal, and Kamptal consistently produce the highest rated wines in the region.

OTHERS
WIEN (VIENNA)
STEIERMARK
NIEDERÖSTERREICH (LOWER AUSTRIA)

Regions

112,300 ACRES (2015)

BURGENLAND

As you move south, the climate is a bit warmer where it's moderated by Neusiedlersee Lake in Burgenland. The warmer temperatures allow for high-quality red wines including Zwiegelt, Blaufränkisch, and St. Laurent.

In Steiermark (Styria), it's cooler and there are some incredible examples of Sauvignon Blanc, a spicy rosé called Schilcher, and Muskateller (an aromatic but dry Muscat Blanc wine).

KAMPTAL
Kamptal DAC

KREMSTAL
Kremstal DAC

WACHAU

WEINVIERTEL
Weinviertel DAC

WAGRAM

Wien
(VIENNA)
🍇 *W. Gemischter Satz DAC*
🍇 *Grüner Veltliner*

VIENNA

BRATISLAVA

TRAISENTAL
Traisental DAC

CARNUNTUM

Niederösterreich
(LOWER AUSTRIA)
🍇 *Grüner Veltliner*
🍇 *Zweigelt*
🍇 *Riesling*
🍇 *Welschriesling*

THERMENREGION

WIENER NEUSTADT

EISENSTADT

Steiermark
(STYRIA)
🍇 *Sauvignon Blanc*
🍇 *Pinot Gris*
🍇 *Welschriesling*
🍇 *Schilcher Rosé*
🍇 *Muskateller*

NEUSIEDLERSEE-HÜGELLAND
Leithaberg DAC

MITTELBURGENLAND
Mittelburgenland DAC

NEUSIEDLERSEE
Neusiedlersee DAC

Burgenland
🍇 *Blaufränkisch*
🍇 *Zweigelt*
🍇 *Grüner Veltliner*
🍇 *Chardonnay*
🍇 *St. Laurent*

SZOMBATHELY

GRAZ

WESTSTEIERMARK
Schilcherland DAC

SÜDBURGENLAND
Eisenberg DAC

SÜDSTEIERMARK

SÜD-OSTSTEIERMARK

MARIBOR

0   25   50 km

0   25 mi

N

Wines to Explore

Austria's lean and laser-like whites—Grüner Veltliner, Riesling, and Sauvignon Blanc—easily match up to the best of France and Germany. The country's red varieties like Zweigelt, Blaufränkisch, and St. Laurent are terrific food-pairing wines given their ample spice, earthiness, and explosive fruit.

Grüner Veltliner

Austria's top variety is made in a wide variety of styles. Wines labeled "Klassik" are typically lighter and more peppery, whereas those labeled with "Reserve" or "Smaragd" (from Wachau) offer more rich, tropical fruit notes. Those aged in oak are quite the find.

 LW STARFRUIT, GOOSEBERRY, SNAP PEA, WHITE PEPPER, CRUSHED ROCKS

Riesling

On first taste, Austrian Riesling seems very similar to German Riesling, with crystalline acidity and explosive fruit aromas. Tasting them side-by-side reveals Austria's slightly more lean profile and focused herbal notes. Niederösterreich is the place to look.

 AW LEMON-LIME, APRICOT, PEAR, LEMON ZEST, TARRAGON

Sauvignon Blanc

An exciting discovery if you visit Austria is the country's Sauvignon Blanc from Steiermark. The wines have mouth-watering acidity and create tension on the palate with ripe, peachy fruit complemented by spicy and minty herbal flavors.

 LW HONEYDEW MELON, CELERY, FRESH HERBS, WHITE PEACH, CHIVE

Wiener Gemischter Satz

Wiener Gemischter Satz is a traditional Vienna white wine blend of at least 3 white varieties from the same vineyard that may include Grüner Veltliner, Pinot Blanc, Gewürztraminer, Graševina (aka Welschriesling), and rare finds like Sämling and Goldburger.

 AW RIPE APPLE, PEAR, MARZIPAN, WHITE PEPPER, CITRUS ZEST

Zweigelt

The most planted red variety of Austria is a cross between St. Laurent (lighter like Pinot Noir) and the more robust Blaufränkisch. The result are spicy, red-fruit-driven reds and rosé wines that can be served chilled and pair perfectly with a hot summer's day.

 LR TART CHERRY, MILK CHOCOLATE, PEPPER, DRIED HERBS, POTTING SOIL

Blaufränkisch

Austria's champion red wine has surprising depth and tannin structure (on good vintages), which suggests it's a worthy contender for cellaring. In its youth it can taste somewhat earthy and spicy with tart fruit notes and becomes more velvety with time.

 MR DRIED CHERRY, POMEGRANATE, ROASTED MEAT, ALLSPICE, SWEET TOBACCO

Reading a Label

After a highly publicized scandal in 1985 when low-quality wines were found containing ethylene glycol, the Austrian Wine Board tightened regulation. Today, Austria has the most rigorous wine quality and labeling standards. Even though it's quite logical, it's still a bit confusing!

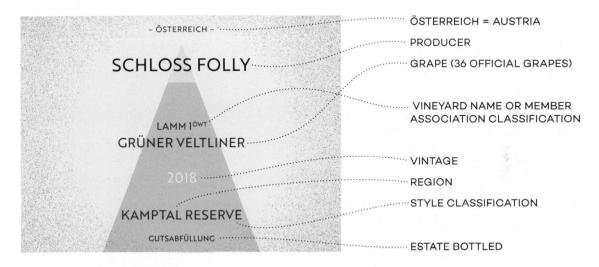

– ÖSTERREICH –

SCHLOSS FOLLY

LAMM 1ÖWT
GRÜNER VELTLINER

2018

KAMPTAL RESERVE

GUTSABFÜLLUNG

ÖSTERREICH = AUSTRIA

PRODUCER

GRAPE (36 OFFICIAL GRAPES)

VINEYARD NAME OR MEMBER ASSOCIATION CLASSIFICATION

VINTAGE

REGION

STYLE CLASSIFICATION

ESTATE BOTTLED

Trocken: Dry wines between 0–9 g/L residual sugar.

Halbtrocken: Off-dry wines between 10–18 g/L RS.

Lieblich: Medium sweet wines with up to 45 g/L RS.

Sweet: Sweet wines with more than 45 g/L RS.

Klassik: Light, zesty wines.

Reserve: Rich wines with 13%+ ABV and hand-harvested.

Wein / Austrian Sekt: No region listed other than Austria? Expect basic table wines.

Landwein: If it's from Weinland, Steirerland, or Bergland it's one step up from table wine using 36 official grapes.

Qualitätswein: This is the top quality marker for Austrian wine. It's indicated by a red-and-white bottle seal that certifies wines passed two

inspections (chemical analysis and tasting). Wines are made with 36 official grapes and labeled with one of the 16 wine regions or 9 states (Niederösterreich, Burgenland, Steiermark, Wien, etc.).

Kabinett: Qualitätswein wines with slightly higher standards.

Prädikatswein: Qualitätswein wines with higher grape ripeness and production rules:

- **Spätlese:** Late harvest picked at or over 22.4 °Brix.
- **Auslese:** Noble rot selected grapes at or over 24.8 °Brix.
- **Beerenauslese:** Noble rot selected grapes at or over 29.6 °Brix.
- **Eiswein:** made with frozen-on-the-vine grapes at or over 29.6 °Brix.
- **Strohwein:** "Straw wine" air-dried grapes to at or over 29.6 °Brix (aka Schilfwein).

- **Trockenbeerenauslese:** (TBA) Noble rot selected grapes at or over 35.5 °Brix.

DAC: Qualitätswein wines from 10 of the 16 wine regions that have officially designated wine styles. (See map.)

Sekt g.U.: Qualitätswein-level sparkling wines with 3 quality tiers: Klassik (9 mos. on lees), Reserve (18 mos. on lees) and Grosse Reserve (30 mos. on lees). Well worth investigating!

Steinfeder: Zesty Wachau whites with up to 11.5% ABV.

Federspiel: Mid-weight Wachau whites with 11.5–12.5% ABV.

Smaragd: Rich Wachau whites with over 12.5% ABV.

1 ÖWT: Listed after a name to designate a special vineyard in Kremstal, Kamptal, Traisental, and Wagram (like Premier Cru).

Chile

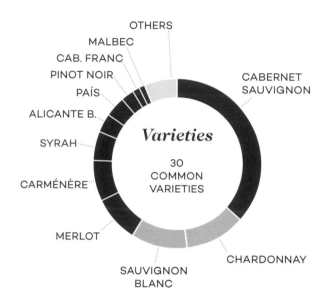

OTHERS
MALBEC
CAB. FRANC
PINOT NOIR
PAÍS
ALICANTE B.
SYRAH
CARMÉNÈRE
MERLOT
SAUVIGNON BLANC
CHARDONNAY
CABERNET SAUVIGNON

Varieties

30 COMMON VARIETIES

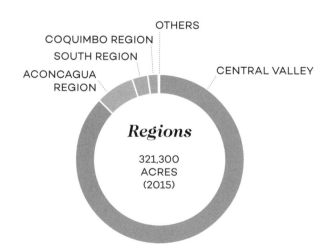

OTHERS
COQUIMBO REGION
SOUTH REGION
ACONCAGUA REGION
CENTRAL VALLEY

Regions

321,300 ACRES (2015)

Francophiles in South America

The French were excited by the prospects of Chile's ideal climate and soils for fine wines and invested in the region early on. Their influence shaped Chile's wine market toward a focus on Bordeaux varieties like Merlot and Cabernet, focusing heavily on exports. Then in the 1990s, it was discovered that much of the country's Merlot was actually a nearly extinct variety called Carménère. Chile suddenly had its own unique wine.

Wine Regions

Chile is a thin strip of land sandwiched between the Pacific Ocean and the Andes mountains. Its position creates a massive air conditioner effect—sucking cool ocean air inland. Each wine region has 3 unique growing zones: The Costas (cooler coastal regions), Entre Cordilleras (warm inland valleys), and Los Andes (exposed mountainous areas).

- The coastal regions are best suited for cool climate grapes like Pinot Noir and Chardonnay. Sauvignon Blanc grows well here too!

- The inland valleys are warmest and known for their soft and supple Bordeaux Blends.

- The high elevation Andes create wines with more structure (tannin and acidity) and this has lead to intriguing Syrah, Cabernet Franc, Malbec, and Cabernet Sauvignon.

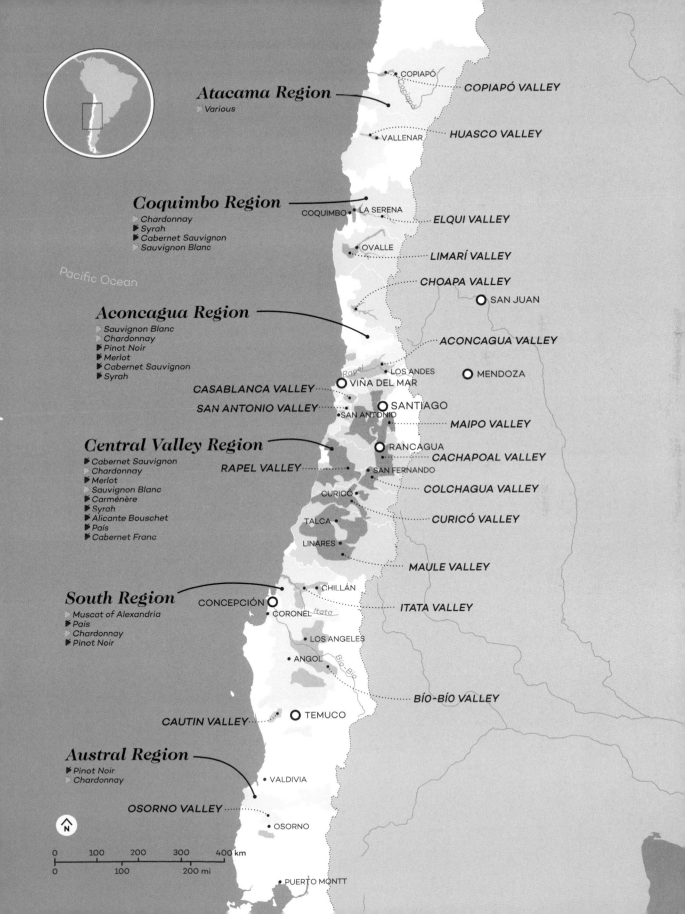

Atacama Region
- Various

Coquimbo Region
- Chardonnay
- Syrah
- Cabernet Sauvignon
- Sauvignon Blanc

Aconcagua Region
- Sauvignon Blanc
- Chardonnay
- Pinot Noir
- Merlot
- Cabernet Sauvignon
- Syrah

Central Valley Region
- Cabernet Sauvignon
- Chardonnay
- Merlot
- Sauvignon Blanc
- Carménère
- Syrah
- Alicante Bouschet
- País
- Cabernet Franc

South Region
- Muscat of Alexandria
- País
- Chardonnay
- Pinot Noir

Austral Region
- Pinot Noir
- Chardonnay

Pacific Ocean

COPIAPÓ — *COPIAPÓ VALLEY*

VALLENAR — *HUASCO VALLEY*

COQUIMBO • LA SERENA — *ELQUI VALLEY*

• OVALLE — *LIMARÍ VALLEY*

CHOAPA VALLEY

○ SAN JUAN

ACONCAGUA VALLEY

• LOS ANDES

○ MENDOZA

CASABLANCA VALLEY ○ VIÑA DEL MAR

SAN ANTONIO VALLEY ○ SANTIAGO
SAN ANTONIO •

MAIPO VALLEY

○ RANCAGUA — *CACHAPOAL VALLEY*

RAPEL VALLEY • SAN FERNANDO

CURICÓ — *COLCHAGUA VALLEY*

TALCA — *CURICÓ VALLEY*

LINARES — *MAULE VALLEY*

• CHILLÁN

CONCEPCIÓN ○ — *ITATA VALLEY*
• CORONEL *Itata*

• LOS ANGELES

• ANGOL *Bío-Bío*

BÍO-BÍO VALLEY

○ TEMUCO

CAUTIN VALLEY

• VALDIVIA

OSORNO VALLEY

• OSORNO

N

| 0 | 100 | 200 | 300 | 400 km |
| 0 | | 100 | | 200 mi |

• PUERTO MONTT

Wines to Explore

Chile specializes in red wine production with a keen focus on Bordeaux varietals, including Cabernet, Merlot, and Carménère, which define Chile's terroir as one of elegance and structure. Beyond this, white wines offer incredible value and grapes like País and Carignan will impress the wine geeks.

Carménère

Carménère is directly related to Cabernet Franc and shares its red fruit flavors and herbaceousness. At the moment, the best wines are found in and around Colchagua, Cachapoal, and Maipo Valleys, where wines are richer and more chocolatey.

 RASPBERRY, PLUM, GREEN PEPPERCORN, MILK CHOCOLATE, BELL PEPPER

Cabernet Sauvignon

The most planted wine grape of Chile is known for producing more elegant and herbal styles of Cabernet. That said, the regions of Apalta, Maipo, and Colchagua show outstanding potential and produce wines with richness, similar to fine Bordeaux.

 DRIED BLACKBERRY, BLACK CHERRY, GREEN PEPPERCORN, DARK CHOCOLATE, PENCIL LEAD

Bordeaux Blend

With several French producers situated in Chile's major wine-growing regions it's no wonder that Bordeaux blends are an important style of wine. The best producers are mostly found in Maipo and Colchagua and produce balanced, age-worthy blends.

 BLACK CURRANT, RASPBERRY, PENCIL LEAD, COCOA POWDER, GREEN PEPPERCORN

Merlot

Chilean Merlot has much more lean fruit and more herbal aromas, especially in the Central Valley, where much of the country's bulk wines are made. That said, Merlot from Cabernet's top regions offer awesome value because they're always overlooked.

 PLUM, BLACK CHERRY, DRIED HERBS, COCOA POWDER

Pinot Noir

The coastal regions, including the famed area Casablanca Valley, and the Southern parts of Chile are where Pinot Noir shines the best. Chilean Pinot exudes flavors of fresh, macerated berries with subtle woodsy notes, often from judicious oaking.

 BLUEBERRY SAUCE, RED PLUM, SANDALWOOD, VANILLA, CLAY POT

Syrah

Syrah shows some of the best potential as an up-and-comer. Wines range in style from succulent reds with black fruit and brooding chocolate notes to wines from higher elevations, which tend to be more elegant with lighter red fruit flavors, higher acidity, and minerality.

 BOYSENBERRY, PLUM SAUCE, MOCHA, ALLSPICE, WHITE PEPPER

Good to Know

🍷 The first wine grapes were planted by Spanish missionaries in the mid-1500s including País (aka Listan Prieto).

🍷 To date, the vineyards in Chile are not affected with phylloxera—a louse that infests *Vitis vinifera* roots.

Cabernet Franc

Cabernet Franc is one of the unsung workhorses of the Chilean Bordeaux Blend and seems to flourish all over the country's varied climates. That said, you'll find a wide range of variation with the best wines mainly coming from Maipo and Maule Valley.

 BLACK CHERRY, ROASTED RED PEPPER, CEDAR, WOOD SMOKE, DRIED HERBS

País

Also known as the Mission grape, and widely planted but rare outside of the country. País has enjoyed a rediscovery with many old vines in Maule and Bío-Bío. Wines are juicy with bright red fruit and crunchy tannins. País is very much the Beaujolais of Chile.

 CANDIED RASPBERRY, ROSE, VIOLET, CHERRY SAUCE, DRIED MEAT

Carignan

A variety with fervent local support due to the high number of century-old vines—some of which are dry farmed and plowed by horse. Wines have both deep concentration and heightened acidity that plays between fruit and savory notes of grilled meats and herbs.

 GRILLED PLUM, DRIED CRANBERRY, NUTMEG, IRON, WHITE PEPPER

Chardonnay

The cooler Costa areas is where you'll find the best Chardonnay. The most popular style is buttery from oak aging, and comes from Casablanca and San Antonio Valleys. The outer regions of Limarí and Aconcagua offer the most minerality and are uniquely salty.

 BAKED APPLE, PINEAPPLE, STARFRUIT, BUTTER, FLAN

Sauvignon Blanc

Chilean Sauvignon Blanc is highly aromatic with zippy acidity. What makes this wine unique is the contrast between its fruit notes of white peach and pink grapefruit by intense green, herbal notes of lemongrass, green pea, and freshly wetted concrete.

LW KIWI, GREEN MANGO, FRESH CUT GRASS, CHERVIL, FENNEL

Viognier

Still a rare find as a single-varietal wine from Chile, Viognier is often blended with Chardonnay to add stone fruit flavors or splashed into Syrah to intensify color (believe it or not!) and aromatics. If you do find one, Chilean Viognier is quite lithe and minerally.

LW HONEYDEW MELON, FENNEL, GREEN ALMOND, ASIAN PEAR, SALINE

France

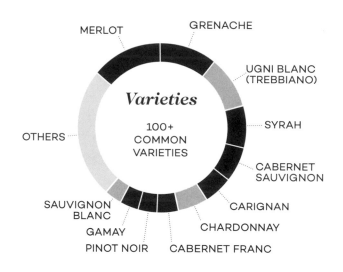

MERLOT · GRENACHE · UGNI BLANC (TREBBIANO) · SYRAH · CABERNET SAUVIGNON · CARIGNAN · CHARDONNAY · CABERNET FRANC · PINOT NOIR · GAMAY · SAUVIGNON BLANC · OTHERS

Varieties

100+ COMMON VARIETIES

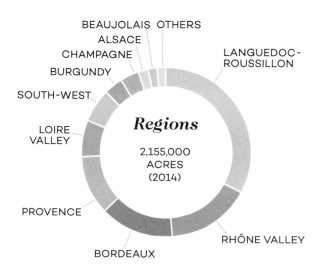

BEAUJOLAIS · OTHERS · ALSACE · CHAMPAGNE · BURGUNDY · SOUTH-WEST · LOIRE VALLEY · PROVENCE · BORDEAUX · RHÔNE VALLEY · LANGUEDOC-ROUSSILLON

Regions

2,155,000 ACRES (2014)

Top wine influencer

The wines of France have had a profound influence on new and developing wine countries. So, even if you haven't had a French wine before, you've had one inspired by France. For example, the varieties of Cabernet Sauvignon, Syrah, Pinot Noir, and Chardonnay originated here, and the French versions have a distinct character unlike any other. Tasting French wine offers a valuable perspective on the evolution of modern wine.

Wine Regions

France can be divided into 11 major wine regions that span a wide variety of climates and territories. Some regions are more well-known than others based on production size, or wide-reaching distribution and influence. Arguably the most influential (and famous) regions of France are Bordeaux, Bourgogne, the Rhône Valley, the Loire Valley, and Champagne. You'll find these aforementioned regions are a great place to explore popular French wine.

If there is one takeaway to remember about French wine it's that its climate conditions vary greatly year to year, causing a high amount of vintage variation (where wines taste different year to year). Vintage variation isn't as noticeable in fine wines from quality producers but it does affect value wines a great deal. Thus, a good rule of thumb is to stock up great values on good vintages!

Champagne
- Champagne

Alsace
- Riesling
- Crémant d'Alsace
- Gewürztraminer
- Pinot Gris
- Pinot Noir

Loire Valley
- Sauvignon Blanc
- Muscadet (Melon)
- Chenin Blanc
- Cabernet Franc

Burgundy
- Chardonnay
- Pinot Noir

Beaujolais
- Gamay

Bordeaux
- Bordeaux Blend
- Sauvignon Blanc
- Sémillon
- Sauternais

Rhône Valley
- Rhône / GSM Blend
- Syrah
- Marsanne-Roussanne
- Viogner

South-West
- Bergerac (Bordeaux Blend)
- Cahors (Malbec)
- Madiran (Tannat)
- Irouléguy (Tannat-Cabernet)
- Jurançon (Gros Manseng)
- Ugni Blanc (Trebbiano Toscano)

Provence
- Rhône / GSM Blend
- Bandol (Mourvèdre)
- Rolle (Vermentino)

Languedoc-Roussillon
- Rhône / GSM Blend
- Crémant de Limoux
- Syrah
- Carignan
- Picpoul

Corsica
- Rhône / GSM Blend
- Syrah
- Nielluccio (Sangiovese)
- Vermetino

LORRAINE

JURA

BUGEY

SAVOIE

VENDÉE

AUVERGNE

REIMS ·
PARIS
STRASBOURG ·
LE MANS ·
ORLEANS
NANTES ·
TOURS ·
DIJON ·
LYON
BORDEAUX ·
TOULOUSE
MONTPELLIER ·
MARSEILLE
NICE

Marne
Seine
Yonne
Loire
Vienne
Saône
Rhône
Dordogne
Garonne
Tarn
Durance
Moselle

N

| 0 | 60 | 120 | 180 km |
| 0 | | 60 | 120 mi |

Wines to Explore

Included here are a dozen of France's most iconic wines, including those of Burgundy and Bordeaux. With each of these wines you'll note a distinct earthy elegance that makes French wines slightly more subtle in flavor and great for pairing with food.

Brut Champagne

Champagne was the first region to produce sparkling wines made with the traditional method. The non-vintage Brut Champagne is the most popular style and it's typically a blend of Chardonnay, Pinot Noir, and Pinot Meunier.

SP   GREEN PEAR, CITRUS, SMOKE, CREAM CHEESE, TOAST

Sparkling Vouvray

Vouvray is the most famous appellation for Chenin Blanc in the Loire Valley. There are wines in all styles from dry to sweet and still to sparkling. Sparkling Vouvray wines are a great way to explore the delicious floral aromas found in Chenin Blanc.

SP   PEAR, QUINCE, HONEYSUCKLE, GINGER, BEESWAX

Sancerre

Sancerre is a well-known appellation for Sauvignon Blanc in the Loire Valley. This region typifies what cool-climate Sauvignon Blanc is all about: linear, mineral-driven, bright-yet-textural with herb-driven flavors, and a tingly finish.

LW   GOOSEBERRY, WHITE PEACH, TARRAGON, LEMON-LIME, FLINT

Chablis

A small northerly region within Bourgogne whose singular focus is Chardonnay, made primarily in an unoaked style that brings out the wine's pure fruit aromas and steely minerality. Expert tip: Many of the high-end Grand Cru wines do see some oak.

LW   STARFRUIT, APPLE, WHITE BLOSSOM, LEMON, CHALK

Alsace Riesling

It's no surprise that the region closest to Germany specializes in Riesling. While there are a range of styles found here, the everyday Alsace Riesling is dry, with aromas of lime, green apple, and grapefruit, with smoky minerality and mouth-watering acidity.

AW   LIME, GREEN APPLE, GRAPEFRUIT ZEST, LEMON VERBANA, SMOKE

White Burgundy

The Côte de Beaune region in Burgundy produces some of the top Chardonnay wines in the world. Wines are often oak-aged, where controlled oxidation produces wines with rich nut and vanilla flavors alongside notes of apple, melon, and white flowers.

FW   YELLOW APPLE, ACACIA BLOSSOM, HONEYDEW MELON, VANILLA, HAZELNUT

Good to Know

▐▌ A "vin de terroir" is a regionally labeled wine with rules defining which grapes are used and how it's made.

▐▌ Most high-end French wines are labeled by appellation ("vin de terroir") and not by variety—except for Alsace.

Côtes de Provence Rosé

One of the world's foremost production regions for rosé produces delicate rosé wines with a pale copper hue. Some of the best wines come from the Côtes de Provence appellation and often have a proportion of Rolle (aka Vermentino) in the blend.

 RS STRAWBERRY, CELERY, WATERMELON, CLAY POT, ORANGE ZEST

Beaujolais

Just south of Burgundy, you'll find decomposing pink granite soils that produce high-quality Gamay wines. The best wines come from the 10 Crus that produce wines with a striking resemblance to Red Burgundy, but for a fraction of the price.

 LR CHERRY, VIOLET, PEONY, PEACH, POTTING SOIL

Red Burgundy

Pinot Noir from the Côte de Nuits and Côte de Beaune are some of the highest-priced wines in the world. What makes them intriguing are their unmistakable earth and floral aromas. Seek out the Bourgogne regional wines on good vintages for a taste.

 LR RED CHERRY, HIBISCUS, MUSHROOM, POTTING SOIL, DRIED LEAVES

Southern Rhône Blends

The dominant grapes in this Southern French favorite include Grenache, Syrah, and Mourvèdre. Red wines deliver bold stewed raspberry, fig, and blackberry flavors with subtle notes of dried herbs and cured meats.

 MR PLUM SAUCE, ANISE, GRAPHITE, LAVENDER, TOBACCO

Northern Rhône Syrah

The world's obsession with Syrah was inspired by the wines from the Northern Rhône. Vineyards grow along the slopes (called Côtes) of the Rhône river and are known for their savory fruit (think olive) and peppery aromas. Expect elegant, tart fruit paired with grippy tannins.

 FR OLIVE, PLUM, BLACK PEPPER, BLACKBERRY, MEAT JUICES

Red Bordeaux Blends

A wine that inspired the world's love affair with Cabernet Sauvignon and Merlot. The best values include the regional Bordeaux Supérieur appellation, which offers savory flavors of graphite, black currant, black cherry, and cigar supported by firm-but-balanced tannins.

 FR BLACK CURRANT, BLACK CHERRY, PENCIL LEAD, LOAM, TOBACCO

Reading a Label

The secret to becoming confident with French wine is to know that most French wines are labeled by region or *appellation*. Each appellation has a set of rules that dictate what grapes are inside the bottle.

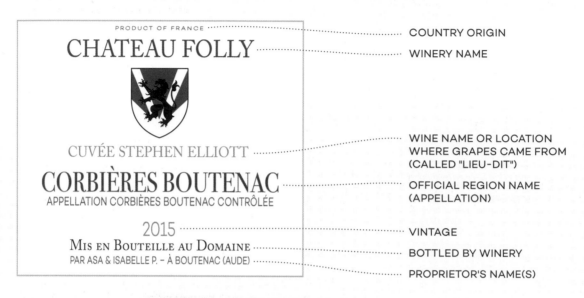

PRODUCT OF FRANCE ········· COUNTRY ORIGIN

CHATEAU FOLLY ········· WINERY NAME

CUVÉE STEPHEN ELLIOTT ········· WINE NAME OR LOCATION WHERE GRAPES CAME FROM (CALLED "LIEU-DIT")

CORBIÈRES BOUTENAC ········· OFFICIAL REGION NAME (APPELLATION)
APPELLATION CORBIÈRES BOUTENAC CONTRÔLÉE

2015 ········· VINTAGE
MIS EN BOUTEILLE AU DOMAINE ········· BOTTLED BY WINERY
PAR ASA & ISABELLE P. – À BOUTENAC (AUDE) ········· PROPRIETOR'S NAME(S)

AOP (AOC)

Appellation d'Origine Protégée/Appellation d'Origine Contrôlée: This is France's most rigid classification that specifies everything from the geographic area, the grapes allowed in the wine, the quality of those grapes and how the vineyards are planted, to the winemaking and aging processes used. There are ~329 appellations, each with a different set of rules overseen by the INAO—the French national committee for wine and alcoholic beverages.

IGP (Vin de Pays)

Indication Géographique Protégée: The everyday French wine. This regional designation is less strict, with more allowed grape varieties but also potentially more variability in quality. There are 74 geographical areas that include 150 unique designations. The most well known (and largest) IGPs include Comté Tolosan, Pays d'Oc, Côtes de Gascogne, and Val de Loire.

Vin de France

Basic table wines of France with no regional specificity. These wines represent the lowest-quality tier of French wine and often include the variety on the label and occassionally the vintage date.

Common Label Terms

2018

GRAND VIN de BOURGOGNE

CHASSAGNE-MONTRACHET
LES BLACHOT-DESSUS

APPELLATION CHASSAGNE-MONTRACHET 1ᴱᴿ CRU CONTROLÉE

Mis en Bouteille à la Proprieté
DOMAINE FOLLY et FILS
Proprietaire-Viticulteur à Chassagne-Montrachet (CÔTE-D'OR), France

CONTAINS SULFITES

750ML   13.5% ALC./VOL

Biologique: Organically produced.

Blanc de Blancs: A white sparkling wine made with 100% white grapes.

Blanc de Noirs: A term for white sparkling wine made with 100% black grapes.

Brut: A term for sweetness level in sparkling wine. Brut indicates a dry style.

Cépage: The grapes used in the wine (Encépagement is the proportions of the blend).

Château: A winery.

Clos: A walled vineyard or vineyard on the site of an ancient walled vineyard. Commonly used in Burgundy.

Côtes: Wines from a slope or hillside (contiguous)—usually along a river.

Coteaux: Wines from a grouping of slopes or hillsides (non-contiguous).

Cru: Translates to "growth" and indicates a vineyard or group of vineyards typically recognized for quality.

Cuvée: Translates to "vat" or "tank" but is used to denote a specific wine blend or batch.

Demi-Sec: Off-dry (lightly sweet).

Domaine: A winery estate with vineyards.

Doux: Sweet.

Élevé en fûts de chêne: Aged in oak.

Grand Cru: Translates to "Great Growth" and is used in Burgundy and Champagne to distinguish the region's best vineyards.

Grand Vin: Used in Bordeaux to indicate a winery's "first label" or best wine they produce. It's common for Bordeaux to have a 1st, 2nd, or 3rd label at varying price tiers.

Millésime: The vintage date. This term is commonly used in the Champagne region.

Mis en bouteille au château/domaine: Bottled at the winery.

Moelleux: Sweet.

Mousseux: Sparkling.

Non-filtré: An unfiltered wine.

Pétillant: Lightly sparkling.

Premiere Cru (1er Cru): Translates to "First Growth" and is the top-tier designation for producers in Bordeaux and the second-best designation for vineyards in Burgundy and Champagne.

Propriétaire: Owner of winery.

Sec: Dry (e.g., not sweet).

Supérieur: A regulatory term commonly used in Bordeaux to describe a wine with higher minimum alcohol and aging requirements than the base.

Sur Lie: A wine that is aged on lees (dead yeast particles), which are known to give a creamy/bready taste and increased body. This term is most commonly found with Muscadet of the Loire.

Vendangé à la main: Hand harvested.

Vieille Vignes: Old vines.

Vignoble: Vineyard.

Vin Doux Naturel (VDN): A wine that is fortified during fermentation (usually a sweet dessert wine).

Bordeaux

The vast majority of Bordeaux produces the eponymous red blend, which features Merlot, Cabernet Sauvignon, and Cabernet Franc. While the most treasured wineries (aka Château) command top prices, most wines can be found for great prices. You just need to know where to look.

Médoc (Left Bank)

The Médoc ("Meh-dok") focuses on Cabernet Sauvignon–based wines grown mostly in gravel and clay soils. Wines tend to deliver earthy fruit flavors, grippy tannin, and a medium to full body. Despite the earthy flavors, the style is clean and polished.

 BLACK CURRANT, BLACKBERRY BRAMBLE, CHARCOAL, ANISE, SMOKE

Libournais (Right Bank)

The Libournais region focuses on Merlot-based wines that, at their best, deliver bold cherry and tobacco flavors supported with refined, chocolatey tannins. The best vineyards are found in Pomerol and Saint-Émilion, where there is a prevalence of clay.

 BLACK CHERRY, TOASTED TOBACCO, PLUM, ANISE, COCOA POWDER

Bordeaux Blanc

Less than 10% of Bordeaux's production is dedicated to white wines made with Sauvignon Blanc, Sémillon and the rare Muscadelle. You'll find a great deal of white Bordeaux growing in the sandy-clay soils of Entre-Deux-Mers.

 GRAPEFRUIT, GOOSEBERRY, LIME, CHAMOMILE, CRUSHED ROCKS

Sauternais

Several subregions, including Sauternes, collect fog from the Garonne river, which causes grapes to grow a special kind of fungus called Botrytis cinerea (aka noble rot). The fungus concentrates the region's white grapes for exceptional sweet wines.

 APRICOT, MARMALADE, HONEY, GINGER, TROPICAL FRUIT

Classifications

Cru Classés *The most expensive wines of Bordeaux.*	**1855**	5-tier classification of 61 producers in Graves and Médoc and 26 producers in Sauternais made in 1855.
	Saint-Émilion	A classification of top-quality producers in Saint-Émilion that is revisited every 10 years.
	Graves	A classification of producers in Graves from 1953 (amended in 1959).
Crus *Médoc-only producer syndicates.*	**Bourgeois**	A group of producers in the Médoc that tests wines to meet quality criteria. A great Cru for hunting values.
	Artisans	A syndicate of small artisan producers of the Médoc.
Bordeaux *Regional wine designations and quality tiers.*	**Appellations**	Wines from a specific designated area (e.g., Blaye, Graves, etc.). There are 37 appellations in this tier.
	Supérieur	Regional wines with higher production standards than Bordeaux AOP.
	AOP	(AOC) Basic regional wines, including sparkling and rosé.

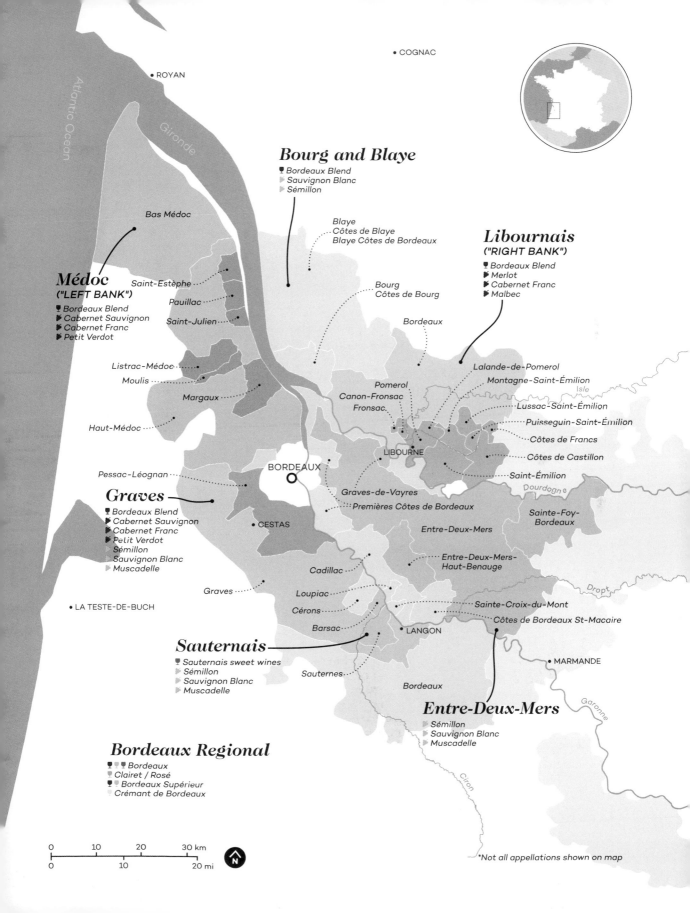

COGNAC

ROYAN

Atlantic Ocean

Gironde

Bourg and Blaye
🍷 *Bordeaux Blend*
🍃 *Sauvignon Blanc*
🍃 *Sémillon*

Bas Médoc

Blaye
Côtes de Blaye
Blaye Côtes de Bordeaux

Libournais
("RIGHT BANK")
🍷 *Bordeaux Blend*
🍇 *Merlot*
🍇 *Cabernet Franc*
🍇 *Malbec*

Médoc
("LEFT BANK")
🍷 *Bordeaux Blend*
🍇 *Cabernet Sauvignon*
🍇 *Cabernet Franc*
🍇 *Petit Verdot*

Saint-Estèphe

Pauillac

Saint-Julien

Bourg
Côtes de Bourg

Bordeaux

Lalande-de-Pomerol
Montagne-Saint-Émilion

Isle

Listrac-Médoc

Moulis

Margaux

Pomerol
Canon-Fronsac
Fronsac

Lussac-Saint-Émilion

Puisseguin-Saint-Émilion

Côtes de Francs

Haut-Médoc

Côtes de Castillon

LIBOURNE

Saint-Émilion

Pessac-Léognan

BORDEAUX

Dourdogne

Graves
🍷 *Bordeaux Blend*
🍇 *Cabernet Sauvignon*
🍇 *Cabernet Franc*
🍇 *Petit Verdot*
🍃 *Sémillon*
🍃 *Sauvignon Blanc*
🍃 *Muscadelle*

Graves-de-Vayres

Premières Côtes de Bordeaux

Sainte-Foy-
Bordeaux

CESTAS

Entre-Deux-Mers

Entre-Deux-Mers-
Haut-Benauge

Cadillac

Drop

LA TESTE-DE-BUCH

Graves

Loupiac

Cérons

Barsac

Sainte-Croix-du-Mont

Côtes de Bordeaux St-Macaire

LANGON

MARMANDE

Sauternais
🍷 *Sauternais sweet wines*
🍃 *Sémillon*
🍃 *Sauvignon Blanc*
🍃 *Muscadelle*

Sauternes

Bordeaux

Garonne

Entre-Deux-Mers
🍃 *Sémillon*
🍃 *Sauvignon Blanc*
🍃 *Muscadelle*

Bordeaux Regional
🍷🍷🍷 *Bordeaux*
🍷 *Clairet / Rosé*
🍷🍷 *Bordeaux Supérieur*
🍾 *Crémant de Bordeaux*

Ciron

0   10   20   30 km
0   10   20 mi

N

*Not all appellations shown on map

Burgundy

(French: "Bourgogne") Burgundy's vineyards can trace their origins back to medieval times, when Cistercian monks planted grapevines in walled vineyards called clos ("klo"). What did the monks plant? Chardonnay and Pinot Noir, of course! These two grapes are now world renowned and Burgundy is considered the benchmark of quality.

Pinot Noir

Along a thin, sloped strip of land called the Côte d'Or, or "golden slope," grows the most sought-after Pinot Noir vineyards in the world. On a great vintage, wines can be highly aromatic, bursting with red fruits, flowers, and subtle mushroom-like funkiness.

 CHERRY, HIBISCUS, ROSE PETAL, MUSHROOM, POTTING SOIL

Chardonnay

Chardonnay is the most planted variety and offers two primary styles. Wines from the Côte de Beaune tend to be richer, using oak aging with flavors of golden apple and hazelnut. The Mâconnais and basic Bourgogne Blanc are lighter and typically lightly oaked.

 YELLOW APPLE, BAKED QUINCE, APPLE BLOSSOM, VANILLA, TRUFFLE

Chablis

Chablis is a much cooler growing region that focuses on Chardonnay. The majority of Chablis is made in a lean and minerally style without oak. However, if you get into the higher end, you'll discover the 10 Grand Cru vineyard sites are bolder and often oak-aged.

 QUINCE, PASSIONFRUIT, LIME ZEST, BRIE RIND, APPLE BLOSSOM

Crémant de Bourgogne

You can find great sparkling wines using the same grapes and process as Champagne under the Crémant de Bourgogne appellation. The recent additions of aging regimes including Éminent (aged 24 months) and Grand Éminent (aged 36 months) promise increased nuttiness.

 WHITE PEACH, APPLE, CHEESE RIND, BAKED BREAD, RAW ALMOND

Classifications

Crus *The most prestigious wines of Burgundy.*	**Grand Cru**	Wines from Burgundy's top vineyard plots (called *climats "klee-maht"*). There are 33 Grand Crus in the Côte d'Or and about 60% of the production is Pinot Noir.
	Premier Cru (1er)	Wines made from exceptional climats of Burgundy. There are 640 official Premier Cru plots. Wines may or may not list the climat on the label but will list the village name and "Premier Cru" or "1er."
Villages *Quality wines from focused areas.*	**Village or Commune Name**	Wines from a village or commune of Burgundy. There are a total of 44 village wines of Burgundy, which include Chablis, Pommard, Pouilly-Fuissé, and the subregional designations of Côte-de-Beaune-Villages and Mâcon-Villages.
Appellation *Introductory wines.*	**"Bourgogne"**	Wines from the overarching *Bourgogne* appellation labeled as Bourgogne, Bourgogne Aligoté, Crémant de Bourgogne, and Bourgogne Hautes Côtes de Beaune.

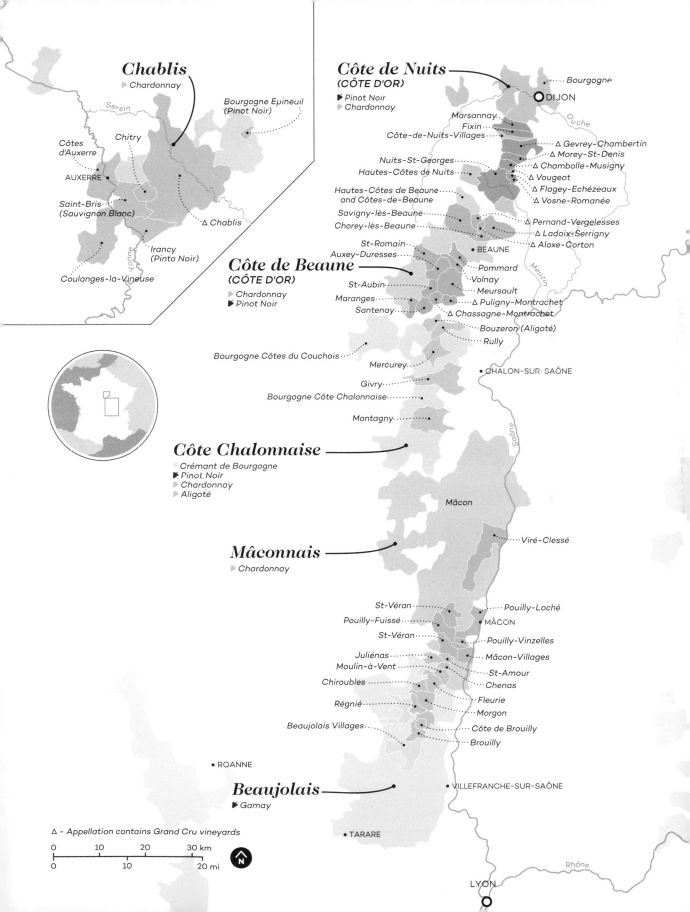

Chablis
▶ Chardonnay

Serein

*Bourgogne Epineuil
(Pinot Noir)*

Chitry

Côtes
d'Auxerre

AUXERRE

Saint-Bris
(Sauvignon Blanc)

△ Chablis

Irancy
(Pinto Noir)

Coulanges-la-Vineuse

Yonne

Côte de Nuits
(CÔTE D'OR)
▶ Pinot Noir
▶ Chardonnay

Bourgogne

DIJON

Ouche

Marsannay
Fixin
Côte-de-Nuits-Villages

Nuits-St-Georges
Hautes-Côtes de Nuits

△ Gevrey-Chambertin
△ Morey-St-Denis
△ Chambolle-Musigny
△ Vougeot
△ Flagey-Echézeaux
△ Vosne-Romanée

Hautes-Côtes de Beaune
and Côtes-de-Beaune
Savigny-lès-Beaune
Chorey-lès-Beaune

△ Pernand-Vergelesses
△ Ladoix-Serrigny
△ Aloxe-Corton

St-Romain
Auxey-Duresses

BEAUNE

Meuzin

Côte de Beaune
(CÔTE D'OR)
▶ Chardonnay
▶ Pinot Noir

St-Aubin

Maranges

Santenay

Pommard
Volnay
Meursault
△ Puligny-Montrachet
△ Chassagne-Montrachet
Bouzeron (Aligoté)
Rully

Bourgogne Côtes du Couchois

Mercurey

CHALON-SUR-SAÔNE

Givry

Bourgogne Côte Chalonnaise

Montagny

Saône

Côte Chalonnaise
▢ Crémant de Bourgogne
▶ Pinot Noir
▶ Chardonnay
▶ Aligoté

Mâcon

Viré-Clessé

Mâconnais
▶ Chardonnay

St-Véran

Pouilly-Fuissé

St-Véran

Juliénas
Moulin-à-Vent
Chiroubles

Régnié

Beaujolais Villages

Pouilly-Loché

MÂCON

Pouilly-Vinzelles
Mâcon-Villages
St-Amour
Chenas
Fleurie
Morgon
Côte de Brouilly
Brouilly

● ROANNE

● VILLEFRANCHE-SUR-SAÔNE

Beaujolais
▶ Gamay

● TARARE

△ - Appellation contains Grand Cru vineyards

| 0 | 10 | 20 | 30 km |
| 0 | 10 | | 20 mi |

N

Rhône

LYON

Champagne

As one of the coolest growing regions of France, Champagne has historically struggled with ripening grapes. Perhaps it's because of this that cellar masters in the 1600s, like Dom Perignon, focused on cutting-edge wine production, leading to the popularization of sparkling wines. There are three primary grapes of Champagne: Chardonnay, Pinot Noir, and Pinot Meunier.

Non Vintage (NV)

Cellar masters are skilled at creating a consistent house blend year in and year out. This is achieved through blending different vats, or "cuvées," from various vineyards and vintages. Non-vintage Champagne is required to age for a minimum of 15 months.

 QUINCE, PEAR, CITRUS ZEST, CHEESE RIND, SMOKE

Blanc de Blancs

Blanc de Blancs means "white of whites" and is a Champagne produced with only white grapes. The majority of Blanc de Blancs are 100% Chardonnay, although a few exceptions include the rare white grapes of Arbane, Pinot Blanc, and Petit Meslier.

 YELLOW APPLE, LEMON CURD, HONEYDEW MELON, HONEYSUCKLE, TOAST

Blanc de Noirs

Blanc de Noirs means "white of blacks" and is a Champagne produced with only black (red) grapes. You'll find these wines to be made with varying proportions of Pinot Noir and Pinot Meunier. Wines tend to have a more golden hue and more red fruit aromas.

 WHITE CHERRY, RED CURRANT, LEMON ZEST, MUSHROOM, SMOKE

Vintage

On very good vintages Cellar masters often create a single-vintage Champagne. While the style varies depending on the producer, they often have more aged flavors of nuts and baked fruits. Vintage Champagne is required to be aged a minimum of 36 months.

 APRICOT, WHITE CHERRY, BRIOCHE, MARZIPAN, SMOKE

Classifications

Crus *Site-specific Champagne.*	**Grand Cru**	The 17 Grand Crus of Champagne are considered to be the best sites for growing Chardonnay, Pinot Noir, and Pinot Meunier. Wines are made into both vintage and non-vintage styles.
	Premier Cru	There are 42 sites considered to be exceptional that garner the Premier Cru (1er) classification.
Vintage *Single-vintage Champagne.*	**"Millesime"**	A Champagne wine produced from a single vintage that's required to age for 36 months. Aging increases tertiary flavors associated with fine Champagne, including flavors of marzipan, brioche, toast, and nuts.
Non-Vintage *Multi-vintage Champagne.*	**"NV"**	The wine maker, or "chef de cave," blends wines from several vintages to produce a consistent house style year in and year out. Non-vintage wines are required to age at least 15 months.

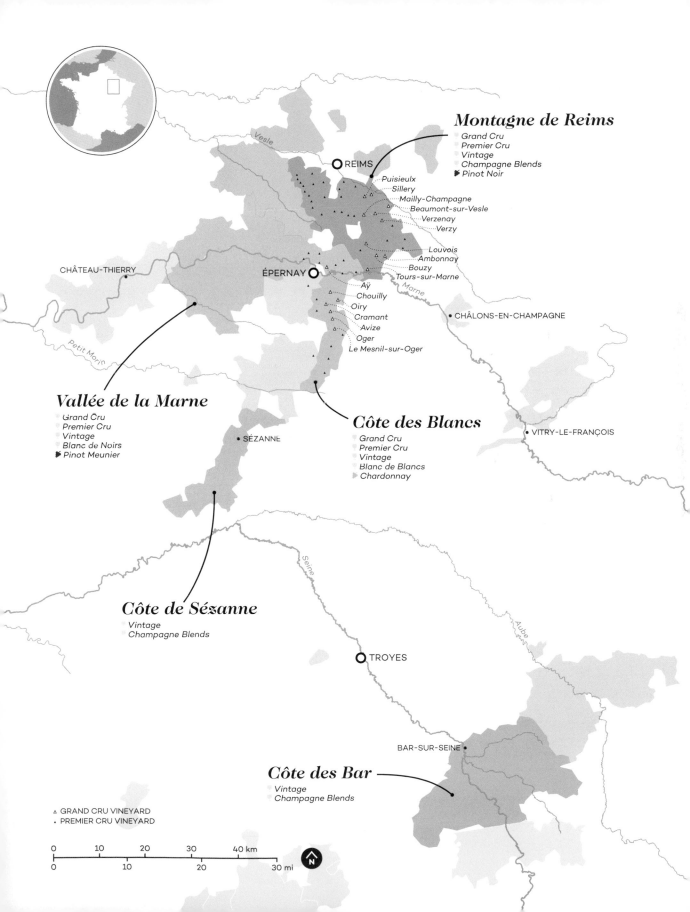

Montagne de Reims
- Grand Cru
- Premier Cru
- Vintage
- Champagne Blends
- ▶ Pinot Noir

REIMS

Vesle

Puisieulx
Sillery
Mailly-Champagne
Beaumont-sur-Vesle
Verzenay
Verzy

Louvois
Ambonnay
Bouzy
Tours-sur-Marne

ÉPERNAY

Aÿ
Chouilly
Oiry
Cramant
Avize
Oger
Le Mesnil-sur-Oger

Marne

CHÂTEAU-THIERRY

CHÂLONS-EN-CHAMPAGNE

Petit Morin

Vallée de la Marne
- Grand Cru
- Premier Cru
- Vintage
- Blanc de Noirs
- ▶ Pinot Meunier

Côte des Blancs
- Grand Cru
- Premier Cru
- Vintage
- Blanc de Blancs
- ▶ Chardonnay

SÉZANNE

VITRY-LE-FRANÇOIS

Seine

Côte de Sézanne
- Vintage
- Champagne Blends

TROYES

Aube

Côte des Bar
- Vintage
- Champagne Blends

BAR-SUR-SEINE

△ GRAND CRU VINEYARD
• PREMIER CRU VINEYARD

0   10   20   30   40 km
0   10   20   30 mi

N

Languedoc-Roussillon

The Languedoc-Roussillon combines the Languedoc and Roussillon regions into the largest vineyard area of France, and it's a great place to hunt for values. Languedoc specializes in red blends made of Syrah, Grenache, Mourvèdre, and Carignan. Additional surprises include great sparkling wines (Crémant de Limoux), dessert wines, and zesty whites.

Languedoc Red Blends

Syrah, Grenache, and Mourvèdre, along with Carignan and Cinsault (a lighter red), are the dominant grapes here. The regions of Saint-Chinian, Faugères, Minervois, Corbières, Fitou, and Pic St. Loup produce incredible quality usually for a fraction of the price as neighboring Rhône.

 BLACK OLIVE, CASSIS, PEPPER, DRIED HERBS, CRUSHED ROCKS

Côtes du Roussillon, etc.

Roussillon lies next to the Spanish border and historically the region was famous for dessert wines made with Muscat Blanc and Grenache. Today, you'll also find excellent dry red wines from places like Coullioure and Côtes du Roussillon Villages, where Grenache features prominently.

 RASPBERRY, CLOVE, OLIVE, COCOA, CRUSHED ROCKS

Languedoc White Blends

Southern France grows an incredible diversity of white grapes, and the best for the warm Mediterranean climate include Marsanne, Roussanne, Grenache Blanc, Picpoul, Muscat Blanc, and Vermentino (also the rare Clairette and Bourboulenc!). Wines are often blends of multiple varieties, so look into the producer to determine the taste.

 FLAVORS VARY

Crémant de Limoux

The first sparkling wines of France can be traced back to 1531 from the Abbey in St-Hilaire in Limoux (not Champagne!). Crémant de Limoux is made with Chardonnay and Chenin Blanc. Try the more rare Blanquette Methode Ancestrale made with regional Mauzac grapes for a window into Limoux's past.

 BAKED APPLE, LEMON, LIME ZEST MASCARPONE, PEACH SKIN

Picpoul de Pinet

Picpoul (aka Piquepoul) means "stings the lip," which likely refers to the grape's naturally high acidity. Wines from Picpoul de Pinet are refreshing and light-bodied with mouthwatering acidity. This wine is an awesome alternative to Pinot Gris and Sauvignon Blanc.

 HONEYDEW MELON, PRESERVED LEMON, LIME, APPLE BLOSSOM, CRUSHED ROCK

Dessert Wines

Roussillon produces several oustanding dessert wines with Grenache and Muscat Blanc. Grapes are picked ripe and then partially fermented, at which point eau de vie (neutral grape spirit) is added, creating a richly textured, grape-sweetened, fortified wine. The French call this winemaking method "Vin Doux Naturel" (or VDN).

- Maury
- Rivesaltes
- Banyuls

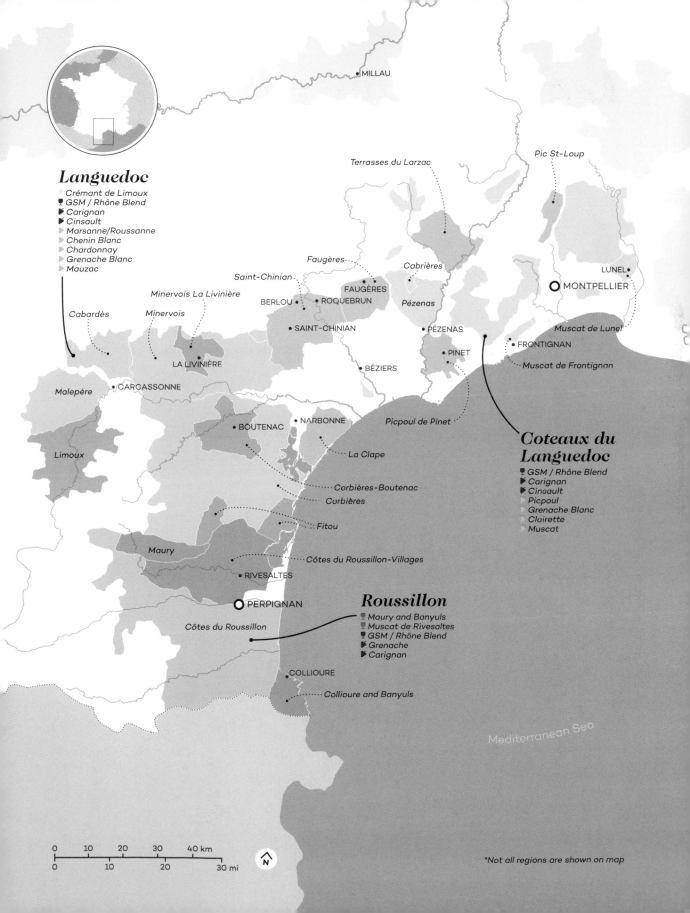

MILLAU

Pic St-Loup

Terrasses du Larzac

Languedoc

🍷 Crémant de Limoux
🍷 GSM / Rhône Blend
🍇 Carignan
🍇 Cinsault
🍷 Marsanne/Roussanne
🍷 Chenin Blanc
🍷 Chardonnay
🍷 Grenache Blanc
🍷 Mauzac

Faugères

Cabrières

LUNEL

Minervois La Livinière

FAUGÈRES

Pézenas

◎ MONTPELLIER

Cabardès

BERLOU ● ● ROQUEBRUN

SAINT-CHINIAN

Saint-Chinian

Muscat de Lunel

Minervois

● SAINT-CHINIAN

PÉZENAS

● FRONTIGNAN

Malepère

● LA LIVINIÈRE

BÉZIERS

● PINET

Muscat de Frontignan

● CARCASSONNE

Picpoul de Pinet

Coteaux du Languedoc

Limoux

● BOUTENAC

● NARBONNE

La Clape

🍷 GSM / Rhône Blend
🍇 Carignan
🍇 Cinsault
🍷 Picpoul
🍷 Grenache Blanc
🍷 Clairette
🍷 Muscat

Corbières-Boutenac

Corbières

● Fitou

Maury

Côtes du Roussillon-Villages

● RIVESALTES

Roussillon

● PERPIGNAN

🍷 Maury and Banyuls
🍷 Muscat de Rivesaltes
🍷 GSM / Rhône Blend
🍇 Grenache
🍇 Carignan

Côtes du Roussillon

● COLLIOURE

Collioure and Banyuls

Mediterranean Sea

0   10   20   30   40 km
0   10   20   30 mi

N

Not all regions are shown on map

Loire Valley

The Loire Valley is a large region that follows the longest river of France and its many tributaries. As a cooler-climate growing area, the Loire is an exceptional place to find lean, racy white wines including those of Chenin Blanc, Sauvignon Blanc, and Muscadet. Red varieties include Cabernet Franc, Gamay, and Côt (Malbec), which produce herbaceous, rustic reds and fruity, dry rosé.

Sauvignon Blanc

Touraine and Centre have a keen focus on Sauvignon Blanc. Of the many appellations that produce Sauvignon Blanc, the most well known wines hail from the vineyards around Sancerre and Pouilly Fumé. It's around this area that Sauvignon Blanc produces higher ripeness and flavors of flint and smoke.

 LW RIPE GOOSEBERRRY, QUINCE, GRAPEFRUIT, FLINT, SMOKE

Chenin Blanc

Chenin Blanc is made into a myriad of styles from dry and sparkling to sweet and still. The grape grows primarily in Touraine and Anjou-Saumur and is found in Crémant de Loire. Notable regions include Vouvray, Montlouis sur Loire, Savennières (oxidative style), and Quarts de Chaume (dessert wines).

 LW PEAR, HONEYSUCKLE, QUINCE, APPLE, BEESWAX

Muscadet (Melon)

Close to the coast, the Nantais region is known for its bracing, minerally white wines made with Melon. About 70–80% of the production is labeled Muscadet de Sèvre et Maine and many producers age their wines on the lees, or "sur lie," to give them a rounder mouthfeel and yeasty aromas.

 LW LIME PEEL, SEA SHELL, GREEN APPLE, PEAR, LAGER

Cabernet Franc

Cabernet Franc (aka Breton) grows throughout the Loire, most notably in the Middle Loire around Chinon and Bourgueil ("bor-goy"). The region is cool, so reds are spicy and herbaceous with distinct bell pepper notes. Surprisingly, wines age quite well, revealing soft baked plum and tobacco flavors.

 MR ROASTED PEPPER, RASPBERRY SAUCE, SOUR CHERRY, IRON, DRIED HERBS

Côt (Malbec)

This is not your typical Argentina Malbec! In the Loire Valley, Malbec is called Côt ("coat") and can be found growing in the Touraine appellation. Wines are known for their rustic taste profile with earthy fruit flavors and herbal notes. Try pairing Côt and cassoulet!

 MR GREEN OLIVE, BLACK CURRANT, TOBACCO, BLACKBERRY BRAMBLE, DRIED HERBS

Loire Sparkling Wines

The Loire Valley has many sparkling wines, including those labeled Crémant de Loire, Vouvray, and Saumur. Sparkling production is found mostly in the Middle Loire and typically features Chenin Blanc, Chardonnay, and Cabernet Franc (for rosé). Wines tend to deliver tart, fresh fruit flavors. Those labeled Pétillant-naturel are made with an ancient method that results in a cloudy, yeasty style with delicate bubbles.

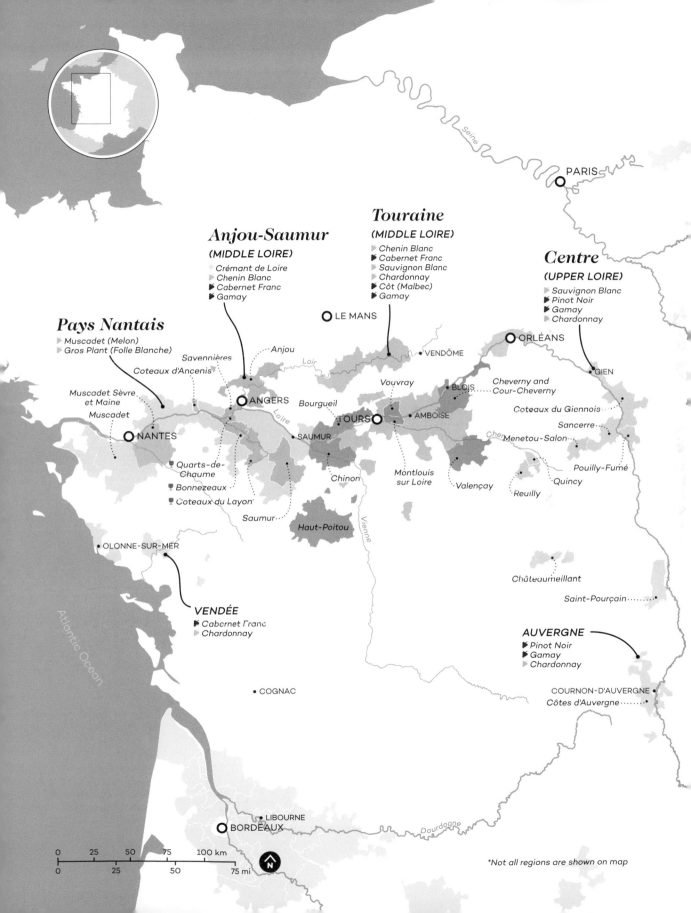

Anjou-Saumur
(MIDDLE LOIRE)

▷ Crémant de Loire
▷ Chenin Blanc
▶ Cabernet Franc
▶ Gamay

Touraine
(MIDDLE LOIRE)

▷ Chenin Blanc
▶ Cabernet Franc
▷ Sauvignon Blanc
▷ Chardonnay
▶ Côt (Malbec)
▶ Gamay

Centre
(UPPER LOIRE)

▷ Sauvignon Blanc
▶ Pinot Noir
▶ Gamay
▷ Chardonnay

Pays Nantais

▷ Muscadet (Melon)
▷ Gros Plant (Folle Blanche)

Savennières
Coteaux d'Ancenis
Anjou
Loir
LE MANS
VENDÔME
Cheverny and
Cour-Cheverny
ORLÉANS
GIEN

Muscadet Sèvre
et Maine
Muscadet
ANGERS
Bourgueil
Loire
Vouvray
BLOIS
Coteaux du Giennois

NANTES
SAUMUR
TOURS
AMBOISE
Sancerre
Menetou-Salon

Quarts-de-
Chaume
Bonnezeaux
Coteaux du Layon
Chinon
Montlouis
sur Loire
Cher
Pouilly-Fumé

Saumur
Valençay
Quincy

Haut-Poitou
Reuilly

OLONNE-SUR-MER

VENDÉE

▶ Cabernet Franc
▷ Chardonnay

Châteaumeillant

Saint-Pourçain

AUVERGNE

▶ Pinot Noir
▶ Gamay
▷ Chardonnay

COGNAC

COURNON-D'AUVERGNE
Côtes d'Auvergne

Vienne

Atlantic Ocean

LIBOURNE
BORDEAUX
Dourdogne

Seine
PARIS

| 0 | 25 | 50 | 75 | 100 km |
| 0 | 25 | 50 | 75 mi |

N

*Not all regions are shown on map

Rhône Valley

Grenache, Syrah, and Mourvèdre are the primary varieties in the Rhône Valley. In the South, Côtes du Rhône blends (red and rosé) can feature up to 18 different grapes in a blend! In the Northern Rhône, single-varietal Syrah is the focus, along with scant plantings of Viognier.

Syrah

Many look to the Northern Rhône regions of Côte Rôtie, Hermitage, and Cornas for the ultimate expression of Syrah. Wines are bold with high tannin and savory olive, plum sauce, and bacon fat flavors. Stock up on Saint-Joseph and Crozes-Hermitage on good vintages for great values.

 OLIVE TAPENADE, PLUM SAUCE, BLACK PEPPER, BACON FAT, DRIED HERBS

Rhône / GSM Blend

Grenache features prominently in the Southern Rhône GSM Blend, but the region is home to many rare varieties including Cinsault, Counoise, Terret Noir, Muscardin, and Marselan, which are often found in small amounts in the fruity-yet-rustic red blend.

 GRILLED PLUM, TOBACCO, RASPBERRY SAUCE, DRIED HERBS, VANILLA

Marsanne Blend

Many white varieties can be found growing across the Rhône valley but the two used most commonly in Côtes du Rhône whites are Marsanne and Roussanne. Marsanne blends tend to be rich and fruity with bolder peach flavors along with an oily texture that finishes similar to oaked Chardonnay.

 APPLE, MANDARIN ORANGE, WHITE PEACH, BEESWAX, ACACIA

Viognier

The two tiny regions of Condrieu and Château-Grillet produce 100% Viognier. Wines often have noticeable sweetness that many believe is the classic expression of this variety. Because of Viognier's increasing international popularity, we're likely to see more Viognier in years to come.

 PEACH, TANGERINE, HONEYSUCKLE, ROSE, RAW ALMOND

Classifications

Crus *17 crus make the top-quality Rhône wines.*	**Northern Rhône**	8 crus make mostly Syrah and 2 others focus on Viognier (Condrieu and Château-Grillet). St-Peray does sparkling.
	Southern Rhône	9 crus south of Montélimar produce red, white, rosé, and sweet wines. Wines are labeled by cru (see map).
Côtes du Rhône Villages *High-quality Southern Rhône blends.*	**Southern Rhône**	Côtes du Rhône Villages is at least 50% Grenache. Of 95 districts that make this wine, 21 may append their village name to the label (e.g., "Chusclan Côtes du Rhône Villages"). Sometimes a village gets upgraded to a cru!
Appellations *Basic regional wines.*	**Côtes du Rhône and others**	171 districts produce basic Côtes du Rhône wines. Additionally, the appellations of Ventoux, Luberon, Grignan les Adhémar, Costières de Nîmes, Clairette de Bellegarde, and Côtes du Vivarais fall into this category.

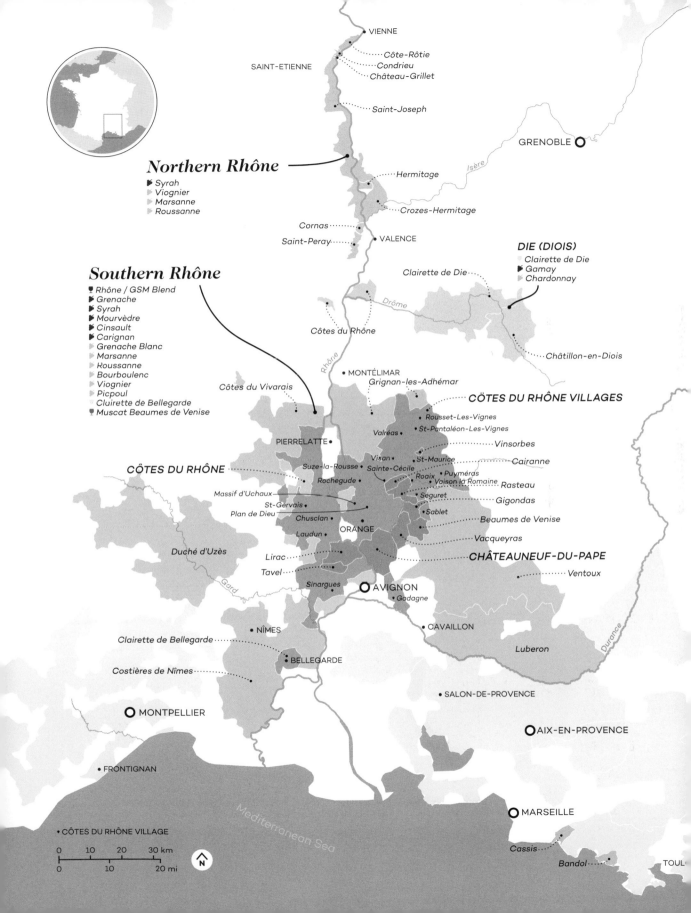

VIENNE

SAINT-ETIENNE

············ Côte-Rôtie
············ Condrieu
············ Château-Grillet

············ Saint-Joseph

GRENOBLE ○

Isère

Northern Rhône

🍷 *Syrah*
🍷 *Viognier*
🍷 *Marsanne*
🍷 *Roussanne*

············ Hermitage

············ Crozes-Hermitage

Cornas ·········
Saint-Peray ········· • VALENCE

DIE (DIOIS)

▫ *Clairette de Die*
🍷 *Gamay*
🍷 *Chardonnay*

Clairette de Die ·········

Drôme

············ Châtillon-en-Diois

Southern Rhône

🍷 *Rhône / GSM Blend*
🍷 *Grenache*
🍷 *Syrah*
🍷 *Mourvèdre*
🍷 *Cinsault*
🍷 *Carignan*
▫ *Grenache Blanc*
▫ *Marsanne*
▫ *Roussanne*
▫ *Bourboulenc*
▫ *Viognier*
▫ *Picpoul*
▫ *Cluirette de Bellegarde*
🍷 *Muscat Beaumes de Venise*

Côtes du Rhône ·········

Rhône

• MONTÉLIMAR
Grignan-les-Adhémar

CÔTES DU RHÔNE VILLAGES

Côtes du Vivarais ·········

PIERRELATTE

Valréas •
Rousset-Les-Vignes •
• St-Pantaléon-Les-Vignes
············ Vinsorbes
············ Cairanne

CÔTES DU RHÔNE

Visan •
Suze-la-Rousse •
Rochegude •
Sainte-Cécile •
St-Maurice •
Roaix • • Puyméras
• Vaison la Romaine
············ Rasteau

Massif d'Uchaux
St-Gervais •
Plan de Dieu
Chusclan •
Laudun •
Seguret •
Sablet •
············ Gigondas
············ Beaumes de Venise

ORANGE

············ Vacqueyras

CHÂTEAUNEUF-DU-PAPE

Duché d'Uzès

Lirac ·········
Tavel ·········
Sinargues •
············ Ventoux

AVIGNON ◎
• Gadagne

Gard

• NÎMES

Clairette de Bellegarde ·········

Costières de Nîmes ·········

BELLEGARDE •

• CAVAILLON

Luberon

Durance

• SALON-DE-PROVENCE

○ MONTPELLIER

◎ AIX-EN-PROVENCE

• FRONTIGNAN

◎ MARSEILLE

Mediterranean Sea

• CÔTES DU RHÔNE VILLAGE

Cassis ·········

Bandol ·········

TOUL

0 10 20 30 km
0   10   20 mi

⊙ N

Germany

The land of Riesling

The Germans have championed single-varietal wines since the first mass plantings of Riesling at Schloss Johannisberg in 1720 (in Rheingau). Since then, Germany has become the world's top Riesling producer, developing a wide range of styles from dry and lean to succulently sweet. Beyond Riesling, the country's cool climate is ideal for light red wines and aromatic whites. And, in recent years, the Germans have lead the way for Europe in their focus on organic and biodynamic wine production.

Wine Regions

Germany has a total of 13 wine regions, or anbaugebiete ("ahn-bow-jeh-beet"), as they're called. The majority of German wine production is found in the Southwestern part of the country.

- In the far southern regions of Baden, Württemberg, and parts of Pfalz, you'll see a strong focus on red wines, particularly Pinot Noir and Blaufränkisch.

- Rheingau, Rheinhessen, Nahe, and Mosel Valley produce the most Riesling. Some of the world's top Riesling wines come from Rheingau and Mosel Valley.

- The Ahr is a tiny region noted in particular for exceptional Pinot Noir.

- Finally, the satellite regions of Sachsen and Saale-Unstrut make remarkable Pinot Blanc.

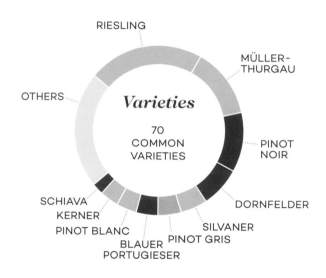

Varieties

70 COMMON VARIETIES

RIESLING · MÜLLER-THURGAU · PINOT NOIR · DORNFELDER · SILVANER · PINOT GRIS · BLAUER PORTUGIESER · PINOT BLANC · KERNER · SCHIAVA · OTHERS

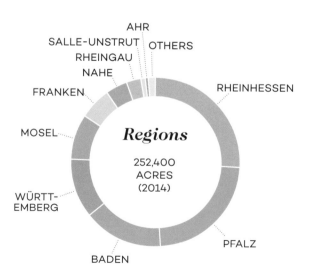

Regions

252,400 ACRES (2014)

AHR · SALLE-UNSTRUT · OTHERS · RHEINGAU · NAHE · FRANKEN · MOSEL · WÜRTT-EMBERG · BADEN · PFALZ · RHEINHESSEN

○ BREMEN

BERLIN ○
● POTSDAM

○ HANNOVER

Sachsen
▶ Müller-Thurgau
▶ Riesling

Saale-Unstrut
▶ Müller-Thurgau
▶ Pinot Blanc

○ LEIPZIG

DRESDEN ○

Mittelrhein
▶ Riesling

COLOGNE ○

Ahr
▶ Pinot Noir
BONN ○

Rheingau
▶ Riesling
▶ Pinot Noir

Rheinhessen
▶ Müller-Thurgau
▶ Riesling
▶ Dornfelder
▶ Silvaner
▶ Blauer Portugieser

Franken
▶ Müller-Thurgau
▶ Silvaner
▶ Bacchus

Mosel
▶ Riesling
▶ Müller-Thurgau
▶ Elbing

FRANKFURT ○
WIESBADEN ●
● MAINZ

● WURZBURG

Nahe
▶ Riesling
▶ Müller-Thurgau
▶ Dornfelder
▶ Silvaner

○ MANNHEIM
● HEIDELBERG

Hessische Bergstrasse
▶ Riesling
▶ Pinot Noir

Pfalz
▶ Riesling
▶ Dornfelder
▶ Müller-Thurgau
▶ Blauer Portugieser
▶ Pinot Noir

● KARLSRUHE

STUTTGART ○

Württemberg
▶ Trollinger (Schiava)
▶ Riesling
▶ Pinot Meunier
▶ Blaufränkisch
▶ Pinot Noir
▶ Dornfelder

● STRASBOURG

Baden
▶ Pinot Noir
▶ Müller-Thurgau
▶ Pinot Gris
▶ Pinot Blanc
▶ Chasselas

○ MUNICH

● FREIBURG

BASEL ●

| 0 | 25 | 50 | 75 | 100 km |

| 0 | 25 | 50 | 75 mi |

N

Wines to Explore

Beyond Riesling, there are several other wine varieties that excel in Germany's cooler climates, including fine reds like Blaufränkisch and Pinot Noir. What's interesting is the distinct spice flavor that carries through all the wines in the country and ties them together.

Sweet Pradikat Riesling

The late-harvested styles of Spätlese, Auslese, BA, and TBA (see p. 239) produce some of the most sought-after sweet Riesling wines in the world. These wines offer surprising depth with contrasting sweet and sour tastes and heady aromas of apricots, lime, and honey.

 APRICOT, HONEY, LIME, YOUNG COCONUT, TARRAGON

Dry Riesling

Dry styles of Riesling are becoming increasingly popular in Germany. You can identify a dry Prädikat Riesling by the term "Trocken" on the label or by investigating the alcohol level. Higher ABV levels typically indicate a more dry style of Riesling.

LW HONEYDEW MELON, WHITE PEACH, LIME, JASMINE, SMOKE

VDP Riesling

An invite-only grower association known to contain some of the best wineries in Germany. VDP also classifies vineyards. The top level is called Grosses Gewächs ("grand growth") and a first-quality vineyard is called Erstes Gewächs ("first growth").

 VARIOUS STYLES AND FLAVORS

Silvaner

Silvaner is a great wine often found at a superb value. The primary regions producing it include Rheinhessen and Franken (where wines are bottled in stubby, green *bocksbeutels*). The best wines offer enticing aromas of sweet stone fruits contrasted with flinty minerality.

LW PEACH, PASSIONFRUIT, ORANGE BLOSSOM, THYME, FLINT

Grauburgunder

(aka Pinot Gris) In Germany, Pinot Gris is often very light-bodied with lovely floral notes accenting flavors of white peach, pear, and minerals. The heightened acidity gives the wine a tingly quality that's complemented with a lush, somewhat oily mid-palate.

 LW WHITE PEACH, OIL, ASIAN PEAR, LIME, WHITE FLOWERS

Weißburgunder

(aka Pinot Blanc) There are many shared flavors between Pinot Gris and Pinot Blanc but overall, Pinot Blanc is much more delicate and subtle in its flavoring. If there is any single wine to pair with high tea and cucumber sandwiches, Pinot Blanc is it.

 LW WHITE PEACH, WHITE FLOWERS, GREEN APPLE, LIME, FLINT

Good to Know

▮▮ Pradikätswein (QmP) wines are not allowed to sweeten grape must (e.g., chaptalize) before/during fermentation.

▮▮ Quality for German wine truly starts at the Qualitätswein (QbA) level and above.

Müller-Thurgau

A cross between Madeleine Angevine and Riesling that ripens a little earlier and thus grows well in Germany's cooler sites. Wines have slightly more tropical fruit notes with slightly less acidity than Riesling, but offer a similar flavor profile at a better price.

 RIPE PEACH, ORANGE BLOSSOM, OIL, LEMON, DRIED APRICOT

Sekt

While there is still some low-quality Sekt in Germany, most isn't exported. The Sekt with amazing potential are those wines labeled Traditionelle Flaschengärung (traditional method) and made with Pinot varieties and Chardonnay. Look into the Pfalz and Rheingau for quality.

 BAKED APPLE, WHITE CHERRY, MUSHROOM, WAX LIPS, LIME

Spätburgunder

(aka Pinot Noir) The warmer regions in the south and Ahr specialize in Pinot Noir. Wines exude sweet fruit flavors that are complemented with subtle earth and leafy notes. Contextually, these Pinot Noir wines taste a little bit new world and old world all at once.

 DRIED BLUEBERRY, RASPBERRY, CINNAMON, DRIED TWIGS, BROWN SUGAR

Lemberger

(aka Blaufränkisch) Hailing mainly from Baden and Württemberg, where the seasons are longer and warmer. Great examples have rich brooding chocolate and berry flavors with firm tannins and spicy acidity. Blaufränkisch is a perfect wine for the fall season.

 CURRANT SAUCE, POMEGRANATE, BROWN SUGAR, DARK CHOCOLATE, WHITE PEPPER

Dornfelder

A popular everyday value in Germany that ranges in quality, so be choosy! When made well, Dornfelder wines exude boisterous, sweet baked berry and vanilla aromas. Wines taste balanced with moderate tannins, spicy acidity, and an earthy-herbal finish.

 RASPBERRY PIE, OREGANO, VANILLA, TART BLUEBERRY, PEPPER, POTTING SOIL

Portugieser

A light red wine that's found in Germany and many countries on the Danube River including Austria, Hungary, Croatia, and Serbia. In Germany it's primarily grown in the Pfalz and Rheinhessen and popular in rosé wines and simple reds.

 DRIED RED BERRIES, PEPPERY SPICE, TOASTED OREGANO

Reading a Label

Once you know the system that identifies quality and ripeness levels on the label, you can hone your skills exploring the differences among Germany's 13 official designated wine regions. The word Germans use for wine region is anbaugebiete ("ahn-baw-jeh-beet").

PRODUCT OF GERMANY

– MOSEL –
WEINGUT FOLLY
2018
SAARBURGER RAUSCH
RIESLING
KABINETT
GUTSABFÜLLUNG
750 ML   D-55555 SAARBURG   PRADIKATSWEIN   8% / VOL

PRODUCER ASSOCIATION
REGION
WINERY
VINTAGE
VILLAGE WHERE THE VINEYARD IS LOCATED. "ER" IS A POSSESSIVE AFFIX.
VINEYARD NAME
VARIETY
RIPENESS LEVEL
BOTTLED BY WINERY
GERMAN CLASSIFICATION

Sweetness Levels

Trocken/Selection: A dry wine with ~9 g/l RS or less. The term "Selection" is specifically for the wines of Rheingau that have been hand-harvested.

Halbtrocken/Classic: A "half-dry" or slightly sweet wine with up to 18 g/l RS (up to 15 g/l RS for "Classic").

Feinherb: An unofficial term to describe an off-dry wine similar to Halbtrocken.

Liebliche: A sweet wine with up to 45 g/l RS.

Süß or Süss: A sweet wine with more than 45 g/l RS.

Other Terms

Anbaugebiete: Germany's 13 protected designation of origin wine regions.

Bereich: A subregion within an Anbaugebiete. For example,

Mosel Valley has 6 subregions: Moseltor, Obermosel, Saar, Ruwertal, Bernkastel, and Burg Cochem.

Grosselage: A group of vineyards. Not the same as VDP.Grosse Lage.

Einzellage: Single vineyard.

Weingut: Winery.

Schloss: Castle or château.

Erzeugerabfüllung: (Gutsabfüllung) Bottled at winery.

Rotwein: Red wine.

Weißwein: White wine.

Liebfraumilch: A cheap, sweet wine (typically white).

Sekt b.A.: Sparkling wines originating from one of the 13 anbaugebiete.

Winzersekt: High-quality single-varietal, estate-grown

sparkling wines made with the traditional method.

Perlwein: Semi-sparkling carbonated wines.

Rotling: Rosé wine made by blending red and white wine varieties.

Fruhburgunder: A variant of Pinot Noir found in Germany, particularly in the Ahr.

Trollinger: Schiava Grossa.

Elbling: A very old, rare white grape found in the Mosel.

Würzgarten: "Spice garden," a common vineyard name.

Sonnenuhr: "Sun dial," a common vineyard name.

Rosenberg: "Rose hill," a common vineyard name.

Honigberg: "Honey hill," a common vineyard name.

Alte Reben: Old vines.

Wine Classifications

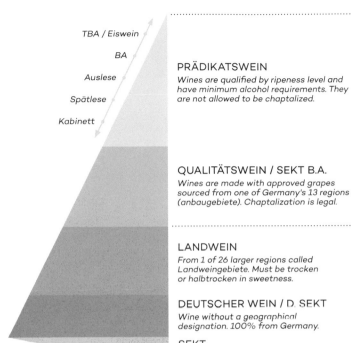

TBA / Eiswein

BA

Auslese

Spätlese

Kabinett

PRÄDIKATSWEIN
Wines are qualified by ripeness level and have minimum alcohol requirements. They are not allowed to be chaptalized.

QUALITÄTSWEIN / SEKT B.A.
Wines are made with approved grapes sourced from one of Germany's 13 regions (anbaugebiete). Chaptalization is legal.

LANDWEIN
From 1 of 26 larger regions called Landweingebiete. Must be trocken or halbtrocken in sweetness.

DEUTSCHER WEIN / D. SEKT
Wine without a geographical designation. 100% from Germany.

SEKT
Non-German sparkling wines with minimum EU quality standards.

VDP

VDP.Grosses Gewächs (GG) / VDP.Grosse Lage*

VDP.Erste Lage*

VDP.Ortswein*

VDP.Gutswein*

*VDP is Prädikatswein or Qualitätswein.

Prädikatswein

Kabinett: The lightest style of Riesling, made from grapes that have a sweetness level of 67–82 Oechsle (148–188 g/L sugar). Kabinett wines range in style from dry to off-dry.

Spätlese: "Late harvest." Grapes have a sweetness level of 76–90 Oechsle (172–209 g/L sugar). Spätlese wines are rich and usually sweeter than Kabinett, although if you see "Trocken" on the bottle it's dry with increased alcohol.

Auslese: "Select harvest." Picked more ripe at 83–110 Oechsle (191–260 g/L sugar). Grapes are hand-selected and have noble rot. Wines are sweeter or dry with high alcohol when labeled "Trocken."

Beerenauslese (BA): "Berry select harvest." Wines are much more rare because the grapes are basically raisinated noble rot grapes picked at 110-128 Oechsle (260+ g/L sugar!). Expect precious dessert wines sold in half-bottles.

Trockenbeerenauslese (TBA): "Dry berry select harvest." The most rare wine of the group, made from raisinated grapes that dried out on the vine picked at 150–154 Oechsle. Very sweet wines.

Eiswein: "Ice wine." Indicates the grapes were frozen on the vine and then pressed. These wines will have between 110–128 Oechsle (260+ g/L sugar!) when picked. Very sweet wines.

VDP

Verband Deutscher Prädikatsweingüter (VDP) is an independent association of ~200 wine estates that classify vineyards.

VDP.Gutswein: "House wine." Labeled with a proprietary, village or regional name and labeled "VDP."

VDP.Ortswein: "Local village wine." High-quality vineyards within a village area labeled with a vineyard site name.

VDP.Erste Lage: "First site." Vineyards designated first class with stricter growing standards. All wines are certified by a tasting panel.

VDP.Grosses Gewächs / VDP. Grosse Lage: "Great site"/ "Great growth." A designation of the best vineyards with increased growing standards. All wines are certified by a tasting panel. Wines labeled Grosses Gewächs (GG) must be dry.

Greece

Varieties
100+
COMMON
VARIETIES

- SAVATIANO
- OTHERS
- RODITIS
- RODITIS (RED)
- AGIORGITIKO
- KOTSIFALI
- MUSCAT BLANC
- XINOMAVRO
- ROMEIKO
- CAB. SAUVIGNON
- MOSCHOMAVRO

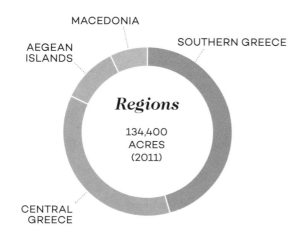

Regions
134,400
ACRES
(2011)

- MACEDONIA
- SOUTHERN GREECE
- AEGEAN ISLANDS
- CENTRAL GREECE

Food wines of all kinds

The secret to understanding Greek wine is appreciating the intensity of flavors found in Greek foods—intensity is a theme in Greek wines as well!

Wine Regions

Northern Greece: Known for elegant, savory reds as well as fresh and fruity whites. Xinomavro from Naoussa is often called "the Barolo of Greece," because of its high tannin and acidity. Assyrtiko, Malagousia, Debina (from Zitsa), and even Sauvignon Blanc are also worth seeking.

Central Greece: A warmer climate producing softer Xinomavro-dominant blends, including those from Rapsani, a region on the slopes of Mount Olympus. Savatiano offers bolder whites, similar to Chardonnay, and Retsina, a traditional white made with Aleppo pine tree sap(!)

Southern Greece: Hot climates produce fruity reds, perfumed whites, and rich dessert wines. Nemean Agiorgitiko can be likened to a fruity Cabernet. Mantineia's Moschofilero is like drinking perfume in a glass. Kefalonian Mavrodaphne is typically rich, sweet red wine. Crete is known for their Greek spin on the GSM blend.

Aegean Islands: The most famous wine island is Santorini, which is the famous home of Greece's most important white: Assyrtiko. The other islands have many rare finds. In Lemnos, an herbaceous red called Limnio is thought to have been mentioned in Aristotle's writings.

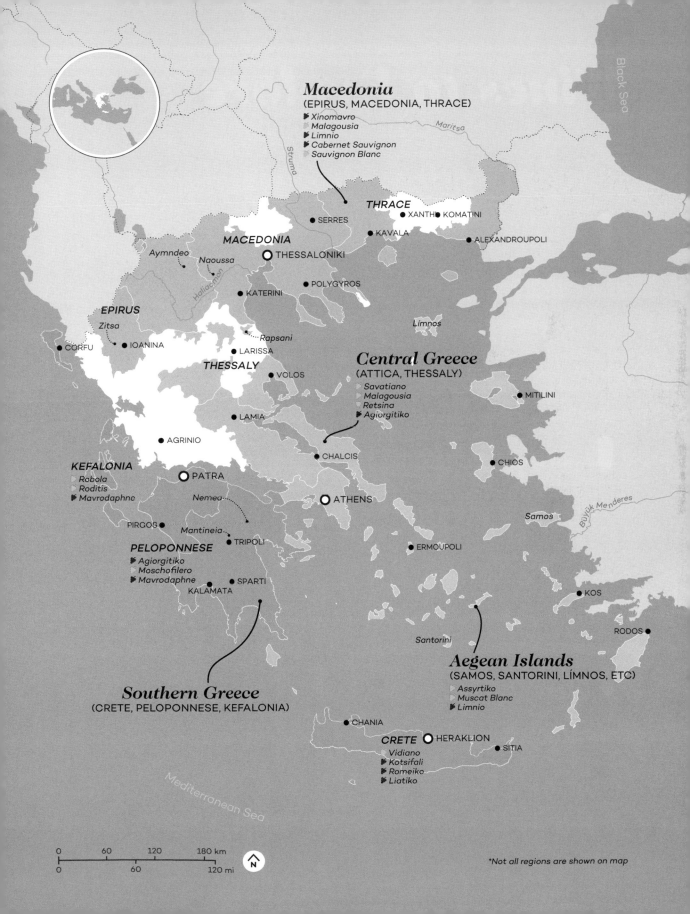

Macedonia
(EPIRUS, MACEDONIA, THRACE)
▶ *Xinomavro*
  Malagousia
▶ *Limnio*
▶ *Cabernet Sauvignon*
  Sauvignon Blanc

Central Greece
(ATTICA, THESSALY)
  Savatiano
  Malagousia
  Retsina
▶ *Agiorgitiko*

Aegean Islands
(SAMOS, SANTORINI, LÍMNOS, ETC)
  Assyrtiko
  Muscat Blanc
▶ *Limnio*

Southern Greece
(CRETE, PELOPONNESE, KEFALONIA)

Kefalonia
  Robola
  Roditis
▶ *Mavrodaphne*

Peloponnese
▶ *Agiorgitiko*
  Moschofilero
▶ *Mavrodaphne*

Crete
  Vidiano
▶ *Kotsifali*
▶ *Romeiko*
▶ *Liatiko*

Black Sea

Maritsa

THRACE
● XANTHI ● KOMATINI
● KAVALA
● ALEXANDROUPOLI

● SERRES

MACEDONIA
◉ THESSALONIKI

Aymndeo Naoussa
Struma
● KATERINI ● POLYGYROS
Haliacmon

EPIRUS
Zitsa
● IOANINA
● CORFU
Rapsani
● LARISSA
THESSALY
● VOLOS

Límnos

● MITILINI

● LAMIA

● AGRINIO

● CHALCIS

● CHIOS

KEFALONIA
◉ PATRA
Nemea
● PIRGOS Mantineia
PELOPONNESE ● TRIPOLI

◉ ATHENS

● ERMOUPOLI

Samos

Büyük Menderes

● KALAMATA ● SPARTI

● KOS

Santorini

● RODOS

Mediterranean Sea

● CHANIA

CRETE ◉ HERAKLION
● SITIA

0   60   120   180 km
0   60   120 mi

N

*Not all regions are shown on map

Wines to Explore

Greece has many wine treasures to discover beyond what's listed here. That said, if it's your first foray into this passionate wine country, the bottles below include some of the most exciting wines being made in Greece right now.

Assyrtiko

"Ah-seer-tee-ko." The champion white of Greece originated on the volcanic island of Santorini. Wines are bone-dry and lean with subtle saltiness. Assyrtiko labeled as Nykteri ("nith-terry") are always oaked and offer more lemon brûlée, pineapple, fennel, cream, and baked pie crust notes.

LW LIME, PASSIONFRUIT, BEESWAX, FLINT, SALINE

Savatiano

"Sav-ah-tee-anno." For the longest time Savatiano was used to make bulk wine. Only recently, select producers have taken special care with Savatiano to create rich, oak-aged white wines with a creaminess and texture like French Chardonnay.

 FW LEMON CURD, LANOLIN, GREEN APPLE, CULTURED CREAM, LEMON CAKE

Malagousia

"Mala-goo-zya." A richer style of white with more fruit and oiliness in a style similar to French Viognier. The grape was single-handedly saved from extinction by the winery Ktima Gerovassiliou in Northern Greece. (The word "ktima" means "winery.") It now grows in Northern and Central Greece.

 FW PEACH, LIME, ORANGE BLOSSOM, LEMON OIL, ORANGE PEEL

Retsina

"Ret-see-nuh." An ancient white wine specialty of Greece made by infusing wines with sap from Aleppo pine trees. When made well, wines offer one-of-a-kind pine flavors with a sappy, honeyed finish. Savatiano grapes make richer styles whereas Roditis and Assyrtiko make leaner styles.

 FW LEMON, PINE DUST, YELLOW APPLE, BEESWAX, GREEN APPLE SKIN

Moschofilero

"Mosh-co-fill-air-oh." A delightfully zesty, aromatic white wine that originated in Mantineia in central Peloponnese. Wines range in style from still to sparkling and from lean, floral, and dry to richer, nuttier, oak-aged wines that age for 10 or more years.

 AW POTPOURRI, HONEYDEW MELON, PINK GRAPEFRUIT, LEMON, ALMOND

Agiorgitiko

"Ah-your-yee-tee-ko." Generous, fruity reds and rosés that are often likened to Merlot. Agiorgitiko is Greece's most planted red and famous from the region of Nemea in Peloponnese, where the best wines are said to grow in the hills close to the commune of Koutsi.

 MR RASPBERRY, BLACK CURRANT, PLUM SAUCE, NUTMEG, OREGANO

Good to Know

🍷 Popular brands include Boutari, D. Kourtakis, Domaine Sigalas, Tselepos, Alpha Estate, Hatzidakis, and Kir Yianni.

🍷 The word Ktima ("tee-mah") is often found on labels and means "estate winery" (e.g., Ktima Gerovassiliou).

Xinomavro

"Keh-see-no-mav-roh." Xinomavro is being hailed as "The Barolo of Greece," where it grows in the regions Naoussa and Amyndeo. It can taste strikingly similar to Nebbiolo with its floral aromas, high acidity, and tannin. Xinomavro is a great choice for new wine collectors.

 RASPBERRY, PLUM SAUCE, ANISE, ALLSPICE, TOBACCO

Rapsani Blends

On the slopes of Mount Olympus, the region of Rapsani grows several red grapes including Xinomavro, Krasato, and Stavroto on schist-dominant soils. Wines offer rich red fruit, tomato, and spice flavors with tannins that build slowly on the palate.

 RASPBERRY, CAYENNE PEPPER, ANISE, SUNDRIED TOMATO, FENNEL

Crete GSM Blends

The most southerly island of Greece has one of the warmest and mildest climates for grape growing. The native grapes of Kotsifali and Mandilaria are often blended together with Syrah for a bold, fruit-forward red that has a soft, friendly finish.

 BLACKBERRY, RASPBERRY SAUCE, CINNAMON, ALLSPICE, SOY SAUCE

Mavrodaphne

"Mav-roh-daf-nee." Most often used in Mavrodaphne of Patras, a late-harvest, sweet red wine that tastes of black raisins and Hershey's Kisses. More recently however, a few producers now make intense, full-bodied dry reds that are reminiscent of Syrah.

 BLUEBERRY, BLACK CHERRY, COCOA POWDER, CLAY DUST, BLACK LICORICE

Vinsanto

A sun-dried sweet wine from Santorini that looks like a red but is made with white grapes (Assyrtiko, Athiri, and Aidani). Wines have high volatile acidity that will burn your nose if you sniff to strongly! Vinsanto is a haunting balance of bitter and sweet.

 RASPBERRY, RAISIN, DRIED APRICOT, MARASCHINO CHERRY, NAIL POLISH

Muscat of Samos

The island of Samos is thought to be where Muscat Blanc originated! On Samos many styles are made from dry to sweet. One of the traditionally popular styles is a mistelle (a blend of fresh Muscat juice and Muscat grappa—a spirit) called Vin Doux.

 TURKISH DELIGHT, LYCHEE, SWEET MARMALADE, MANDARIN ORANGE, DRY HAY

Hungary

OTHERS

Varieties
~70
COMMON
VARIETIES

BLAUFRÄNKISCH

GRAŠEVINA

FURMINT

CSERSZEGI
FŰSZERES

BIANCA

CABERNET
SAUVIGNON

CHARDONNAY

MÜLLER-
THURGAU

ZWEIGELT

MERLOT

HARSLEVELU

Making sweet wine history

During the 1700s the world saw Hungary as the benchmark of fine wine. Sweet white wines were the most in-demand style and Tokaji Aszú ("Toe-kye Ah-zoo") was the most sought-after dessert wine in the world. To this day, you can still find these lip-smacking, age-worthy whites, but now they are not all Hungary has to offer.

Hungary is in the midst of a wine renaissance—combining traditional winemaking with modern sensibility. With 22 wine regions and hundreds of varieties, there's a lot to know. The top 4 regions are a great place to start.

Wine Regions

Eger: Known for a wine called "Bull's Blood," a red blend with robust tannin and jammy berry flavors.

Tokaj: The oldest classified wine region in the world, a UNESCO Heritage site, and home to the golden sweet wine, Tokaji Aszú. Furmint is the most important Tokaj grape and is increasingly available in dry styles that taste similar to dry Riesling!

Villány: In the south, Villány is a fantastic place for red wines, particularly Kékfrankos (aka Blaufränkisch), Cabernet Franc, and Merlot. Cabernet Franc is especially good here.

Somló: A tiny wine region with volcanic soils that makes incredibly elegant, smoky white wines with a rare grape called Juhfark ("Yoo-fark").

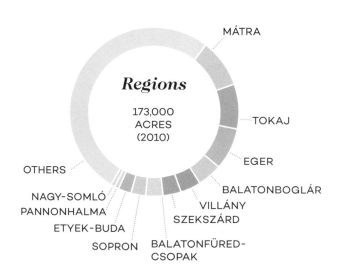

MÁTRA

Regions
173,000
ACRES
(2010)

TOKAJ

EGER

BALATONBOGLÁR

VILLÁNY

SZEKSZÁRD

BALATONFÜRED-
CSOPAK

SOPRON

ETYEK-BUDA

PANNONHALMA

NAGY-SOMLÓ

OTHERS

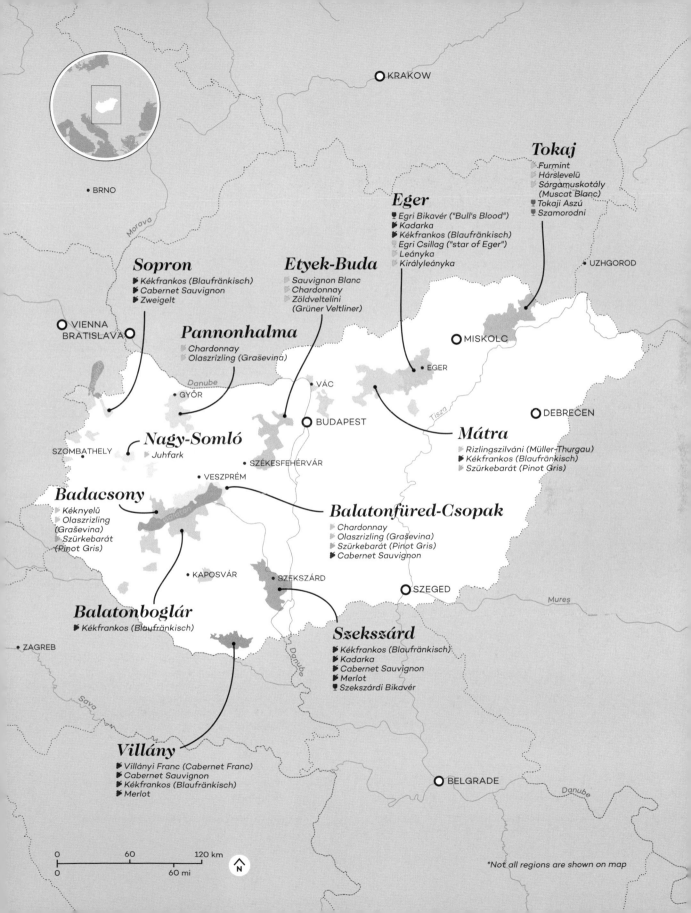

KRAKOW

BRNO

Sopron
🍷 Kékfrankos (Blaufränkisch)
🍷 Cabernet Sauvignon
🍷 Zweigelt

Tokaj
🍷 Furmint
🍷 Hárslevelü
🍷 Sárgamuskotály
   (Muscat Blanc)
🍷 Tokaji Aszú
🍷 Szamorodni

Eger
🍷 Egri Bikavér ("Bull's Blood")
🍷 Kadarka
🍷 Kékfrankos (Blaufränkisch)
🍷 Egri Csillag ("star of Eger")
🍷 Leányka
🍷 Királyleányka

Etyek-Buda
🍷 Sauvignon Blanc
🍷 Chardonnay
🍷 Zöldveltelíni
   (Grüner Veltliner)

UZHGOROD

Pannonhalma
🍷 Chardonnay
🍷 Olaszrizling (Graševina)

VIENNA
BRATISLAVA

MISKOLC

VÁC

GYŐR

EGER

Nagy-Somló
🍷 Juhfark

BUDAPEST

DEBRECEN

SZOMBATHELY

Mátra
🍷 Rizlingszilváni (Müller-Thurgau)
🍷 Kékfrankos (Blaufränkisch)
🍷 Szürkebarát (Pinot Gris)

SZÉKESFEHÉRVÁR

VESZPRÉM

Badacsony
🍷 Kéknyelű
🍷 Olaszrizling
   (Graševina)
🍷 Szürkebarát
   (Pinot Gris)

Balatonfüred-Csopak
🍷 Chardonnay
🍷 Olaszrizling (Graševina)
🍷 Szürkebarát (Pinot Gris)
🍷 Cabernet Sauvignon

KAPOSVÁR

SZEKSZÁRD

SZEGED

Balatonboglár
🍷 Kékfrankos (Blaufränkisch)

ZAGREB

Mures

Szekszárd
🍷 Kékfrankos (Blaufränkisch)
🍷 Kadarka
🍷 Cabernet Sauvignon
🍷 Merlot
🍷 Szekszárdi Bikavér

Villány
🍷 Villányi Franc (Cabernet Franc)
🍷 Cabernet Sauvignon
🍷 Kékfrankos (Blaufränkisch)
🍷 Merlot

BELGRADE

Danube

0   60   120 km
0   60 mi

N

*Not all regions are shown on map

Wines to Explore

The Northern parts of Hungary excel at white wines and elegant reds with noticeable tannin. As you travel south, you'll find plump, fruit-forward reds with varieties like Cabernet Franc and Blaufränkisch (known as Kékfrankos) producing outstanding examples. Here are just a few you absolutely must know about:

Furmint

("foor-meent") The most important grape of Tokaj is increasingly made into dry styles. The cool climate and clay soils give this wine a rich and somewhat waxy profile. The wine's acidity is so high that wines taste bone-dry even with 9 grams of residual sugar!

LW PINEAPPLE, HONEYSUCKLE, LIME PEEL, BEESWAX, SALINE

Nagy Somló

The rare white grape, Juhfark ("you-fark") or "sheep's tail" grows on an extinct volcano above Lake Balaton. It was long believed that if a woman drank this smoky white, she'd conceive a male heir. Wines are intensely smoky and fruity at the same time with a subtle bitter note on the finish.

LW STAR FRUIT, GREEN PINEAPPLE, LEMON, VOLCANIC ROCKS, SMOKE

Egri Csillag

Egri Csillag ("egg-ree chee-log") means "the Star of Eger" and is a super aromatic white blend containing at least 4 different grapes including natives like Furmint, Hárslevelü ("harsh-level-ooo"), Leányka ("lay-anka") and Királyleányka ("key-rai lay-anka"). A fantastic value.

 AW TROPICAL FRUIT, LYCHEE, CITRUS ZEST, HONEYSUCKLE, ALMOND

Tokaji Aszú

Exceptional sweet white wines made with noble rot in the region of Tokaj with up to 6 different grapes, including Furmint, Hárslevelü, Kabar, Kövérszőlő, Zéta, and Sárga Muskotály ("shar-guh-moose-koh-tie"). This wine region is so special historically that it's earned its own page. →

 DS HONEY, PINEAPPLE, BEESWAX, GINGER, TANGERINE, CLOVE

Egri Bikavér

("egg-ree BEE-kah-vaer") or "Bull's Blood" blends from Eger have a distinctly volcanic and high tannin profile with sweet, spiced plum aromas. You'll find the grapes of Kardarka (plummy, jammy), Kékfrankos (aka Blaufränkisch) and Cabernet Franc feature prominently in this blend.

 MR PLUM, RASPBERRY, BLACK TEA, ASIAN 5-SPICE, CURED MEAT

Villány Red Blends

A much warmer region producing Bordeaux-style blends made with Cabernet Franc, Merlot, Cabernet Sauvignon, and the regional Kékfrankos (Blaufränkisch). Expect more plummy, spiced berry, and fruitcake notes with wines aged for extended periods in Hungarian oak.

 MR CANDIED CURRANTS, BLACKBERRY FRUITCAKE, PLUM SAUCE, VOLCANIC ROCKS

Tokaji

During the 1700s, Tokaji was one of the most important wine regions of the world. The production of Tokaji depends on a necrotrophic fruit fungi called noble rot, or Botrytis cinerea. The mold develops on the berries in moist conditions and then dries when the sun comes out. This process of rotting and drying causes the grapes to shrivel and become sweet. Hungarians call berries with noble rot "Aszú" grapes.

Grapes

- Furmint ("foor-meent")
- Hárslevelü ("harsh-level-lou")
- Sárga Muskotály (aka Muscat Blanc)
- Kövérszőlő ("kuh-vaer-sue-lou")
- Zéta ("zay-tuh")
- Kabar ("kah-bar")

Styles

Aszú

Wines produced with a blend of Aszú (noble rot) grapes and regular grape must. Required to have 18 months oak aging (minimum) and 19% potential alcohol (actual ABV is around 9% ABV—the rest is sweetness).

- Aszú = min. of 120 g/L RS
- 6 Puttonyos = minimum of 150 g/L RS

Szamorodni

A wine made without separating noble rot grapes from regular grapes. The term translates to "made by itself."

- Édes = sweet, with ≥ 45 g/L sugar
- Száraz = dry, with < 9 g/L sugar—usually made in a nutty, oxidative style.

Eszencia

(rare) A drink made solely from Aszú grapes. Wines rarely are above 3% ABV. Eszencia is so sweet (450+ g/L RS) it's traditionally served in a tablespoon!

Fordítás

(rare) A wine produced by blending the used pomace (seeds, skins, etc.) from an Aszú fermentation with non-Aszú grapes.

Máslás

(rare) A wine produced with grape must, pomace, or wine blended with the used wine lees (dead yeast and leftover wine) from Aszú wine.

Italy

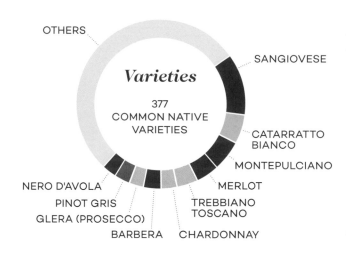

Varieties

377 COMMON NATIVE VARIETIES

- OTHERS
- SANGIOVESE
- CATARRATTO BIANCO
- MONTEPULCIANO
- MERLOT
- TREBBIANO TOSCANO
- CHARDONNAY
- BARBERA
- GLERA (PROSECCO)
- PINOT GRIS
- NERO D'AVOLA

Regions

1,705,000 ACRES (2016)

- OTHERS
- SICILY
- PUGLIA
- VENETO
- TUSCANY
- EMILIA-ROMAGNA
- PIEDMONT
- ABRUZZO
- LOMBARDY
- FRIULI-V. G.
- LE MARCHE

Covered in vines

There are more than 500 native wine varieties, of which at least 175 make up Italy's everyday wines. Thus, Italy is one of the hardest countries to master! Despite the complexity, if you taste the primary wines from the larger regions of Northwest, Northeast, Central, and Southern Italy, you will gain an understanding of what to expect, and more important, what wine regions you'd like to explore more!

Wine Regions

Northwest: The regions of Lombardy, Piedmont, Liguria, and Aosta Valley have mostly intermediate to cool climates, meaning the season is slightly shorter and thus red wines tend to be more elegant, aromatic, and earthy in style. Whites sparkle with ample acidity.

Northeast: The regions of Veneto, Emilia-Romagna, Trentino-Alto Adige, and Friuli-Venezia Giulia have cooler climates and the warmer areas are influenced by the Adriatic Sea. Reds offer more fruit (although still elegant) and the best white wines are found in the hills, such as the Soave grape, Garganega.

Central: The Mediterranean climate in Tuscany, Umbria, Marche, Lazio, and Abruzzo is why red varieties shine here, including Sangiovese and Montepulciano.

Southern and Islands: Italy's warmest regions: Molise, Campania, Basilicata, Puglia, Calabria, and the islands of Sicily and Sardinia. Reds lean toward more ripe fruit flavors and white wines tend to have a fuller body.

Lombardy
Franciacorta
◗ Croatina
◗ Pinot Noir
◗ Barbera
◗ Chiavennasca (Nebbiolo)

Trentino-Alto Adige
Pinot Grigio
Gewürztraminer
Trento
◗ Schiava
◗ Lagrein
◗ Teroldego

Friuli-Venesia Giulia
Pinot Grigio
Friulano (Sauvignon Vert)
Ribolla Gialla
Prosecco
◗ Merlot
◗ Refosco
◗ Schioppettino

VALLE D'AOSTA
Petite Arvine
◗ Petite Rouge

• AOSTA

• BERGAMO
• MILAN

Veneto
Prosecco
Garganega (Soave)
Pinot Grigio
◗ Valpolicella Blend
◗ Merlot

• TRIESTE

• VERONA
• VENICE

• TURIN
• ASTI

• PARMA
• MODENA

Emilia-Romagna
🍷 Lambrusco
◗ Sangiovese
◗ Barbera
Trebbiano Toscano

• BOLOGNA

• GENOA

LIGURIA
Vermentino
◗ Rossese

• NICE

Le Marche
Verdicchio
◗ Lacrima di Morro
◗ Montepulciano

• FLORENCE

Piedmont
◗ Nebbiolo
◗ Barbera
◗ Dolcetto
Moscato d'Asti
Gavi (Cortese)
◗ Brachetto
Arneis

Tuscany
🍷 Chianti/Brunello
◗ Sangiovese
◗ Bordeaux Blend
🍷 Vin Santo
Trebbiano Toscano
Vermentino

• SIENA

• PERUGIA

Abruzzo
◗ Montepulciano
◗ Sangiovese

• L'AQUILA

MOLISE
◗ Montepulciano
🍷 Tintilia del Molise

Umbria
Orvieto (Grechetto)
◗ Sagrantino
◗ Sangiovese
◗ Merlot

• ROME

• CAMPOBASSO

Puglia
◗ Primitivo
◗ Negroamaro

• BARI

Lazio
Malvasia
Grechetto
◗ Cesanese
🍷 Bordeaux Blend

• BENEVENTO

• NAPLES
• SALERNO

• OLBIA

Campania
◗ Aglianico
Malvasia
Falanghina
Fiano

CALABRIA
◗ Gaglioppo
◗ Greco Nero
Greco Bianco

• CROTONE

• CAGLIARI

Mediterranean Sea

Sardegna
◗ Cannonau (Grenache)
Vermentino
◗ Carignan
Nuragus

Siciliy
◗ Nero d'Avola
◗ Nerello Mascalese
◗ Frappato
Grillo
Inzolia
Catarrato Bianco
🍷 Marsala

• MARSALA

• PALERMO

• MESSINA
• REGGIO DI CALABRIA

• CATANIA

• SIRACUSA
• RAGUSA

• TUNIS

0   50   100   150   200 km
0   50   100   150 mi

N

Wines to Explore

Many believe Italian wines are food wines because of their distinct savory flavors and spicy acidity. These attributes give Italian wines the structure to pair with a wide variety of foods. In all, Italy has hundreds of native varieties, so think of these 12 wines as a great place to start exploring the country's wide array of wines.

Chianti Classico

The Classico designation means the wine comes from the historic boundaries of Chianti. Wines are primarily Sangiovese but also may contain Canaiolo, Colorino, Cabernet, and Merlot. The Riserva and Gran Selezione are the area's finest wines and age 2 and 2.5 years respectively.

 PRESERVED CHERRY, AGED BALSAMIC, ESPRESSO, DRY SALAMI

Montepulciano d'Abruzzo

The region of Abruzzo offers some of the finest expressions of Italy's second-most planted red wine variety. The best wines age in oak and exhibit deep black-fruit flavors often with grippy tannin, so be sure to seek out those aged 4 or more years.

 SWEET PLUM, BOYSENBERRY, TOBACCO, ASH, DRIED MARJORAM

Nero d'Avola

The champion red wine of Sicily can have a strikingly similar taste profile to Cabernet Sauvignon with a full body, boisterous black and red fruit notes, and structured tannins ideal for aging. Of course, quality varies depending on the producer, so choose wisely.

 GRILLED HERBS, BLACK CURRANT, DRIED HERBS

Primitivo

Even though Primitivo is genetically identical to Zinfandel, you'll find the wines of Puglia have decidedly more earthiness to counteract the grape's uber-sweet fruit. The finest examples can be found in and around Primitivo di Manduria in Puglia.

 PLUM SAUCE, LEATHER, DRIED STRAWBERRY, ORANGE PEEL, CLOVE

Nebbiolo

The variety of the renowned Barolo region in Piedmont smells and looks like a light-bodied red wine until you taste it and are greeted by its intense, mouth-gripping tannins. Outside of Barolo, wines have lighter tannin, and are great introduction to variety.

 CHERRY, ROSE, LEATHER, ANISE, CLAY DUST

Aglianico

A rare grape found growing in the volcanic soils of Campania and Basilicata. Wines have a bold, savory taste with grippy tannins that smooth out slowly over a period of 10 or so years, eventually revealing soft, cured meat, and tobacco flavors.

 WHITE PEPPER, LEATHER, SPICED PLUM, CHERRY, ASH

Good to Know

ǁ The word "Classico" on labels is most commonly used to signify the original boundaries of a wine region.

ǁ *Native Grapes of Italy* (d'Agata 2014) lists ~500 native grapes, and *Wine Grapes* (Robinson et al. 2012) lists 377.

Valpolicella Ripasso

While most people know the star wine, Amarone della Valpolicella, the Ripasso of Valpo offers a similar taste of cherries and chocolate for a fraction of the price. The best wines generally have a higher proportion of Corvina and Corvinone—the area's best grapes.

 SOUR CHERRY PRESERVES, DARK CHOCOLATE, DRIED HERBS, BROWN SUGAR, WHITE PEPPER

Vermentino

A workhorse white grape that grows all over the French and Italian Rivieria as well as in Sardinia. Wines offer more heavyweight body and flavors that play between ripe fruit and grassy herbs. Seek out an oak-aged version for a full-bodied, nutty style.

LW RIPE PEAR, PINK GRAPEFRUIT, SALINE, CRUSHED ROCKS, GREEN ALMOND

Pinot Grigio

In Northern Italy is where you'll find Italy's top examples of Pinot Grigio (aka Pinot Gris). Wines have subtle tart fruit characteristics supported by delightfully high, tingling acidity. The best regions include Alto Adige and Collio in Friuli-Venezia Giulia.

LW GREEN APPLE, UNRIPE PEACH, THYME, LIME ZEST, QUINCE

Soave

The Garganega variety is the primary grape of both Soave ("Swah-vay") and Gambellara. While the wines are lithe and minerally on release, they slowly gain peach, marzipan, and tangerine aromas as they age for 4–6 years.

LW HONEYDEW MELON, TANGERINE ZEST, FRESH MARJORAM, GREEN ALMOND, SALINE

Prosecco Superiore

Italy's most popular bubbly is made with Glera grapes. And, while most Prosecco is mass-produced, beer-like fizz, you can find exceptional quality from the hilly zones of Colli Asolani and Valdobbiadene Superiore (including the subzones of Rive and Cartizze).

 WHITE PEACH, PEAR, ORANGE BLOSSOM, VANILLA CREAM, LAGER

Moscato d'Asti

A frizzante (lightly sparkling), highly aromatic sweet white wine from Piedmont that has some of the lowest alcohol levels of all wine (5.5% ABV). These wines are loved for their outstanding aromas and succulent sweet taste that pairs well with fruity desserts and cake.

 CANDIED LEMON, MANDARIN ORANGE, ASIAN PEAR, ORANGE BLOSSOM, HONEYSUCKLE

Reading a Label

Italian wine labels are the most challenging to understand because there is no single rule that defines how they're labeled. Additionally, the Italian wine classification system hasn't kept up with the innovations and new quality styles coming out of Italy today. Fortunately, there is a way!

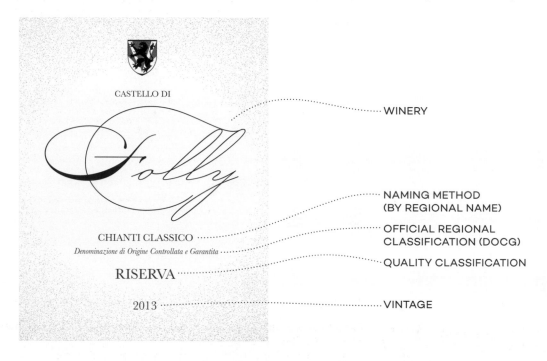

CASTELLO DI

Folly

CHIANTI CLASSICO
Denominazione di Origine Controllata e Garantita

RISERVA

2013

WINERY

NAMING METHOD
(BY REGIONAL NAME)

OFFICIAL REGIONAL
CLASSIFICATION (DOCG)

QUALITY CLASSIFICATION

VINTAGE

Naming Methods

Italians have 3 different ways of telling you what 's inside the bottle:

- **By variety,** as in *"Vermentino di Sardinia"* or *"Sagrantino* di Montefalco."
- **By region,** such as "Chianti" or "Barolo."
- **By made-up name**, such as "Sassicaia" (sass-ah-kye-yuh), an IGT from Tuscany.

Label Terms

Secco: Dry.

Abboccato: Off dry.

Amabile: Semi-sweet.

Dolce: Sweet.

Poggio: Hill or elevated place.

Azienda Agricola: Estate winery.

Azienda Vinicola: Winery that buys most of its grapes.

Castello: Castle or château.

Cascina: Winery (farmhouse).

Cantina: Winery (cellar).

Colli: Hills.

Fattoria: Wine farm.

Podere: Rural wine farm.

Tenuta: Estate.

Vigneto: Vineyard.

Vecchio: Old.

Uvaggio: Wine blend.

Produttori: "Producers." Usually a cooperative.

Superiore: Usually associated with a regional classification that offers a slight bump in quality. For example, Prosecco Valdobbiadene Superiore.

Classico: A classic or historic wine zone within a region. For example, Soave Classico and Chianti Classico are made within the original boundaries of these two wine regions.

Riserva: A wine that's been aged for longer than the standard denomination. Aging varies from region to region, but generally it's a year or more.

Italian Wine Classifications

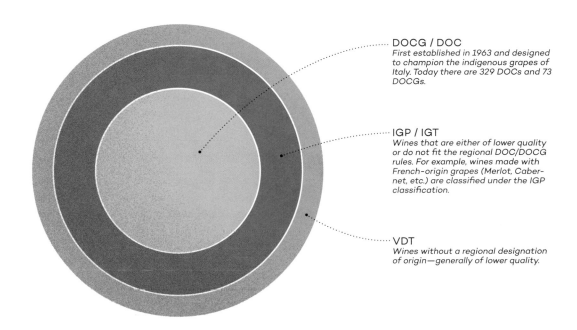

DOCG / DOC
First established in 1963 and designed to champion the indigenous grapes of Italy. Today there are 329 DOCs and 73 DOCGs.

IGP / IGT
Wines that are either of lower quality or do not fit the regional DOC/DOCG rules. For example, wines made with French-origin grapes (Merlot, Cabernet, etc.) are classified under the IGP classification.

VDT
Wines without a regional designation of origin—generally of lower quality.

DOCG/DOC
33%

(2014)

VDT
26%

IGP
35%

DOCG—Denominazione di Origine Controllata e Garantita

73 regions are ranked as Italy's top quality tier. DOCG wines meet both basic DOC standards along with more rigorous growing, aging, and quality specifications defined by each region.

DOC—Denominazione di Origine Controllata

329 officially designated wine regions. Wines must use official grape varieties and have minimum quality standards. Most DOC wines are decent everday drinkers.

IGP / IGT—Indicazione di Geografica Tipica

Most IGP are table wines from larger geographical areas, but you'll also find regional wines made with non-Italian grapes, including French-origin Merlot, Cabernet Franc, and Syrah. These declassified grape wines can be of exceptional quality and often use a made-up name. The "Super Tuscans" from the Bolgheri region of Tuscany are a good example. IGP can offer great value.

VdT—Vino da Tavola

Basic table wines with no regional designation.

Northwest Italy

Northwest Italy includes the regions of Piedmont, Lombardy, Liguria, and Aosta Valley. For wine collectors, the area is most famed for its robust, high tannin red wines of Nebbiolo, which can age for decades before reaching their prime. For everyday drinkers, you'll find a plethora of earthy reds and minerally, elegant white wines that pair excellently with Italian foods.

Nebbiolo

Nebbiolo is known by many names. In Valtellina, it's called Chiavennasca and the wines are lighter and more tart. A similar style comes from Northern Piedmont, where the grape is called Spanna. In Southern Piedmont you'll find the boldest Nebbiolo wines with rich fruit and grippy tannin.

 BLACK CHERRY, ROSE, LEATHER, ANISE, CLAY POT

Barbera

As an everyday red Barbera is a perfect match with pepperoni pizza. At their best, wines offer spiced and sour cherry flavors with an unmistakable aroma of melted licorice. Explore the regions of Barbera d'Alba, Barbera d'Asti, and Barbera del Monferrato Superiore for the best quality.

 SOUR CHERRY, LICORICE, DRIED HERBS, BLACK PEPPER, ESPRESSO

Dolcetto

Dolcetto is loved for its soft blackberry and plum flavors with firm-finishing tannins that simulate dark chocolate. With lower acidity, it's usually best to drink Dolcetto within 5 years of release. Of the wine regions to try, Dogliani DOCG is the only one that doesn't specify Dolcetto on the label.

 PLUM, BLACKBERRY, DARK CHOCOLATE, BLACK PEPPER, DRIED HERBS

Moscato Bianco

(Muscat Blanc) This highly perfumed grape is used in a variety of styles and sweetness levels. Moscato d'Asti is delicately "frizzante," Asti Spumante is fully effervescent, and there is also a dried "Passito" style found in Strevi. Look in Asti, Loazzolo, Strevi, and Colli Tortonesi for this wine.

 ORANGE BLOSSOM, MANDARIN ORANGE, RIPE PEAR, LYCHEE, HONEYSUCKLE

Franciacorta

One of Italy's great sparkling wines is produced using the traditional Champagne method (labeled "Metodo Classico"). The region sits on glacial clay-loam soils and wines are mostly Chardonnay with Pinot Blanc and Pinot Noir. Expect rich fruit and a creamy mousse.

 LEMON, PEACH, WHITE CHERRY, RAW ALMOND, TOAST

Brachetto

One of Piedmont's most delightfully fruity and sweet red wines offers up aromas of strawberry purée, cherry sauce, milk chocolate, and candied orange peel. On the palate, wines are juicy and often made in a creamy, sparkling style to accent the sweetness in the wine. This is one of a few reds that pairs perfectly with chocolate.

 BLACK PLUM, RASPBERRY, OLIVE, RED PEPPER FLAKE, COCOA

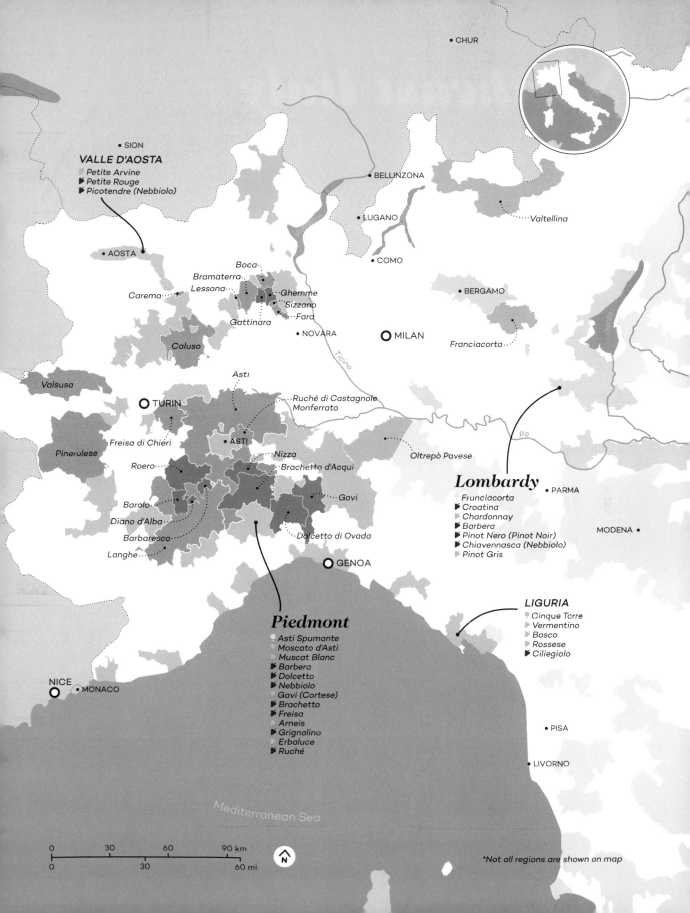

• CHUR

• SION

VALLE D'AOSTA
🍷 Petite Arvine
🍷 Petite Rouge
🍷 Picotendre (Nebbiolo)

• AOSTA

• BELLINZONA

• LUGANO

Valtellina

• COMO

Boca
Bramaterra
Lessona
Carema
Ghemme
Sizzano
Gattinara
Fara

• BERGAMO

Caluso

• NOVARA

○ MILAN

Franciacorta

Valsusa

Asti

○ TURIN

Ruché di Castagnole
Monferrato

Freisa di Chieri

• ASTI

Po

Pinerolese

Roero

Nizza

Brachetto d'Acqui

Oltrepò Pavese

Lombardy

🍷 Franciacorta
🍷 Croatina
🍷 Chardonnay
🍷 Barbera
🍷 Pinot Nero (Pinot Noir)
🍷 Chiavennasca (Nebbiolo)
🍷 Pinot Gris

• PARMA

Gavi

Barolo
Diano d'Alba
Barbaresco
Dolcetto di Ovada
Langhe

• MODENA

○ GENOA

LIGURIA
🍷 Cinque Terre
🍷 Vermentino
🍷 Bosco
🍷 Rossese
🍷 Ciliegiolo

Piedmont

🍷 Asti Spumante
🍷 Moscato d'Asti
🍷 Muscat Blanc
🍷 Barbera
🍷 Dolcetto
🍷 Nebbiolo
🍷 Gavi (Cortese)
🍷 Brachetto
🍷 Freisa
🍷 Arneis
🍷 Grignolino
🍷 Erbaluce
🍷 Ruché

○ NICE
• MONACO

• PISA

• LIVORNO

Mediterranean Sea

| 0 | 30 | 60 | 90 km |
| 0 | | 30 | 60 mi |

N

*Not all regions are shown on map

Northeast Italy

Northeastern Italy encompasses the regions of Veneto, Trentino-Alto Adige, Friuli-Venezia Giulia, and Emilia-Romagna. It's here that you'll find Prosecco, Lambrusco, Italy's best Pinot Grigio, and the well regarded red wines of Valpolicella. Beyond this, there are many delightful wine discoveries made with esoteric varieties as well as common French grapes like Merlot and Sauvignon Blanc.

Valpolicella

Around Verona you'll find one of Italy's most famous reds: Amarone della Valpolicella. There are many grapes in Valpolicella, but Corvina and Corvinone are the favorites in this blend. For Amarone, grapes dry until they lose 40% of their weight, increasing the intensity of the wine.

 CHERRY, CINNAMON, CHOCOLATE, GREEN PEPPERCORN, ALMOND

Soave

"Swa-vay" and neighboring Gambellara specialize in white wines made with Garganega. The region's powdery, volcanic tufa soils in Soave Classico lend to minerally, dry whites that are shockingly similar in style to Chablis. Wines gain texture with 4+ years of aging and reveal tangerine notes.

 LEMON, GREEN PEAR, GREEN ALMOND, CHERVIL, WHITE PEACH

Pinot Grigio

The regions of Alto Adige and Friuli are famous for Pinot Grigio. In the alpine, Alto Adige, wines are more floral with piercing acidity. In Friuli, you'll find them to offer peach and chalky flavor. Investigate Colli Orientali and Collio for great quality.

 LEMON, WHITE PEACH, CRUSHED ROCKS, SALINE, LIME ZEST

Prosecco

Prosecco uses the tank method to produce a fruity sparkling wine meant to be drunk in its youth. In the Prosecco region, you'll find the best wines come from the hilly areas in Valdobbiadene around Treviso and Colli Asolani, where the vines produce more concentrated grapes. An Extra Dry style is a great place to start with Prosecco.

 PEAR, HONEYDEW MELON, HONEYSUCKLE, CREAM, YEAST

Trento

Trentino is a region that's quickly becoming known for sparkling wines made with Chardonnay. Grapes are trained onto overhead trellises called pergola, which help ripen grapes in these cool alpine valleys. Trento sparkling wines are known for their rich, creamy texture.

 YELLOW APPLE, CRUSHED GRAVEL, BEESWAX, CREAM, TOASTED ALMOND

Lambrusco

The most famous sparkling red of Italy (and Emilia-Romagna) is actually a group of no less than 8 varieties. Because of this, there are a range of styles, from delicate rosé wines of Lambrusco di Sorbara to rich plummy reds with noticeable tannin made with Lambrusco Grasparossa. Try them all!

 CHERRY, BLACKBERRY, VIOLET, RHUBARB, CREAM

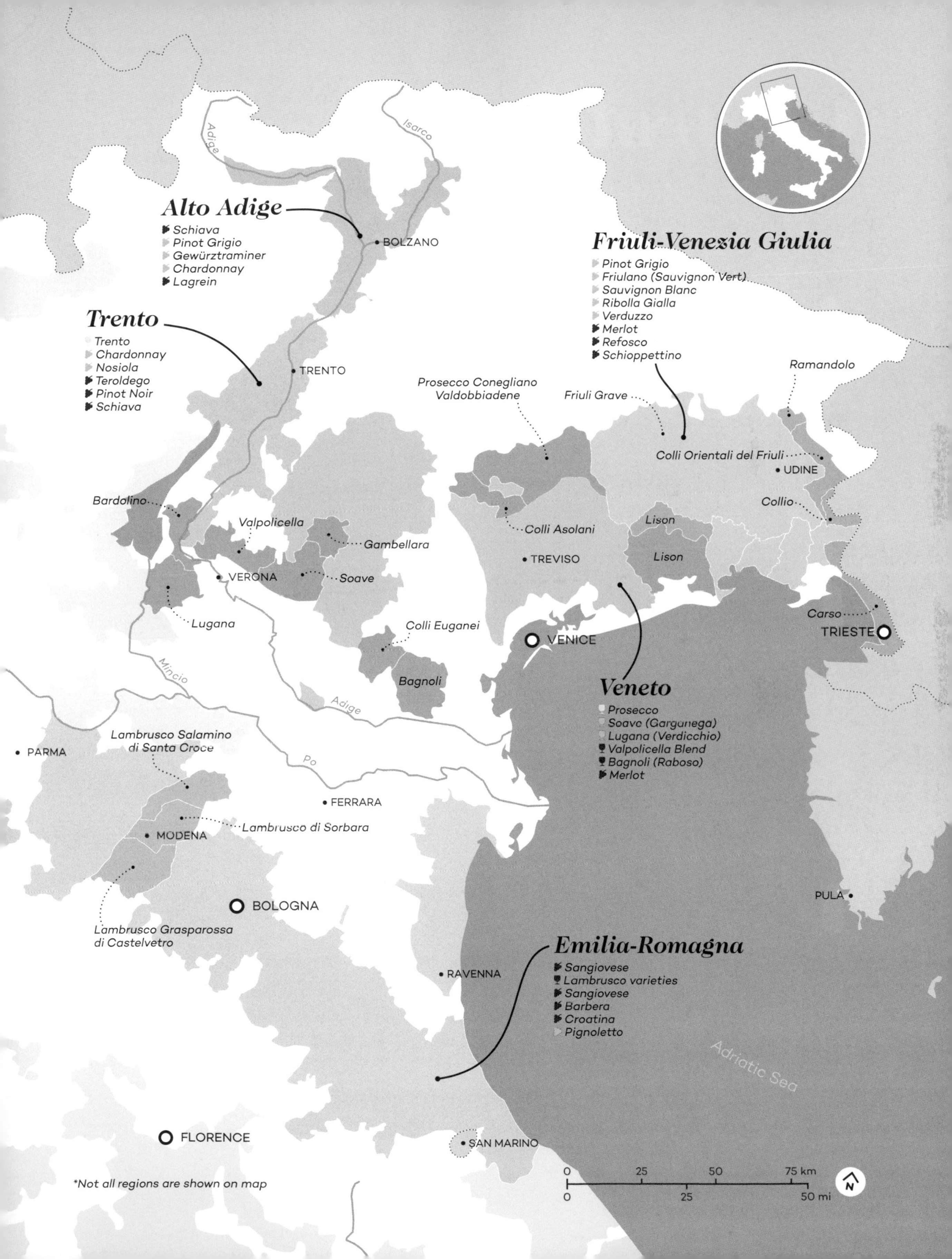

Alto Adige
Schiava
Pinot Grigio
Gewürztraminer
Chardonnay
Lagrein
BOLZANO
Adige
Isarco
Trento
Trento
Chardonnay
Nosiola
Teroldego
Pinot Noir
Schiava
TRENTO
Friuli-Venezia Giulia
Pinot Grigio
Friulano (Sauvignon Vert)
Sauvignon Blanc
Ribolla Gialla
Verduzzo
Merlot
Refosco
Schioppettino
Ramandolo
Prosecco Conegliano Valdobbiadene
Friuli Grave
Colli Orientali del Friuli
UDINE
Collio
Bardolino
Valpolicella
Gambellara
Colli Asolani
Lison
Lison
TREVISO
VERONA
Soave
Lugana
Carso
TRIESTE
Colli Euganei
VENICE
Mincio
Bagnoli
Adige
Veneto
Prosecco
Soave (Garganega)
Lugana (Verdicchio)
Valpolicella Blend
Bagnoli (Raboso)
Merlot
Lambrusco Salamino di Santa Croce
PARMA
Po
FERRARA
Lambrusco di Sorbara
MODENA
PULA
BOLOGNA
Lambrusco Grasparossa di Castelvetro
Emilia-Romagna
Sangiovese
Lambrusco varieties
Sangiovese
Barbera
Croatina
Pignoletto
RAVENNA
Adriatic Sea
FLORENCE
SAN MARINO
*Not all regions are shown on map
0 25 50 75 km
0 25 50 mi
N

Central Italy

Central Italy includes the regions of Tuscany, Le Marche, Umbria, Abruzzo, and parts of Lazio. This is red wine country. Getting to know the region can be challenging because of the confusing names. For example, Vino Nobile di Montepulciano is made with Sangiovese, not Montepulciano!

Sangiovese

Sangiovese is the champion grape of Chianti and Montalcino in Tuscany. Wines range from earthy to fruity but consistently deliver trademark spiciness and subtle balsamic notes. Look to Montecucco, Carmignano, Morellino di Scansano, and Montefalco Rosso (in Umbria) for great values.

 BLACK PLUM, RASPBERRY, OLIVE, RED PEPPER FLAKE, COCOA

Montepulciano

While most Montepulciano is made economically into easy-drinking food wines, it has potential for much more. In Abruzzo, well-made wines are bold with ample tannin and play between fruit and savory, meaty flavors. Look into Colline Teramane for quality.

 DRIED BLACKBERRY, SMOKY BACON, VIOLET, LICORICE, MARJORAM

Grechetto

Found inland in Umbria and Northern Lazio, this medium-weight white grape could be mistaken for a dry rosé if tasted blind. The region most known for Grechetto is Orvieto, but you can also find wines labeled simply by variety.

 WHITE PEACH, HONEYDEW, STRAWBERRY, WILD FLOWERS, SEASHELL

Super Tuscan Blends

This made-up term describes red wine blends made with French-origin grapes like Cabernet Sauvignon, Merlot, Cabernet Franc, and Syrah. These blends are labeled with the lowly IGT classification because they don't follow the DOC law. Still, many of Tuscany's most expensive wines are in this category.

 BLACK CHERRY, LEATHER, GRAPHITE, VANILLA, MOCHA

Vermentino

A great white from the coastal regions of Tuscany and Liguria (and Sardinia!). Wines are richer in style and more unctuous on the palate with flavors that play between ripe fruit and fresh, grassy herbs that finish bitterness that tastes like green almonds.

 GRAPEFRUIT, PRESERVED LEMON, FRESH CUT GRASS, RAW ALMOND, DAFFODIL

Verdicchio

A delightful, delicate white wine that's most known by the regional wine Verdicchio dei Castelli di Jesi from Le Marche. Verdicchio offers pretty floral aromas that complement its citrus and stone fruit tastes. Another region worth investigating for richer examples are wines labeled Lugana from Veneto.

 PEACH, LEMON CURD, ALMOND SKIN, OILY, SALINE

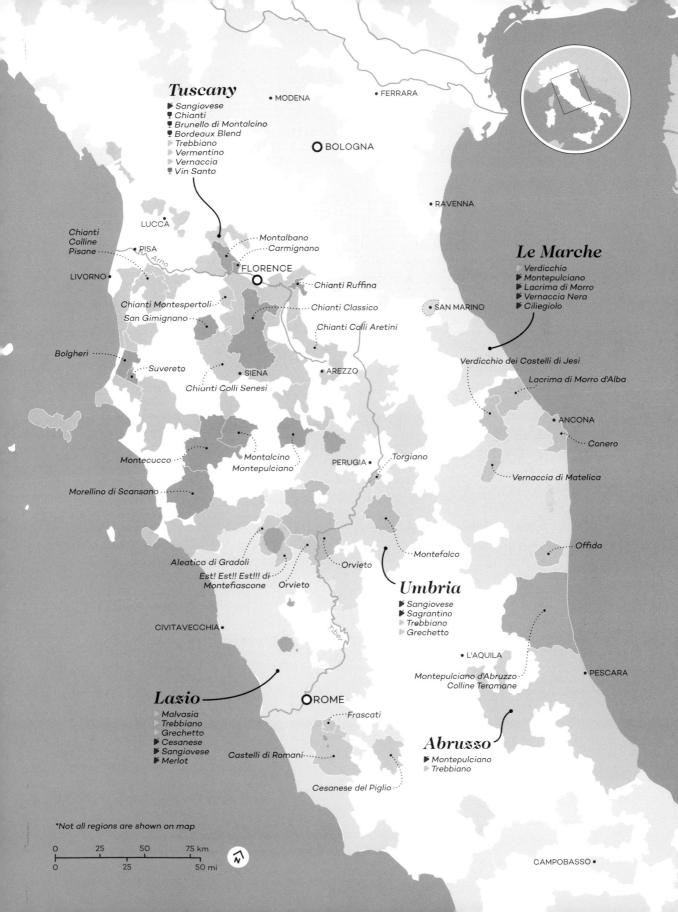

Tuscany
- 🍖 *Sangiovese*
- 🍷 *Chianti*
- 🍖 *Brunello di Montalcino*
- 🍷 *Bordeaux Blend*
- 🍶 *Trebbiano*
- 🍶 *Vermentino*
- 🍶 *Vernaccia*
- 🍷 *Vin Santo*

MODENA •   • FERRARA

◎ BOLOGNA

• RAVENNA

Chianti
Colline
Pisane

LUCCA •

• PISA

Arno

LIVORNO •

Chianti Montespertoli
San Gimignano

Bolgheri ····

···· *Suvereto*

FLORENCE ◎

···· *Montalbano*
···· *Carmignano*

···· *Chianti Ruffina*

···· *Chianti Classico*

Chianti Colli Aretini

• SAN MARINO

Le Marche
- 🍶 *Verdicchio*
- 🍖 *Montepulciano*
- 🍖 *Lacrima di Morro*
- 🍖 *Vernaccia Nera*
- 🍖 *Ciliegiolo*

Verdicchio dei Castelli di Jesi

Lacrima di Morro d'Alba

• SIENA

Chianti Colli Senesi

• AREZZO

• ANCONA

···· *Conero*

Montecucco

Morellino di Scansano

Montalcino
Montepulciano

PERUGIA •   • *Torgiano*

Vernaccia di Matelica

···· *Offida*

Aleatico di Gradoli

Est! Est!! Est!!! di
Montefiascone

Orvieto

···· *Orvieto*

···· *Montefalco*

Umbria
- 🍖 *Sangiovese*
- 🍖 *Sagrantino*
- 🍶 *Trebbiano*
- 🍶 *Grechetto*

Tiber

CIVITAVECCHIA •

• L'AQUILA

Montepulciano d'Abruzzo
Colline Teramane

• PESCARA

Lazio
- 🍶 *Malvasia*
- 🍶 *Trebbiano*
- 🍶 *Grechetto*
- 🍖 *Cesanese*
- 🍖 *Sangiovese*
- 🍖 *Merlot*

◎ ROME

···· *Frascati*

Castelli di Romani ····

Cesanese del Piglio

Abruzzo
- 🍖 *Montepulciano*
- 🍶 *Trebbiano*

CAMPOBASSO •

*Not all regions are shown on map

| 0 | 25 | 50 | 75 km |
| 0 | | 25 | 50 mi |

Southern Italy / Islands

We may envision Tuscany first for Italian wine, but the truth is, the island of Sicily and the region of Puglia are the two largest wine regions of Italy. Red grapes grow well in the hot climate and produce wines with bold, fruit-forward flavors and high alcohol. White grapes are often reserved for rich dessert wines. One thing is for certain: Southern Italy is a great place for value.

Primitivo

(Zinfandel) Grows almost exclusively in Puglia. Wines are boldly fruity with baked berry flavors balanced by Italy's trademark dusty and leathery minerality. High-quality wines should have high alcohol (~15% ABV). Try Primitivo di Manduria for a classic example.

 BAKED BLUEBERRY, FIG, LEATHER, BLACKBERRY BRAMBLES, CLAY POT

Negroamaro

It translates to "black bitter" but Negroamaro is surprisingly fruity and not too tannic. The Puglian regions of Salice Salento, Squinzano, Lizzano, and Brindisi are known for their particularly lush Negroamaro wines. Expect ripe, baked plum and raspberry flavors with subtle notes of baking spice and herbs.

 PLUM SAUCE, BAKED RASPBERRY, ALLSPICE, HERBS, CINNAMON

Cannonau

Technically it's Grenache, but Cannonau is unlike most Grenache. Wines are rustic, with leather, tobacco, and toasted herb notes that give way to roasted fruit and allspice flavors. The spice and fruit remind you that it's still Grenache, but everything else is distinctly Italian.

 TOBACCO, LEATHER, DRIED RASPBERRY, GRAPHITE, ALLSPICE

Aglianico

An age-worthy red that thrives on volcanic soils, Aglianico is not for the faint of heart. Wines are intensely rustic, meaty, and tannic and sometimes take a decade to come around. Look for Aglianico del Vulture, Taurasi, Aglianico del Taburno, and Irpinia—all known for quality.

 WHITE PEPPER, BLACK CHERRY, SMOKE, GAME, SPICED PLUM

Nero d'Avola

Nero d'Avola was resurrected in the late 1990s and has since become Sicily's champion red wine. Quality Nero d'Avola can be compared in style and richness to Cabernet Sauvignon but with more red fruit notes. The grape is drought resistant and can be dry-farmed.

 BLACK CHERRY, BLACK PLUM, LICORICE, TOBACCO, CHILI PEPPER

Nerello Mascalese

Even though Sicily is far more productive with Marsala, it's hard not to mention up-and-coming red grapes. Nerello Mascalese has striking similarities to Pinot Noir and it grows best on the volcanic soils of Mount Etna.

 DRIED CHERRY, ORANGE ZEST, DRIED THYME, ALLSPICE, CRUSHED GRAVEL

MOLISE
- Montepulciano
- Tintilia del Molise

Biferno .... •   San Severo

Puglia
- Primitivo (Zinfandel)
- Negroamaro
- Sangiovese
- Montepulciano
- Trebbiano
- Nero di Troia

• PESCARA

• L'AQUILA

• CAMPOBASSO   • FOGGIA

BARLETTA

• BARI

Brindisi

Salice Salento

Squinzano

BRINDISI

Falanghina del Sannio ....

• BENEVENTO

Aglianico del Taburno ....

Taurasi

Fiano del Avellino ....

Greco di Tufo ....

• POTENZA

Aglianico del Vulture

• TARANTO

• LECCE

Lizzano

Primitivo di Manduria

NAPLES

• SALERNO

Campania
- Aglianico
- Falanghina
- Fiano
- Greco Bianco
- Malvasia

Basilicata
- Aglianico

Cirò ....

Tyrrhenian Sea

Calabria
- Gaglioppo
- Greco Nero
- Magliocco
- Greco Bianco

• CROTONE

• CATANZARO

Sicily
- Marsala
- Catarratto Biano
- Grillo
- Inzolia
- Chardonnay
- Nero d'Avola
- Nerello Mascalese
- Frappato
- Syrah

• VIBO VALENTIA

Greco di Bianco ....

Greco di Bianco ....

• MESSINA

• REGGIO DI CALABRIA

Sardinia

Vermentino di Gallura ....

• OLBIA

• SASSARI

Sardinia
- Vermentino
- Cannonau (Grenache)
- Monica Nera
- Nuragus

• PALERMO

Etna ....

• MARSALA

• CATANIA

Cerasuolo di Vittoria ....

• SIRACUSA

• RAGUSA

Not all regions are shown on map

0	50	100	150 km
0		50	100 mi

CAGLIARI

New Zealand

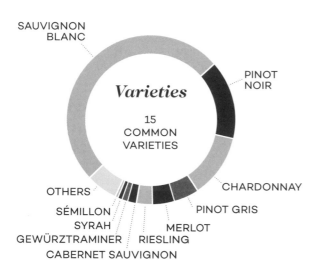

SAUVIGNON BLANC

Varieties

15 COMMON VARIETIES

PINOT NOIR

CHARDONNAY

PINOT GRIS

MERLOT

RIESLING

CABERNET SAUVIGNON

GEWÜRZTRAMINER

SYRAH

SÉMILLON

OTHERS

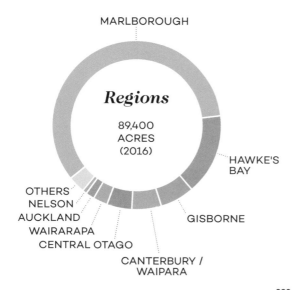

MARLBOROUGH

Regions

89,400 ACRES (2016)

HAWKE'S BAY

GISBORNE

CANTERBURY / WAIPARA

CENTRAL OTAGO

WAIRARAPA

AUCKLAND

NELSON

OTHERS

The greenest wine country

New Zealand reigns as the "Sauvignon Blanc capital of the world" with nearly 50,000 acres planted throughout the country. On the whole, New Zealand produces excellent cool-climate varieties including Sauvignon Blanc, Chardonnay, Riesling, Pinot Noir, and Pinot Gris. What's interesting is New Zealand's unparalleled commitment to sustainability. To date, 98% of vineyards are above the ISO 14001 sustainability standard and 7% operate organically. This is no small feat, considering it's harder to be organic in a cool climate.

Wine Regions

The cooler regions of Marlborough, Nelson, and Wairarapa make Sauvignon Blanc with passionfruit aromas and such high acidity, that it's not uncommon to see some residual sugar, even if you can't taste it. Marlborough's Pinot Noir is restrained and herbaceous, and Riesling and Pinot Gris are quite the find.

Despite the southerly latitude of Central Otago, the region is sunny and dry and produces great Pinot Noir. You'll find these wines typically have sweet dark berry notes supported by a gravelly minerality, and clove-like spice. Yum!

On the North Island, from Hawke's Bay north, there are surprising red wines including elegant and plummy Syrah and Merlot. Gisborne is known for rich and creamy Chardonnay, which, when made well, has enough acidity to age for 5–10 years. Surprising finds here include Gewürztraminer and Chenin Blanc.

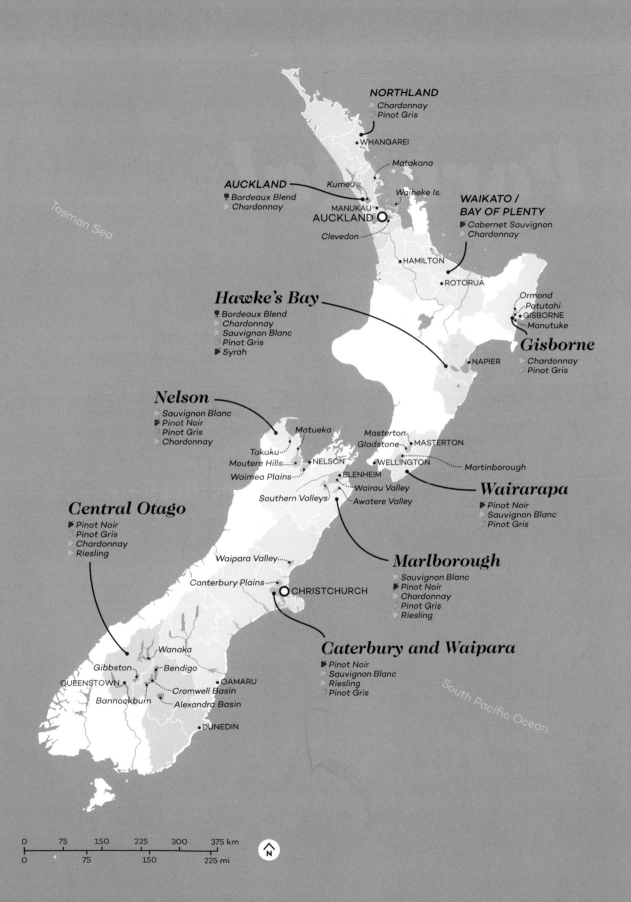

NORTHLAND
🍷 Chardonnay
🍷 Pinot Gris

● WHANGAREI

Matakana

AUCKLAND
🍷 Bordeaux Blend
🍷 Chardonnay

Kumeu

Waiheke Is.

MANUKAU

**WAIKATO /
BAY OF PLENTY**
🍷 Cabernet Sauvignon
🍷 Chardonnay

AUCKLAND ◯

Clevedon

● HAMILTON

● ROTORUA

Hawke's Bay
🍷 Bordeaux Blend
🍷 Chardonnay
🍷 Sauvignon Blanc
🍷 Pinot Gris
🍷 Syrah

Ormond
Patutahi
● GISBORNE
Manutuke

Gisborne
🍷 Chardonnay
🍷 Pinot Gris

● NAPIER

Nelson
🍷 Sauvignon Blanc
🍷 Pinot Noir
🍷 Pinot Gris
🍷 Chardonnay

Motueka

Takaka
Moutere Hills
Waimea Plains

● NELSON

Masterton
Gladstone

● MASTERTON

● WELLINGTON

Martinborough

BLENHEIM
Wairau Valley

Southern Valleys

Awatere Valley

Wairarapa
🍷 Pinot Noir
🍷 Sauvignon Blanc
🍷 Pinot Gris

Central Otago
🍷 Pinot Noir
🍷 Pinot Gris
🍷 Chardonnay
🍷 Riesling

Waipara Valley

Canterbury Plains

Marlborough
🍷 Sauvignon Blanc
🍷 Pinot Noir
🍷 Chardonnay
🍷 Pinot Gris
🍷 Riesling

◯ CHRISTCHURCH

Wanaka

Gibbston

Bendigo

QUEENSTOWN

● OAMARU

Cromwell Basin

Bannockburn

Alexandra Basin

Caterbury and Waipara
🍷 Pinot Noir
🍷 Sauvignon Blanc
🍷 Riesling
🍷 Pinot Gris

● DUNEDIN

Tasman Sea

South Pacific Ocean

0   75   150   225   300   375 km
0   75   150   225 mi
N

Portugal

Cornucopia of native grapes

Portugal is a treasure trove of unique wines and grape varieties that are not well known outside the country. However, long ago, the country was at the leading edge of wine technology and can claim one of the world's first demarcated wine regions (Port, since 1757). So, when you combine the country's longstanding wine traditions with the cornucopia of indigenous varieties, it makes Portugal one of the most exciting places for enthusiasts on the hunt for high quality and great value.

Varieties

77 COMMON NATIVE VARIETIES

- TINTA RORIZ (TEMPRANILLO)
- OTHERS
- TOURIGA FRANCA
- CASTELÃO
- TOURIGA NACIONAL
- FERNÃO PIRES
- TRINCADEIRA
- SÍRIA (ROUPEIRO)
- TINTA BARROCA
- ARINTO
- BAGA

Wine Regions

The climate changes drastically across Portugal, making a variety of wine styles.

In the Northwest, the region of Vinho Verde is much cooler and ideal for zippy, low alcohol whites. Inland however, you'll find dense, full-bodied reds and Port made with Touriga Nacional from the world-famous Douro Valley.

In Central and Southern Portugal there are a diverse range of wine varieties. Whites include age-worthy Arinto, and aromatic Fernão Pires. For reds, Trincadera and Alfrocheiro tend to be more elegant whereas Baga, Alicante Bouschet, and Jaen (aka Mencía) can be quite bold.

Lastly, the islands of Madeira and the Azores make profound, salty dessert wines, including the uniquely crafted Madeira, which is one of the most age-worthy wines in the world.

Regions

470,000 ACRES (2016)

- OTHERS
- BAIRRADA
- SETÚBAL
- TEJO
- DÃO
- ALENTEJO
- LISBOA
- BEIRA INTERIOR
- VINHO VERDE
- DOURO VALLEY

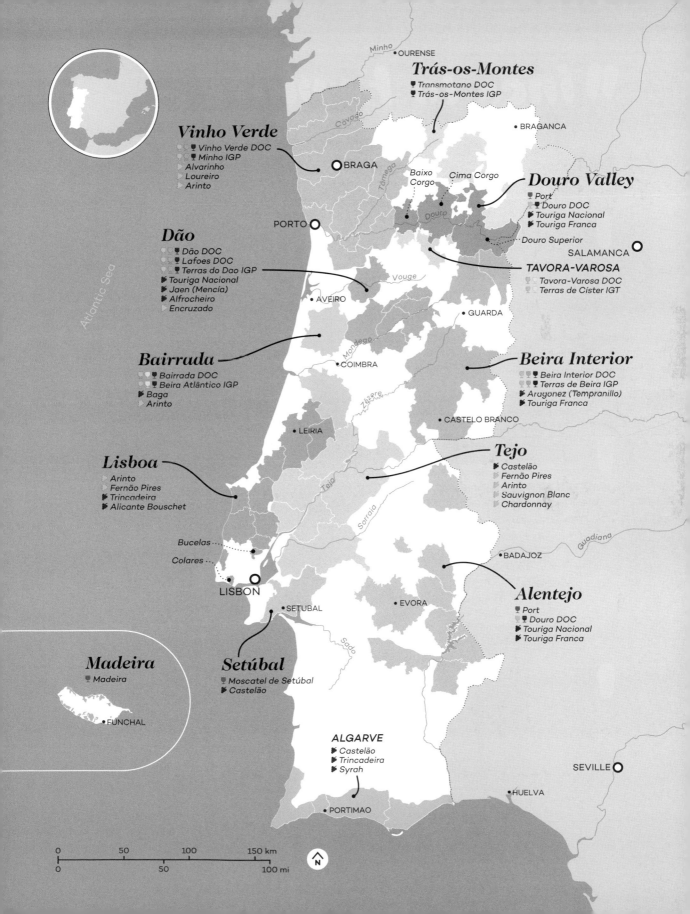

Trás-os-Montes
- 🍷 *Transmotano DOC*
- 🍷 *Trás-os-Montes IGP*

• OURENSE
Minho

• BRAGANCA

Vinho Verde
- 🍷 *Vinho Verde DOC*
- 🍷 *Minho IGP*
- *Alvarinho*
- *Loureiro*
- *Arinto*

○ BRAGA

Baixo Corgo   Cima Corgo

Douro Valley
- 🍷 *Port*
- 🍷 *Douro DOC*
- 🍷 *Touriga Nacional*
- 🍷 *Touriga Franca*

PORTO ○

Douro Superior

SALAMANCA ○

Dão
- 🍷 *Dão DOC*
- 🍷 *Lafoes DOC*
- 🍷 *Terras do Dao IGP*
- 🍷 *Touriga Nacional*
- 🍷 *Jaen (Mencía)*
- 🍷 *Alfrocheiro*
- *Encruzado*

TAVORA-VAROSA
- 🍷 *Tavora-Varosa DOC*
- 🍷 *Terras de Císter IGT*

• AVEIRO

Vouge

• GUARDA

Bairrada
- 🍷 *Bairrada DOC*
- 🍷 *Beira Atlântico IGP*
- 🍷 *Baga*
- *Arinto*

• COIMBRA

Mondego

Beira Interior
- 🍷 *Beira Interior DOC*
- 🍷 *Terras de Beira IGP*
- 🍷 *Aragonez (Tempranillo)*
- 🍷 *Touriga Franca*

Zêzere

• CASTELO BRANCO

• LEIRIA

Lisboa
- *Arinto*
- *Fernão Pires*
- 🍷 *Trincadeira*
- 🍷 *Alicante Bouschet*

Tejo

Tejo
- 🍷 *Castelão*
- 🍷 *Fernão Pires*
- *Arinto*
- *Sauvignon Blanc*
- *Chardonnay*

Sorraia

Bucelas ·····
Colares ·····

Guadiana

• BADAJOZ

LISBON

Sado

• EVORA

Alentejo
- 🍷 *Port*
- 🍷 *Douro DOC*
- 🍷 *Touriga Nacional*
- 🍷 *Touriga Franca*

Madeira
- 🍷 *Madeira*

Setúbal
- 🍷 *Moscatel de Setúbal*
- 🍷 *Castelão*

• SETUBAL

• FUNCHAL

ALGARVE
- 🍷 *Castelão*
- 🍷 *Trincadeira*
- 🍷 *Syrah*

SEVILLE ○

• HUELVA

• PORTIMAO

Atlantic Sea

| 0 | 50 | 100 | 150 km |
| 0 | 50 | | 100 mi |

N

Wines to Explore

The climate extremes in Portugal deliver both lean, minerally whites and robust, high-tannin reds. Of the hundreds of indigenous varieties to dive into, Touriga Nacional is a great place to start. This grape has risen the ranks from Port blending grape to sumptuous, single-varietal dry red wine.

Douro Reds

The Douro is home to dozens of native varieties, including Touriga Franca, Touriga Nacional, Tinta Barroca, Tinta Roriz (Tempranillo), and Tinta Cão. Today, dry "tinto" blends are on the rise. Wines have dense fruit and chocolate flavors supported by robust tannins.

 BLUEBERRY, RASPBERRY, DRIED DRAGON FRUIT, DARK CHOCOLATE, CRUSHED ROCK

Dão Reds

The Dão is mountainous and thus wines are more spicy and tannic. The varieties of interest include Jaen (Mencía), Touriga Nacional, Tinta Roriz, Alfrocheiro, and Trincadeira. Blends are common but single-varietal-focused wines tend to get the highest praise.

 CHERRY SAUCE, BLACKBERRY BRAMBLES, GINGER CAKE, COCOA POWDER, DRIED HERBS

Touriga Nacional

Considered to be one of Portugal's champion varieties, Touriga Nacional originated in the Douro Valley and can now be found throughout the country. Wines have mouth-coating intensity with distinct floral aromas of violets. Expect bold fruit, high tannins, and a long finish.

 BLUEBERRY, RED PLUM, VIOLET, GRAPHITE, VANILLA

Alicante Bouschet

Around Alentejo and Lisboa you'll find a "tenturier" grape called Alicante Bouschet with both red skins and red flesh. Although the variety originated in France, Portugal offers an ideal climate for this grape, making bold, smoky reds that are akin to Syrah.

 SUGARPLUM, BLACKBERRY BRAMBLES, BROWN SUGAR, CLOVE, GRANITE

Arinto

A top Portuguese white variety that grows all over the country but shows exceptional potential in Tejo and Alentejo. Arinto can be extremely light and minerally upon release, but with 5–10 years of aging it develops complexity and richness on par with aged Riesling.

 QUINCE, LEMON, BEESWAX, HONEYSUCKLE, PETROLEUM

Antão Vaz

A very rare white wine that originated from the Vidigueira region in Alentejo that was of little importance until modern French winemaking techniques were brought in. Antão Vaz quickly showed itself to be a star with striking similarities to Chardonnay.

 YELLOW APPLE, WHITE FLOWERS, LEMON OIL, BEESWAX, HAZELNUT

Good to Know

❚❚ Port producers are required to declare a vintage year. Then, the wine must be approved by the Port Wine Institute.

❚❚ Tawny Port is a special kind of Port wine that's aged oxidatively in barrels for many years. The older the better!

Verdelho

A white grape grown on both the Azores and Madeira and used in rich, salty dessert wines but also popular in the Iberian peninsula (and even California and Australia) as a steely white. This is a must-try for those who enjoy Sauvignon Blanc.

LW   GOOSEBERRY, PINEAPPLE, WHITE PEACH, GINGER, LIME

Alvarinho

(Albariño) The Vinho Verde region shares many of the same varieties as Rias Baixas in Spain. Alvarinho is usually made into a low-alcohol and slightly fizzy white Vinho Verde, but the serious examples show a rich, oily mid-palate with complexity and depth.

LW   GRAPEFRUIT, LIME BLOSSOM, HONEYSUCKLE, LIME, CUCUMBER SKIN

Fernão Pires

Half of Portugal refers to this aromatic white wine as Fernão Pires and the other half calls it Maria Gomez. Regardless of what you choose, what makes Fernão Pires special is the contrast between its sweet floral aromas, light body, and dry taste.

 AW   ASIAN PEAR, FRESH GRAPE, LYCHEE, LEMON-LIME, POTPOURRI

Madeira

The single-varietal wines, including Sercial, Verdelho, Malmsey, and Bual, are the best styles (from dry to sweet). Bual (aka Boal) is the classic, sweetest choice—the wine plays with flavors of sweet, sour, salty, nutty, and umami all at once.

 DS   BLACK WALNUT, RIPE PEACH, WALNUT OIL, BURNT SUGAR, SOY SAUCE

Port

There are a variety of Port styles to choose from but the style that cannot be missed is the Vintage or LBV (late-bottled vintage) Port. Wines burst with sweet red berry flavors supported with fine, graphite-like tannins. Try with blue cheese for a perfect pairing.

 DS   CANDIED RASPBERRY, BLACKBERRY JAM, CINNAMON, CARAMEL, MILK CHOCOLATE

Moscatel de Setúbal

Two varieties of Muscat (Muscat of Alexandria and Moscatel Roxo) make up the base of this golden sweet fortified wine that uses oxidation to achieve its intense caramel and nutty flavors. Wines aged more than 10 years are well worth trying.

 DS   DRIED CRANBERRY, FIG, CARAMEL, CINNAMON, VANILLA

South Africa

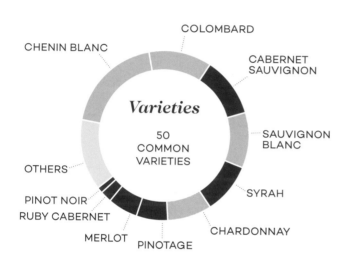

CHENIN BLANC
COLOMBARD
CABERNET SAUVIGNON

Varieties

50 COMMON VARIETIES

SAUVIGNON BLANC

OTHERS

PINOT NOIR
RUBY CABERNET

SYRAH

MERLOT
PINOTAGE
CHARDONNAY

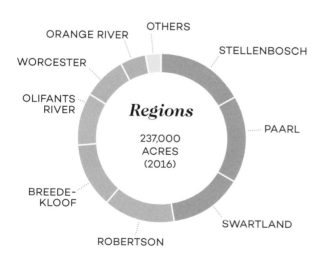

ORANGE RIVER
OTHERS
STELLENBOSCH

WORCESTER

OLIFANTS RIVER

Regions

237,000 ACRES (2016)

PAARL

BREEDE-KLOOF

SWARTLAND

ROBERTSON

Old world meets new world

Wine grapes first arrived in South Africa by way of the Dutch East India Company. And, by the mid-1700s, the country's Chenin Blanc–based dessert wine, Constantia, was famous across Europe. What makes South Africa unique is its warm climate paired with ancient granite soils (over 600 million year old), which result in bold red and white wines with high aromatic intensity.

Wine Regions

With the exception of Lower Orange River and Douglas in the Northern Cape, nearly all South African wine comes from the Western Cape.

The Coastal Region has a hot climate, making it an ideal place for bold red wines, including Cabernet, Pinotage, and Syrah. There are several cooler microclimates too, producing lush styles of Chardonnay and Sémillon. Highlights include wines from the regions of Stellenbosch, Paarl, and Swartland.

Breede and Olifants River Valleys are still very much considered the value wine areas of the country. You'll also find many thousands of acres of white varieties, including Chenin Blanc, that are used for brandy production.

Cape South Coast is tiny, but shows some of the highest potential for great quality, cool-climate wines, including those of Pinot Noir, Chardonnay, and even sparkling wines (from Elgin). The region is very spread out and producers here are very individualized and unique.

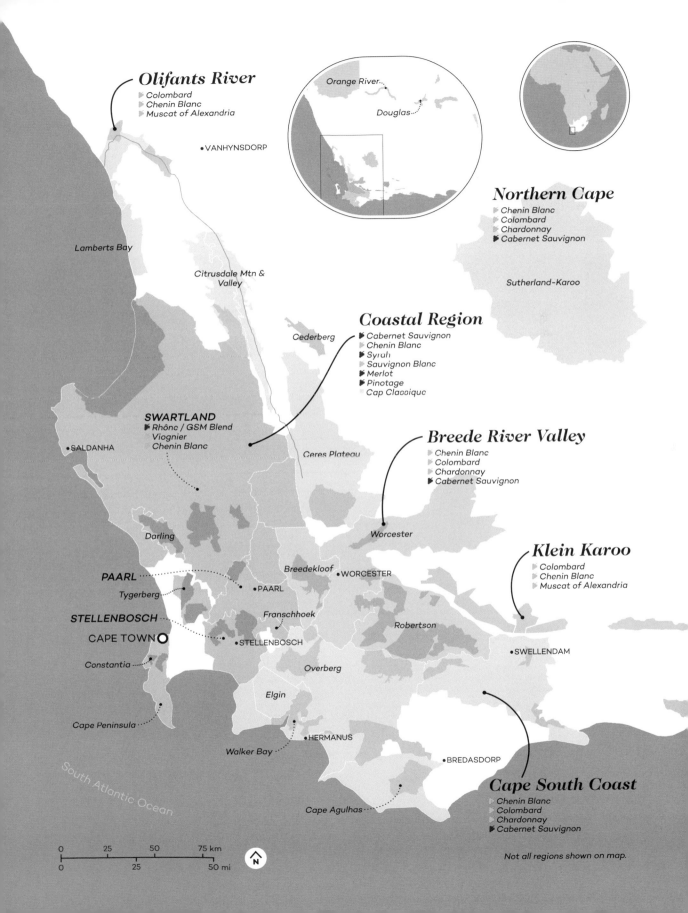

Olifants River
▷ Colombard
▷ Chenin Blanc
▷ Muscat of Alexandria

• VANHYNSDORP

Lamberts Bay

Citrusdale Mtn & Valley

Orange River
Douglas

Northern Cape
▷ Chenin Blanc
▷ Colombard
▷ Chardonnay
▶ Cabernet Sauvignon

Sutherland-Karoo

Cederberg

Coastal Region
▶ Cabernet Sauvignon
▷ Chenin Blanc
▶ Syrah
▷ Sauvignon Blanc
▶ Merlot
▶ Pinotage
▷ Cap Classique

Ceres Plateau

SWARTLAND
▶ Rhône / GSM Blend
  Viognier
  Chenin Blanc

• SALDANHA

Breede River Valley
▷ Chenin Blanc
▷ Colombard
▷ Chardonnay
▶ Cabernet Sauvignon

Worcester

Darling

Breedekloof • WORCESTER

Klein Karoo
▷ Colombard
▷ Chenin Blanc
▷ Muscat of Alexandria

PAARL
Tygerberg

STELLENBOSCH
CAPE TOWN ◯

• PAARL

Franschhoek

Robertson

• STELLENBOSCH

• SWELLENDAM

Constantia

Overberg

Elgin

Cape Peninsula

Walker Bay • HERMANUS

• BREDASDORP

South Atlantic Ocean

Cape Agulhas

Cape South Coast
▷ Chenin Blanc
▷ Colombard
▷ Chardonnay
▶ Cabernet Sauvignon

0   25   50   75 km
0   25   50 mi

Ⓝ

Not all regions shown on map.

Wines to Explore

South African wines offer flavors that seem to be both both new and old world. The ancient granite soils in the Western Cape produce astounding minerality and aromatics, while the ample sunshine makes for rich, fruit-forward flavors. The quality and value of South African Cabernet Sauvignon, Chenin Blanc, and Syrah are remarkable.

Cabernet Sauvignon

The most-planted red grape offers a range of styles and quality levels. Top-quality examples easily rival the best in the world with their structured tannin and big, varied aromas. Even on the low end, South African Cabernet Sauvignon is known to over-deliver.

 BLACK CURRANT, BLACKBERRY, BELL PEPPER, DARK CHOCOLATE, VIOLET

Pinotage

South Africa's own grape variety is very difficult to grow and make and thus, the variety has suffered a poor reputation. Fortunately, several estates have taken extra care with this grape and produce rich, lush, and smoky wines which are shockingly affordable.

 BLUEBERRY, SPICED PLUM, ROOIBOS, SWEET AND SOUR, TOBACCO SMOKE

Bordeaux Blends

Where there is great Cabernet you'll also find exceptional Bordeaux-style blends. South African blends are elegant and savory, resembling more of an old-world style that you might imagine coming from Italy or France.

 BLACK CURRANT, COCOA POWDER, GREEN PEPPERCORN, TOBACCO, CIGAR BOX

Rhône / GSM Blends

Swartland is a rugged, dry region with many old vines of Grenache, Syrah, and Mourvèdre. It produces juicy and fleshy reds with sweet black fruits, olive, and pepper flavors supported by robust tannins. A region with serious potential.

 BLUEBERRY, BLACKBERRY, DARK CHOCOLATE, BLACK OLIVE, SWEET TOBACCO

Syrah

A surprising find from South Africa that's only just becoming well-known outside the country. The region's granite-based soils boost peppery aromas, and in Swartland, Franschhoek, and Jonkershoek they're known for their elevated, age-worthy tannin.

 CHERRY SYRUP, MENTHOL, BLACKBERRY BRAMBLES, CLAY DUST, SWEET TOBACCO

Chardonnay

Traditionally, Chardonnay performs best in cooler climates, but there are a few microclimates that excel for this variety in South Africa. Regions that focus on this variety include Elgin in Cape South Coast and Banghoek ward within Stellenbosch.

 PINEAPPLE, YELLOW APPLE, GRAHAM CRACKER, PIE CRUST, TOASTED ALMOND

Good to Know

🍾 In South Africa, "Estate Wines" are from registered vineyards farmed as single units (there are 207 in total).

🍾 South Africa's growing season starts in September and the majority of harvest happens in February.

Crisp Chenin Blanc

While everyone else looks to France and Vouvray, South Africa hums along making some of the best Chenin Blanc wines in the world for a fraction of the price. The dry styles are a delightfully tart and refreshing alternative to Sauvignon Blanc.

LW   LIME, QUINCE, APPLE BLOSSOM, PASSIONFRUIT, CELERY

Rich Chenin Blanc

The more serious Chenin Blanc wines of South Africa often receive extended aging regimes in oak, where they develop sweet, candied apple notes and meringue-like creaminess on the palate. The Chenin Blanc Challenge cites top wines each year.

 AW   PASSIONFRUIT, BAKED APPLE, HONEYCOMB, NECTARINE, LEMON MERINGUE

Sauvignon Blanc

Where there is good Chenin Blanc you can bet there is good Sauvignon Blanc as well. Wines are savory but punch a pucker on the palate with moderate body. Some producers will even oak their wines to deliver even more body.

LW   WHITE PEACH, GOOSEBERRY, HONEYDEW MELON, LOVAGE, GRANITE

Viognier

Viognier is still quite small in terms of production but it's well-distributed throughout the country. You'll find it often blended with other white varieties where it adds heady floral aromas and increases the mid-weight oiliness in the palate. Viognier grows very well in South Africa's climate!

 FW   LEMON, APPLE, VANILLA, VIOLET, LAVENDER

Sémillon Blends

A unique specialty in South Africa are Sémillon-based blends. Many are aged in oak to produce a full-bodied, creamy, and savory white wine. The region most focused on this style is Franschhoek, which is a slightly cooler area producing wines with high aromatics.

 FW   MEYER LEMON, LANOLIN, YELLOW APPLE, BREAD AND BUTTER PICKLES, HAZELNUT

Cap Classique

An association created in 1992 dedicated to producing high-quality sparkling wines made with the traditional Champagne method. Chardonnay, Pinot Noir, Pinot Meunier, and the unique addition of Chenin Blanc give these wines sweet citrus-like notes.

 SP   ORANGE BLOSSOM, MEYER LEMON, YELLOW APPLE, CREAM, ALMOND

Spain

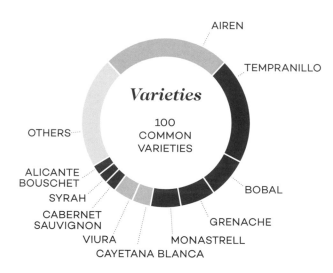

Varieties
100 COMMON VARIETIES

- AIREN
- TEMPRANILLO
- BOBAL
- GRENACHE
- MONASTRELL
- CAYETANA BLANCA
- VIURA
- CABERNET SAUVIGNON
- SYRAH
- ALICANTE BOUSCHET
- OTHERS

Regions
2,409,000 ACRES (2016)

- GALICIA
- OTHERS
- ANDALUCÍA
- CASTILLA-LA MANCHA
- ARAGON
- LA RIOJA
- CATALONIA
- CASTILLA Y LEÓN
- EXTREMADURA
- VALENCIA

Gateway to the old world

Spanish wines feature a dichotomy between bold fruit and dusty minerality that makes them fall between old-and new-world styles. The country boasts the highest vineyard acreage in the world, but yields are relatively low given the wide vine spacing and limited water use. Spain is the origin country of several top varieties like Tempranillo, Garnacha, and Monastrell. There are other varieties, like Petit Verdot, that seem to perform better here than in their country of origin.

Wine Regions

Spain can be organized into 7 overarching areas by climate.

"Green" Spain: The coolest areas include País Vasco and Galicia. Expect minerally, refreshing whites like Albariño, elegant reds like Mencía, and crisp rosado.

Catalonia: Catalonia has two notable specialties: Cava and Spanish GSM / Rhône blends. You must try a red from Priorat at least once in your life.

North Central Spain: The Ebro and Douro River Valleys are famous for Tempranillo wines, but you'll also find amazing Garnacha, Viura, and Verdejo.

Central Plateau: Known mostly for bulk production, but there are several surprising finds, including old vine Garnacha and Petit Verdot. This area is primed for rediscovery.

Valencia Coast: You must not miss the smoky, bold Monastrell wines from Yecla, Alicante, and Jumilla.

Southern Spain: Sherry country.

The Islands: A tiny area with curious finds like Listán Negro (a fruity, dry red) and Moscatel (an aromatic dessert wine).

Atlantic Ocean

Galicia
- Albariño
- Mencía
- Godello

PAÍS VASCO
- 🍷 Txakoli

La Rioja
- Tempranillo
- Garnacha
- Viura

NAVARRA
- Tempranillo
- Garnacha

Aragon
- Garnacha
- Tempranillo
- Macabeo (Viura)

MONTPELLIER

BORDEAUX

SANTANDER

• LA CORUA

BILBAO

• LEON

HARO

PAMPLONA

• VIGO

Castilla y León
- Tempranillo
- Verdejo
- Mencía

VALLADOLID

ZARAGOZA

BARCELONA

• PORTO

MADRID

Catalonia
- Cava
- Garnacha
- Tempranillo
- Merlot

Plà i Llevant
Binissalem
PALMA

EXTREMADURA
- Tempranillo

Castilla-La Mancha
- Airén
- Tempranillo
- Bobal

VALENCIA

MAJORCA
- Manto Negro
- Callet

LISBON

ALICANTE

• CORDOBA

MURCIA

Valencia
- Monastrell
- Bobal

CARTAGENA

SEVILLE

• GRANADA

Mediterranean Sea

MALAGA

Andalucía
- 🍷 Sherry
- Palomino Fino
- Pedro Ximinez
- Muscat of Alexandria

TANGIER

CANARY ISLANDS
- Listán Negro
- Listán Blanco (Palomino Fino)
- Listán Prieto (País)

CASABLANCA

Ycoden-Daute-Isora
Valle de la Orotava
Tacoronte-Acentejo

La Palma

Lanzarote

Valle de Güimar

La Gomera

El Hierro

Albona

Gran Canaria

TENERIFE Is.

0   75   150   225 km
0   75   150 mi

N

Wines to Explore

It's impossible not to mention the regions of Rioja and Ribera del Duero, who champion Spain's top red grape, Tempranillo. Also, Garnacha and Monastrell originated in Spain and arguably find their ultimate expression here. In the south, Sherry is a dry aperitif wine with no worldly comparison. Finally, Cava, Albariño, and Verdejo show how this country expresses white and sparkling wines.

Reserva Rioja

(Wree-yo-ha) Tempranillo-based wines that soften and become more complex with aging. The Rioja classifications of Reserva (1 year in oak/2 in bottle) and Gran Reserva (2 years in oak/3 in bottle) are a great way to taste the best of what Rioja has to offer.

 DUSTY CHERRY, DILL, DRIED FIG, GRAPHITE, SWEET TOBACCO

Ribera del Duero / Toro

Two growing regions withstand sweltering summers in the Duero river valley to produce rich and tannic Tempranillo wines (called Tinto Fino or Tinta del Toro here) that exude sweet black fruit paired with scorched earthiness. Several of the world's top Tempranillo estates are found here.

 RASPBERRY, LICORICE, GRAPHITE, EXOTIC SPICES, ROAST MEAT

Catalonian GSM Blends

The regions close to Barcelona, including Priorat, Montsant, Terra Alta, and others produce their own variant of the GSM / Rhône Blend. What makes these wines intriguing is the frequent use of Cabernet and Merlot to add richness.

 BAKED CURRANTS, MOCHA, LEATHER, SAGE, SCHIST ROCKS

Garnacha

The true origins of Grenache are Spanish, suggesting we immediately adopt Garnacha as the grape's official name! The regions of Aragon and Navarra produce fruity styles whereas old vine *Vinos de Madrid* have increased tannin and elegance.

 RASPBERRY, CANDIED GRAPEFRUIT PEEL, GRILLED PLUM, DRIED HERBS

Bobal

A variety that's planted in vast numbers throughout the Castilla–La Mancha, where it's often used in basic bulk "Tinto" blends. That said, a few producers make single-varietal wines that show how delightfully fruity and aromatic this everyday drinker can be.

 BLACKBERRY, POMEGRANATE, LICORICE, DARJEELING TEA, COCOA POWDER

Monastrell

Another Spanish-origin grape that the rest of the world calls by its French name, "Mourvèdre." Incredibly dense, nearly opaque Monastrell wines can found in Southern Valencia, Alicante, Yecla, Jumilla, and Bullas. This Spanish delight is not to be missed!

 GRILLED PLUM, LEATHER, CAMPHOR, BLACK PEPPER, CLAY POT

Good to Know

❚❚ Spain champions the use of American oak in the Gran Reserva Rioja (Tempranillo) classification.

❚❚ We may think of Grenache and Mourvèdre as French grapes, but the origins are believed to be Spanish.

Mencía

A lighter-bodied, age-worthy red that's grown in cooler, mountainous areas in Northwest Spain. The fruitiest styles are found in Bierzo and wines become more elegant/herbal as you move westward from Bierzo to Valdeorras to Ribera Sacra.

 MR — DRIED HERBS, BLACK PLUM, SPICY RED CURRANT, COFFEE, GRAPHITE

Garnacha Rosado

A striking, ruby-colored rosé that's made in a richer and more oily style than the famous onion-skinned rosé wines of Provence. The Garnacha-focused regions within Aragon and Navarra excel at rosado and always offer great value.

 RS — CHERRY, CANDIED GRAPEFRUIT, ORANGE OIL, GRAPEFRUIT PITH, CITRUS

Verdejo

A lean and lithe white that grows mostly in Rueda, where sandy soils lend to wines with zesty, citrus aromatics and a highly mineral, saline taste. You'll often find Rueda wines include a blend of Sauvignon Blanc and Verdejo. The perfect taco wine.

 LW — LIME, HONEYDEW MELON, GRAPEFRUIT PITH, FENNEL, WHITE PEACH

Albariño

One of Spain's champion whites that grows best in the cooler climates of Rias Baixas (Rhee-yus By-shus). You'll note wines become richer and more grapefruit-driven (vs. citrus and saline) from the inland areas, where there are more clay-based soils.

 LW — LEMON ZEST, HONEYDEW MELON, GRAPEFRUIT, BEESWAX, SALINE

Cava

Spain's answer to Champagne is made with the traditional method and includes the Spanish natives of Macabeo (aka Viura), Xarello, and Paralleda. Even though the wines are often much more affordable than Champagne, the quality levels are technically similar.

 SP — QUINCE, LIME, YELLOW APPLE, CHAMOMILE, ALMOND CREAM

Sherry

Sherry wines include several special styles that age in partially filled barrels in order to develop a surface yeast called *flor*. The flor eats the glycerol in the wine and it results in a leaner, more delicate, and salty tasting wine. Manzanilla and Fino Sherry are two flor wines worth exploring.

 DS — JACKFRUIT, SALINE, PRESERVED LEMON, BRAZIL NUT, ALMOND

Reading a Label

Today, it's common to find the grape variety listed on a bottle of Spanish wine. There are a few exceptions of course, including the classic regions of Rioja and Ribera del Duero, which are perhaps better characterized by the aging classifications of Crianza, Reserva, or Gran Reserva.

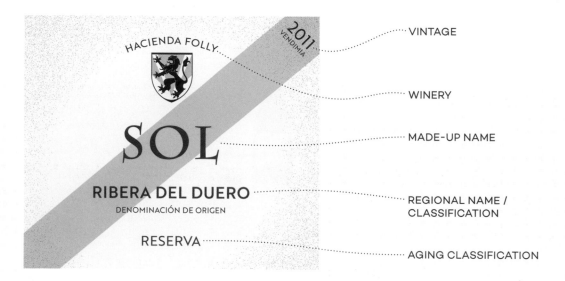

HACIENDA FOLLY

2011 VENDIMIA

SOL

RIBERA DEL DUERO
DENOMINACIÓN DE ORIGEN

RESERVA

VINTAGE

WINERY

MADE-UP NAME

REGIONAL NAME / CLASSIFICATION

AGING CLASSIFICATION

Naming Methods

Spain has 4 different ways to communicate what's inside the bottle:

- **By variety,** such as "Monastrell" or "Albariño."
- **By region,** such as "Rioja D.O.C.a" or "Priorat D.O.Q."
- **By made-up name,** such as "Unico" or "Clio."
- **By style,** (common in Sherry) such as "Fino" or "Oloroso."

Regional Wines

Rioja: Tempranillo-dominant red wines and Viura-dominant white wines.

Ribera del Deuro and Toro: Tempranillo-dominant wines.

Priorat: Red blends with a variety of possible grapes including Garnacha, Carignan, Syrah, Cabernet Sauvignon, Merlot, and others.

Aging Classification

Aging terminology can help you find the style you like. Generally speaking, the longer the wine ages, the more aged flavors it gains and the richer it becomes. Some regions have longer aging minimums:

Joven: Wine spends little or no time in oak. Applies to DOP wines only and also includes wines without an aging level listed, such as basic Rioja.

Crianza: Red: 24 months aging with at least 6 months (1 year in Rioja and Ribera del Duero) in barrel. White/Rosé: 18 months aging with at least 6 months in barrel.

Reserva: Red: 36 months aging with at least 12 months in barrel. White/Rosé: 24 months aging with at least 6 months in barrel.

Gran Reserva: Red: 60 months aging with at least 18 months. (2 years in Rioja and Ribera del Duero) in barrel. White/Rosé: 48 months aging with at least 6 months in barrel.

Roble: Means "oak." This term is a bit misleading because it's usually a young wine that's only spent a small amount of time in oak.

Noble: (rare) 18 months in barrel.

Añejo: (rare) 24 months in barrel.

Viejo: (rare) 36 months aging and must demonstrate oxidative character (tertiary flavors).

Spanish Wine Classifications

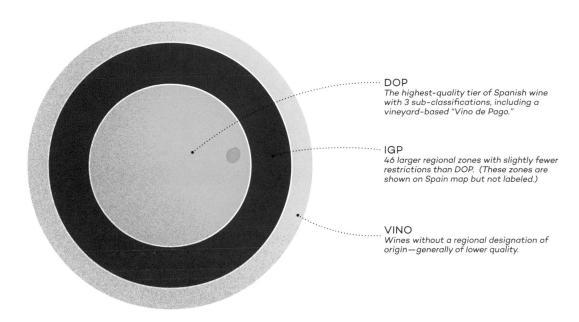

DOP
The highest-quality tier of Spanish wine with 3 sub-classifications, including a vineyard-based "Vino de Pago."

IGP
46 larger regional zones with slightly fewer restrictions than DOP. (These zones are shown on Spain map but not labeled.)

VINO
Wines without a regional designation of origin—generally of lower quality.

Vino de Pagos (VP)

- Arínzano *(Navarra)*
- Aylés *(Cariñena)*
- Calzadilla *(Castilla-La Mancha)*
- Campo de la Guardia *(Castilla-La Mancha)*
- Casa del Blanco *(Castilla-La Mancha)*
- Chozas Carrascall *(Utiel-Requena)*
- Dehesa del Carrizal *(Castilla-La Mancha)*
- Dominio de Valdepusa *(Castilla-La Mancha)*
- El Terrerazo *(Valencia)*
- Finca Élez *(Castilla-La Mancha)*
- Florentino *(Castilla-La Mancha)*
- Guijoso *(Castilla-La Mancha)*
- Los Balagueses *(Valencia)*
- Otazu *(Navarra)*
- Prado de Irache *(Navarra)*

DOP—Denominación de Origen Protegida

The highest-quality tier of Spanish wine. There are 3 main sub-classifications of DOP:

Vino de Pago (VP): ("DO Pago") This is a single-vineyard wine. Currently, there are 15 Vino de Pagos, mainly in Castilla-La Mancha and Navarra. Be wary, some wineries use "Pago" on the label but are not from an official Vino de Pago.

DOCa / DOQ: (Denominación de Origen Calificada) A more rigorous quality standard that requires wineries must be located within the region where wines are labeled. Rioja and Priorat are currently the only DOCa.

DO: (Denominación de Origen) Quality wines made in one of the 79 official wine regions.

IGP

Good everyday wines. Wines from larger regional zones with slightly lower requirements than DOP. Wines are labeled Indicación Geográfica Protegida or IGP and sometimes labeled Vino de la Tierra (VdiT). There are 46 IGPs of Spain, including the productive Castilla-La Mancha IGP.

Vino

(or Vino de Mesa or "table wine") Basic table wines of Spain with no regional specificity. Many wines are labeled simply Tinto ("red") or Blanco ("white") and can be off-dry to improve the taste.

Northwest Spain

The Northwest region is much cooler than rest of Spain. Rías Baixas and País Vasco are the coolest, specializing in zesty whites and lean, elegant reds. Moving south, the Cantabrian Mountains stop the Atlantic chill and thus, the Duero River Valley experiences both hot summers and icy winters. This combination results in some of the boldest Tempranillo wines of Spain.

Albariño

Albariño is a specialty of Rías Baixas ('Rhee-yus By-shus"). Vineyards close to the coast are more sandy and produce much more lean styles with noticeable salinity. Inland, there is more clay and sunshine, producing richer wines with more grapefruit and peach flavors.

 LEMON ZEST, GRAPEFRUIT, HONEYDEW, NECTARINE, SALINE

Mencía

An up-and-coming Iberian variety that's loved for it's piercing, pure red fruit flavors, graphite-like minerality, and age-worthy tannin structure. Mencía is the specialty of Bierzo, Valdeorras, and Ribeira Sacra. Wines are richer from Bierzo and become more elegant as you move west.

 TART CHERRY, POMEGRANATE, BLACKBERRY, LICORICE, CRUSHED GRAVEL

Ribera del Duero & Toro

Extreme weather shifts in the Duero River Valley result in high tannin, ripeness, and intensity in Tempranillo wines. The most famous regions include Ribera del Duero and Toro, where Tempranillo is labeled as Tinto Fino and Tinta del Toro respectively.

 BLACKBERRY, FIG, DILL, SWEET TOBACCO, CLAY DUST

Verdejo

The Rueda region specializes in an intriguing white variety made into both oaked and unoaked styles. Unoaked styles champion Verdejo's lime and grassy flavors and are often bottled in high-shouldered bottles. Oaked styles waft flavors of lemon curd and almond.

 LIME, HONEYDEW, GRAPEFRUIT PITH, FENNEL, WHITE PEACH

Txakoli

In Basque Country (aka País Vasco) you'll find the Spanish equivalent of Vinho Verde. Txakoli ("Cha-koli") are mostly white wines of Hondarrabi Zuri that have high acidity, low alcohol, and light bubbles. Reds use Hondarrabi Beltza—a rarity related to Cabernet.

 LIME, QUINCE, BREAD DOUGH, VANILLA, CITRUS ZEST

Godello

("Go-dey-yo") A rare white wine with surprising quality found mostly from Valdeorras, Ribiero, and Bierzo. Good Godello is often likened to white Burgundy, with apple and peach flavors complemented by subtle spice from oak aging, and a long tingly finish.

 YELLOW APPLE, CITRUS ZEST, LEMON CURD, NUTMEG, SALINITY

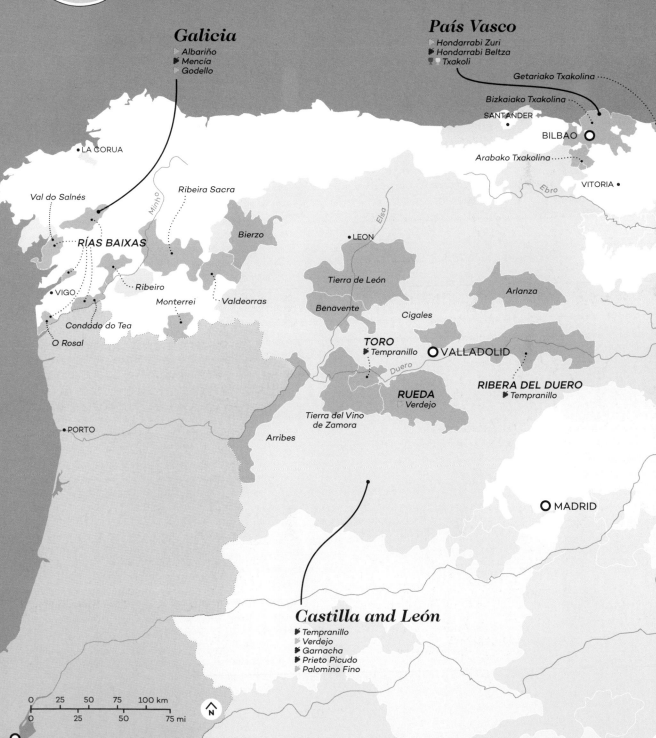

Atlantic Ocean

Galicia
▷ Albariño
▶ Mencía
▷ Godello

País Vasco
▷ Hondarrabi Zuri
▶ Hondarrabi Beltza
🍷 Txakoli

Getariako Txakolina ·············

Bizkaiako Txakolina ·············

SANTANDER

BILBAO ⊙

Arabako Txakolina ·············

VITORIA

Ebro

Elsa

LA CORUA

Minho

Ribeira Sacra

Val do Salnés

Bierzo

LEON

RÍAS BAIXAS

Tierra de León

Arlanza

Ribeiro

VIGO

Monterrei

Valdeorras

Benavente

Cigales

Condado do Tea

TORO
▶ Tempranillo

⊙ VALLADOLID

O Rosal

Duero

RIBERA DEL DUERO
▶ Tempranillo

RUEDA
Verdejo

PORTO

Tierra del Vino
de Zamora

⊙ MADRID

Arribes

Castilla and León
▶ Tempranillo
▷ Verdejo
▷ Garnacha
▶ Prieto Picudo
▷ Palomino Fino

| 0 | 25 | 50 | 75 | 100 km |
| 0 | | 25 | 50 | 75 mi |

N

Northeast Spain

Northeastern Spain can be split into two major zones: the Ebro River watershed and the coastal hills that run from Tarragona to the Spanish border. The Ebro River Valley is famous for its robust, fruity reds and rosés of Tempranillo, Garnacha, and Carignan. The coastal hills produce Cava and elegant, mineral-laced red blends that often include Cabernet Sauvignon, Syrah, and Merlot.

Rioja Reserva

The renowned Rioja wine region is famous for its age-worthy Tempranillo. Wines are more elegant from Rioja Alta and Rioja Alavesa's limestone-clay soils. Wines are richer and meatier from Rioja Baja, where clay soils have more iron.

 FR   CHERRY, ROASTED TOMATO, PRUNE DILL, LEATHER, VANILLA

Priorat Blends

Priorat became famous in the 1990s when a few producers created a uniquely Spanish Bordeaux-style blend using Garnacha, Carignan, Syrah, Merlot, and Cabernet Sauvignon. "Priorat blends" can also be found from Montsant, Costers del Segre, and Terra Alta.

 MR   BAKED RASPBERRY, COCOA, CLOVE, PEPPER, CRUSHED GRAVEL

Garnacha

Even though Garnacha (Grenache) is grown throughout Aragon, Navarra, Rioja, and much of Catalunya, you'll find the regions of Campo de Borja and Calatayud specialize in single-varietal wine. Wines have lighter tannin and unmistakable pink grapefruit notes.

 MR   RASPBERRY, HIBISCUS, CANDIED GRAPEFRUIT, CLAY DUST, DRIED HERBS

Carignan

You'll find Carignan (aka Mazuelo, Samso, or Cariñena) is often blended with Garnacha and occasionally Syrah, Merlot, and Cabernet Sauvignon to achieve incredible depth. Look into the regions of Emporda, Montsant, Priorat, Penedès, and Cariñena for quality.

 MR   BLACK PLUM, RASPBERRY, OLIVE, RED PEPPER FLAKE, COCOA

Rioja Blanco

Viura is commonly used in Cava, where it's called Macabeo, but in Rioja it's famous for its rich, age-worthy whites. Rioja Blanco is classified by age: Crianza (1 year), Reserva (2 years), and Gran Reserva (4 years). Each wine also must age 6 months in oak.

 FW   ROASTED PINEAPPLE, PRESERVED LIME, HOREHOUND CANDY, HAZELNUT, CANDIED TARRAGON

Cava

Cava offers exceptional value for a sparkling wine made with the same production method as Champagne. Macabeo is the most important variety by far, but you'll also find Xarello and Paralleda for whites, and Trepat and Garnacha commonly used to make Cava rosado.

 SP   YELLOW APPLE, LIME, QUINCE, BREAD DOUGH, MARZIPAN

La Rioja
- Tempranillo
- Garnacha
- Vlura
- Carignan
- Graciano

○ BILBAO

Navarra
- Tempranillo
- Garnacha
- Merlot
- Cabernet Sauvignon

Aragon
- Tempranillo
- Garnacha
- Viura
- Cabernet Sauvignon
- Merlot
- Syrah

• VITORIA

Rioja Alavesa

• PAMPLONA

Somontano

PERPIGNAN •

• ANDORRA

HARO
LOGRONO

Rioja Alta

Rioja Baja

Segre

Empordà

Pla de Bages

Alella

Campo de Borja

○ ZARAGOZA

Ebro

Costers del Segre

Conca de Barberà

• MATARO

○ BARCELONA

Cariñena

Calatayud

Penedès

• TARRAGONA

Tarragona

PRIORAT

Montsant

Catalunya
- Cava
- Macabeo (Viura)
- Xarello
- Parellada
- Garnacha
- Syrah

Terra Alta

• CASTELLO

Valencia

Balearic Sea

PALMA •

Utiel-Requena

○ VALENCIA

Valencia
- Monastrell
- Bobal
- Merseguera
- Tempranillo
- Garnacha
- Cabernet Sauvignon

Valencia

• ALBACETE

Alicante

Yecla

Alicante

Jumilla

• ALICANTE

Bullas

○ MURCIA

Murcia
- Monastrell
- Syrah

• LORCA

• CARTAGENA

| 0 | 25 | 50 | 75 | 100 km |

| 0 | 25 | 50 | 75 mi |

N

Southern Spain

A great deal of Spain's value wine comes from Central Spain, particularly from Castilla-La Mancha and parts of Valencia (including Castilla VT). Still, you can find excellent quality reds here, usually at great prices. As you move farther South, you get into dominant plantings of Palomino Fino and Pedro Ximenez, which are used for Sherry of all kinds from dry to sweet.

Monastrell

Monastrell (aka Mourvèdre) is thought to have originated in Murcia, where it produces rich and smoky wines. On the high end, wines deliver subtle violet and black pepper aromas on top of rich blueberry fruit. Look to Alicante, Jumilla, Yecla, and Bullas.

 BLACKBERRY, BLACK PEPPER, VIOLET, BLACK PEPPER, SMOKE

Bobal

A super value red that's not well known outside of Spain. Wines deliver soft plum and chocolate flavors with occasional rustic, meaty undertones. Look to Valencia in the regions of Utiel-Requena (including Pago Finca Terrerazo) and Manchuela for great quality.

 BLACK CHERRY, BLUEBERRY, DRIED GREEN HERBS, VIOLET, COCOA

Garnacha

Even though the region is quite small in size, we'd be remiss not to mention Garnacha from Vinos de Madrid and Méntrida. There are many old vines planted in granite soils and high elevations, resulting in complex, high tannin, and age-worthy Grenache.

 BLACK CHERRY, BLACK PEPPER, GRAPHITE, CINNAMON, DESSERT SAGE

Cabernet Blends

Across La Mancha and Valencia you'll find French varieties, including Cabernet Sauvignon, Syrah, and Petit Verdot. The grapes are often blended with the native Garnacha or Monastrell to produce incredibly rich, chocolatey wines. Look in Jumilla and Valencia.

 BLACKBERRY, BLACK CHERRY, DARK CHOCOLATE, GRAPHITE, CLAY DUST

Sherry

Despite what you might think, most Sherry isn't sweet, it's salty and nutty. The fortified wine is made mostly with Palomino Fino grapes that grow on chalky-white albariza soils around Jerez. When it's sweet (like Cream Sherry), it's blended with Pedro Ximenez.

 JACKFRUIT, PRESERVED LEMON, BRAZIL NUT, LANOLIN, SALINE

Montilla-Moriles PX

Montilla-Moriles is a wine region in Andalucía that specializes in a white grape called Pedro Ximenez (PX). PX is one of the sweetest dessert wines in the world! Aging oxidizes the wine to a deep dark brown and sweetness gives it the viscosity of warm maple syrup.

 RAISIN, FIG, WALNUT, CARAMEL, NUTELLA

Vinos de Madrid
- Monastrell
- Garnacha
- Syrah

Castilla–La Mancha
- Airén
- Bobal
- Monastrell
- Tempranillo

Extremadura
- Tempranillo
- Cabernet Sauvignon
- Syrah

Andalucía
- Palomino Fino
- Pedro Ximinez
- Muscat of Alexandria
- Sherry

• GUADALAJARA

Mondéjar

Uclés

CASTELLO •

MADRID

Méntrida

Ribera del Júcar

Togus/Tajo

• TOLEDO

VALENCIA

La Mancha

Manchuela

Guadiana

• ALBACETE
Almansa

• MÉRIDA

Valdepeñas

Ribera del Guadiana

ALICANTE •

• LINARES

MURCIA

Condado de Huelva

• CÓRDOBA

• JAÉN

• LORCA

• CARTAGENA

Guadalquivir

SEVILLE

Montilla-Moriles

• GRANADA

• ALMERIA

Málaga and
Sierras de Málaga

Manzanilla

• SANLÚCAR DE BARRAMEDA

MALAGA

• JEREZ

• MARBELLA

• CADIZ

Sherry

Málaga and
Sierras de Málaga

Alboran Sea

ALGECIRAS • GIBRALTAR

• CEUTA

TANGIER

• MELILLA

0   25   50   75   100 km

0   25   50   75 mi

N

United States

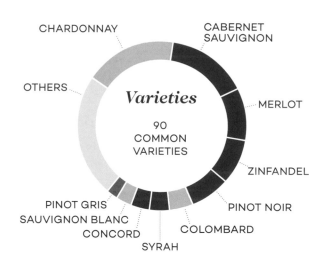

CHARDONNAY

CABERNET
SAUVIGNON

OTHERS

Varieties

90
COMMON
VARIETIES

MERLOT

ZINFANDEL

PINOT GRIS
SAUVIGNON BLANC
CONCORD

PINOT NOIR

COLOMBARD

SYRAH

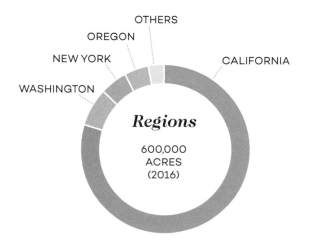

OTHERS

OREGON

NEW YORK

CALIFORNIA

WASHINGTON

Regions

600,000
ACRES
(2016)

Fruit-forward gems

It's difficult to characterize the wines of the United States given the varied landscape from coast to coast. That said, 80% of US wine is made in California, which is famous for its bodacious, fruit-forward wines that focus on French varieties like Cabernet Sauvignon, Merlot, Chardonnay, and Pinot Noir.

Beyond California, Washington (state), Oregon, and New York represent the largest up-and-comers at 17% of US wine. Finally, the last fraction represents the remaining 46 states, notably Arizona, New Mexico, Virginia, Texas, Colorado, Idaho, and Michigan (to name a few), which represent the frontier of US wine.

Wine Regions

California is characterized by a climate similar to the Mediterranean, making it ideal for full-bodied red wines. That said, areas closer to the Pacific Ocean receive layers of fog that allow great success with cooler-climate varieties, including whites and Pinot Noir.

Washington wine grows primarily on the eastern side of the state, which is dry and sunny. This area offers fruity red wines with sweet-tart acidity.

Oregon's Willamette Valley is ideal for Pinot Noir, Pinot Gris, and Chardonnay.

New York grows mostly Concord (mostly for juice, not for wine), but the state is quickly becoming known for Riesling, elegant Merlot-based blends, and rosé.

Northwest
- Bordeaux Blend
- Chardonnay
- Pinot Noir
- Pinot Gris
- Riesling

Northeast
- Concord
- Riesling
- Ice Wine
- Merlot

California
- Chardonnay
- Cabernet Sauvignon
- Pinot Noir
- Merlot
- Syrah

Midwest
- Norton
- Chambourcin
- Vidal Blanc

Southwest
- Cabernet Sauvignon
- Merlot
- Chardonnay

Southeast
- Muscadine / Scuppernong

Hudson Bay

VANCOUVER
SEATTLE
PORTLAND

MONTREAL
OTTAWA
TORONTO
DETROIT
CHICAGO
NEW YORK
WASHINGTON, D.C.
CHARLOTTE
JACKSONVILLE
MIAMI

SAN FRANCISCO
SAN JOSE
DENVER
LOS ANGELES
SAN DIEGO
PHOENIX
ENSENADA
DALLAS
AUSTIN

MONTERREY
SALTILLO

Gulf of Mexico

Pacific Ocean

MEXICO CITY
ACAPULCO

0 200 400 600 800 km
0 200 400 600 mi

N

Fraser Valley

Similkameen Valley
Okanagan Valley (Canada)

VANCOUVER

BRITISH COLUMBIA
🍷 Riesling
🍷 Sparkling Wine

SEATTLE

Washington
🍷 Bordeaux Blend
🍷 Chardonnay
🍷 Sauvignon Blanc
🍷 Syrah
🍷 Riesling

Willamette Valley

Columbia Valley

PORTLAND

WALLA WALLA

Oregon
🍷 Pinot Noir
🍷 Pinot Gris
🍷 Chardonnay
🍷 Riesling

BOISE

IDAHO
🍷 Bordeaux Blend
🍷 Riesling

Snake River Valley

North Coast

California
🍷 Chardonnay
🍷 Cabernet Sauvignon
🍷 Pinot Noir
🍷 Merlot
🍷 Syrah
🍷 Zinfandel

Napa Valley

Sonoma

SAN FRANCISCO

Sierra Foothills

Madera

Central Coast

Paso Robles

Grand Valley   DENVER

GRAND JUNCTION

West Elks

COLORADO
🍷 Cabernet Franc

Malibu Coast

LOS ANGELES

Temecula

ARIZONA
🍷 Cabernet Sauvignon

NEW MEXICO
🍷 Cabernet Sauvignon
🍷 Sparkling Wine

SAN DIEGO

Verde Valley

PHOENIX

Middle Rio
Grande Valley

ENSENADA

Valle de Guadalupe
(Mexico)

Sonoita

Texas High Plains

CIUDAD JUÁREZ

TEXAS
🍷 Cabernet Sauvignon
🍷 Chardonnay

Escondido

Texas Hill Country

AUSTIN

SAN ANTONIO

CHIHUAHUA

Pacific Ocean

Valle de Parras
(Mexico)

SALTILLO

ONTARIO, CANADA
🍷 Cabernet Franc
🍷 Ice Wine
🍷 Riesling
🍷 Chardonnay
🍷 Baco Noir

MONTRÉAL

Prince Edward County

Niagara Peninsula   TORONTO
Niagara Escarpment
Lake Erie North Shore   *Finger Lakes*
North Fork
The Hamptons
Hudson Valley
DETROIT   *Lake Erie*   NEW YORK   **NEW YORK**
🍷 Concord
Lake Michigan Shore   🍷 Riesling
CHICAGO   🍷 Bordeaux Blend
PHILADELPHIA
Lake Wisconsin   **NEW JERSEY**
🍷 Bordeaux Blend
PITTSBURGH   BALTIMORE   *Outer Coastal Plain*
COLUMBUS
Middleburg

MIDWEST   *Ohio River Valley*   *Shenandoah Valley*
🍷 Norton
🍷 Chambourcin   *Monticello*
🍷 Vidal Blanc
🍷 Chardonel   **VIRGINIA**
Augusta   🍷 Bordeaux Blend
🍷 Chardonnay
🍷 Viognier
Upper Mississippi River Valley
Yadkin Valley

Ozark Mountain
CHARLOTTE

SOUTHEAST
🍷 Muscadine / Scuppernong

Atlantic Ocean

JACKSONVILLE

HOUSTON

Gulf of Mexico

N
0   150   300   450   600 km
0   150   300   450 mi

Wines to Explore

California is first known for bold Cabernet Sauvignon, oaked Chardonnay, and Pinot Noir. The up-and-coming wines of Syrah, Petite Sirah, and Zinfandel all highlight California's fruit-forward style. The wines included from Oregon, Washington, and New York are the top wines from these states.

CA Cabernet Sauvignon

California's most famous Cabernet wines come from the North Coast region, which includes Sonoma and Napa Valley. At their best, wines offer lush black fruit flavors that unravel into layers of cedar, dusty minerality, and tobacco-laced tannins.

 BLACKBERRY, BLACK CHERRY, CEDAR, BAKING SPICES, GREEN PEPPERCORN

CA Zinfandel

In 1994, Zinfandel was shown to share the same DNA as Italian Primitivo and Croatian Tribidrag. Zinfandel bursts with candied fruit and tobacco but is often surprisingly dry with minerally tannins and high alcohol. Sonoma and Lodi offer a fantastic comparison.

 BLACKBERRY, PLUM SAUCE, ASIAN 5-SPICE, SWEET TOBACCO, GRANITE

CA Petite Sirah

California is the world's top producer of the French grape. Petite Sirah performs particularly well in the state's warmer climates, including the Inland Valleys, where wines have rich, saucey, black fruit flavors supported by firm, cocoa-like tannin.

 SUGARPLUM, BLUEBERRY, DARK CHOCOLATE, BLACK PEPPER, HERBS

CA Chardonnay

The best Chardonnay grows mostly in coastal regions and valleys up and down the coast that receive cooling breezes and morning fog from the Pacific. Wines offer a richer body, with flavors of pineapple and tropical fruits that are often complemented with toasty oak.

 YELLOW APPLE, PINEAPPLE, CRÈME BRÛLÉE, VANILLA, CARAMEL

CA Pinot Noir

The cooler coastal areas in the North and Central Coast produce some of the boldest, fruit-forward examples of Pinot Noir on the planet. That said, more producers are pulling back to produce elegant, almost Burgundy-like wines. Either way, it's not to be missed.

 BLACKBERRY, DRIED BLUEBERRY, CLOVE, ROSE, COLA

CA Syrah & GSM Blends

You can find great Syrah all over the state, but the Central Coast is by far the most dedicated to Rhône varieties. The best wines have deep black fruit, peppery flavors, and dusty minerality. Santa Barbara and Paso Robles are great places to start looking.

 BLACKBERRY, BLUEBERRY PIE, CRACKED PEPPER, MOCHA, BAY LEAF

Good to Know

❚❚ Single-varietal wines must contain 75% of the listed variety. Oregon Pinot Noir / Pinot Gris require 90%.

❚❚ A wine that is labeled as an estate wine must use grapes grown on the winery's property.

WA Syrah & GSM Blends

Even though Rhône varieties like Syrah and Grenache are not Washington's most popular grapes, they show great potential here. Wines are generous and bold, with sweet-tart red fruit, rich meaty flavors, and spicy alcohol.

 BLACK CURRANT, BRANDIED CHERRY, BACON FAT, DARK CHOCOLATE, GRAPHITE

WA Bordeaux Blends

Even though there is a heavy focus on Cabernet Sauvignon in Washington, the most age-worthy wines include a blend of Merlot and other Bordeaux varieties. These wines offer pure black cherry fruit with lovely floral, minty, and violet-like overtones.

 RASPBERRY, LICORICE, GRAPHITE, EXOTIC SPICES, ROAST MEAT

OR Pinot Noir

Just over 50% of Oregon's vineyards are planted to Pinot Noir, which grows exceptionally well in the Willamette Valley. Wines offer rich, red berry aromas that are complemented by a light body, juicy acidity, and spice flavors often derived from oak aging.

 POMEGRANATE, RED PLUM, ALLSPICE, VANILLA, BLACK TEA

OR Pinot Gris

Pinot Gris is Oregon's most important white wine and grows quite well in the southern Willamette Valley. You'll find these wines to have focused peach and pear flavors, with an oily mid-palate, and a tingly, citrus-driven finish.

LW NECTARINE, RIPE PEAR, CITRUS BLOSSOM, LEMON OIL, ALMOND CREAM

NY Riesling

New York has great potential for Riesling and minerally white wines, but the icy winters make grape growing difficult in most areas except those close to bodies of water (rivers, lakes, and the ocean). This is where you'll find New York's best wines.

 RIPE PEACH, YELLOW APPLE, LIME, LIME PEEL, CRUSHED ROCKS

Sparkling Wines

There aren't many producers making sparkling wines in the United States but those who do produce great quality. You'll find exceptional producers in the North Coast of California and Oregon and surprising values coming out of New Mexico and Washington State.

 LEMON, WHITE CHERRY, ORANGE BLOSSOM, CREAM, RAW ALMOND

California

Califorrna wine started quite humbly 240 years ago at the Mission de Alcalá in San Diego. Then, after the gold rush in 1849, wineries began to populate Sonoma and Napa Valley and the industry took off. Today, California makes 80% of US wine. The lion's share is dedicated to just 7 grapes: Cabernet Sauvignon, Chardonnay, Merlot, Zinfandel, Pinot Noir, Pinot Gris, and Sauvignon Blanc.

North Coast

The North Coast may not be the most productive region, but it is the most famous. The inland regions of Napa Valley and Clear Lake produce great full-bodied reds, including Cabernet Sauvignon. The coastal areas in Sonoma and Mendocino are excellent for cooler-climate grapes such as Chardonnay and Pinot Noir, as well as sparkling wines.

Central Coast

The Central Coast is responsible for many of the great values coming from California. The fog layer that comes in from the coast makes adjacent regions ideal for Chardonnay and Pinot Noir. More inland it's much hotter, such as in Paso Robles, where you'll find outstanding Syrah and Rhone / GSM Blends.

Sierra Foothills

A hilly region that was first populated by gold miners gave way to provincial farmers planting a melting pot of grape varieties. Wines are typically bold with bombastic fruit flavors. There is a focus on Zinfandel here, but varieties like Barbera and Syrah show serious potential.

Inland Valleys

California's large central valley produces a great deal of the food America eats. It's here that you'll find the large scale wine producers, including the world's largest producer: Gallo. Overall, quality isn't high but there are some exceptions, including the old vines of Lodi.

South Coast

Plantings in the South Coast are sparse because land is expensive. Still, you'll find some rare old Zinfandel vineyards planted in East L.A., and a growing wine tourism industry in Temecula. Chardonnay and Cabernet are popular but acidity is low due to the hot climate.

Redwoods

An extremely small wine-growing area with only a couple dozen acres of grapes and very few remaining commercial wineries. The climate is cooler here and thus there are several acres of aromatic white wine varieties, including Riesling and Gewürztraminer.

MEDFORD

CRESCENT CITY

Willow Creek

Trinity Lakes

Seiad Valley • MT. SHASTA

EUREKA

WINNEMUCCA

REDDING

Redwoods

▹ Sauvignon Blanc
▹ Gewürztraminer

Dos Rios
Covelo

North Coast

❦ Cabernet Sauvignon
▹ Chardonnay
❦ Pinot Noir
❦ Merlot
❦ Zinfandel

MENDOCINO

Clear Lake

North Yuba

UKIAH

Capay Valley

• RENO

Mendocino

Dunnigan Hills

• YUBA CITY

Sonoma Valley

Eldorado
Fair Play
CA Shenandoah Valley
Fiddletown

SACRAMENTO

Napa Valley

NAPA

Clarksburg

Lodi

Sierra Foothills

❦ Zinfandel
❦ Barbera
❦ Syrah
❦ Petite Sirah

SAN FRANCISCO

OAKLAND

Livermore Valley

• MODESTO

Inland Valleys

❦ Zinfandel
❦ Petite Sirah
❦ Cabernet Sauvignon
▹ Muscat of Alexandria

Santa Cruz Mountains

SANTA CRUZ

SALINAS
MONTEREY

Madera

• FRESNO

Monterey

LAS VEGAS •

Paso Robles

Central Coast

▹ Chardonnay
❦ Cabernet Sauvignon
❦ Pinot Noir
❦ Zinfandel
❦ Syrah

PASO ROBLES

SAN LUIS OBISPO

Edna Valley
Arroyo Seco

SANTA MARIA •

Santa Maria Valley

Santa Ynez Valley

• SANTA BARBARA

Leona Valley

Sierra Pelona Valley

Cucamonga Valley

South Coast

❦ Cabernet Sauvignon
▹ Chardonnay

Malibu Coast

LOS ANGELES

• PALM SPRINGS

LONG BEACH

Temecula Valley

Pacific Ocean

OCEANSIDE

San Pasqual

Ramona Valley

SAN DIEGO

YUMA

TIJUANA

MEXICALI

| 0 | 60 | 120 | 180 km |
| 0 | 60 | | 120 mi |

N

North Coast, CA

In 1976, a British wine importer held a blind tasting with several French wine critics that included top Bordeaux and Napa Valley wines. Two Napa Valley wines ended up making top scores and the "Judgement of Paris" went down in California wine history. Since then, Sonoma and Napa Valley have become benchmark regions for fine wines made with French varieties.

Cabernet Sauvignon

The most important variety in the North Coast shows rich fruit and dusty minerality when grown in volcanic-clay soils. The regions of Napa Valley, Clear Lake, and much of Sonoma (try regions close to Mayacamas) make some of the highest-rated Cabernet in the world.

 BLACK CURRANT, BLACK CHERRY, GRAPHITE, CIGAR BOX, MINT

Merlot

Merlot is similar to Cabernet Sauvignon, but with bolder cherry flavors and smoother, finer tannins. The grape performs excellently all over the North Coast (at better values than Cabernet!), and will generally be more elegant and herbal from coastal areas and Mendocino.

 CHERRY, VANILLA, CEDAR, PENCIL LEAD, TOASTED NUTMEG

Pinot Noir

The areas that collect morning fog, including Carneros, Russian River Valley, Sonoma Coast, and Mendocino, are more ideal for cooler-climate grapes like Pinot Noir and Chardonnay. Wines deliver sweet red fruit and finish on subtle notes of black tea and allspice.

 CHERRY, PLUM, VANILLA, MUSHROOM, ALLSPICE

Zinfandel

Zinfandel finds some of its richest and most minerally styles from several hot spots (literally, warmer areas) within the North Coast. Watch out for Sonoma's Rockpile AVA and Napa's Howell Mountain AVA, which produce some of the most coveted Zinfandel in the state.

 BLACKBERRY BRAMBLE, COCOA, RASPBERRY SAUCE, CRUSHED ROCKS, SWEET TOBACCO

Chardonnay

As the second most planted variety, Chardonnay loves cooler growing areas and performs exceptionally well in Sonoma, Mendocino, and Southern Napa. This grape is also a popular choice for North Coast sparkling wines, which deliver apple and almond cream flavors.

 BAKED PEAR, PINEAPPLE, BUTTER, HAZELNUT, CARAMEL

Sauvignon Blanc

A less-planted grape from the North Coast making high-quality wines with rich fruity flavors of white peach, orange blossom, and pink grapefruit—very unlike other Sauvignon. Blanc regions. Look to Sonoma and Mendocino, where cooler temperatures maintain acidity.

 WHITE PEACH, PINK GRAPEFRUIT, ORANGE BLOSSOM, HONEYDEW MELON, MEYER LEMON

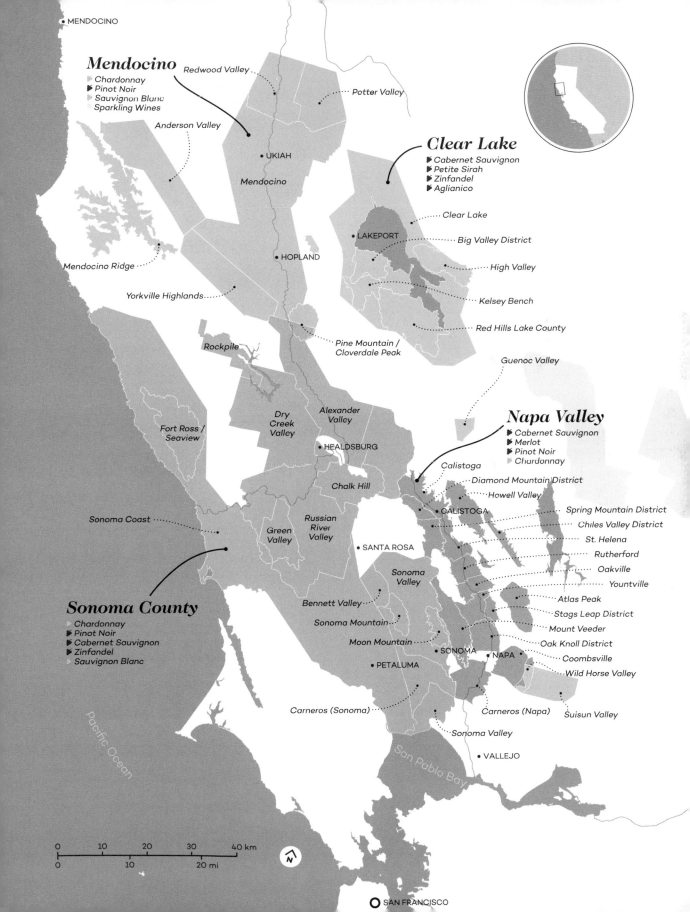

MENDOCINO

Mendocino
- Chardonnay
- Pinot Noir
- Sauvignon Blanc
- Sparkling Wines

Redwood Valley

Potter Valley

Anderson Valley

UKIAH

Mendocino

Mendocino Ridge

HOPLAND

Yorkville Highlands

Rockpile

Clear Lake
- Cabernet Sauvignon
- Petite Sirah
- Zinfandel
- Aglianico

Clear Lake

LAKEPORT

Big Valley District

High Valley

Kelsey Bench

Red Hills Lake County

Pine Mountain /
Cloverdale Peak

Guenoc Valley

Fort Ross /
Seaview

Dry
Creek
Valley

Alexander
Valley

HEALDSBURG

Chalk Hill

Calistoga

Napa Valley
- Cabernet Sauvignon
- Merlot
- Pinot Noir
- Chardonnay

Diamond Mountain District

Howell Valley

Sonoma Coast

Green
Valley

Russian
River
Valley

SANTA ROSA

Sonoma
Valley

CALISTOGA

Spring Mountain District

Chiles Valley District

St. Helena

Rutherford

Oakville

Yountville

Atlas Peak

Stags Leap District

Mount Veeder

Oak Knoll District

Coombsville

Wild Horse Valley

Bennett Valley

Sonoma Mountain

Moon Mountain

Sonoma County
- Chardonnay
- Pinot Noir
- Cabernet Sauvignon
- Zinfandel
- Sauvignon Blanc

SONOMA

NAPA

PETALUMA

Carneros (Sonoma)

Carneros (Napa)

Suisun Valley

Sonoma Valley

VALLEJO

Pacific Ocean

San Pablo Bay

0   10   20   30   40 km
0   10   20 mi

N

SAN FRANCISCO

Central Coast, CA

The Central Coast includes Monterey, Paso Robles, and Santa Barbara. The vineyards in ocean-facing valleys receive abundant morning fog and are best for cool-climate grapes. Farther inland, it's hotter and better for sun-loving varieties like Syrah. Central Coast has many commercial growers making value wines, but there is also outstanding quality from smaller producers.

Chardonnay

Chardonnay takes up the largest vineyard area in the Central Coast, most of which is average quality. That said, there is great Chardonnay here, particularly from Santa Barbara and the regions closer to the coast within Monterey. Wines are often made in a rich, oaked style.

 MANGO, LEMON CURD, WHITE BLOSSOM, TOASTED ALMOND, CRÈME BRÛLÉE

Pinot Noir

The Central Coast is an amazing area for Pinot Noir, especially from the subregions of Santa Cruz Mountains, Santa Lucia Highlands, Sta Rita Hills, Mount Harlan, and Santa Maria Valley. Expect bold, juicy red fruit flavors supported with spice and vanilla notes.

 RED CHERRY, RASPBERRY, ALLSPICE, DARJEELING TEA, VANILLA

Cabernet Sauvignon

The second-most planted variety in the Central Coast performs best inland, where the fog burns off early and it's sunny enough to properly soften the tannins. One region that makes particularly plush and rich styles of Cabernet Sauvignon worth exploring is Paso Robles.

 BLACK RASPBERRY, BLACK CHERRY, MOCHA, VANILLA, GREEN PEPPERCORN

Zinfandel

In the Central Coast region, Zinfandel is best from Paso Robles, where it's hot enough to ripen this variety. Wines take on a much juicier and typically lighter style (with less tannin) than in the North Coast.

 RASPBERRY, PEACH PRESERVES, CINNAMON, SWEET TOBACCO, VANILLA

Syrah

An up-and-coming grape that shows excellent quality potential where it grows in the limestone-dominant clay soils of Paso Robles, Santa Barbara, and eastern parts of Monterey. Wines are often rich, meaty, and peppery, with boysenberry and olive flavors.

 BOYSENBERRY, BLACK OLIVE, PEPPER STEAK, BACON FAT, SMOKE

Rhône / GSM Blend

A winery called Tablas Creek started importing Rhône varieties in the early 1990s to Paso Robles. The Grenache, Syrah, and Mourvèdre blends created an explosion of interest for Rhône-style wines made in America. Tablas Creek now has a nursery that supplies baby vines to the entire state.

 RASPBERRY, PLUM, LEATHER, COCOA POWDER, SAGE FLOWER

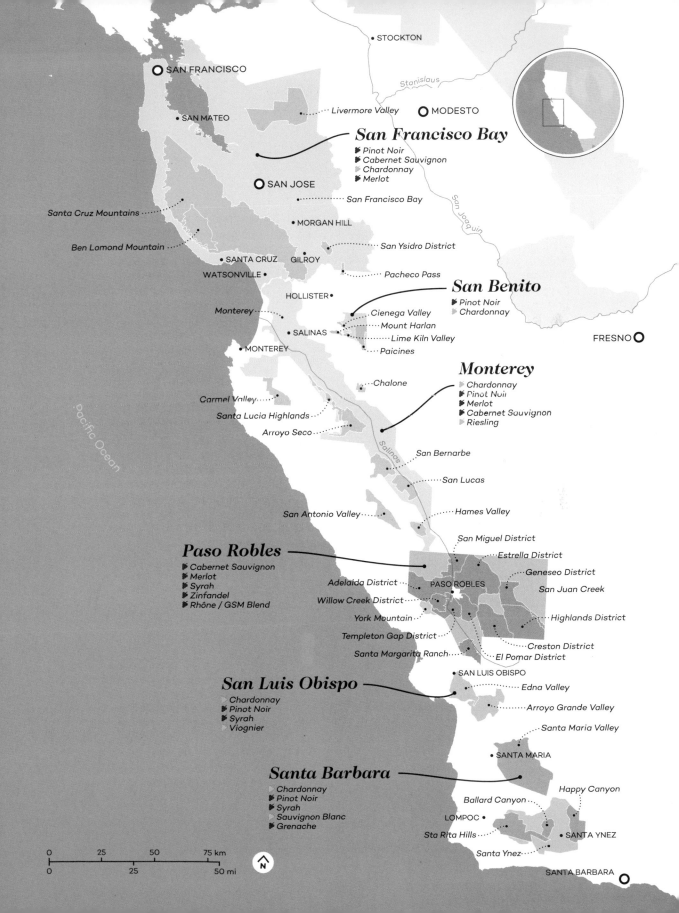

STOCKTON

SAN FRANCISCO

SAN MATEO

Livermore Valley   MODESTO

Stanislaus

San Francisco Bay

🍇 *Pinot Noir*
🍇 *Cabernet Sauvignon*
🍇 *Chardonnay*
🍇 *Merlot*

SAN JOSE

San Francisco Bay

San Joaquin

Santa Cruz Mountains   • MORGAN HILL

Ben Lomond Mountain

San Ysidro District

• SANTA CRUZ   GILROY
WATSONVILLE •

Pacheco Pass

HOLLISTER •   ## San Benito

Monterey   Cienega Valley   🍇 *Pinot Noir*
                    Mount Harlan   🍇 *Chardonnay*
• SALINAS   Lime Kiln Valley

MONTEREY   Paicines

Pacific Ocean   ## Monterey

                    Chalone   🍇 *Chardonnay*
                                      🍇 *Pinot Noir*
Carmel Valley   🍇 *Merlot*
                                      🍇 *Cabernet Sauvignon*
Santa Lucia Highlands   🍇 *Riesling*

Arroyo Seco

                    Salinas

                    San Bernarbe

                    San Lucas

San Antonio Valley   Hames Valley

                              San Miguel District

Paso Robles   Estrella District

🍇 *Cabernet Sauvignon*   Geneseo District
🍇 *Merlot*
🍇 *Syrah*   Adelaida District   San Juan Creek
🍇 *Zinfandel*   PASO ROBLES
🍇 *Rhône / GSM Blend*   Willow Creek District

                    York Mountain   Highlands District

                    Templeton Gap District   Creston District

                    Santa Margarita Ranch   El Pomar District

                                          • SAN LUIS OBISPO

San Luis Obispo   Edna Valley

Chardonnay
🍇 *Pinot Noir*   Arroyo Grande Valley
🍇 *Syrah*
Viognier   Santa Maria Valley

                                          • SANTA MARIA

Santa Barbara

Chardonnay   Ballard Canyon   Happy Canyon
🍇 *Pinot Noir*
🍇 *Syrah*   LOMPOC •   • SANTA YNEZ
Sauvignon Blanc
🍇 *Grenache*   Sta Rita Hills

                    Santa Ynez

                                          SANTA BARBARA

0   25   50   75 km
0   25   50 mi

N

Oregon

Most Oregon vineyards are found in the Northern Willamette Valley, which was first planted with Burgundy grapes (Pinot and Chardonnay) starting in the 1960s. The region grew slowly, mostly with small wineries and rigorous standards (Oregon requires varietal wines contain 90% of the listed grape!). Overall, wines can be characterized by their tart fruit and subtle, elegant flavors.

Pinot Noir

The most important Oregon wine is very unlike its Californian neighbors. Wines tend to be lighter bodied with more piercing tart red fruit flavors, allspice, and earthy, forest-floor notes. The subregions around Dundee Hills are the epicenter of production.

 CHERRY, POMEGRANATE, POTTING SOIL, VANILLA, ALLSPICE

Pinot Gris

Even though Pinot Gris is the second-most planted variety in Oregon it might be the most underrated. Oregon Pinot Gris are surprisingly rich and somewhat smoky, with white peach and meyer lemon flavors. The style can be likened to those coming from Germany or New Zealand.

 WHITE PEACH, MEYER LEMON, HONEYSUCKLE, LIME PITH, CLOVE

Chardonnay

Chardonnay is a rarity to find outside of the state but still manages to get international attention because of its likeness to white Burgundy. The cooler climate gives the wines a much lighter body with leaner fruit, more mineral notes, and higher acidity.

 YELLOW APPLE, MEYER LEMON, PRESERVED LEMON, BUTTERED TOAST, SOUR CREAM

Riesling

There isn't much Riesling in the state, which is a shame because when made well, these wines are quite similar in taste and style to Riesling from the Pfalz in Germany. Several producers are experimenting with more dry styles to great success.

 DRIED APRICOT, GREEN APPLE, LIME ZEST, HONEYCOMB, PETROL

Cabernet Sauvignon

Eastern Oregon and Southern Oregon are very unlike the Willamette Valley, with much warmer, dry, sunny weather. Thus, varieties like Cabernet Sauvignon, Cabernet Franc, and Syrah are becoming increasingly popular.

 BLACK CURRANT, BLACK CHERRY, GREEN PEPPERCORN, VANILLA, TOBACCO LEAF

Tempranillo

Even though Tempranillo plantings are incredibly rare in Oregon, this grape shows potential grown in Southern Oregon. The climate seems to be surprisingly similar to Rioja Alta, producing wines with elegant flavors of cherry, leather, and dill.

 BLACK CHERRY, BLACKBERRY, LEATHER, DILL, SWEET TOBACCO, GRAPHITE

SEATTLE

OLYMPIA

YAKIMA

RICHLAND

WALLA WALLA
The Rocks District
Walla Walla

PENDLETON

LA GRANDE

ASTORIA

Chehalem Mountains

Ribbon Ridge

TILLAMOOK

VANCOUVER

PORTLAND

Columbia Gorge

Dundee Hills

DUNDEE

Yamhill-Carlton

McMinnville

SALEM

Eola-Amity Hills

CORVALLIS

ALBANY

Columbia Valley

▶ *Cabernet Sauvignon*
▷ *Pinot Gris*
▶ *Syrah*

John Day

JOHN DAY

Willamette Valley

▶ *Pinot Noir*
▷ *Pinot Gris*
▷ *Chardonnay*
▷ *Riesling*

EUGENE

Willamette

ONTARIO

Elkton

Red Hills Douglas County

COOS BAY

Umqua Valley

ROSEBURG

SNAKE RIVER VALLEY

▶ *Cabernet Sauvignon*
▶ *Merlot*

Southern Oregon

▶ *Pinot Noir*
▷ *Pinot Gris*
▶ *Cabernet Sauvignon*
▶ *Syrah*
▶ *Tempranillo*

Rogue

Rogue Valley

Klamath

GRANTS PASS

MEDFORD

ASHLAND

Applegate Valley

CRESCENT CITY

Pit

Sacramento

Trinity

EUREKA

0   60   120 km

0   60 mi

N

Washington

Most people think of Washington as a rainy place. However, the Cascade Mountains stop the clouds from going east and the rest of the state is sunny and dry (some areas are as dry as the Gobi Desert!). Most vineyards are found within the Columbia Valley AVA, where bold red wines are becoming known for their great quality and affordable prices.

Cabernet Sauvignon

The most planted variety in Washington grows best in hotter sites. Horse Heaven Hills, Red Mountain, and Walla Walla produce excellent examples. Wines are noted for their rich raspberry, black cherry, and cedar flavors that have yogurt-like creaminess.

 BLACK CHERRY, RASPBERRY, CEDAR BOX, CREAM, MINT

Merlot

It was Merlot that first put Washington on the map for wine in the 1990s. Merlot has proven to be especially well-suited for the region's extreme diurnal shift (e.g., hot days, cold nights) and makes rich, full-bodied wines with pure cherry fruit flavors and subtle mint notes on the finish.

 BLACK CHERRY, SPICED PLUM, BAKING SPICES, VIOLET, MINT

Bordeaux Blends

Even though single-varietal wines will always be in high demand, some of Washington's very best red wines are blends. The varieties of Cabernet, Merlot, Petit Verdot, Malbec, and even Syrah go into regionally blended wines that have increased body, depth, and complexity.

 BLACK CHERRY, PLUM, MOCHA, BAKING SPICES, VIOLET

Syrah

They say that "Syrah likes a view" and this grape is quickly becoming the focus of several Washington wine regions with sloping views. You'll find it performs well in Yakima, Horse Heaven Hills, and Walla Walla. The highest-quality wines manage to be smoky, rich, and tart at the same time.

 PLUM, BLACK OLIVE, BACON FAT, COCOA POWDER, WHITE PEPPER

Riesling

Riesling was one of the first wines to become popular outside of Washington state. The variety does well in the cooler growing areas, including Naches Heights, Ancient Lakes, and Yakima Valley. More and more producers are making dry styles similar to Alsace Riesling.

 MEYER LEMON, GREEN MELON, GALA APPLE, HONEYCOMB, LIME

Sauvignon Blanc

Where there is good Cabernet and Merlot, you can expect to see great Sauvignon Blanc as well! Wineries occasionally blend this grape with Sémillon and oak-age these wines to produce a rich, creamy white with more savory notes of lemon balm and tarragon.

 WHITE PEACH, GREEN MELON, LEMON BALM, TARRAGON, GRASS

Okanagan Valley (BC) ···· ● KELOWNA

Similkameen Valley (BC) ····

● PENTICTON

Salish Sea

○ VANCOUVER Fraser

···· Fraser Valley (BC)

● ABBOTSFORD

Columbia Valley

Straight of Juan de Fuca

● VICTORIA

PUGET SOUND
▶ Madeleine Angevine
▶ Müller-Thurgau
▶ Melon

🍷 Bordeaux Blend
▶ Chardonnay
▶ Riesling
🏹 Syrah
▶ Sauvignon Blanc
🏹 Cabernet Franc

Columbia

Lake Chelan ····

● EVERETT

SPOKANE ●

BREMERTON ●   ○ SEATTLE

● WENATCHEE

Ancient Lakes

● TACOMA

Wahluke Slope

● OLYMPIA

Yakima

● CENTRALIA

Naches Heights ····

● YAKIMA

Snake

Yakima Valley ····

Rattlesnake Hills ····

RICHLAND ●

Snipes Mountain ····

KENNEWICK ●

Red Mountain ····

···· Walla Walla

Horse Heaven Hills ····

● WALLA WALLA

Columbia Gorge ····

● VANCOUVER

○ PORTLAND

Pacific Ocean

John Day

● SALEM

Willamette

0   50   100   150 km

0   50   100 mi

N

References & Sources

This section includes useful references, including wine terminology, additional resources, further reading, sources, and index.

Wine Terms

LEGEND:

⚑ Technical Term

🍷 Tasting Term

📑 Winemaking Term

🍃 Grape / Region Term

🍷 ABV

The abbreviation of alcohol by volume, listed by percent on a wine label (e.g., 13.5% ABV).

⚑ Acetaldehyde

A toxic organic chemical compound that is produced in our bodies in order to metabolize ethyl alcohol. The cause of alcohol poisoning.

📑 Acidification

A wine additive process common in warm- and hot-climate growing regions to increase acidity by adding tartaric or citric acid. Acidification is less common in cool-climate regions and more common in hot climates in the United States, Australia, and Argentina.

⚑ Amino Acids

Organic compounds that are the building blocks of proteins. Red wine contains 300–1300 mg/L of amino acids, of which proline accounts for up to 85%.

🍃 Appellation

A legally defined geographical location used to identify where (and how) grapes are grown and made into wine.

⚑ Aroma Compounds

Chemical compounds with very low molecular weights, making it possible for them to be carried into the upper nasal passage. Aroma compounds are derived from grapes and fermentation and are volatilized by the evaporation of alcohol.

🍷 Astringent

A drying mouthfeel typically caused by tannins, which bind to salivary proteins, causing them to depart the tongue/mouth. It results in a rough sandpapery sensation in the mouth.

🍃 AVA

American Viticultural Area. A legally designated grape-growing region in the United States.

🍃 Biodynamics

At its core, Biodynamics is an energy management system. Biodynamics was popularized in the 1920s by an Austrian philosopher name Rudolf Steiner. It is a holisitic, homeopathic manner of farming that uses natural composts, or preparations, and times farming work, including harvests, with celestial (moon and sun) cycles. There are two certifying bodies for biodynamic wines: Demeter International and Biodyvin. Certified biodynamic wines may contain up to 100 ppm sulfites, but other than the strict farming rules, will not taste any different than standard wines.

📑 Brix (symbol °Bx)

Relative density scale for sucrose dissolved in grape juice used for determining the potential alcohol level of a wine. ABV is about 55–64% of the Brix number. For example, 27°Bx will result in a dry wine with 14.9–17.3% ABV.

📑 Carbonic Maceration

A winemaking method where uncrushed grapes are placed in a sealed vat and topped with carbon dioxide. Wines created without oxygen have low tannin and color with juicy fruit flavors and bold yeast aromas. This practice is common with entry-level Beaujolais wines.

📑 Chaptalization

A wine additive process common in cool climates where sugar is added when grape sweetness isn't high enough to produce the minimum alcohol level. Chaptalization is illegal in the United States but common in cool climate areas such as regions in France and Germany.

📑 Clarification / Fining

A process after fermentation where proteins and dead yeast cells are removed. To clarify, either a protein, such as casein (from milk) and egg whites or a vegan clay-based agent like bentonite or kaolin clay are added. These fining agents bind to the particles and pull them from the wine, making it clear.

🍃 Clone

Wine grapes are cloned for their beneficial traits much like other agricultural products. For example, there are over 1,000 registered clones of the Pinot cultivar.

Wine Terms

♠ Diacetyl

An organic compound found in wine that tastes like butter. Diacetyl comes from oak aging and malolactic fermentation.

♠ Esters

Esters are one type of aroma compound found in wine, which are caused by alcohol reacting with acids in wine.

♀ Fortified Wine

A wine that's stabilized by the addition of spirits, typically made of neutral, clear grape brandy. For example, about 30% of Port wine is spirit, which raises the ABV to 20%.

♠ Glycerol

A colorless, odorless, viscous, sweet-tasting liquid that is a byproduct of fermentation. In red wines there are about 4–10 g/L and noble rot wines contain 20+ g/L. Glycerol has been considered to add a positive, rich, oily mouthfeel to wine, however, studies have shown that other traits, like alcohol level and residual sugar, have a greater effect on mouthfeel.

♠ Grape Must

Freshly pressed grape juice that still contains the seeds, stems, and skins of a grape.

▤ Lees

Sediment from dead yeast particles left in wine after the fermentation.

▤ Malolactic Fermentation (MLF)

MLF isn't technically a fermentation but a bacteria called Oenococcus oeni that converts one type of acid (malic acid) to another type of acid (lactic acid). MLF makes wine taste smoother and creamier. Nearly all red wines and some white wines, like Chardonnay, go through Malo. It is responsible for creating the compound diacetyl, which smells like butter.

♀ Minerality

A non-scientific term used to describe flavors that smell or taste like rocks or organic matter (soil). Minerality was thought to be presence of trace minerals in wine. Recent research suggests the majority of mineral-like aromas in wine are due to sulfur compounds derived from fermentation.

♀ Natural Wine

A generalized term used to describe wines that are produced with sustainable, organic, and/or biodynamic viticulture. Wines are processed using minimal or no additives, including sulfur dioxide (sulfites). Because of the lack of clarification and fining, natural wines are typically cloudy and some may still contain yeast sediment. Generally speaking, natural wines are fragile and sensitive and should be stored carefully.

⚘ Noble Rot

Noble rot is a fungal infection caused by Botrytis cinerea, common in areas with high humidity. It is considered a flaw in red grapes and wines but in white grapes it is appreciated for making sweet wines with flavors of honey, ginger, marmalade, and chamomile.

▤ Oak: American

American white oak (Quercus alba) grows in the Eastern United States and is primarily used in the Bourbon industry. American oak is known for adding flavors of coconut, vanilla, cedar, and dill. Since American oak tends to be more loose-grained, it's known to impart robust flavors.

▤ Oak: European

European oak (Quercus robur) is sourced primarily in France and Hungary. Depending on where it is grown it can range from medium grained to very fine grained. European oak is known for adding flavors of vanilla, clove, allspice, and cedar.

♀ Off-Dry

A term to describe a wine that is slightly sweet.

♀ Orange Wine

A term used to describe a style of white wine where the grape must is fermented with the skins and the seeds, much like a red wine. The lignin in the seeds dyes the wine a deep orange color. This style of wine is traditionally known from eastern Friuli-Venezia Giulia, Italy, and in Brda, Slovenia.

⚘ Organics

Organic wine must be made with organically grown grapes and processed using a short list of acceptable additives. EU allows organic wines to use sulfur dioxide (SO2) and US organic wines do not allow the use of SO2.

Oxidation / Oxidized

When wine is exposed to oxygen, a chain of chemical reactions occur that alter the compounds. One obvious change is an increased level of acetaldehyde, which smells similar to bruised apples in white wine and nail polish remover in red wines. Oxidation is the opposite of reduction.

pH

A figure that expresses the acidity or alkalinity in a substance numbered from 1–14, where 1 is acid, 14 is alkaline, and 7 is neutral. Wine's average range is about 2.5–4.5 pH and a wine with a pH of 3 is ten times more acidic than a wine with a pH of 4.

Phenols

A group of several hundred chemical compounds found in wine that affect the taste, color, and mouthfeel of wine. Tannin is a type of phenol called a polyphenol.

Phylloxera

A microscopic louse that eats Vitis vinifera roots and kills vines. It first spread throughout Europe in the 1880s and devastated the majority of the world's vineyards except for a few places with sandy soils (the louse cannot thrive in sand). The only solution was to graft Vitis vinifera vines onto other vine species' rootstocks, including Vitis aestivalis, Vitis riparia, Vitis rupestris, and Vitis berlandieri (all native American species). To date, there is still no cure for grape phylloxera.

Reduction

When wine doesn't receive enough air during fermentation, the yeast will substitute its need of nitrogen with amino acids (found in grapes). This creates sulfur compounds that can smell like rotten eggs, garlic, burnt matches, rotten cabbage, or sometimes positive traits like passionfruit or wet flint rocks. Reduction is not caused by "sulfites" being added to wine.

Residual Sugar (RS)

The sugar from grapes left over in a wine after a fermentation stops. Some wines are fermented completely dry, and some are stopped before all the sugar is converted to alcohol to create a sweet wine. Residual Sugar ranges from nothing to upward of 400 grams per liter for very sweet wines.

Sommelier

("Sa-muhl-yay") A French word used for wine steward. A "master sommelier" is a US trademark term owned by Court of Masters Sommeliers that's reserved for those who pass the 4th level of their certification exam.

Sulfites

Sulfites, sulfur dioxide, or SO2 is a preservative that is either added to wine or present on grapes before fermentation. Wines range from about 10 ppm (parts per million) to 350ppm—the legal US limit. Wines must label if they contain more than 10 ppm.

Sulfur Compounds

Sulfur compounds affect the aroma and taste of wine. In low levels they offer positive aroma characteristics, including mineral-like flavors, grapefruit, or tropical fruit. In higher levels, sulfur compounds are considered a fault when they smell of cooked eggs, garlic, or boiled cabbage.

Terroir

("Tear-woh") Originally a French word that is used to describe how a particular region's climate, soils, aspect (terrain), and traditional winemaking practices affect the taste of the wine.

Typicity / Typicality

A wine that tastes typical of a particular region or style.

Vanillin

The primary extract of the vanilla bean, also found in oak.

Vinification

The creation of wine by fermentation of grape juice.

Vinous

A tasting term to describe a wine that has a freshly fermented flavor.

Volatile Acidity (VA)

Acetic acid is the volatile acid in wine that turns wine to vinegar. In small levels it adds to the complexity of flavor and in high levels it causes the wine to spoil.

Additional Resources

Vintage Charts

Variations in weather conditions do affect the size and quality of the wine grape crop each vintage. Vintage variation is common in areas with very cool climates and very hot climates where grapes may not acheive optimal ripeness by harvest. Vintage variation affects the quality of both value wines and collectible wines.

Below are our favorite vintage resources:

- bbr.com/vintages
- robertparker.com/resources/vintage-chart
- jancisrobinson.com/learn/vintages
- winespectator.com/vintagecharts

Wine Ratings

Wine ratings are useful when you know what wine you want (be it a Mendoza Malbec or a Tempranillo from Ribera del Duero) but do not know which bottle to buy. The most useful wine ratings will include tasting notes and aging estimates.

Critic rating sites:

- Wine Enthusiast Magazine (free)
- Decanter (free)
- Wine Spectator (paid)
- Wine Advocate (paid)
- James Suckling (paid)
- Vinous (paid)

Consumer rating sites:

- CellarTracker (donation)
- Vivino (free)

Further Reading

Beginner / Intermediate

Other great beginner and intermediate books worth investigating (from easiest to hardest).

- *The Essential Scratch & Sniff Guide to Becoming a Wine Expert*
- *How to Drink Like a Billionaire*
- *Kevin Zraly's Windows on the World*
- *The Wine Bible*
- *Taste Like a Wine Critic*
- *I Taste Red*

Regional Wine Guides

Organized guides that include lists of wineries, wines, and rankings. Good for if you plan to travel to a region and want to pick out specific wineries to visit.

- *Gambero Rosso's Italian Wine*
- *Platter's South African Wine Guide*
- *Falstaff Ultimate Wine Guide Austria*
- *Halliday Wine Companion (Australia)*
- *Asian Wine Review*

Reference Books

Reference books for the wine professional.

- *Wine Grapes*
- *Native Wine Grapes of Italy / Italian Wine Unplugged*
- *Wine Atlas of Germany*
- *The Oxford Companion to Wine*

Technical / Winemaking Books

Essential textbooks for winemakers.

- *Principles and Practices of Winemaking*
- *Understanding Wine Chemistry*
- *Grape Grower's Handbook*

Wine Certifications

If you're interested in working in wine or becoming a wine educator consider the following certification courses to validate your knowledge:

- **Court of Masters Sommeliers (CMS):** Great for sommeliers, educators, and hospitality.
- **Wine and Spiritis Education Trust (WSET):** Great for sommeliers, educators, and hospitality.
- **Society of Wine Educators (SWE):** Great for educators, consumers, and wine retailers.
- **International Sommelier Guild (ISG):** Great for sommeliers and hospitality professionals.
- **Wine Scholar Guild (WSG):** In-depth programs for French, Italian, and Spanish wine.

Online Resources

Need more information about a wine, grape, region, or topic? Here are some great places to look online for answers:

- winefolly.com (free)
- wine-searcher.com (free)
- guildsomm.com (free and paid)
- jancisrobinson.com (free and paid)

Special Thanks

This book would not have been possible without the existence of freely accessible research and data that was accomplished by individuals and groups at universities and research centers throughout the world, such as:

- Adelaide University (Australia)
- University of California Davis
- Geisenheim University (Germany)
- Fondazione Edmund Mach
- The Wine Institute
- International Organisation of Vine and Wine
- Southeast University (Nanjing, China)

It would also not have been possible to make this book without the many contributions from the community of wine professionals who have independently categorized, organized, studied, questioned, researched, rated, ranted, wrote about, illustrated, and simplified the many sub-topics of wine.

Finally, a few thank-yous:

- Sandy Hammack
- Margaret Puckette
- Bob and Sheri
- Robert Ivie
- Kym Anderson
- Geoff Kruth
- Matt Stamp
- Jason Wise
- Brian McClintic
- Dustin Wilson
- Kevin Zraly
- Rick Martinez
- Evan Goldstein
- Rajat Parr
- Lisa Perrotti-Brown
- Dlynn Proctor
- Brandon Carneiro
- Ian Cauble
- Frédéric Panaïotis
- Matteo Lunelli
- Jancis Robinson
- Karen MacNeil
- Sofia Perpera
- Ryan Opaz
- Ana Fabiano
- Morgan Harris
- Bryan Otis
- Athena Bochanis
- Courtney Quattrini
- Ben Andrews
- Micah Huerta

Sources

Anderson, Kym. *Which Winegrape Varieties are Grown Where? A Global Empirical Picture.* Adelaide: University Press. 2013.

Robinson, Jancis, Julia Harding, and Jose F. Vouillamoz. *Wine Grapes: A Complete Guide to 1,368 Vine Varieties, Including Their Origins and Flavors.* New York: Ecco/HarperCollins, 2012. Print.

D'Agata, Ian. *Native Wine Grapes of Italy.* Berkeley: U of California, 2014. Print.

Waterhouse, Andrew Leo, Gavin Lavi Sacks, and David W. Jeffery. *Understanding Wine Chemistry.* Chichester, West Sussex: John Wiley & Sons, 2016. Print.

Fabiano, Ana. *The Wine Region of Rioja.* New York, NY: Sterling Epicure, 2012. Print.

"South Africa Wine Industry Statistics." Wines of South Africa. SAWIS, n.d. Web. 8 Feb. 2018. <wosa.co.za/The-Industry/Statistics/SA-Wine-Industry-Statistics/>.

Dokumentation Österreich Wein 2016 (Gesamtdokument). Vienna: Österreich Wein, 18 Sept. 2017. PDF.

Hennicke, Luis. "Chile Wine Annual Chile Wine Production 2015." Global Agricultural Information Network, 2015, Chile Wine Annual Chile Wine Production 2015.

"Deutscher Wein Statistik (2016/2017)." The German Wine Institute, 2017.

"ÓRGA NOS DE GESTIÓN DE LAS DENOMINACIONES DE ORIGEN PROTEGIDAS VITIVINÍCOLAS." Ministerio De Agricultura y Pesca, Alimentación y Medio Ambiente.

Arapitsas, Panagiotis, Giuseppe Speri, Andrea Angeli, Daniele Perenzoni, and Fulvio Mattivi. "The Influence of Storage on the chemical Age of Red Wines." Metabolomics 10.5 (2014): 816-32. Web.

Ahn, Y., Ahnert, S. E., Bagrow, J. P., Barabási, A., "Flavor network and the principles of food pairing" *Scientific Reports.* 15 Dec. 2011. 20 Oct. 2014. <nature.com/srep/2011/111215/srep00196/full/srcp00196.html>.

Klepper, Maurits de. "Food Pairing Theory: A European Fad." *Gastronomica: The Journal of Critical Food Studies.* Vol. 11, No. 4 Winter 2011: 55-58

Hartley, Andy. "The Effect of Ultraviolet Light on Wine Quality." Banbury: WRAP, 2008. PDF.

Villamor, Remedios R., James F. Harbertson, and Carolyn F. Ross. "Influence of Tannin Concentration, Storage Temperature, and Time on Chemical and Sensory Properties of Cabernet Sauvignon and Merlot Wines." *American Journal of Enology and Viticulture* 60.4 (2009): 442-49. Print.

Lipchock, S V., Mennella, J.A., Spielman, A.I., Reed, D.R. "Human Bitter Perception Correlates with Bitter Receptor Messenger RNA Expression in Taste Cells 1,2,3." *American Journal of Clinical Nutrition.* Oct. 2013: 1136–1143.

Shepherd, Gordon M. "Smell Images and the Flavour System in the Human Brain." Nature 444.7117 (2006): 316-21. Web. 13 Sept. 2017.

Pandell, Alexander J. "How Temperature Affects the Aging of Wine" *The Alchemist's Wine Perspective.* 2011. 1 Nov. 2014. <wineperspective.com/STORAGE%20TEMPERATURE%20&%20AGING.htm>

"pH Values of Food Products." *Food Eng.* 34(3): 98-99

"Table 1: World Wine Production by Country: 2013-2015 and % Change 2013/2015" *The Wine Institute.* 2015. 9 February 2018. <wineinstitute.org/files/World_Wine_Production_by_Country_2015.pdf>.

Index

Note: Page numbers in **bold** indicate primary information about grapes/wines. When **bold** page numbers stand alone, for more information, see main entry of the referenced grape/wine. Page numbers in parentheses indicate noncontiguous references.

About the Authors

Madeline Puckette cofounded the website Wine Folly (winefolly.com) in 2011 with her partner, **Justin Hammack**. A certified sommelier with a background in design, Puckette developed methods to simplify wine using information design. Hammack developed the site's infrastructure to be a free, open-resource for wine knowledge.

Wine Folly's infographics, articles, and videos quickly made it the world's most popular wine blog. Puckette and Hammack also developed tools for professional trade organizations including The Wines of France and The Guild of Sommeliers.

In 2015, they launched their first book, *Wine Folly: The Essential Guide to Wine*, which was a *New York Times* bestseller and an Amazon pick for Top Cookbook of 2015. The very same year, Madeline Puckette was featured in the Jason Wise documentary, *Somm: Into the Bottle*.

Winefolly.com now offers a host of educational products including wine maps, posters, and tasting tools as well as a free learning resource. The site has been featured in *Forbes*, *The New York Times*, *The Wall Street Journal*, and *Lifehacker*, to name a few, and it continues to bring a new generation into wine.